C

Social and developmental psychology are often viewed as distinct subdisciplines, each with its own theories and methodologies. This book seeks to bridge that divide by proposing an integrative framework that considers various levels of analysis, from the individual to the societal. It emphasises the interplay of fundamental concepts such as intra- and intergroup conflict and change across these levels. By revisiting and renewing foundational theories of development, the book introduces the concept of 'genetic social psychology'. This approach is applied to the complex case of the Cyprus conflict, as well as other conflict and post-conflict scenarios, uncovering transformative possibilities for both theory and practice. Ultimately, this work advocates for a broader, more cohesive understanding of psychological processes in social contexts, addressing contemporary challenges and enhancing our grasp of human behaviour.

CHARIS PSALTIS is Professor of Social and Developmental Psychology at the University of Cyprus. His books include *Social Relations in Human and Societal Development* (with Alex Gillespie and Anne-Nelly Perret-Clermont), *Interaction, Communication and Development* (with Anna Zapiti) and *History Education and Conflict Transformation* (with Mario Carretero and Sabina Čehajić-Clancy). In 2024 he received the International Society of Political Psychology (ISPP) Nevitt Sanford Award for his professional contributions to the field of political psychology.

BRADY WAGONER is Professor of Psychology at the University of Copenhagen, Aalborg University and Oslo New University College. His books include *The Constructive Mind: Bartlett's Psychology in Reconstruction*, *The Psychological of Radical Social Change* (with Fathali M. Moghaddam and Jaan Valsiner) and *Handbook of Culture and Memory*. He has received the Alexander von Humboldt Award in 2021 for his lifetime contributions to research.

The Progressive Psychology Book Series

This book is part of the Cambridge University Press book series, Progressive Psychology, edited by Fathali M. Moghaddam. As the science of human behavior, psychology is uniquely positioned and equipped to try to help us make more progress toward peaceful, fair, and constructive human relationships. However, the enormous resources of psychology have not been adequately or effectively harnessed for this task. The goal of this book series is to engage psychological science in the service of achieving more democratic societies, toward providing equal opportunities for all. The volumes in the series contribute in new and unique ways to highlight how psychological science can contribute to making justice a more central theme in health care, education, the legal system, and business, combatting the psychological consequences of poverty, ending discrimination and prejudice, better understanding the failure of revolutions and limits on political plasticity, and moving societies to more openness. Of course, these topics have been discussed before in scattered and ad hoc ways by psychologists, but now they are addressed as part of a systematic and cohesive series on Progressive Psychology.

CONFLICT AND CHANGE

Integrating Social and Developmental Psychology

EDITED BY

CHARIS PSALTIS

University of Cyprus

BRADY WAGONER

University of Copenhagen

Aalborg University

CAMBRIDGE
UNIVERSITY PRESS

CAMBRIDGE
UNIVERSITY PRESS

Shaftesbury Road, Cambridge CB2 8EA, United Kingdom

One Liberty Plaza, 20th Floor, New York, NY 10006, USA

477 Williamstown Road, Port Melbourne, VIC 3207, Australia

314–321, 3rd Floor, Plot 3, Splendor Forum, Jasola District Centre, New Delhi – 110025, India

103 Penang Road, #05-06/07, Visioncrest Commercial, Singapore 238467

Cambridge University Press is part of Cambridge University Press & Assessment, a department of the University of Cambridge.

We share the University's mission to contribute to society through the pursuit of education, learning and research at the highest international levels of excellence.

www.cambridge.org
Information on this title: www.cambridge.org/9781009393126

DOI: 10.1017/9781009393133

When citing this work, please include a reference to the DOI 10.1017/9781009393133

First published 2026

A catalogue record for this publication is available from the British Library

A Cataloging-in-Publication data record for this book is available from the Library of Congress

ISBN 978-1-009-39312-6 Hardback
ISBN 978-1-009-39315-7 Paperback

This book is dedicated to the memory of Gerard Duveen and Ivana Marková with the wish for a better world for our children Maximos and Leon

Contents

Figures

Tables

Contributors

CHRISTINA ALEXOPOULOS University of Cyprus, Cyprus

ALICIA BARREIRO, FLACSO, Argentina

ANGELA BERMÚDEZ, University of Deusto, Spain

MARIO CARRETERO, University Autonoma de Madrid, Spain

JOSÉ ANTONIO CASTORINA, FLACSO, Argentina

ALEX GILLESPIE, London School of Economics, UK

IVANA MARKOVÁ, University of Stirling, UK

CATHY NICHOLSON, London School of Economics, UK

CHARIS PSALTIS, University of Cyprus, Cyprus

GORDON SAMMUT, University of Malta, Malta

BRADY WAGONER, University of Copenhagen, Denmark

TANIA ZITTOUN, University of Neuchatel, Switzerland

Series Foreword

Why is theorising so limited in mainstream psychology? Why do mainstream psychological theories have so little of consequence to say about enormously important topics such as conflict and change? Why is it that when we want to understand conflict and change, we do not reach for explanations from mainstream psychology? The answer to these questions is that theorising in mainstream psychology is still shackled to limited and flawed ideas about what constitutes scientific research methodology.

In order to try to position itself as a science, mainstream psychology has adopted the causal model and the experimental laboratory method as the gold standard. Psychological theorising has been stunted by this incorrect perspective, which still largely dominates academic psychology. The result is the almost complete neglect of vitally important topics such as conflict and change, as well as democracy and dictatorship, which are seen as far too complex to study through one-hour experiments.

This volume represents an exciting and serious effort to apply a 'from societies to cells,' rather than the reductionist 'from cells to societies,' type of analysis to conflict and change. We are reminded of the deceptively simple Gestalt motto, 'The whole is more than the sum of its parts.' The overall picture that emerges is of a valuable historically grounded effort to break out of traditional disciplinary boundaries and come to grips with conflict and change in everyday life. A next step is to better understand limitations and possibilities for change. This brings to mind the concept of *political plasticity*, limitations on how fast, how much and in what ways political behaviour does (or does not) change. Such limitations are in part psychological, having to do with basic cognitive processes such as categorisation, but they also include biological, social, cultural and economic factors. Genetic social psychology as discussed in this volume seems poised to fruitfully take on the challenge of exploring the limitations and possibilities of change.

Fathali M. Moghaddam
Georgetown University

Acknowledgements

This book would not have been possible if Brady Wagoner had not given me the opportunity to present the vision of a genetic social psychology at the annual Niels Bohr lecture at the Centre for Cultural Psychology of Aalborg University on 23–24 August 2021, and without his enthusiasm to turn both the talk and the various commentaries on it into a book. I also want to thank Brady for inviting the commentaries and handling their editing, as well as giving me feedback and ideas about the revision of the first part of the book where I propose genetic social psychology as a past and future discipline. By the time the book went to press, social psychology lost a great mind and person, Ivana Marková, who contributed to this volume a commentary. We will miss the intellectually engaging discussions with such a deep thinker. I would like to thank Alex Gillespie, Tania Zittoun, José Antonio Castorina, Mario Carretero, Alicia Barreiro, Cathy Nicholson, Gordon Sammut, Christina Alexopoulos and Angela Bermúdez for their valuable commentaries in this book. Christina Alexopoulos, Pavlos Pavlou and Costas M. Constantinou read an earlier version of the book and made valuable comments for revisions. I also benefited a lot from insightful comments by Anne-Nelly Perret Clermont on Piaget and emotion. Anne-Nelly has always supported my career and enriched my ideas with her wisdom, and I take the opportunity now to thank her for everything. Similarly, I want to thank Jaan Valsiner for his support throughout these years in his various travels and intellectual exchanges, with the more recent one being in the context of the Cultural Psychology European Doctoral Network in Sociocultural Psychology (CuPsyNet) in 2023 in Cyprus, which enriched the analysis of my autobiographical narrative in this book. I also want to thank Professor Fathali M. Moghaddam for his hospitality in publishing this book in his Cambridge University Press Progressive Psychology series and for the series foreword in this volume, as well as David Repetto and Sari Wastell at the Press, our project manager Shreyasi Saha and our copy editor Mark Fox for their hard work and endless patience in bringing this process to fruition. I thank Cyprus Dialogue Forum for the reproduction of the very helpful infographic about the chronology of negotiations in Cyprus for the solution of the Cyprus issue and the journalist Sefa Karahasan for his generosity in allowing the use of his beautiful photo as the image for the cover of the book.

This volume is the result of a journey initiated at the start of this century at the University of Cambridge. In 2000, as soon as I started my studies for an MPhil in Social and Developmental Psychology at the Department of Social and Developmental Psychology at the University of Cambridge, I met Tania Zittoun, Alex Gillespie and Flora Cornish. We all worked around issues related to social and developmental psychology and formed a small reading group that I now recognise as the first arena for the formation of my theoretical ideas. Brady Wagoner later joined our group, and we were all greatly influenced in our ideas and appreciation of an integrative approach to social and developmental psychology by the late Gerard Duveen's depth of intellect, who supervised our work. In the same context of ideas around the MPhil in Social and Developmental Psychology in later years, we had the opportunity to work together with Anna Zapiti, Irini Kadianaki and Seamus Power, whom I also want to thank for their valuable contributions to the development of research and ideas reported here. I view the proposal presented in this book as continuing along the vision proposed by the late Gerard Duveen as genetic social psychology.

Turning my attention to issues related to the Cyprus conflict and intergroup relations was the result of my engagement with the work of Chara Makriyianni on history teaching in post-conflict Cyprus and my work at the Oxford Centre for the Study of Intergroup Conflict under the supervision of Professor Miles Hewstone whom I would like to thank for the introduction to the world of the study of intergroup relations from a social psychological perspective. Chara was influential on my thinking in more ways than one, as she was later to become my wife. Our initiative with other colleagues to establish the first bicommunal non-governmental organisation in divided Cyprus relating to history teaching (the Association for Historical Dialogue and Research [AHDR]) and my engagement with themes of interest to civil society, conflict resolution and peace making would be impossible without her inspirational influence. AHDR has been a learning experience for me, and I want to thank all founding members of AHDR and more recent personnel for their continuing efforts for the reunification of Cyprus, critical historical approach and peace education, as well as the various research projects that we had the chance to co-operate on.

Throughout these years various funding bodies supported our work, and I would like to thank them all, in alphabetical order: A.G. Leventis Foundation, Cambridge Commonwealth Trust, Corpus Christi College Research Scholarship, Cyprus Research and Innovation Foundation, EU under the Cypriot Civil Society in Action I Programme, Grow Civic Programme financed by the European Union in the Turkish Cypriot community, LSE Hellenic Observatory, Nuffield Foundation, UNDP-Act and the University of Cyprus for its internal funding and Onisilos post-doctoral grants. I also want to thank the Deputy Ministry of Research, Innovation and Digital Policy for funding the European Social Survey in Cyprus. I also extend my gratitude to the International Society for Political Psychology for the 2024 Nevitt Sanford Award for Professional Contributions to Political Psychology.

Special thanks go to my good friend and research partner, Professor Neophytos Loizides of Warwick University, since through our collaboration and his support with various projects funded by Leverhulme Trust (RF-2014-401), the US Institute of Peace (G-1703-172) and the British Academy (AF16002) we were able to collect many of the data used for this book in both communities of Cyprus and to publish together various papers mentioned in this volume. Neophytos and the other members of our team from other disciplines beyond psychology (Edward Morgan Jones, Laura Sudulic, Djordje Stefanovic, Raluca Popp), as well as Daniella Donno and Deniz Yucel, helped me to expand my horizons into the importance of the political, sociological and international relations perspective beyond my original training in education and psychology.

Data collection with large representative samples in both communities of Cyprus would not have been possible without the help of Andrea Nicolaou, Evangelos Georgiou and Maria Perivolaraki working with me at the University Centre for Field Studies of the University of Cyprus (UCFS). I also want to thank the field researchers working at UCFS and Evangelos Georgiou who prepared the table in Appendix C of the book.

The contributions of Huseyin Cakal and Maria Ioannou from the Oxford Centre for the Study of Intergroup Conflict to this research programme are invaluable. I want to thank Eliz Tefik, Mine Yucel, Huseyin Cakal, Shenel Husnu and Deniz Yucel for their co-operation over these years in making possible research in the Turkish Cypriot community of Cyprus, thus giving voice to the views of all Cypriots across the existing divide. Huseyin and Shenel should also be thanked along with Irini Kadianaki, Maria Ioannou, Eleni Lytras, and Kyriakos Pachoullides for their efforts and inspiration to work together for the benefit of social psychology in Cyprus beyond ethnic divisions and for the establishment of the Cyprus Association of Social Psychology (CASP) in 2007. I also want to thank Huseyin Cakal, Irini Kadianaki, Marios Kyriakides, Eleni Lytra, Orkun Yetkili, Maria Ioannou, Andreas Michael, Nazife Fuat and Dize Irkad, who, as the new board of CASP in a constitutional assembly in 2019, unanimously decided to change the constitution of CASP to have a board of a federal structure with two co-presidents.

Feedback from PhD students in our genetic social psychology lab at the University of Cyprus has been very valuable, and I want to thank them for that. I specifically want to thank Eleni Anastasiou for preparing the index of the book. Post-doctoral researchers at our lab, Maria Avraamidou, Christiana Karayianni and Dora Georgiou, contributed various ideas relating to the study of media, communication and transitional justice.

I also want to thank Ayse Uskul, Borja Martinovic and Neophytos Loizides who honoured me with being part of their successful European Research Council (ERC) applications (HONORLOGIC, OWNERS and PEACERETURN, respectively), and for including me as the Cyprus partner in their international networks. Similarly, I want to thank Laurent Licata for leading the COST action 1205 that brought together for the first time historians, history teachers and social psychologists, and Mario Carretero for leading MAKINGHISTORIES of similar interdisciplinary composition more recently. The writing up of this book was also supported by MAKINGHISTORIES, 101086106, Marie Curie Staff Exchange (EU). Participation in all these networks has greatly enhanced the interdisciplinarity of my proposal in this book.

Finally, as always, I want to thank my family and in-laws for their support in bringing up our son Maximos and for their resilience as internally displaced persons after 1974 in offering the next two generations of our family everything they could.

Charis Psaltis

Introduction: Contextualising Conflict and Change

Charis Psaltis and Brady Wagoner

Setting the Scene: Internal Conflicts and Joint Collective Action

The picture on the cover of the book was taken on 7 March 2020 next to the Greek Cypriot checkpoint by a journalist who was in the UN-patrolled buffer zone at the centre of divided Nicosia. It depicts both Greek Cypriot and Turkish Cypriot demonstrators who were jointly protesting the closure of this checkpoint one week earlier on Saturday, 29 February 2020, by the authorities of the Republic of Cyprus over coronavirus disease (COVID-19) concerns. The Greek Cypriot police clashed with Turkish Cypriot protesters in Nicosia a week later, on 7 March, as demonstrators denounced, twice in a week, the closure of the Ledra Street checkpoint in the UN-controlled buffer zone between the Republic of Cyprus and the internationally unrecognised Turkish Republic of Northern Cyprus. Greek Cypriot police reportedly used pepper spray or tear gas on some Turkish Cypriot protesters near the checkpoint. One week earlier some 200 Greek Cypriot protesters at the pedestrian Ledra Street checkpoint barged through the same police barricades, scuffling with officers, and crossed to the north, despite efforts to stop them. There they were joined by Turkish Cypriot protesters.

It is worth noting that on the day of these protests there was no reported confirmed case of COVID-19 in either the south or the north of the Cyprus divide. This fact, the protesters argued, suggested that COVID-19 was being used as an excuse to close the checkpoints and prevent free movement on the island. In the minds of the protesters there was a series of developments after the most recent failure at Crans Montana Switzerland to resolve the Cyprus problem in July 2017 that suggested Nicos Anastasiades, president of the Republic of Cyprus and Greek Cypriot leader in the negotiations to solve the Cyprus issue, was becoming comfortable with the idea of partitioning Cyprus. They thought he started negotiating the partition of Cyprus with Turkey behind closed doors without any mandate from the people who elected him to do so and was undermining the agency of the pro-reconciliation and pro-BBF (Bizonal Bicommunal Federation) Turkish Cypriot leader Mustafa Akinci by taking unilateral actions of this kind. Interestingly, in the same period, pro-federalist Akinci was also undermined by Turkey's pressing for the abandonment of the BFF model in favour of a two-state solution in Cyprus. This shift in policy by Turkey was accompanied by increasing tensions in the Eastern Mediterranean around the contested areas of the Exclusive Economic Area (EEZ) and hydrocarbon findings and antagonising Greece in the Aegean Sea.

This was the first time any of the crossings have been shut for any reason after 2003 when some checkpoints opened for the first time since the war of 1974 and the complete geographical division of Cyprus. The first crossing point to open was the Ledra Palace in April 2003, but Ledra Street did not open until April 2008 when the Greek Cypriot leader Demetris Christofias and the Turkish Cypriot leader Mehmet Ali Talat were the Cyprus interlocutors, both coming from leftsist, pro-reconciliation and pro-BBF parties.

The protestors on 29 February 2020 and 7 March 2020 held banners 'Open all and more checkpoints. Reunite Cyprus', 'Unite Cyprus Now' and 'Stop the divisionist virus'. The image of a Turkish Cypriot female protestor making a hand gesture in the form of a heart captured very well the demonstrators' vision of their island as that of love and not of war and division, and it was an apt expression of the feelings and affective state of that part of society: the bicommunal movement and activists that valued intercommunal contacts, friendships and social relationships. They experienced this closure of checkpoints as a direct attack on their vision and efforts for reunification.

This act was an expression of a position in the representational field of the Cyprus issue discovered by bicommunal research since 2007 (Psaltis, 2012a), only four years after the opening of the checkpoints, but its clarity and importance in the consciousness of people as a motivation for joint collective action were the result of a process of a historical change that took almost a generation after the opening of the checkpoints. It was catalysed by the disappointment of the Crans Montana failure where the two communities of Cyprus came very close to a commonly agreed peace plan the principles of which were proposed by the UN Secretary General Antonio Guterres as the 'Guterres framework'. But probably more important here was the uneasy feeling that potentially corrupt politicians were ready to partition Cyprus for their own financial interests.

One had to go back in the history of Cyprus to the British colonial era, to the miners' strike in 1936 and all-female spinners' strike in 1938 (Rappas, 2009), to point out an event in which both Greek Cypriots and Turkish Cypriots were involved in joint collective action against an administration. But the particular event depicted on the cover of the book also exhibited some unnerving parallels with the joint revolts of the two communities against corrupt local elites that went back to the era of Ottoman rule. These elites colluded with the Ottoman rulers to financially exploit the islanders from both communities. At other times the same elites even made fortunes by breaking sanctions exporting wheat to Malta when the local people were starving to death (Hadjykiriakos, 2023).

Had the Greek Cypriots known more about the Ottoman history of Cyprus, they would perhaps join the Ledra Street demonstrations in bigger numbers. As it has been noted by many historians (Hadjianastasis, 2009; Michael, 2009; Hadjikiriakos, 2023), the Ottoman history of Cyprus is a blind spot in both history teaching at Greek Cypriot schools and official historiography, as it is exhausted in the stereotype of "300 years of dark slavery" aligned with the ethnocentric narrative of Greeks of Cyprus who have to face the aggression of barbaric Turks throughout time immemorial (Papadakis, 2008).

In bicommunal circles in 2020 there was a lot of discussion about the Greek Cypriot leader Nicos Anastasiades losing his focus on the effort to reunite Cyprus due to both Russian influence and his involvement in the 'golden passport programme', through the law office carrying his name in Limassol and run by close family members (Drousiotis, 2020, 2021, 2022). Officially titled 'the Cyprus Investment Programme', the passport programme was a citizenship-by-investment scheme that was highly criticised by the European Union (EU). It produced the highest number of per-capita investment citizenship cases globally (Rakopoulos, 2023), making millions for a network of Greek Cypriot lawyers, politicians and real estate agents who served this industry in the south of the divide. According to Rakopoulos (2023), because of this investment policy and its associated returns, the programme was particularly popular, and about 6,000 rich people (mostly Russian oligarchs) had become citizens since 2013 through it by buying property on the island in excess of 2.5 million euros per investor. Most investment was in real estate in Limassol whose skyline recently has been transformed by newly built skyscrapers. Due to this real estate bubble in Limassol most Cypriots can no longer build a new house or even rent because of astronomic land and rent prices.

Just a few months after the Ledra Street incidents, in August and October 2020, *Al Jazeera* published a series of investigative journalism pieces under the title 'The Cyprus Papers',[1] naming beneficiaries related to the golden passport programme of the Republic of Cyprus, which included convicted criminals or people awaiting trial in their home countries. Due to the reactions from the revealed scandal related to a member of parliament and the speaker of parliament and threats of sanctions from the EU, the programme was discontinued in November 2020. The Cypriot president said this was his worst experience in a political career spanning 40 years but did not admit to any corruption criticism and did not resign from office until the end of his term in February 2023.

In the meantime, Turkey intervened in the Turkish Cypriot elections in October 2020 and managed to get the nationalist leader Ersin Tatar elected. Tatar was involved before in the Polly Peck scandal in the United Kingdom[2] when Asil Nadir was sentenced to 10 years in prison after he was found guilty of stealing £29 million from his company Polly Peck during the 1980s. Tatar denied any corruption criticisms after he was elected. Together with Turkey, Tatar changed their policy to supporting a two-state solution in Cyprus, calling the BBF model supported by the UN and the Security Council resolutions and the EU 'dead'. Such hardening of positions went hand in hand with renewed tensions in the Aegean between Greece and Turkey that escalated after the Crans Montana failure. These were tensions over territorial and airspace claims in and over the Aegean Sea. Despite being NATO allies, Greece and Turkey have been at odds on maritime issues concerning the Aegean Sea since the 1970s, but the more recent contestation included delimitation of the EEZ in the Eastern Mediterranean. In the summer of 2022, the two countries came to the brink of a full-blown naval and air military confrontation.

After the change of leadership in the Greek Cypriot community in February 2023 and elections in Greece and Turkey in the same year, there is a new dynamic emerging in the Eastern Mediterranean which seems to be related to an effort by the USA and the EU to lessen Russian influence in the Eastern Mediterannean and to bring back stability in the Eastern Mediterranean, especially since 24 February 2022 when Russia invaded Ukraine. With this war ongoing, the last thing western powers would obviously like to see is war between two NATO countries.

In early 2024, both leaders in Cyprus requested a joint meeting with the UN Secretary General who also appointed Ms. María Angela Holguín Cuéllar of Colombia as his Personal Envoy on Cyprus to assume the good

1 See https://interactive.aljazeera.com/aje/2020/cyprus-papers/index.html.
2 See https://lgcnews.com/pm-tatar-will-not-face-arrest-in-uk-letter-confirms/.

offices role on his behalf to search for common ground on the way forward and to advise him on the Cyprus issue. By the end of 2024, an agreement has been reached between the two leaders to attempt opening new checkpoints and also to hold a multiparty meeting with guarantor powers sometime in 2025.

It is thus hoped that another opportunity might be on the horizon to resolve the Cyprus problem and once again the international community will try to understand what the Cypriots want in terms of the future of their island. Do they want reunification of Cyprus or its partition? Do they still support the BFF model? If yes, what is the specific content of BBF that could be accepted in referendums in the two communities so that the peace package would gain legitimacy with the people? These pertinent questions come 60 years after intercommunal strife in 1964 and 50 years after the complete geographical division of Cyprus in 1974. Last year also marks 20 years since Cyprus joined the EU in 2004 with the EU *aquis* suspended in the north of Cyprus pending a solution of the Cyprus problem, and about the same time since opening of checkpoints in 2003.

The protests depicted on the cover of the book were the manifestation of the joint collective action by members of both communities, and it is an important case of internal ideological conflict over co-operation across the dividing line in Cyprus. This subtype of collective action is understudied in the field of collective action where the main interest is collective action defined by social psychologists as any action that individuals undertake as psychological group members, and with the subjective goal to improve their group's condition (Van Zomeren, 2013). Even analyses of protracted or intractable conflicts (Bar-Tal, 2023) usually paint a homogeneous picture of two conflicting ethnic groups discussing their collective memory (Bar-Tal, 2014) and ethos of conflict (Bar-Tal, 2023) as a system of beliefs that represents the ethnic group as a whole, masking the heterogeneity within ethnic groups on how they represent the conflict and the out-group (s) of that conflict (Psaltis, 2016). It is our firm belief that any understanding of the process of conflict transformation of an ethnic conflict and change needs to delve deeper into issues of heterogeneity (Psaltis, 2012b; Duveen, 2007) and understand change from one position in the representational field to another. Geopolitical analyses of conflicts and the realist school of international relations homogenise this picture even more by treating the nation state and its national interests as the unit of analysis where the public and the people lose any agency to resist what is defined by the elites as the national interest (Trimikliniotis, 2020), ending up ossifying the conflict itself. Given that ethnic conflicts are usually resolved by a peace deal or agreement legitimised by popular vote on a peace plan through referendums (Loizides, 2014), understanding this heterogeneity within each of the conflicting groups in order to design or institutionalise a peace plan acceptable by both sides of the conflict is actually not a luxury but a necessity (see Loizides et al., 2022). Similar previous efforts to chart the views of the the two communities in Cyprus through polling were valuable in helping the UN and negotiators to formulate policy proposals (Lordos, 2009; Sozen et al., 2010) but did not offer an integrative theoretical framework to make sense of their data from a social, developmental or historical perspective. It is our contention in this book that in understanding conflict and change an integrative and interdisciplinary social developmental psychology that takes historical time seriously into account can contribute a lot in this effort.

The joint protests that occurred at the Ledras checkpoint on 7 March 2020 in this sense represented a change of mentality that was being prepared for since the openings of a checkpoint between the divided island at that very spot in 2008 and in the first opening of the checkpoints in 2003. While the ethnic *conflict* of 1963–1964 and the war of 1974 in Cyprus has had lasting consequences in the minds of people (e.g., how they see the other community, their representations and attitudes about the past, present and future of Cyprus), 17 years of contact had led to profound transformations and opened up new possibilities of conflict transformation that people were witnessing during the events depicted on the cover of the book.

The ex-minister of education in Cyprus, Andreas Demetriou, who is a professor of developmental psychology, along with historian Antonis Liakos and political scientist Niyazi Kizilyürek (Demetriou et al., 2021), recently proposed in the *Journal of Intelligence* a developmental/historical theory which propounds an educational programme 'for raising Mandelas'. They argue that no theory of intelligence or intellectual development suffices to generate solutions for serious social or political problems, and we need to focus our attention on the study of how we can cultivate wisdom. They propose that to be useful for this sake, any theory would have to be much broader, accounting for individual and social development on several fronts, such as (1) individual mental development and (2) the contribution of individual development to the functioning of the social groups and institutions at various levels, such as family, city, nation, and humanity, increasingly distancing from an individual's own life. They note that currently, no comprehensive theory exists that would do justice to these interactions. We fully agree with their claims, and we see this book and the proposal for a genetic social psychology as a contribution in this direction. However, to fully comprehend this shift, a new form of psychological theory is needed premised on a social relational epistemology. In the place of an individualist epistemology focused on abstract and timeless central processing mechanisms, we must start from people embedded in complex social relationships and history, recognising the microgenetic processes of communication and dialogue as the motor for ontogenetic and sociogenetic change.

Our approach highlights the nature and conditions of social and psychological change starting from the study of microgenetic processes. Moreover, change must be understood as occurring at interrelated levels of analysis, namely interpersonal interaction (microgenesis), a person's life course (ontogenesis) and society at large in historical time (sociogenesis). At each level, people are shaped by a history of interactions and ideas accumulated up to that point but also use that history to set goals for the future. Thus, psychology should study not only people's current beliefs and behaviours but also the *possibilities* they strive for. In this book, the Cyprus conflict will serve as a rich case study to develop a broader theoretical framework that can be used to understand the processes of change and conflict transformation in other cases. Furthermore, we believe this wider approach is better equipped to tackle other major issues of our day.

Transformation of Conflict and the Path to Reconciliation and Institution Building

The shift in peace and conflict studies towards a focus on 'conflict transformation' rather than solely on 'conflict resolution' represents a significant and positive development (Galtung & Tschudi, 2001; Lederach, 1997). This evolution, as noted by scholars such as Kelman (2008), facilitates a deeper comprehension of the complexities surrounding conflicts, emphasising a more holistic approach compared to the somewhat narrower scope of conflict resolution. Conflict transformation is distinguished by its comprehensive focus not only on ceasing direct violence but also on fostering a sustained commitment to positive peace. This includes addressing structural issues such as inequality, social exclusion and exploitation, as well as cultural violence manifested through prejudices, distrust and perceived threats. Essentially, conflict transformation seeks to modify the underlying systems, structures and relationships that perpetuate violence and injustice.

Theoretical frameworks that extend beyond mere conflict management and resolution underscore the necessity of understanding the mechanisms that facilitate the transformation of conflict from destructive expressions to constructive engagements. These models view conflict as an inherent aspect of daily life, which should be navigated through dialogue, creativity and peaceful means. According to Constantinou (2015), conflict resolution and transformation are complementary, with the latter often serving as a precursor to effective resolution, particularly in prolonged conflicts.

Central to both conflict resolution and transformation is the concept of reconciliation (Nadler & Shabel, 2015), which is pivotal both as a process and as an outcome. Reconciliation reduces the likelihood of violent conflict in scenarios marked by structural inequalities, political instability or transitional periods. It also enhances the durability of peace agreements. Recent contributions from social psychology have been instrumental in enriching our understanding of reconciliation. Kelman (2005, 2008) and others have highlighted the importance of trust in achieving a peace settlement that addresses justice and inequality, thereby ensuring its sustainability.

The emotional dynamics of intergroup reconciliation have been conceptualised as processes of emotion regulation (Čehajić-Clancy et al., 2016) involving a shift towards positive affective states towards former adversaries. This perspective integrates insights from the fields of emotion regulation and intergroup reconciliation, suggesting the modulation of emotions such as hatred, anger, guilt, hope and empathy to facilitate profound psychological transformations. These include changes in beliefs, emotions, identities and behavioural intentions, grounded in theories like the *Intergroup Emotions Theory* (Smith, 1993) or *Integrated Threat Theory* (Stephan et al., 2009).

Critiques have emerged, arguing that viewing reconciliation merely as emotional regulation oversimplifies the process (Shnabel & Ulrich, 2016; Volhard & Twali, 2016), neglecting the necessity for structural and societal changes. This critique aligns with the broader discourse on conflict transformation, which encompasses both societal and individual dimensions of change. From the perspective of social representations, reconciliation involves a shift from a position in the representational field of mistrust and prejudice to one of trust, understanding and reduced threats, facilitated by meaningful intergroup contact and supported by legal and societal structures (Psaltis, 2012a).

Theories focusing on transformative processes view social and national identities as socially constructed, aligning with recent advances in social and developmental psychology. These theories advocate for understanding human and societal change as transformations in social relations, offering a broader perspective than traditional social identity theory, which focuses primarily on categorisation processes. This approach underscores the importance of the transformation of historical master narratives of conflict and social representations (Nasie et al., 2014; Hilton & Liu, 2017; Psaltis et al., 2017) in shaping intergroup relations, highlighting the potential for in-depth societal transformation.

In the case of Cyprus, where an ethno-political conflict of contested sovereignty and power struggle between the two communities (Kızılyürek, 2019) turned into a territorial conflict, ethnic cleansing and violation of international law, sustainable peace can only be achieved by reaching an agreement that safeguards some preconditions that follow the basic principles of the conflict transformation approach: (1) it is supported by the international community, international law and UN resolutions; (2) it satisfies the basic needs and thus accepted by both communities of Cyprus; (3) it entails a compromise for both communities so that no one community will feel they lost at the expense of the other; and (4) it resolves historical structural inequalities and injustices.

As it will become clear from the findings presented in the first part of the book, the only type of solution that satisfies these preconditions in the case of Cyprus is Bizonal Bicommunal Federation (henceforth BBF), since it was the type of solution agreed by the leaders of the two communities in the high-level agreements since 1977, it is the type of solution supported by numerous UN Security Council resolutions, and, as we will see, it is a solution that can be accepted by a majority of voters in both communities.

From the perspective of conflict transformation, there is therefore a clear route to be followed: there needs to be a cultivation of a reconciliation ethos (Shnabel & Ulrich, 2016) in large parts of both communities of Cyprus that will make possible the transformation of co-operative ingroup norms into the setting up of the institution of a federal state. In this process some key outcomes are of crucial importance: the reduction of prejudice in both communities of Cyprus (Hunsu & Lajunen, 2015; Husnu et al., 2018; Yucel & Psaltis, 2020a), the cultivation of trust (Kende et al., 2022; McKeown & Psaltis, 2017), transformation of collective identities (Psaltis & Cakal, 2016), acceptance of renewed cohabitation (Yucel & Psaltis, 2020b), reconciliation (Trimikliniotis, 2023) and acceptance of BBF itself (Psaltis et al., 2020; Loizides et al., 2022) as a model of governance. In this process the reflection, deconstruction and transformation of master narratives of conflict and representations of the past in Cyprus are key (Makriyianni & Psaltis, 2007; Papadakis, 2008; Psaltis et al., 2011; Klerides & Zembylas, 2017). In this book we will propose a multilevel framework to understand processes of change as conflict transformation at different timescales that integrates the most recent findings from the field of intergroup relations in not only social and political psychology but also developmental psychology and history.

UNDERSTANDING CHANGE: THE NEED FOR AN INTEGRATIVE FRAMEWORK

Most of social psychology today remains acontextual and ahistorical, and as the late Gerard Duveen of the Department of Social and Developmental Psychology at Cambridge University always used to say, 'We generally lack good theories of change in the social sciences.' His striving for understanding change inspired both editors of this volume, as he supervised both of our PhDs. He had a vision of creating an integrative social-developmental psychology that he called *genetic social psychology*. Social and developmental psychology have typically been understood as two separate subdisciplines – with their own theories, methods and canonical studies – that only occasionally overlap. Despite their centrality, there have been few attempts in recent decades to articulate a broader integration of the two.

This integration would require an expansive interdisciplinary vision that takes account of different levels of analysis (from individual to societal) and their relationships to each other. Moreover, it will have to explore how the fundamental concepts of conflict and change play out on different levels and timescales. This book aims to provide a vision for integration on the foundations of earlier concepts of development (or genesis) in philosophy, history, social and developmental psychology, and their renewal to meet the big challenges of the 21st century and our living in times of accelerated historical change after the 1950s (McNeill & Engelke, 2016) that is not only affecting the survival of the human species in the Anthropocene through climate change but also increasing inequalities, global injustices and intergroup conflict, bringing back the spectre of a new cold war, divisions of East and West, North and South, and eventually the real threat of nuclear extinction.

With China as the new challenger of US financial and military world dominance, the centre of financial gravity of the world is once again turning towards the eastern border of the EU, the Eastern Mediterranean and the Near East. But this time it seems the international antagonisms are not around trade routes described by the Annales historian Fernand Braudel (1949) in his *The Mediterranean and the Mediterranean World in the Age of Philip II*, but around energy routes, pipelines of hydrocarbons (Faustmann & Sözen, 2021; Sozen, 2023) and electricity, posing important questions about the ability of states around the Mediterranean to overcome their historical divisions, 'banal imperialism' (Constantinou, 2021) and animosities to co-operate in finding win–win solutions while at the same time posing important questions about sustainability and clean energy alternatives in these troubled times of climatic change.

Fernard Braudel was not only successful in bringing to global attention the land–sea continuity of the Mediterranean as a key geography for the development of early capitalism in the second half of the sixteenth century. He also inspired generations of first-rate Cypriot diaspora historians (Hadjikyriacou, 2023; Kitromilides, 2019; Zanou, 2018) to reconceptualise the Mediterranean as a fluid space of both antagonism and co-operation and add their voices to historians who are not afraid to deconstruct national myths and are interested in promoting co-operation in our area (Hadjidimitriou, 2021; Katsikas, 2021; Ktoris, 2013; Kızılyürek, 2019; Pavlou, 2015; Perikleous, 2010; Varnava, 2024). Moreover, Braudel's discussion of the multiplicity of timescales and promotion of interdisciplinary thinking are key in any serious attempt to approach issues of historical change. Braudel distinguishes the structures of *La longue durée* (The Long Duration), Conjuctures and Events. Despite these useful distinctions, Braudel's approach can be criticised on at least two fronts: first, his downplaying of human agency and importance of psychology in his interdisciplinary approach; and second, and perhaps more fundamentally considering the work of McNeill and Engelke (2016) on accelerated historical change, that his tripartite distinction might no longer be relevant in the 21st century of fast ecological changes, internet communication and globalization.

It seems like the first problem is due to the disciplines of psychology and history traditionally being strange bedfellows. This is in spite of late 19th-century arguments for modelling psychology on history, as Wilhelm Dilthey had done and even partially Wilhelm Wundt in his *Völkspsychologie.* In an insightful discussion between social psychologists and historians in an edited volume by Tileagă and Byford (2014) entitled *Psychology and History: Interdisciplinary Explorations*, it was made clear that there exists a historical divide between psychology and history. The editors note that despite sharing a common interest in understanding human behaviour and societal phenomena, the two disciplines have often operated in isolation, each with its distinct methodologies, theoretical frameworks and epistemological underpinnings. This separation has led to a lack of substantive dialogue and collaboration between these disciplines.

Methodologically, psychology's reliance on empirical, often experimental methods contrasts with history's focus on narrative and interpretive analysis of past events. This methodological divergence has been a significant barrier to interdisciplinary work. As we show in this volume, the first barrier can be overcome through the application of mixed methods. There is also a difference in temporal focus. Historians typically engage with long-term processes and changes over extended periods, while psychologists often concentrate on immediate or short-term human behaviours and mental processes. This difference in temporal scales can make it challenging to integrate insights from the two fields. We believe that historical timescales like the ones proposed by Braudel and the ones that we will propose in our approach as microgenesis, ontogenesis and sociogenesis can be both overlapping and complementary. But maybe even more important in any analysis of conflict and change is the question of *what* changes, *how* (through which mechanisms) and the *quality or depth* of that change.

For example, Moghaddam (2018) recently discussed transitions from dictatorships or totalitarian regimes to democracies observing that historically there are actually only a few rare successful instances of such transitions to what he calls 'actualised democracies'. He defines actualised democracies as a democracy where there is full, informed, equal participation in wide aspects of political, economic and cultural decision-making independent of financial investment and resources. He makes the distinction between first-, second- and third-order societal change. First-order change takes place without altering either the formal law or the informal normative system that justifies unequal treatment on the basis of group membership. Second-order change involves change in formal law to make illegal unequal treatment on the basis of group membership, but the informal normative system continues to allow unequal treatment on the basis of group membership. Third-order change involves a transformation of both the formal and informal systems: it is a change of systems, from one system to another, rather than a change only within a system.

The editors and contributors in the Tileagă and Byford (2014) volume discuss fields of fruitful interdisciplinary exchange between history and psychology, such as the study of collective memory, stereotypes, prejudice, identity formation and social representations, where insights from both disciplines can mutually enrich understanding. These examples demonstrate how interdisciplinary research can lead to more comprehensive and nuanced perspectives. In this book we aim to extend this discussion through the case study of divided Cyprus and historical transformation of social representations of each community about the other community, prejudice, trust and the potential of renewed cohabitation as well as representations of the past in the last 20 years. Perhaps more ambitiously, we would like to outline the programmatic contours of a once and future discipline that integrates social and developmental psychology in the study of different timescales and different quality of change that our late supervisor Gerard Duveen called genetic social psychology. This approach is a kind of history from below that resonates with the position about the role of history proposed by Duveen's favourite author, Walter Benjamin.

Such an approach was applied in the historical work of E. P. Thompson (1974) in his study of the labour class in the United Kingdom, and in Cyprus in the study of the labor class in the transition from the Ottoman to the British period by the late historian Rolandos Katsianounis (1996). The present book will play a similar function in giving voice to laypeople from the two communities beyond the elite views or the views of some politicians in Cyprus that might have their own agendas, individualist considerations of becoming billionaires or perceptions about the Cyprus problem. At the end of the day we are interested in the views of the people that will be voting in a referendum in both communities if we ever get to an agreed package by the leaders of the two communities. This is the voice that on various occasions has been suppressed, hijacked[3] or distorted by the elites and media conglomerates in Cyprus with an anti-federalist agenda (Avraamidou & Psaltis, 2022).

The social developmental theoretical framework advanced in this book offers valuable insights to the Progressive Psychology book series it belongs to, as it shares with it some key concerns such as ending discrimination and prejudice, combating the psychological consequences of interethnic conflict, protecting children in conflict zones, moving societies to more openness and consolidating and deepening democracy. It avoids the pitfalls of cultural relativism as it builds up its unit of analysis from deep, universal central processes of an epistemological triad of *subject–object–other* and the changing socially constructed social relational configurations through well-defined and empirically validated processes of changing social representations in human groups and communities in specific sociocultural and historical settings. This approach makes possible finding oneself in history as it relates past, present and future, giving agency not only to the historical subjects under study but also to the researchers doing the study. In this way the approach developed here aligns with the 'social psychology of the

[3] An example of this hijacking is reported by investigative journalist Makarios Drousiotis (2022) in his most recent book, *Crime in Crans Montana*. He reports an incident (pp. 284–285) where Anastasiades' PR manager, who was also the in-between with a Russian oligarch close to Putin was informing Anastasiades about an alleged rejection of the peace package under negotiation according to a poll he completed in February 2017. This poll was actually never published even in dailies, so in fact nobody can judge its quality (or even its existence).

world making' model that we have recently proposed (Power et al., 2023). Any representation of the past not only refers to the past but also shapes the present and imagines the future, as we are positioned actors in research and not just objects.

Why Cyprus as a starting point? Cyprus is a small island where one can know more about the internal dynamics and policymaking even at the highest echelons of power. Some say nothing stays secret in Cyprus. Indeed, the owner of one of the biggest nationalist media conglomerates (Hadjicostis, 2023), in a book where he reveals discussions he had with previous presidents of the Republic of Cyprus, reveals that Anastasiades was indeed seriously thinking about a two-state solution in Cyprus at some point. Was he in alignment or complete disagreement on his judgement in relation to what the Greek Cypriot voters wanted? The findings reported in this book will not only answer this question by showing the big discrepancy between his elite ideas and the public but also identify moments in his own governance when efforts for bottom-up change, grassroots initiatives, everyday diplomacy (Constantinou, 2015) and track II diplomacy met top-down decisions by his leadership that made a significant positive impact, like the establishment of the Bi-communal Technical Committee of Education or the programme Imagine.

The geographical position of Cyprus also allows it to be a test case of influences at the international and geopolitical levels of superpowers of the world. In terms of a case of conflict transformation, it is also a middle case between an active conflict (e.g., Israel) and a post–peace accord case (e.g., Northern Ireland, Colombia), and in that sense there are dynamics that could either take Cyprus forward or turn it back whilst helping to understand both ends of the spectrum. We will thus be using Cyprus as an illustrative example to highlight broader concepts and issues important to social and developmental theory in the real world. We see the proposal of genetic social psychology as being complementary to other recent efforts by researchers to synthesise findings from cultural evolution, religion studies, economics, anthropology and psychology (Henrich, 2015, 2020) in our understanding of changes in humanity. Data from Cyprus will further contribute to reducing dependence of our theories built almost exclusively from Western-educated industrial rich democracies (WEIRD) societies (Henrich, 2020).

Preview of the Book

Part I of the book is structured in five chapters written by Charis Psaltis. In Chapter 1 he discusses the philosophical and theoretical foundations of genetic social psychology. He returns to the work of sociologist Lucien Goldmann to broaden the theoretical and methodological purview of genetic social psychology as originally proposed by Gerard Duveen. In Chapter 2 he explores the ontogenesis of prejudice using the framework outlined in Chapter 1. This leads into Chapter 3 on sociogenetic changes, highlighting the role of values in society and through time. In Chapter 4, he applies the broader framework specifically to the Cyprus issue, analysing the microgenesis, ontogenesis and sociogenesis of the conflict, especially how 'otherness' is conceived by both communities. Special emphasis is made on understanding how children in the two communities of Cyprus become politically socialised into a protracted conflict of a deeply divided society through the educational system. Given his particular interest in ontogenetic changes, he reviews work covering childhood, adolescence and adulthood in relation to the development of prejudice and representations of the Cyprus problem. In Chapter 5, he discusses the methodology of articulation of microgenetic, ontogenetic and sociogenetic processes and offers a qualitative analysis of an autobiographical account of his changing representations of the Cyprus problem and the other community as well as a quantitative way of disentangling age, period and cohort effects.

Part II of the book contains several commentaries and extensions on the integrative approach developed in Part I. In Chapter 6 Ivana Marková revisits the epistemological foundations of some of the ancestors of genetic social psychology and particularly the common threads binding these approaches together, which are the concepts of the dialectics of genesis and structure, part–whole relations, and temporality. Marková discusses the way these common threads were linked with the fundamental epistemological questions that had already preoccupied philosophers such as Immanuel Kant, Georg W. F. Hegel and Karl Marx. In her commentary she suggests that while the questions about the nature of knowledge bind these philosophers together, their proposed answers surpass their common links because, depending on their epistemological presuppositions, their answers are based on diverse concepts concerning the nature of knowledge. Consequently, these answers were reflected in different ways in the contributions of Piaget, Goldmann, Moscovici and Duveen in their studies of the dialectics of genesis and structure.

In his commentary in Chapter 7 Alex Gillespie claims that addressing the human-made problems of the 21st century requires rethinking the aims of social and developmental psychology. It requires scholarship that seeks not merely to describe how humans develop but one that aims to intervene in how humans develop. More fundamentally, it requires resisting the widespread idea that there are causes of human behaviour (socialisation, history, culture) that push us mechanically from the past into the future and instead focus on humans as world-makers. Either by accepting the status quo or resisting it, humans must take responsibility for the world of tomorrow. The question for social psychology is not what causes human behaviour or even how human behaviour changes and develops, but rather what type of people we want to be. Such a pragmatic and genetic social and developmental psychology would be doubly genetic: it is not only about change but also about enabling humans to critically reflect on and collectively guide these changes. Specifically, it needs to critically challenge and expand the possible, ensure that world-making tools are fairly distributed, and create theories of human behaviour that encourage a richer humanity.

In Chapter 8 Tania Zittoun discusses what she calls 'the ambitious project of a genetic social psychology' that proposes to integrate various strands of psychology around a case study, along the tripartite concepts of sociogenesis, microgenesis and ontoegenesis. In her commentary she retraces three variations of the tripartite model (microgensis, ontogenesis and sociogenesis) and highlights conceptual ambiguities they maintain around the issues of affects and their model of the subject. She also indicates how her own work in sociocultural psychology has developed in parallel to the genetic social psychology proposed, and how both approaches seem to concur on the importance of studying complex case studies. Third, drawing on the two previous points, she emphasises the role of affects in the case study reported in the first part of the book, and she argues that it needs an adequate model of the person. She concludes by proposing that a better integration of the two lines of theorisation may lead us to a richer theory of human development.

In Chapter 9 Christina Alexopoulos proposes some theoretical bridges between psychoanalysis and genetic social psychology. She shows how psychoanalysis deals with individual and collective trauma, in relation to the unconscious reproduction of what has caused a psychic breakthrough for the subject and the group, with each aftermath re-semantising painful past experiences. Archaic fears and defence mechanisms are common to everyone before giving way to more evolved modes of functioning. Confrontation with major traumatic experiences can undo the symbolic capacities acquired during human development and plunge the subject and the group into archaic modes of functioning: projection of the bad object outside the group, splitting between an all-good self-image and an all-bad image of the other, denial of the suffering of the outside group. This regressive logic traps the actors in a victimisation likely to lead to further violence or to maintain a climate of permanent threat. She shows that working on the dual recognition of trauma means that the experiences are not hidden; that the point of view of the other, whether inside or outside the group, is integrated; and that a narrative of the past that leaves room for internal and external polyphony is passed on to future generations. This leads to the expression of internal conflict within oneself and one's community, rejecting a monolithic vision of identity and history.

In Chapter 10 Gordon Sammut proposes that divergent perspectives are typically rooted in contrasting worldviews which, in their own right, help to establish a certain social order and structure social relations in determined ways. Worldviews not only grant meaning to individual existence but also help communities to pursue collective goals that advance their members' mutual interests. In their turn, individuals establish communities and participate in collective actions in pursuit of their own interests. In his commentary he argues that human action is characteristically self-interested and oriented towards social relations at the service of collective projects. These collective projects are legitimated by common sense that grants meaning to social objects and events. Processes of social representation serve to fashion objectifications that do not challenge a community's underlying project. In this way, overcoming conflict requires unpacking contrasting action strategies in terms of projects supported by logical perspectives – that is, perspectives that make sense to the individuals involved. He also proposes an argumentation analysis protocol that serves to identify convergent claims between groups with contested visions, thus providing the building blocks for mutually satisfactory solutions revealing targets for social representation transformative interventions.

In Chapter 11 Cathy Nicholson argues that the concern of genetic social psychology is to understand the possibilities for change through different kinds of contact between members of groups in protracted conflicts. This is pursued through an interacting multilayer lens that takes the individual self as a unit, set within a particular intrapersonal, intergroup and societal ideological context. The role of asymmetry is central to the contact hypothesis, yet often ignored, in determining how each group perceives the other and acts on that contact whether through planned or random meetings resulting in positive, negative or ambiguous outcomes. Her own work on the Israeli–Palestinian conflict stands at the foundation for her chapter, using empirical findings from a range of settings to discuss the role of intergroup prejudice affecting contact and how this might usefully map onto the processes of microgenesis, ontogenesis and sociogenesis of social representations of the conflict. This conflict situation is compared and contrasted with the one described by Psaltis (this volume) to arrive at a general model of intergroup conflict and contact within the framework of genetic social psychology.

In Chapter 12 Angela Bermudez offers an autobiographical narrative relating to her trajectory and experience of working in various conflict and post-conflict settings which culminates in a proposition of how to study from a critical stance the normalisation of violence in historical narratives and texbooks. She also makes some linkages with genetic social psychology proposed in this book.

In Chapter 13 Alicia Barreiro, Antonio Castorina and Mario Carretero return to the work of Doise (1986) and his four levels of analysis to discuss the challenge of a dialectical articulation between the individual and society. In their commentary they discuss different ways in which this tension was translated into research in genetic social psychology as well as present their own variant of revised genetic psychology, making links with history teaching and representations of the past. They also touch on some fundamental epistemological issues of interdisciplinarity and the call for a clarification of the ontological and epistemological commitments of genetic social psychology.

In the Conclusion Psaltis answers with a rejoinder to the various commentaries and discusses the relevance of his work for Cyprus and other post-conflict settings.

REFERENCES

Bar-Tal, D. (2014). Collective memory as social representations. *Papers on Social Representations, 23*(1), 5–11.

(2023). *Sinking into the honey trap: The case of the Israeli-Palestinian conflict.* Washington, DC: Westphalia Press.

Braudel, F. (1949/2023). *The Mediterranean and the Mediterranean world in the age of Philip II* (Vol. 2). Oakland: University of California Press.

Čehajić-Clancy, S., Goldenberg, A., Gross, J. J., & Halperin, E. (2016). Social-psychological interventions for intergroup reconciliation: An emotion regulation perspective. *Psychological Inquiry, 27*(2), 73–88.

Constantinou, C. M. (2008). On the Cypriot states of exception. *International Political Sociology,* 2(2), 145–164. https://doi.org/10.1111/j.1749-5687.2008.00041.x.

(2015). Conflict transformation and homodiplomacy. In C. Psaltis, A. Gillespie, & A. Perret-Clermont (Eds.), *Social relations in human and societal development* (pp. 114–133). London: Springer.

(2021). Why Greeks and Turks fight. *Current History, 120*(824), 105–111.

Demetriou A., Liakos A., & Kizilyürek N. (2021). How wisdom emerges from intellectual development: A developmental/historical theory for raising Mandelas. *Journal of Intelligence,* 9(3), 47. https://doi.org/10.3390/jintelligence9030047

Doise, W. (1986). *Levels of explanation in social psychology: European monographs in social psychology.* Cambridge: Cambridge University Press.

Drousiotis, M. (2020). *The gang: The corrupt system of power in Cyprus – The haircut and the entanglement of politicians and lawyers.* Alphadi [in Greek].

(2021). *Crime at Crans Montana: How and why the gang thwarted the Cyprus solution – Corruption, incompetence and foreign dependencies.* Alphadi [in Greek].

(2022). *Mafia State: How the gang abolished the rule of law in Cyprus – Oligarchs / Money Laundering / Corruption / Stake outs.* Alphadi [in Greek].

Duveen, G. (2007). Culture and social representations. In J. Valsiner & A. Rosa (Eds.), *The Cambridge handbook of sociocultural psychology* (pp. 543–559). Cambridge: Cambridge University Press.

Faustmann, H., & Sözen, A. (2021). Cyprus: Political developments and data in 2020. *European Journal of Political Research Political Data Yearbook, 60*(1), 84–102.

Galtung, J., & Tschudi, F. (2001). Crafting peace: On the psychology of the transcend approach. In D. Christie, R. Wagner, & D. Winter (Eds.), *Peace, conflict, and violence: Peace psychology for the 21st century* (pp. 210–222). Hoboken, NJ: Prentice-Hall.

Hadjianastasis, M. (2009). *Cyprus in the Ottoman period: Consolidation of the Cypro-Ottoman elite, 1650–1750.* Ottoman Cyprus: A Collection of Studies on History and Culture. Wiesbaden: Harrassowitz Verlag.

Hadjidemetriou, T. (2021). *Republic of Cyprus 1959–1964: State and parastate [in Greek].* Athens: Papazisis.

Hadjikostis, C. (2023). *7 presidential portraits [in Greek].* Thessaloniki: Germanos.

Hadjikyriacou, A. (2021). Economic geographies. In R. Bavaj, K. Lawson, & B. Struck (Eds.), *Doing spatial history* (pp. 252–273). London: Routledge.

(2023). *Earthly island: The Mediterranean and Cyprus in the Ottoman era of revolts [in Greek].* Thessaloniki: Psifides.

Henrich, J. (2015). *The secret of our success: How culture is driving human evolution, domesticating our species, and making us smarter.* Princeton, NJ: Princeton University Press.

(2020). *The weirdest people in the world: How the West became psychologically peculiar and particularly prosperous.* New York: Farrar, Straus & Giroux.

Husnu, S., & Lajunen, T. (2015). Predictors of intergroup bias in Turkish Cypriots. *International Journal of Intercultural Relations, 44,* 63–71.

Husnu, S., Mertan, B., & Cicek, O. (2018). Reducing Turkish Cypriot children's prejudice toward Greek Cypriots: Vicarious and extended intergroup contact through storytelling. *Group Processes & Intergroup Relations, 21*(1), 178–192.

Katsiaounis, R. (1996). Labour, society and politics in Cyprus during the second half of the nineteenth century. PhD thesis, Kings College of University of London.

Katsikas, S. (2021). *Islam and nationalism in modern Greece, 1821-1940*. Oxford: Oxford University Press.

Kelman, H. C. (2005). Building trust among enemies: The central challenge for international conflict resolution. *International Journal of Intercultural Relations, 29*(6), 639–650.

(2008). Reconciliation from a social-psychological perspective. In A. Nadler, T. Malloy, & J. Fisher (Eds.), *Social psychology of intergroup reconciliation: From violent conflict to peaceful co-existence* (pp. 15–32). Oxford: Oxford University Press.

Kende, J., Psaltis, C., Reiter, J., Fousiani, K., Cakal, H., & Green, E. (2022). Past and present intergroup contact and conflict among inhabitants of former mixed villages of Cyprus: The role of individual and collective experiences in predicting attitudes and trust. *Political Psychology, 43*(4), 751–768.

Klerides, E., & Zembylas, M. (2017). Identity as immunology: History teaching in two ethnonational borders of Europe. *Compare: A Journal of Comparative and International Education, 47*(3), 416–433.

Ktoris, S. (2013). *Turkish Cypriots: From marginalisation to partnership, 1923-1960* [in Greek]. Athens: Papazisis.

Kızılyürek, N. (2019). *A history of violence and resentment: The genesis and evolution of ethnic conflict in Cyprus* [in Greek]. Nicosia: Heterotopia.

Kitromilides, P. (2019). *Insular destinies: Perspectives on the history and politics of modern Cyprus*. Routledge: Taylor & Francis.

Lederach, J. P. (1997). *Building peace: Sustainable reconciliation in divided societies*. Washington, DC: United States Institute of Peace Press.

Liu, J. H., & Hilton, D. J. (2005). How the past weighs on the present: Social representations of history and their role in identity politics. *British Journal of Social Psychology, 44*, 537–556.

Loizides, N. (2014). Negotiated settlements and peace referendums. *European Journal of Political Research, 53*, 234–249. https://doi.org/10.1111/1475-6765.12043.

Loizides, N., Psaltis, C., Morgan-Jones, E., Sudulich, L., Popp, R., & Baykiz, T. (2022). Citizens and peace mediations in divided societies: Identifying zones of agreement through a conjoint survey experiment. *Journal of Conflict Resolution, 66*(9), 1619–1649.

Lordos, A. (2009). Rational agent or unthinking follower?: A survey-based profile analysis of Greek Cypriot and Turkish Cypriot referendum voters. In T. Diez & N. Tocci (Eds.), *Cyprus: A conflict at the crossroads* (pp. 17–47). Manchester: Manchester University Press.

Makriyianni, C., & Psaltis, C. (2007). History teaching and reconciliation. *Cyprus Review, 19*, 43–69.

Makriyianni, C., Psaltis, C. & Latif, D. (2011). History teaching in Cyprus. In E. Erdmann & W. Hasberg (Eds.), *Facing mapping, bridging diversity: Foundations of a European discourse on history education, part 1* (pp. 91–138). Frankfurt Wochen Schau Wissenschaft.

Marková, I., & Gillespie, A. (Eds.). (2011). *Trust and conflict: Representation, culture and dialogue*. London: Routledge.

McKeown, S., & Psaltis, C. (2017). Intergroup contact and the mediating role of intergroup trust on outgroup evaluation and future contact intentions in Cyprus and Northern Ireland. *Peace and Conflict: Journal of Peace Psychology, 23*(4), 392.

McNeill, J. R., & Engelke, P. (2016). *The great acceleration: An environmental history of the Anthropocene since 1945*. Cambridge, MA: Harvard University Press.

Michael, M. N., Gavriel, E., & Kappler, M. (Eds.). (2009*). Ottoman Cyprus: A collection of studies on history and culture (Vol. 4)*. Wiesbaden: Otto Harrassowitz Verlag.

Moghaddam, F. M. (2018). The road to actualized democracy: A psychological exploration. In B. Wagoner, I. Bresco de Luna, & V. Glavenau (Eds.), *The road to actualized democracy: A psychological exploration* (pp. 3–23). Charlotte, NC: Information Age Publishing.

Nadler, A., & Shnabel, N. (2015). Intergroup reconciliation: Instrumental and socio-emotional processes and the needs-based model. *European Review of Social Psychology, 26*, 93–125.

Nasie, M., Bar-Tal, D., Pliskin, R., Nahhas, E., Haperin, E. (2014). Overcoming the barrier of narrative adherence in conflicts through awareness of the psychological bias of naive realism. *Personal and Social Psychology Bulletin, 40*, 1543–1557.

Papadakis, Y. (2008). A comparison of schoolbooks on the "history of Cyprus". *History & Memory*, 20(2), 128–148.

Pavlou, P. (2015). *State, ideology, politics and education in Cyprus 1959–1974* [in Greek]. Athens: Papazisis.

Perikleous, C. (2010). *Republic of Cyprus: 50 years painful road [in Greek]*. Athens: Papazisis.

Power, S. A., Zittoun, T., Akkerman, S., Wagoner, B., Cabra, M., Cornish, F., et al. (2023). Social psychology of and for world-making. *Personality and Social Psychology Review*, 10888683221145756.

Psaltis, C. (2012a). Intergroup trust and contact in transition: A social representations perspective on the Cyprus conflict. In I. Marková & A. Gillespie (Eds.), *Trust and conflict: Representations, culture and dialogue* (pp. 83–104). London: Routledge.

(2012b). Culture and social representations: A continuing dialogue in search for heterogeneity in social developmental psychology. *Culture & Psychology, 18*(3), 375–390.

(2016). Collective memory, social representations of intercommunal relations, and conflict transformation in divided Cyprus. *Peace and Conflict: Journal of Peace Psychology, 22*(1), 19.

Psaltis, C., & Cakal, H. (2016). Social identity in a divided Cyprus. In S. McKeown, R., Haji, & N. Ferguson (Eds.), *Understanding peace and conflict through social identity theory* (pp. 229–244). Cham: Springer.

Psaltis, C., Cakal, H., Loizides, N., & Kuşçu Bonnenfant, I. (2020). Internally displaced persons and the Cyprus peace process. *International Political Science Review, 41*(1), 138–154.

Psaltis, C., Carretero, M., & Čehajić-Clancy, S. (2017). *History education and conflict transformation: Social psychological theories, history teaching and reconciliation*. Berlin: Springer Nature.

Rakopoulos, T. (2023). *Passport island.* Manchester: Manchester University Press.

Rappas, A. (2009). The labor question in colonial Cyprus, 1936–1941: Political stakes in a battle of denominations. *International Labor and Working-Class History*, *76*(1), 194–216.

Shnabel, N., & Ullrich, J. (2016). Putting emotion regulation in context: The (missing) role of power relations, intergroup trust, and groups' need for positive identities in reconciliation processes. *Psychological Inquiry*, 27(2), 124–132.

Smith, E. R. (1993). Social identity and social emotions: Toward new conceptualizations of prejudice. In D. M. Mackie & D. L. Hamilton (Eds.), *Affect, cognition, and stereotyping: Interactive processes in group perception* (pp. 297–315). San Diego, CA: Academic Press.

Sözen, A. (2023). Cyprus: Leveraging the energy factor to support peacemaking. *FrankfurtWochen Schau WissenschaftConflict Resolution in the Mediterranean: Energy as a Potential Game-Changer*, 37, 37–50, https://diplomeds.org/wp-content/uploads/2023/04/Cyprus-Leveraging-the-Energy-Factor-to-Support-Peacemaking.pdf.

Sözen, A., Lordos, A., Kaymak, E., & Christou, S. (2010). *Next steps in the peace talks: An island-wide study of public opinion in Cyprus*. Cyprus 2015. Available at: http://cyprus2015.org/index.php?option=com_phocadownload&view=category&id=1%3Apublic-opinion-poll&Itemid=34&lang=en.

Stephan, W. G., Ybarra, O., & Rios Morrison, K. (2009). Intergroup threat theory. In T. Nelson (Ed.), *Handbook of prejudice* (pp. 43–59). Mahwah, NJ: Lawrence Erlbaum Associates.

Thompson, E. P. (1974). Patrician society, plebeian culture. *Journal of Social History*, 7(4), 382–405.

Tileagă, C., & Byford, J. (Eds.). (2014). *Psychology and history: Interdisciplinary explorations*. Cambridge: Cambridge University Press.

Trimikliniotis, N. (2020). The national question, partition and geopolitics in the 21st century: The Cyprus problem, the social question and the politics of reconciliation. In R. Latham, K. B. Murray, J. von Bargen, & A. T. Kingsmith (Eds.), *The radical left and social transformation: Strategies of Augmentation and Reorganization* (pp. 147–164). London: Routledge.

(2023). Sitas, the poet-sociologist of spaces for struggles and reconciliation: reconnecting postcolonial Cyprus to South Africa and the world. *Journal of Contemporary African Studies*, *41*(3), 291–308.

Trimikliniotis, N., and U. Bozkurt. (2012b). Rethinking the postcolonial Cypriot statehood: The Cyprus problem, class struggle and ethnic conflict. In N. Trimikliniotis & U. Bozkurt (Eds.), *Beyond a divided Cyprus: A state and society in transformation* (pp. 47–66). New York: Palgrave MacMillan.

Trimikliniotis, N., Georgiou, M., Kaymak, E., Koulaxi, A. M., Mevsimler, M., Charalambous, G., ... & Achiri, E. (2023). Mobile citizenship, states of

exception, and (non) border regimes in the pandemic and post-Covid19 Cyprus. London: Hellenic Observatory.
Trimikliniotis, N., & Tsianos, V. (2023). A refugee crisis or a crisis of anti-immigrant politics? Hostile refugee reception, the pandemic and new solidarities in Cyprus. In V. Ioakimidis & A. Wyllie (Eds.), *Social work's histories of complicity and resistance: A tale of two professions* (pp. 183–203). Bristol: Policy Press.
Van Zomeren, M. (2013). Four core social-psychological motivations to undertake collective action. *Social and Personality Psychology Compass*, *7*(6), 378–388.
Varnava, A. (2009). *British imperialism in Cyprus, 1878-1915: The inconsequential possession*. Manchester: Manchester University Press.
(2024). Revisiting the road to Cypriot independence. *European Review of History*, *31*(4), 612–634.
Vollhardt, J. R., & Twali, M. S. (2016). Emotion-based reconciliation requires attention to power differences, critical consciousness, and structural change. *Psychological Inquiry*, *27*, 136–143.
Yucel, D., & Psaltis, C. (2020a). The effects of direct and indirect contact on prejudice: 2007 and 2017 results among Greek Cypriots and Turkish Cypriots. *European Societies*, *22*(5), 610–635.
(2020b). Intergroup contact and willingness for renewed cohabitation in Cyprus: Exploring the mediating and moderating mechanisms. *Group Processes & Intergroup Relations*, *23*(4), 578–597.
Zanou, K. (2018). *Transnational patriotism in the Mediterranean, 1800-1850: Stammering the nation*. Oxford: Oxford University Press.

PART I

Genetic Social Psychology
A Once and Future Discipline

CHAPTER 1

Theoretical Foundations
Understanding Genesis

Charis Psaltis

On Genesis

The term *genetic* as a method of scientific study of the emergence, development or change of a phenomenon or an organism has a long history that can be traced back to the writings of presocratics like Anaximander and Heraclitus where one can identify the interest in the study of a changing world as a process rather than as a collection of static objects. Aristotle also believed that we cannot really understand something unless we understand its development (Kaplan, 1967). Nevertheless, a first clear vision of the genetic method as the study of the development of an organism can be located in the work of Goethe, who articulated an organismic theory of development, which was the key inspiration for the seminal work of the 20th-century developmental psychologist Heinz Werner (Wagoner, 2024).

The more recent and direct predecessors of the theoretical framework being developed here can be found in Jean Piaget's genetic epistemology, Lucien Goldmann's genetic structuralism, Serge Moscovici's genetic model of social influence and, more recently, Gerard Duveen, who was working in Cambridge until his untimely passing in 2008 towards a *genetic social psychology*, greatly inspired by the vision of his first PhD supervisor Hans Furth, for an integrative social developmental psychology situated in historical time.

There is a common thread that binds all the aforementioned thinkers together, specifically the grasp of the totality of an object of study through an investigation of its development through time. This dialectic of genesis and structure refers directly to some of the more fundamental epistemological questions with which not only classical philosophy but also the modern philosophy of Kant, Hegel and Marx engaged. Indeed, by returning to the philosophical roots of these ideas when disciplinary boundaries were not as sharply defined as today one realises that the dimension of historical change is inextricably intertwined with what is proposed here. While it is very ambitious indeed to be proposing an interdisciplinary field of study that merges social and developmental psychology with history, we do believe that such a new discipline is what can help psychology out of what Valsiner (2013) described as its deep crisis, caused by its success in amassing large quantities of empirical evidence while rarely addressing the question 'what for?'

Indeed, the value of such accumulation of empirical evidence for the generalising power of science is specifically questioned by Valsiner (2013, p. ix), who highlights the life work of the late Gerard Duveen as 'a good illustration of what kind of scholarship could bring psychology out of its crisis of limited generalization value' and explicitly describes Duveen's life project of genetic social psychology as 'the idea that will live'; hence the optimistic and future-oriented subtitle of Part I of this book, 'a once and future discipline'.

Vygotsky and Piaget in Context

From an epistemological point of view one can go back to the enlightenment ideas and Kant to get a clear sense of the limits of human knowledge because of its constrained nature through both sensations and deductive thinking. However, for Kant sensations are worked on and given form by the a priori categories (space, time, etc.), and in that sense these categories themselves were not constructed but given. True dialectical thinking, as argued by Lucien Goldmann (1959, 1967, 1969), can only be found in the more sociological and historical thinking of Hegel and Marx, who offer the tools to understand the socially constructed nature of these categories themselves. Moving from philosophy to psychology, the elaboration of this dynamic and transformative view of genesis and structure is later taken on by Piaget, Vygotsky, Moscovici, and Duveen in the 20th century. Genesis relates to the Greek word *γέννησις and γίγνεσθαι*, the first meaning the process of being born or created and the second the process of change and transformation. In that sense it refers to the beginning of something new and its tranformation. But, of course, nothing is completely new; new structures are built on old structures, and in that sense there is also continuity. As pointed out by Piaget, there is no genesis without structure and no structure without genesis. The main research interest then becomes the study of how structure A transforms into structure B.

In the psychological field Vygotsky (1962, 1978) dealt with a similar problem of the emergence of higher psychological functions and scientific concepts, but his formula of the general genetic law of cultural development – the Janet–Vygotsky law according to Valsiner (2000, p. 40) – was somewhat different from Piaget's. Vygotsky proposed a clearer directional sociogenetic view compared to Piaget's interactivist view. Whilst Vygotsky's emphasis was on mediation by signs and sign systems, for Piaget knowledge was built through the subject's action on objects. The internalisation formula offered by Vygotsky from social speech to thought was, according to Moscovici (1990, p. 179), 'too good to be true', and Duveen (1997) argued it failed to grasp the mediating role of social identity.

There is an open debate about how Marxist Vygotsky really was (Kozulin, 1990; Elhammoumi, 2002; Sève, 2018), but what has become clear by now is that there is a Western reading of Vygotsky that attempted to sanitise Vygotsky from Marx so that his writings could be more easily accepted in the West during the Cold War era. Piaget also fell victim to an individualist reading of his work, especially in his reception in the United States (Hsueh, 2009). These kinds of processes of sociogenetic transformation of a theory in their reception in a new context is easily rendered intelligible through a reading of the second part of Moscovici's (1976/2008) book on psychoanalysis, where he describes the way any new ideas are domesticated in a local setting. In his case it was the study of the reception of the scientific theory of psychoanalysis by different interest groups and ideologies (liberal press, church and the communist party) in French society in the latter part of the 1950s.

In fact, it can be shown that both Piaget and Vygotsky proposed a thoroughly dialectical theory, where logic and consciousness emerge from the activity of the psychological subject in his/her social and historical environment. However, the universalist overtones of Piaget's theory relegate the role of sociocultural variations to a secondary role of acceleration or deceleration of cognitive and moral development through a single path from sensorimotor, through pre-operational and concrete operational, to formal operational thinking. We do believe in the universality of the distinction between social relations of constraint and co-operation as the prototype of relations between child–adult (constraint/unilateral respect) and child–child (peer/mutual respect) dyads. In any society of this world such relations are present and have predictable consequences for the cognitive and moral development of the child. Their manifestation in both one-on-one interpersonal relations and part–whole relations (the way individuals are embedded in groups), we claim, introduces most of the variability in ways of thinking, values and morality observed in different geographies and historical points in human evolution systematised recently by Harvard Professor Joseph Henrich (2016, 2020).

Henrich synthesised many findings from anthropology, economics and human and cultural evolution, which cry out for the existence of this important distinction and its consequences in various societies. Although he has not a single citation to Piaget's work and his social psychology, the historical processes Henrich identified (urbanisation, forms of religiosity, kin-based society organisation and political economy, etc.) relating to cultural evolution can all be considered distal predictors of outcomes (cognitive and moral development) identified by Piaget. Henrich is, however, missing the *mediating* and crucial role of relations of constraint and co-operation (Psaltis, 2015a, 2015b; Psaltis et al., 2015; Psaltis & Zapiti, 2014). Such relations are essential to ontogenesis, though in a more messy and complex way than the one foreseen by Piaget (1932, 1995) where varieties of conflicting asymmetries can still create conditions of equilibration and re-equilibration (Psaltis & Duveen, 2006, 2007) and the coordination of perspectives through a process of true engagement of the subject and *participation* in the co-construction of knowledge.

The crucial role of social relations of co-operation in leading thinking to gradually becoming less and less dependent on content as later structures emerge through reflection on the psychological actions of the subject towards the object, rather than the object itself, is key here. At the same time, it is clear from reading Piaget's *Psychogenesis* (Garcia & Piaget, 1989) that these structures (e.g. mathematics) are not historically unchanged universals but are also the result of historical evolution. Vygotsky's cultural historical theory, strongly influenced by Marxist theory, lays fewer universalist claims but is rather weak in formulating the role of social relations in human development. This is something rather unexpected from a Marxist (see Psaltis & Zapiti, 2014) and recognised as one of the weakest points of Vygotskian theorising by Marxist psychologists and philosophers also (Seve, 2018; Wartkofsky, 1984). It requires rectification in the form of future efforts to build psychology's own capital (Elhamoummi, 2002). Despite developments of the post-Vygotskian tradition in the three generations of cultural historical activity theory (CHAT) (Engerström, 2008) that expanded the purview of our understanding of human development as embedded in interacting activity systems, this theoretical expansion clearly failed to capitalise on the strong epistemological foundations of Piaget's theory as well as the theorisation of the role of social relations of power asymmetries in these activity systems.

For Piaget the genetic process of the transformation of structure A to structure B entails a process of disequilibrium and re-equilibration of cognitive structures. Equilibrium is the idea that makes possible the synthesis between genesis and structure. In a discussion that took place in a symposium on 26 July 1959 on genesis and structure with Derrida, Goldmann and Gadillac (Gandillac, Goldman & Piaget, 1965), Piaget gave the example of transition from pre-operational to operational thinking on the conservation of mass, suggesting that conflict of centrations (focusing on only one aspect of a situation at one time) on different dimensions of clay (length, thickness) under transformation is the reason for transition from structure A to structure B. As rightly pointed out by Duveen (2002), this is one of the weakest parts of Piaget's theory, and the reason for this is that it carries too much of an idealist-Hegelian overtone of consciousness being in a position to fix its own inconsistencies by reflection within the same structures of a self-regulated system (that is, conflicting cognitive schemes resolving their inconsistencies within the cognitive system). However, in the same discussion Piaget importantly makes a clear linkage between equilibrated structures and the agency of the child. Piaget's own words are instructive here:

> The equilibrium thus defined is not something passive, but on the contrary something mostly active. It takes an activity that is all the greater as the balance is greater. It is very difficult to maintain a balance of mental point of view. The moral balance of a person presupposes a strength of character to resist disturbances, to preserve values we care about, etc. Balance here is synonymous with activity. (Piaget, 1968, p. 151)

Knowing Piaget's social psychology and methodology in clinical interviews, one would expect to see some linkage between the capacity to resist an adult's counter-suggestion and its cultivation through relations of co-operation, but Piaget does not make this link in his example here.

Such a link could relate to Piaget's distaste for authorities, ideologies or institutions imposing their views on people and the negative implications stemming from relations of constraint for both the cognitive and moral development of the person. The weakness seen by Duveen in Piaget here is created from Piaget's hesitation to create a closer link between his relations of co-operation and equilibration as a process of co-construction with others and not simply an autoregulation of one's own structures. This is one of the manifestations of the 'social' occupying an unstable element in Piaget's thinking (see Duveen & Psaltis, 2008). There is an interplay between self-regulation and other-regulation that Piaget's interest in the epistemic subject did not allow to be empirically investigated. The linkage can be rendered intelligible by the embedding of the epistemic subject in group life and a network of social interactions, where the positions held by an individual for an object are intertwined with the representations of the other and self in the *subject–object–other* triad in both symmetrical and asymmetrical relationships.

Knowledge and Social Structures

From an epistemological point of view, any genetic theory needs to be able to distinguish between surface and depth knowledge. In the Marxist tradition (although Marx never elaborated any epistemological framework himself), the proletariat are those who act on objects, and consciousness is formed by action in the world. This is why the Piagetian notion is compatible with Marxism, and one can see here why Goldmann was so keen on pointing out the similarities between Piagetian genetic epistemology and Marxism on various occasions (Goldmann, 1966; Zimmerman, 1978). Ultimate knowledge of seemingly hidden realities, essences behind appearances such as Kant's elusive 'thing-in-itself' was given only to those who had created that reality (in the way an artist can understand the work he or she has created). Only they could overcome the analytic contradiction of surface and depth dialectically. This distinction between depth and surface knowledge is crucial in Piaget, who proposed a distinction between empirical and reflective abstraction. It is also found in his distinction between relations of constraint and relations of co-operation, where he relates forms of knowing with different qualities of social relations. It is again later found in Moscovici's (1976) dual genetic model of social influence, as well as in the work of Social Genevans (Doise, Mugny & Perret-Clermont, 1975; Doise & Mugny, 1984) who discussed two ways of resolving socio-cognitive conflict (epistemic/constructivist versus relational), further deepening the original insights of Piaget (1932) in his *Moral Judgment of the Child* and his *Sociological Studies* (Piaget, 1995) in this direction.

In the work of other genetic theorists more sociologically and critically minded than Piaget, such as Moscovici and the Social Genevans (Doise et al., 1975), the consequences of symmetrical or asymmetrical forms of social relations on consciousness also became the target of empirical study. The Social Genevans made a distinction between two ways of resolving socio-cognitive conflict: *relational regulation*, which looked like conformity and did not lead to real cognitive change; and *epistemic regulation*, which looked like the reconstruction of knowledge in Piagetian terms towards more equilibrated structures. There is a parallel here with Lucien Goldmann's description of how the *subject–other* relationship can be downgraded into a *subject–object* relation through processes of *objectification*, *reification* or *alienation*. Similar ideas can be found in the field of the study of intergroup relations today with *dehumanisation* or *infrahumanisation* where out-group members in an antagonistic context often lead in forms of non-recognition of others as thinking subjects or even, in worst cases (linked to genocidal tendencies), denigrating them as non-humans.

This strong sense of a dual process of social influence is found more recently in the work of Gerard Duveen, who was convinced that there are two opposing ways in which representations change. In viewing social representations theory as a genetic theory, Duveen and Lloyd (1990) argue that a genetic perspective is implied in the conception of social representations, in the sense that the structure of any particular social representation is a construction, and thus the outcome of some developmental process. Three types of transformations, associated with social representation as a process, are proposed: *sociogenesis*, which concerns the construction and transformation of the social representations of social groups about specific objects in historical time; *ontogenesis*, which concerns the development of individuals in relation to social representations during a lifetime; and *microgenesis*, which concerns the evocation and (re)construction of social representations in social interaction in micro-time.

A careful reading of the oeuvre of Duveen's first PhD supervisor Hans G. Furth leaves no doubt that Duveen's vision of integrating social and developmental psychology came from him. Furth was born in 1920 in Austria and was well known for his significant contributions to our understanding of cognitive development. His early work was deeply influenced by Piaget's theory and focused on the cognitive abilities of deaf children and, later on, the role of language and social interaction in cognitive development (Furth, Baur & Smith, 1976). He was also a psychoanalyst, and he tried to marry Piagetian ideas with Freud's theory. His early life was significantly impacted by the political upheaval of the time as he fled Austria after the Anschluss with Nazi Germany in 1938 at the formative age of 18, eventually making his way to the United States after spending years in displacement in Croatia, Switzerland and the United Kingdom. This experience of displacement and adaptation to new cultures and languages would later influence his professional work and perspectives. He also served for about a decade as a monk in the Carthusian order until his departure to Canada where he got a master's degree in clinical psychology from the University of Ottawa in 1954. He later received a doctorate in psychology from Portland State University in the United States in 1960 and that same year became a professor of psychology at the Catholic University of America in Washington, DC. In the mid-1960s he worked while on sabbatical at the University of Geneva with Piaget. In 1973–1974 Furth spent time at the University of Sussex in the UK where he crossed paths with Duveen (Jovchelovitch, 2010; Lloyd, 2010).

It was a period when Furth began to integrate more complex societal elements into his analysis of cognitive development (Furth et al., 1976). He started to examine how children's understanding of social structures, such as family dynamics, racial categories and gender roles, emerged and evolved. This period marked a shift from focusing solely on individual cognitive processes to a more holistic view that included the impact of societal factors. Furth's work on symbol formation (Furth, 1987), particularly in relation to Freud and Piaget, also influenced Duveen. This work highlighted his interest in how children use symbols to make sense of the world. This was a crucial part of Furth's theory, as it linked cognitive development with cultural and societal influences. He argued that children form symbols not only to understand their immediate environment but also to navigate and make sense of larger societal constructs. In this process of symbol formation, the affective domain and desire occupied a key position. The perception of society and history is constituted by social significations as something new, qualitatively different from preceding forms of social reality. Piaget's symbol competency is, for Furth, precisely the organ to create this newness in evolution: an understanding of human society and history. In brief, according to Furth, children around the age of two, along with a first glimmer of historical time and of social categories such as sex, 'race' and generations, develop the symbolic competency to create signifiers. Here the emphasis is on the active child who assimilates a given society-culture with a framework the child has developed from within. In this respect the child is able to bring novelty to the given social reality.

As Sandra Jovchelovitch (2010, p. xvii) wrote about Duveen's connection to Hans Furth,

> But in line with his teacher and early supervisor, Hans Furth, Duveen problematised this agency [of the child] by introducing the dynamic of desire in the constitution of the epistemic subject. To know-my-object is also to want-my-object. This insight probed a long-term commitment to the deep psychology of Freud, which was never too far from Duveen's thinking and way of seeing the world. In writing about the development of representation and culture in the pretend-play of young children he goes back to the links between knowledge and desire to show how the drive that

moves the child to create and construct the world as innovator is not far from libidinal organisation.

In Furth's last book, *Desire for Society* (1996), he explores more complex themes, such as how children's cognitive development is affected by the political and economic structures of society, which includes examining how children understand and internalise societal norms, values and beliefs. In this work Furth also shows his admiration for the work of Cornelius Castoriadis and his notion of the 'radical imaginary', in this way pointing to the role of social scientists in not only studying societies but also transforming them in the direction of more equal and peaceful ones. The last chapter can be seen as his legacy to the future generation of social scientists (Furth died three years after the book's publication). It is titled 'Postlude: The nightmare of history', and it starts with the words of Walter Benjamin: 'There has never been a document of culture which was not at the same time a document of barbarism.' In this chapter Furth claims that humanity needs to be guided by the memory of two historical events, Auschwitz and Hiroshima, corresponding to a condemnation of the morality of total annihilation which was made possible by nuclear weapons. The historical consciousness that connects these two historical events with the imagination of destroyed earth in the future, he proposes, can guide humanity towards the creation of a peaceful future. The notion of historical consciousness and historical thinking is crucial for the development of the current theoretical framework that wants to understand processes of ethnic conflict transformation and change, and we will have a lot more to say about this in what follows.

From Learning and Cognitive Development to Ethnic Conflict

Under the influence of his second supervisor, Barbara Lloyd, Duveen took it on himself to explore the ontogenesis of social representations of gender in childhood in the years after his PhD (Lloyd & Duveen, 1992). His personal friendship with Serge Moscovici offered him an unparalleled understanding of the theory of social representations, and his developmental take on this theory was truly original. Since 2000, under the supervision of Duveen at Cambridge, we began to explore the role of social representations of gender and social interaction in learning and cognitive development in the educational context. This work in epistemological terms could be described as moving from the study of the epistemic subject in Piaget towards the study of the social psychological subject (Moscovici,

Jovchelovitch & Wagoner, 2013), introducing a study of the role of social identity and gender asymmetry dynamics into the co-construction of knowledge around cognitive tasks. This work was later extended at the University of Cyprus as one strand of the 'third generation of research in peer interaction and cognitive development' (Leman & Duveen, 1999; Psaltis, 2005a; Psaltis & Duveen, 2006, 2007; Duveen & Psaltis, 2008; Psaltis, Duveen & Perret-Clermont, 2009; Psaltis, 2011, 2012a, 2012b; Psaltis & Zapiti, 2014). In this chapter it will be further extended into a study of the articulation of microgenetic, ontogenetic and sociogenetic processes (Psaltis, 2015), through the study of intergroup relations between Greek Cypriots and Turkish Cypriots in the 20-year period from 2003 to 2023, which is a second line of research we have been working on since 2005 at the Oxford Centre for the Study of Intergroup Conflict.

In the first line of research, we observed peer interaction in the educational context of collaborative problem solving in 6–7-year-olds in Cyprus. These social interactive processes were connected to the sociocultural and historical context of social representations of gender related to asymmetrical structures of patriarchy and with the culture of honour that favours a passive femininity, allowing males more space in the public space and control over objects whilst retaining the strengths of a structural analysis of Piagetian constructivism. These series of studies explored the interplay of representations and identities through the articulation of intrapersonal with interpersonal, intergroup and ideological/social representational dynamics (Perret-Clermont, 1980; Doise, 1986), building on Piagetian insights into the role of social relations in cognitive development (Piaget, 1932) and functionalist-structuralist reading of Piaget and his social psychology (Kitchener, 2002, 2009, 2014), together with the empirical work of the social Genevans on peer interaction and cognitive development (Doise, Mugny & Perret-Clermont, 1975; Perret-Clermont, 1980).

Some critical engagement with the initial ideas we developed with Duveen came from another scholar influenced in his work by both Piaget and Moscovici – Antonio Castorina in Buenos Aires. Castorina proposed a similar model to the one presented here that he calls *revised genetic psychology*; however, he is sceptical of the merging of the disciplines of social and developmental psychology, not because of epistemological incompatibility, but out of respect for their own traditions, methodologies, theories and questions posed.

Castorina made his positive yet critical and constructive expositions in two papers. In the first (Castorina, 2010) – a tribute to Duveen shortly after the former's untimely death – Castorina outlines the points he seems to appreciate in Duveen's work. He writes, 'The leitmotif of Duveen's work has been the process through which children assimilate the beliefs of their communities and thus acquire their social identity, which in turn enables them to become social actors' (p. 18.1). Duveen, according to Castorina, (1) elucidates the dialectical process of the development of representations, (2) acknowledges Vygotsky's contribution to the Theory of Social Representations while questioning some aspects of his concept of culture, (3) shows the correlative construction of subject and object in the dialectics of knowledge and (4) establishes the conditions for social representations to be accepted by developmental psychologists.

In this commentary Castorina wrote something that both we and Patrick Leman (2010) found objectionable in his rendering of Duveen's work, namely 'the significance of some of [Duveen's] empirical studies which link psychological development to social identity' as describing a process of *individuation* in social psychology. I believe there is no place in genetic social psychology for individuation (which I take here as meaning social representations forming a sense of individuality). There are at least two reasons for this: (1) Duveen was describing the process of ontogenesis of social representations as the emergence of the social actor and the internalisation of a social identity, not a personal or ego identity; (2) Duveen was interested in the social psychological and not the psychological subject.

Even in the original genetic psychology of Piaget the epistemic subject, the study of which was Piaget's research interest, is not an individual subject but a mere abstraction dealing with the coordination of actions irrespective of whether these take place intra- or interpersonally. Already in his PhD thesis (Duveen, 1983) on a discussion of the epistemic subject Duveen makes clear that the epistemic subject is not an individual subject. Piaget used the example of two individuals building a bridge as an example of co-operation, and Duveen cited the example of two individuals moving a piano that Lucien Goldmann gave to discuss the trans-individual subject, a unit that cannot be reduced to one or the other psychological subject but characterises the dyad. Still, what the epistemic subject was missing (given that it is an abstraction), according to Duveen, was valorisation and resistance, which appear on the scene once we bring into play the subjects belonging to the social group where one shares social representations about an object. This is why, later on, we suggested the idea of operativity in context (Psaltis, Duveen & Perret-Clermont, 2009), and I think we have demonstrated this through the dynamics of social interaction in our own work (Psaltis & Duveen, 2006, 2007) in an Fm dyad (a dyad where the female was a conserver interacting with a male that was a non-conserver) and how it facilitates a conflict of asymmetries that creates the space for the construction of true novelty. In that sense the social gender identity dynamics are co-constructed and do not characterise any individual property.

This brings us to the second criticism voiced by Castorina (2017). In this paper we see both points of agreement and disagreement between Castorina's revised genetic psychology and what is proposed here as genetic social psychology. On the one hand, we agree with Castorina that there is epistemological compatibility between Moscovici's social representations theory and Piaget's genetic psychology, which goes against the position of Ivana Marková (2010) who argued that the two approaches are epistemologically incompatible. Nevertheless, even within a social constructivist epistemology there is still an issue of how much similarity or difference one sees between the construction of scientific knowledge and the construction of understanding and representations of social objects such as gender, ethnicity, a social problem and so forth.

Castorina makes too strong a distinction when he is stating that above all, social representations are inherently evaluative and shaped through social discourse, not limited by the argumentative logic of concepts. Duveen would certainly accept that in the case of scientific knowledge, we have the construction of what Leslie Smith (2013) called 'necessary knowledge' – a kind of knowledge that has a logical necessity absent in the case of representations discussed in this chapter. I feel Castorina is overstretching the differences between genetic psychology and social representations. On this point Duveen talks about relative autonomy and never fails to remind his readers that Moscovici was inspired the notion of representations from his reading of Piaget's *The Child's Construction of the World*. We argued for the embedding of the epistemic subject in the social psychological subject, which means that operative structures can still be found in social representations. Social representations, however, will not be exhausted by them. For example, the binary distinction of gender or race relations in early childhood do appear to be regulated by cognitive developmental constraints of the pre-operational stage. But in older children we see that there is an interplay between the cognitive and the social that cannot be empirically disentangled, as for example when the part–whole relationships become a prerequisite for the understanding of relations between Cypriots and the other community, Greece and Turkey, that of course do not necessarily relate to positive or negative attitudes towards these groups.

Castorina claims that values cannot be organised in the logical sequence that could be given precisely by the structure of a research conducted within developmental psychology, which is true. Still, in the ontogenesis of social representations that Duveen studied (Gender, Friendships, Economy) there was a clear developmental path that was largely defined by two orientations, the practical and the reflective, directly related to the transition from the pre-operational to operational thinking. So, in terms of content, we do agree that there is no evaluative criterion to judge one value over another. However, in terms of structure, there is a clear developmental course suggested by theorising in genetic social psychology.

Castorina in his 2017 paper also states that the claim that genetic social psychology does not differ from developmental psychology, or that the latter always implies the former, is debatable. While, according to Castorina, introducing social representations in developmental psychology can reformulate genetic psychology itself when studying children's social ideas, it is not acceptable to claim that 'the operating Piagetian structures, as Duveen states (1997) and following Moscovici (1989/2000) could actually be understood as social representations' (Psaltis & Zapiti, 2014, p. 38).

Regarding the first statement by Castorina, I think that we never intended to make such a claim, especially when so many varieties of developmental psychology exist. But on the second point I feel that I need to defend our position in Psaltis and Zapiti (2014).

I think that here we see a re-emergence of the individual–social antinomy that I discussed earlier on the issue of individuation under a different guise. In his 'Psychological Development as a Social Process,' Duveen (1997), citing Guida de Abreau's work on social representations of mathematics, writes: '[W]e do not usually think of children's internalization of representations of mathematics as being linked to specific social identities, but this can indeed be the case' (p. 55). He goes on to give the work of Carugati (1990) on the study of social representations of intelligence as another example. In this way he wanted to show that valorisation, the symbolic value of social representations and social stakes are inextricably interlinked with the development of operative structures. The process of 'socially representing' is at play when children co-construct their operational structures. Duveen's favourite example was the work of Doise and Mugny (1984) on social interaction and cognitive development that offered for him the most convincing evidence in this direction. This is the work that we extended in our work with Duveen in Cambridge and later expanded with Anna Zapiti at the University of Cyprus. This was the culmination of work 'which condensed many years of experimental and ethnographic research in Geneva, Sussex and Cambridge on how the construction of the mental is not only permeated by social interaction but dependent on it' (Jovchelovitch & Wagoner, 2013).

Having already explored the contours of a model of transition from pre-operational to operational thought in children through the study of varying forms of communication, such processes could be expanded to a more general model of the role of social relations and communicative forms (Duveen, 2002; cf. Castorina, 2010; Jovchelovitch, 2010; Leman, 2010) in the transition from representations of belief to representations of knowledge in the public sphere (see Duveen, 2008; Moscovici, 2000) and sociogenetic processes (Wagner, 1994) if scaled up.[1] One field of research that affords the exploration of sociogenetic processes in historical time is that of conflict transformation in societies and changing representations of conflict and its roots. In this sense the Cypriot context of a divided and post-conflict society is an ideal setting for the expansion of these ideas to an exploration of sociogenetic processes beyond what Henrich (2020) calls WEIRD societies (Western, Educated, Industrial, Rich, Democratic). Drawing more on conflict and post-conflict settings in such synthetic efforts as the one by Henrich will allow more decentring from a WEIRD way of looking at systems of values, ideas and practices in historical time and cultural evolution.

In our first line of research we did not have the opportunity to study sociogenetic processes. We instead concentrated on the links between microgenesis and ontogenesis in childhood, exploring the interplay between social representations of gender and the co-construction of new knowledge around cognitive Piagetian tasks in 6–7 and 9–10 years age groups. The lack of emphasis on sociogenetic processes in our first line of research left us open to criticism raised by Nicolopoulou and Weintraub (2009) that the third generation of research in peer interaction and cognitive development did not yet offer a comprehensive sociocultural framework for the study of human development. In what follows we aim at opening a window to the study of sociogenetic processes through the study of longer-term changes that take place in historical time complementing recent formulations of cultural evolution by Henrich (2016, 2020).

Thus, more recent work in our Genetic Social Psychology Lab at the University of Cyprus has as its main aim the articulation of the three processes of genesis (microgenesis, ontogenesis, sociogenesis) (Psaltis,

[1] Moscovici's (2000, p. 136) distinction is between (1) social representations 'whose kernel consists of beliefs which are generally more homogenous, affective, impermeable to experience or contradiction, and leave little scope for individual variations' and (2) social representations founded on knowledge 'which are more fluid, pragmatic, amenable to the proof of success or failure, and leave a certain latitude to language, experience, and even to the critical faculties of individuals', which clearly relates back to his social influence model of minority influence and through that to Piaget's (1932; 1967/1995) social psychological model of relations of constraint vs relations of co-operation.

2015). Our main research interest (intergroup contact between the two communities in Cyprus) was initiated at the Oxford Centre for the Study of Intergroup Conflict in 2005, but the theoretical articulation offered below is a direct continuation of the work at Cambridge. It explores the role of social interaction in the reduction of prejudice based on Allport's (1954) contact hypothesis and its recent developments. Here, we have been exploring the effects of social interaction, termed *intergroup contact* in mainstream social psychology (Allport, 1954), between Turkish Cypriots and Greek Cypriots on the reduction of prejudice and promotion of trust at different ages (Psaltis, 2012a; Tausch, Hewstone, Kenworthy, Psaltis, Schmid, Popan, Cairns & Hughes, 2010). More recently we have also embarked on interdisciplinary work with history educators and historians exploring the interplay between representations of history and social psychological theories of intergroup relations (Psaltis, 2012a; Psaltis, Lytras & Costache, 2011; Lytras & Psaltis, 2011; Psaltis, Carretero & Cehajic-Clancy, 2017) as well as deepening the exploration of the internal heterogeneity of social identity positions within conflicting societies as they produce and represent cultural artefacts valorised as symbols (Psaltis, Beydola, Filippou & Vrachimis, 2014) or structure their oral historical accounts about life in formerly mixed villages in Cyprus (Psaltis, Cabrera, Lytras, Filippou, Cakal & Makriyianni, 2014; Kende, Psaltis, Reiter, Fousiani, Cakal & Green, 2022).

The transition from the study of social representations of gender to the study of social representations of ethnic conflict clarified for me the developmental dimension of what is often argued by feminist writings in the field of peace and conflict studies (Hadjipavlou & Mertan, 2010, 2019; Demetriou & Hadjipavlou, 2021) when they approach militarism and nationalism as dimensions of patriarchy. The 'womb' of asymmetrical social relations of constraint is not only relations between children and adults but also relations between girls and boys in early childhood. The first instances of microgenetic marginalisation of girls from boys take place in early childhood (Duveen & Lloyd, 1990), and variations of this marginalisation are later found in hierarchical institutions related to the reproduction of the nation and traditional culture (army, church, political parties). The issue of the marginalisation and sidelining of women from decision-making processes is a phenomenon that can be traced back to the social interaction of students as young as 6–7 years in Cyprus, as we found. Traditional perspectives or honour cultures (Uskul et al., 2023) oppose the political/public sphere to that of the domestic or personal and equate the first with men and the second with women. Such perspectives have long been superseded by both feminist thought and democratic precepts. The public–private distinction has been shown to perpetuate militarism and sexism, making gender inequalities appear 'natural'. In both cases of gender and ethnic asymmetries the position of submission is that which ends up in marginal or non-existent *participation* by the subject, leading to the transmission of a superficial layer of beliefs that minimises the possibilities for knowledge construction and overcoming of asymmetries.

Engagement with the issue of ethnic conflict made more imperative the theoretical understanding of processes of power and the political dimension of party politics, especially as they relate to sociogenetic changes in the social representations of the Cyprus issue when attempting an understanding of sociogenetic changes in the period since the opening of the checkpoints in 2003. In this sense, the articulations between Doise's intergroup and ideological level of analysis concern not only intergroup relations between the two communities in Cyprus but also intragroup political processes, policies and ideologies relating to the valorisation of bicommunal relations and the solution of the Cyprus problem. This has also led us to interdisciplinary work with political scientists and sociologists (Psaltis, Cakal, Loizides & Kuşçu-Bonnenfant, 2020) exploring the views of the internally displaced persons (IDPs) in the two communities as well as policy implications of our work for the negotiation of a settlement and decision-making processes on a referendum for the solution of the Cyprus issue (Loizides et al., 2022). In this research we revealed not only the feeling of loss by IDPs but also their marginalisation from ongoing discussion to resolve the problem and the feeling of injustice in their own community.

In theoretical terms, the broad vision of Furth, the theoretical and methodological sociological insights of Goldmann – one of Duveen's favourite sociologists – and our recent work on historical thinking and historical consciousness in this extension of the theory are crucial. The work of Goldmann is key not only because he applied Piagetian insights to sociological theorising but also because his sociological outlook brings to our attention the significant structures that constrain the agency of the individual as he/she is embedded in the transindividual subject (dyads, groups, social classes) and the understanding of the role of social relationships more generally in the formation of consciousness.

Lucien Goldmann's Genetic Structuralism

Goldmann (1959, 1967, 1969) criticised Marxist interpretations that reduced explanations of societal consciousness to the economy and relations to the means of production. He offered the crucial insight that the predominance of relations to the means of production is only a recent symptom of late capitalism through processes of reification, and that we should be seeing such relations only as one of various expressions of social relations that generally have always been at the centre of the production of societal consciousness throughout humanity's history. This is a politically crucial insight because it suggests that any social critique that concentrates solely on relations through the means of production would be playing strictly in the field of capitalism and not offering a truly critical theory that would manage to transform society at its core. Similarly, Serge Moscovici emphasised the importance of social psychological theorising beyond the monopoly of social class to the study of the relations between various minorities in the context of the conflict with dominant ideologies and views. This broadening of view beyond the narrow focus on social class calls for an understanding of intergroup relations, asymmetries of power and phenomena that have been at the epicentre of study in social psychology after the Second World War. We find the same broadening of the study of social relations in the work of Duveen where he explored beyond the ontogenesis of the representations of social relations of production and the economy to include the ontogenesis of social representations of friendships and gender. In all of these works his emphasis was on the transition from pre-operational to operational understandings of social relationships. One of the main problems caused by asymmetrical social relations is that of reification as shown by Lukacs and later by Goldmann (1967). Thus, a critique of the situation we are currently living in should be performed through an analysis of how reification (in its various forms) works in the formation of consciousness.

According to Petrovic (1991), reification in the Marxists tradition is

> the act (or result of the act) of transforming human properties, relations and actions into properties, relations and actions of man-produced things which have become independent (and which are imagined as originally independent) of man and govern his life. Also transformation of human beings into thing-like beings which do not behave in a human way but according to the laws of the thing-world. Reification is a 'special' case of alienation, its most radical and widespread form characteristic of modern capitalist society. (p. 463)

These, however, are not the only possible subject–object distortions. Both anthropologists and Piaget identified different mentalities in ontogenetic and historical lines of development. One characteristic form of mentality is the one described by Levy-Bruhl as guided by the logic of participation and by Piaget as magical thinking. In this connection the link between magical thinking and existential anxieties is clear. Non-differentiation between subject and object is a specific structure that serves a specific function of soothing existential anxieties. This totality between structure and function was central in both Piaget's and Goldmann's genetic theorising. Egocentric thinking was one of the manifestations of subject–object non-differentiation and the difficulties in overcoming egocentrism in Piaget related to asymmetrical relations of constraint, whilst on the contrary, relations of co-operation (based on mutual respect) help to overcome egocentrism through decentration. Duveen (2002) also suggested that 'belief' is a certain form of understanding that is sustained by relations of *constraint*. On the contrary, 'knowledge' (a more flexible and less rigid form of understanding) is sustained by relations of *co-operation*. In his studies of the ontogenesis of representations of friendship, economy and gender (see Duveen's essays in Moscovici, Jovchelovitch & Wagoner, 2013) he identified a number of structural differences between two orientations that broadly overlapped with Piaget's stages of pre-operational and operational thinking.

For example, in friendships he identified an action-oriented understanding in younger children and a conceptual understanding in older children. In terms of understanding of time and what could be described as early forms of historical consciousness, younger children were trapped in the here and now: a friend was the one who was playing with them. In the older children there was differentiation of time with friendships attaining a history and a move of knowledge from the 'periphery to the centre' which entailed a more complex understanding of the subjective characteristics of friends (traits, characteristics) and of their intentions, thus differentiating action from its meaning.

Duveen also believed that the genetic study of the development of representations should entail the effort to articulate Doise's (1986) four levels of analysis. He criticised the social cognition paradigm for only exploring the intrapersonal level of analysis. In his work on friendships it was clear that he suggested the study of the subjective understandings of social relations by children but also an understanding of the possible structures of social relationships in social interaction. He considered this dual emphasis necessary because of the lack of a clear endpoint of development that was there for Piaget in his effort to understand the development of scientific thinking but could not be established in the case of the understanding of social relations causing a methodological recursivity problem. This was also done by Piaget (1923) himself in his first book on thought and language but also suggested as the key to understanding society as comprised of various forms of social relations and the rules of their transformations (Piaget, 1995). In my own work with Duveen (Psaltis & Duveen, 2006, 2007) we moved further in this direction by identifying varying types of conversation as a microgenetic process that we related with various forms of social recognition and cognitive change, in an effort to typify these forms of social interaction and articulate all four levels of analysis suggested by Doise (1986).

As I will show later, the original work of Piaget and Weil (1951) offers a broad framework for synthesising many of the theories and empirical findings about the development of prejudice in childhood and for understanding the totality of interethnic relations and consciousness beyond the narrow focus of prejudice and prejudice reduction that has become mainstream (see relevant critique by Dixon & Levine, 2012). The use of the iceberg metaphor for the system of values ideas and practices as a position of an individual in the representational field employed by Duveen and Lloyd (1990) and Daniel Bar-Tal in his idea of the ethos of conflict in the context of interethnic conflict in Israel is useful here: We are interested not only in the tip of the iceberg in this system of thinking, which could be a single isolated attitude or feeling towards an out-group (e.g. prejudice), but in the greater, submerged part of the iceberg that is comprised by values, ideas and practices (threats, stereotypes, identifications, perspective taking, trust, representations of the past) of a group or the transindividual subject in Goldmann's terms that sustains positive or negative emotions towards an out-group. This position in the representational field also extends in time as it refers to past, present and future and as such, it is a form of *historical consciousness*.

Historical consciousness is a concept that deals with people's understanding of the relation between the past, present and future, and it has become central recently in history as a discipline, and researchers from across the world deploy the concept in a variety of approaches to history didactical research (Thorp, 2014). Historical consciousness is becoming influential in policymaking too. In Sweden, the Netherlands and a number of states of the German Federation, for instance, (Grever & Adriaansen, 2019), the history curricula state that the primary aim of teaching history in schools is to develop the historical consciousness of pupils, since it influences their identities and conceptions of morality. However, this field of study has rarely made links to the literature discussed here. Indirectly one could bring up some theoretical links in the work of Rüsen (2004) who theorises about the way narrations of history exhibit different forms of historical consciousness through different uses of history that can be placed on a developmental ladder. First, a *traditional narration* makes use of history to maintain or uphold tradition. Second, an *exemplary narration* uses history to generate rules of conduct so that history teaches us how to lead our lives. Third, the *critical narration* uses the historical example to criticise historical and contemporary societies and cultures. Finally, the *genetic narration* uses history to explain continuity and change in historical and contemporary societies and cultures. One can easily recognise in Rüsen's theorising the links with Piaget's social psychology.

Historical Thinking, Historical Culture and Transformative History Teaching

The development of historical thinking through history teaching is expected to influence the significant structure of Goldmann or what we call the position in the representational field, because, as stated by various researchers (e.g. Lee, 2011; Shemilt, 2011; Seixas, 2017), progression in historical thinking is transformative in the way it changes how people see the world, the present and future. But genetic social psychology proposes a more powerful, broader and more enriched conception of history teaching which goes well beyond traditional descriptions of the disciplinary approach. It not only proposes the merging of the historical thinking literature with the historical consciousness literature, as recently proposed by Seixas (2017), but it also suggests the transformation of history teaching into an interdisciplinary endeavour that we called *transformative history teaching* (Psaltis, Carretero & Cehajic-Clancy, 2017). This entails the study of all processes of genetic change (microgenesis, ontogenesis and sociogenesis) and particularly the change in time of the system of representations of the past, which is very similar to what was described by Mario Carretero (2017) as *historical culture* being the result of influences from three different fields: history teaching, academic history and popular history.

What is discussed as social representations of the past by Liu and Hilton (2005) and Psaltis (2016) is also examined within the social sciences under the concept of 'historical culture' (Carretero, 2017). This term offers a different perspective on how various groups emotionally and effectively engage with their history. The term 'culture' in this context is better seen as a system of social representations (Duveen, 2007; Psaltis 2012b), steering clear of any static, rigid or essentialist implications often associated with 'culture'. The way the past is represented is not static but a living process of public and internal dialogue. This involves sharing, negotiating and discussing interpretations of the past from various angles, including academic, educational and public history, as seen in monuments, commemorations, museums, films and historical novels (Papadakis, 2008; Carretero, 2017). In post-ethnic conflict settings like Cyprus or, for that matter, any context where conflict along any other line of categorisation exists, transformative history teaching becomes essential, as it facilitates the change of social representations of the past. These changes can take the form of what has been described by Barreiro and Castorina (2017) as dialectical inferences in the ontogenesis of social representations or the more disciplinary approaches of the progression of historical thinking (Seixas, 2017).

Genetic social psychology emphasises the importance of different actors involved in conflict transformation – such as policymakers, educators, civil society and grassroots organisations – to actively reconstruct their perceptions of the past. This reconstruction should not simply replace one dominant narrative with another overly simplistic or strategically essentialist narrative. Instead, there's a need for a more epistemologically sophisticated approach to history teaching. This approach should transcend collective memory or history taught merely as heritage (Lowenthal, 1998; Makriyianni & Psaltis, 2007). It should embrace more decentred and multi-perspective knowledge forms, as suggested by Piaget's genetic epistemology, which are more advanced than one-sided victimisation narratives. Additionally, fostering historical literacy and an epistemological understanding of history (Nasie et al., 2016) enables a more informed, critical and reflective view on various historical interpretations and representations. The key message here is the shift from disciplinary to interdisciplinary history teaching. History teachers, equipped with knowledge of social psychological theories, can engage more effectively with historical texts and concepts such as historical significance, continuity and change, cause and consequence, as well as the ethical dimensions of historical interpretations outlined by Seixas (2005). This enhanced approach to teaching expands the concept of historical literacy to include the study of historical culture (Grever & Stuurman, 2007) and historical consciousness (Rüsen, 2004) in the classroom. This inclusion enables students to reflect on the role of collective memory and history teaching in conflict transformation and to understand how various forms of historical consciousness link the past, present and future (Van Alphen & Carretero, 2015; Psaltis, 2016). It involves understanding how attributions of past wrongdoings (Doosje & Branscombe, 2003) are connected to processes like moral disengagement, apology, guilt, shame or regret (Imhoff et al., 2012); how realistic and symbolic threats can hinder prejudice reduction, confidence building and reconciliation; and how intergroup contact can lead to reconciliation. This type of history teaching, which is interdisciplinary and transformative, not only promotes historical thinking but also aids in conflict transformation.

Actual and Potential Consciousness: Utopias, Imagination, Hope and Historical Consciousness

To return to Goldmann and his theorising of totality, one of the most important insights was his distinction between actual and potential consciousness. Actual consciousness refers to the consciousness of the transindividual subject (groups, classes, etc.) which is structured and reflects the everyday world view of a group. In contrast, potential consciousness is captured by an articulated philosophy, ideology or work of art or literature that crystallises in the clearest way possible the structural part–whole relations of the world view of the transindividual subject. In that sense it could be argued that potential consciousness is an orientation towards an ideal world view. In terms of social representations theory, we could say that the actual consciousness is expressed in the messy and polyphasic, sometimes inconsistent everyday practices of individuals as an expression of values and ideas that is context dependent, whilst in sociological or social psychological analyses or works of art or literature, the potential consciousness is expressed in its clearest way as a structured abstraction of those values, ideas and practices and a clear consistent and coherent world view. Both forms of actual and potential consciousness contain various types of narration as proposed by Rüsen (2004). In particular, the two lower levels of historical consciousness (traditional and exemplary) are forms of reification where human constructions (historical narratives) come to dominate the life of the person and where the past dominates the present, forming a relation of constraint with the representation of the past in the dominant role. In contrast, the two higher forms, the critical and the exemplary, free the person from the constraints of the past either through a critical stance on hegemonic narratives or a better grasp of both continuity and change. Thus, one could see how the two higher forms of historical consciousness directly relate to future utopias and the hope (Leshem, 2017, 2019) for a better future, whilst the former two are past oriented and conservative in which the past becomes sacred, filled with nationalist symbols and heroes (Psaltis et al., 2014) and a rising sense of collective threat and existential anxieties through the cultivation of collective victimhood (Psaltis, 2016; Smeekes, McKeown & Psaltis, 2017).

In this way positions in the representational field include in themselves the seed of either conservation or change in sociogenetic processes. The motor of change is the process of microgenesis in social interaction, and in the case of war or civil conflict it takes the form of intergroup contact (Allport, 1954) or semantic forms of contact (Gillespie, 2020) that refer to various ways of coming into contact with the perspective and ideas of the outgroup even if this does not happen through direct physical contact.

Intergroup Contact and Its Varieties as a Microgenetic Process

The origins of the idea of microgenesis can be traced in the German context of the 1920s and 1930s with the work on *Aktualgenese* by Sander, Krueger and Werner (Catan, 1986; Psaltis, 2015; Valsiner & Van Der Veer, 2000; Wagoner, 2009). Werner was actually the first to use the term 'microgenesis' in the English language in 1956 as an approximate translation of the German term *Aktualgenese*, although the concept as a method informed his work since the 1920s (Catán, 1986). For Werner microgenesis referred to 'any human activity such as perceiving, thinking, acting etc. as an unfolding process, and this unfolding or "microgenesis" whether it takes seconds or hours or days occurs in developmental sequence' (Werner, 1956, p. 347). In his 1926 book *The Comparative Psychology of Mental Development*, he presented the microgenetic method as a way of uniting the contents and methods of experimental and developmental psychology as a means of overcoming the dualism between experimental psychology and *Volkerpsychology* promoted by Wundt. Werner was interested in formulating general developmental laws that would apply to phenomena on all developmental levels (e.g. ontogenesis, ethnogenesis), and he was clearly inspired by Goethe's insights about the importance of the study of genetic processes and his organismic theory (Wagoner, 2024).

Closer to the theoretical model developed here, the microgenetic process is the evocation of social representations in social interaction as well as the process of socio-cognitive conflict of perspectives which emerges in social interaction that creates a rupture in the taken-for-granted and introduces doubt (Duveen & Lloyd, 1990; Duveen, 2002) in the thinking or consciousness of the individual. The way of resolving this socio-cognitive conflict (superficial conformity to the other or reconstructive coordination of perspectives) is of crucial importance, as it might or might not lead to change depending on the degree of experience and elaboration of this conflict. Thus, the motor of any change in the transindividual subject

(subject–other–object triad), the significant structure of Goldmann, is microgenesis. This is the changing triad that comprises the basic epistemological unit of analysis in the social constructivist framework of genetic social psychology.

People communicate through social interaction, and thus social representations are *evoked* through the social identities asserted in the activity of individuals. A process of negotiation and *(re)construction* of both social representations and identities is also taking place within social interaction. From the genetic point of view, microgenesis thus holds a privileged and central position, as it is the motor for ontogenesis and sociogenesis of social representations (Duveen & Lloyd, 1990). Microgenesis is defined as 'the genetic process in all social interaction in which particular social identities and the social representations on which they are based are elaborated and negotiated' (Duveen & Lloyd, 1990, p. 8).

As shown in our previous collaboration with Duveen, such configurations create asymmetrical expectations of control in the triad. In that sense the triad metaphor (see Figure 1.1) (Zittoun et al., 2007) is not a symmetrical but an asymmetrical triad imbued with power relations. In this triad any discussion about an *object* of representation is a socio-cognitive process implicating coordinations of actions and operations by both *subject* and *other* as well as pragmatic moves (through the use of words, gestures and actions) that position the psychological *subject* vis-a-vis the *other*. Thus, in the subject–object–other triad social interactive microgenetic moments are moments of potential change of all three points in the

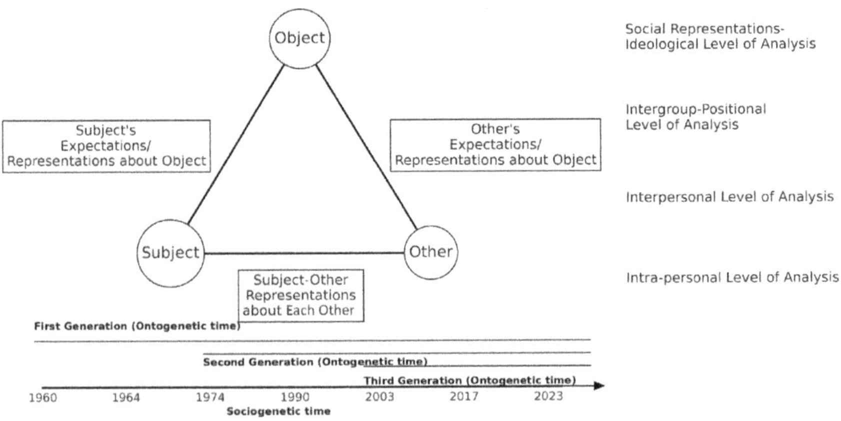

Figure 1.1 The processes to be studied by genetic social psychology.

triangle as well as their relationship. This position is always suggestive of forms of social recognition, and in our past work we have identified recognition of the other as a thinking subject but also instrumental recognition (Psaltis & Duveen, 2007). These forms of recognition regulate the participation and engagement of subject and other in less or more symmetrical social relationships as originally described by Piaget (1932) as social relations of constraint (asymmetrical-based on unilateral respect) and relations of co-operation (symmetrical-based on mutual respect) (see Figure 1.1). In our work exploring the effects of intergroup contact on prejudice reduction, trust building and political positions on a compromise solution when measuring the quality of contact we have always included measurements directly related to the notion of relations of co-operation as positive quality of contact ('when meeting with a member of the other community, I feel that this is based on mutual respect') to facilitate theoretical links between our two lines of research.

The definition by Duveen and Lloyd (1990) is focused on change as a form of construction through socio-cognitive conflict in social interaction, but it is unique because it implicates in this process social identity and social representations *as they are enacted*. According to this perspective, the *evocation* of social representations in social interaction occurs in the ways in which individuals construct an understanding of the situation and *position* themselves and their interlocutors as social subjects in the field of social representations. This process can run smoothly along the lines of the 'taken for granted', but it can also lead to ruptures (see Zittoun, Gillespie, Duveen, Ivinson & Psaltis, 2003). The opening of the checkpoints in 2003 in Cyprus was exactly such a critical historical juncture or rupture point, as we will see in later chapters, that made possible a different form of microgenetic processes taking not only the usual form of intragroup social interaction but making possible intergroup social interactions.

However, this potential for change also comes from indirect forms of contact when, for example, a member of one group does not have an out-group friend but his or her best in-group friend does (Zhou et al., 2019). Beyond this extended form of friendship there is now a burgeoning literature about other indirect forms of contact (Harwood, 2017). Indirect contact covers a broad array of possibilities, which can be subdivided in the following forms: (1) vicarious contact which occurs when we observe contact between an in-group and an out-group member but do not participate in it; (2) mediated contact which is when some of the contact process occurs via a technologically mediated channel (e.g. computer based such as email, texting, conferencing, social media, or TV based such as parasocial contact with an out-group actor in a TV series); and (3) imagined contact which refers to mental visualisations or simulations of contact to operate in similar ways to 'real' contact (Miles & Crisp, 2014). The mechanisms often identified as mediating the prejudice reduction effects are increase of trust, empathy, perspective taking, self-disclosure, recognition of out-group heterogeneity and decrease of inter-group anxiety, realistic and symbolic threats, and stereotypes. Sometimes such mediating processes are also related to collective identity recategorisation processes (Aberson, 2019; Pettigrew et al., 2011).

From the perspective of genetic social psychology, the aforementioned processes only touch upon a part of the significant structure of the subject–object–other triad (see Figure 1.1). They are mostly focused on the subject–other relationship and its quality but have much less to say about the subject–object and the other–object relationship as well as about the role of intragroup contacts and communication. Kadianaki and Gillespie (2015) have also identified a crucial role for self-reflection as a motor for the microgenetic transformation of social representations through the emergence of doubt (Duveen, 2002) in the subject. The meeting with alterity is key in creating self-reflection and can take the following forms: (1) rupture with the physical world (alterity in action), (2) social contact (alterity in other), (3) movement between contexts (alterity in self) and (4) semiotic dialogicality (alterity in the structure of knowledge).

The work of Gillespie (2008, 2020) on semantic contact also points to the way others (both in-group and out-group members) often propose disruptive and disagreeable views of the world (alternative representations of the object) that go against the dominant representations of a society. In this case there is often the phenomenon of resistance (Duveen, 2001) by dominant groups who attempt to raise defensive mechanisms against possible change of the representation of the object by the subject. Gillespie (2020) identifies three layers of defence that take the form of semantic barriers: *avoiding*, *delegitimising* and *limiting*. Semantic barriers are meanings used to reinforce the semantic boundary between the self's views and the views of others, thus protecting the self's universe of meaning from being destabilised. The first layer of semantic barriers avoids acknowledgement of the motives, beliefs or feelings of the out-group. The second layer of semantic barriers acknowledges the existence of the out-group's perspective but works to delegitimise that perspective to such an extent that it can be dismissed. The final and deeper layer of defence acknowledges to some extent the legitimacy of the out-group perspective but works to limit its destabilising impact.

Thus, microgenetic processes of change in social representations need to be seen as potentially engaging all parts of the triad in the significant structure of a position in the representational field, and it concerns a process of possible resistance or reorganisation towards a holistic structure with a certain coherence that involves changes in how self is understood (identity), changes in the subject–other relationship, changes in the representation of the other (e.g. deconstruction of negative stereotypes) and changes in representations about a conflict itself (e.g. an ethnic conflict and its history). Such processes of microgenesis can take the form of intragroup social interaction but also the form of intergroup contact and are shaped by sociogenetic processes of public and mass-mediated communication within and across groups (Wagner, 1994). Of course, one of the main lessons of the first line of research at Cambridge was that the depth of such change varies and directly relates to the quality of social interaction or contact. In that sense not all microgenetic processes lead to ontogenetic or sociogenetic change. In this book we are mostly interested with the articulation of microgenesis with ontogenesis (Chapter 2) and sociogenesis (Chapter 3) at different levels of analysis (Psaltis, 2015) as they relate to the representation of the Cyprus issue identifying instances of rupture and change but also of continuity.

REFERENCES

Aberson, C. L. (2019). Indirect effects of threat on the contact–prejudice relationship: A meta-analysis. *Social Psychology*, 50(2), 105–126. https://doi.org/10.1027/1864-9335/a000364.

Allport, G. W. (1954). *The nature of prejudice*. Garden City, NY: Doubleday.

Barreiro, A., & Castorina, J. A. (2017). Dialectical inferences in the ontogenesis of social representations. *Theory & Psychology*, 27(1), 34–49.

Carpendale, J. I., & Lewis, C. (2020). Tomasello's tin man of moral obligation needs a heart. *Behavioral & Brain Sciences*, 43, 19–20.

Carretero, M. (2017). The teaching of recent and violent conflicts as challenges for history education. In C. Psaltis, M. Carretero, & S. Čehajić-Clancy (Eds.), *History education and conflict transformation* (pp. 341–377). Cham: Palgrave Macmillan, https://doi.org/10.1007/978-3-319-54681-0_14.

Carugati, F. (1990). From social cognition to social representations in the study of intelligence. In G. Duveen & B. B. Lloyd (Eds.), *Social representations and the development of knowledge* (pp. 126–143). Cambridge: Cambridge University Press.

Castorina, J. A. (2010). The ontogenesis of social representations: A dialectic perspective. *Papers on Social Representations*, *19*, 18.1–18.19.

(2017). Relationships between revisited genetic psychology and the theory of social representations: A critical analysis. *Papers on Social Representations*, 26 (1), 5.1–5.22.

Catán, L. (1986). The dynamic display of process: Historical development and contemporary uses of the microgenetic method. *Human Development*, 29, 252–263.

Demetriou, O., & Hadjipavlou, M. (2021). The impact of women's activism on the peace negotiations in Cyprus. In S. Byrne & A. McCulloch (Eds.), *Power-sharing pacts and the women: Peace and security agenda* (pp. 50–65). London: Routledge.

Dixon, J., & Levine, M. (Eds.). (2012). *Beyond prejudice: Extending the social psychology of conflict, inequality and social change*. Cambridge: Cambridge University Press.

Doise, W. (1986). *Levels of explanation in social psychology: European monographs in social psychology*. Cambridge: Cambridge University Press.

Doise, W., & Mugny, G. (1984). *The social development of the intellect*. Oxford: Pergamon.

Doise, W., Mugny, G., & Perret-Clermont, A. N. (1975). Social interaction and the development of cognitive operations. *European Journal of Social Psychology*, *5*, 367–383.

Doosje, B., & Branscombe, N. R. (2003). Attributions for the negative historical actions of a group. *European Journal of Social Psychology*, *33*(2), 235–248.

Duveen, G. (1983). From social cognition to the cognition of social life: An essay in decentration. Unpublished PhD Thesis. University of Sussex.

(1997). Psychological development as a social process. In L. Smith, P. Tomlinson, & J. Dockerell (Eds.), *Piaget, Vygotsky and beyond* (pp. 52–69). London: Routledge.

(2001). Representations, identities, resistance. In K. Deaux & G. Philogène (Eds.), *Representations of the social: Bridging theoretical traditions* (pp. 257–270). London: Blackwell Publishing.

(2002). Construction, belief, doubt. *Psychologie et Societé*, *3*, 139–155.

(2007). Culture and social representations. *The Cambridge handbook of socio-cultural psychology* (pp. 543–559). Cambridge: Cambridge University Press.

(2008). Social actors and social groups: A return to heterogeneity in social psychology. *Journal for the Theory of Social Behaviour*, *38*, 370–374.

Duveen, G., & Lloyd, B. (1990). Introduction. In G. Duveen & B. Lloyd (Eds.), *Social representations and the development of knowledge* (pp. 1–10). Cambridge: Cambridge University Press.

Duveen, G., & Psaltis, C. (2008). The constructive role of asymmetries in social interaction. In U. Mueller, J. Carpendale, N. Budwig, & B. Sokol (Eds.), *Social life and social knowledge: Toward a process account of development* (pp. 183–204). Mahwah, NJ: Lawrence Erlbaum.

Elhammoumi, M. (2002). To create psychology's own capital. *Journal for the Theory of Social Behaviour*, *32*(1), 89–104.

Engeström, Y. (2008). Enriching activity theory without shortcuts. *Interacting with Computers*, *20*(2), 256–259.

Furth, H. G. (1987). *Knowledge as desire: An essay on Freud and Piaget*. New York: Columbia University Press.

(1996). *Desire for society: Children's knowledge as social imagination*. Plenum Press: NY and London.
Furth, H. G., Baur, M., & Smith, J. E. (1976). Children's conception of social institutions: A Piagetian framework. *Human Development*, *19*(6), 351–374.
Gandillac, M., Goldmann, L., & Piaget, J. (Eds.). (1965). *Entretiens sur les notions de genèse et de structure*. Berlin: De Gruyter.
Garcia, R., & Piaget, J. (1989). *Psychogenesis and the history of science*. New York: Columbia University Press.
Gillespie, A. (2008). Social representations, alternative representations and semantic barriers. *Journal for the Theory of Social Behaviour*, *38*(4), 375–391.
(2020). Semantic contact and semantic barriers: Reactionary responses to disruptive ideas. *Current Opinion in Psychology*, *35*, 21–25.
Goldmann, L. (1959). *Recherches dialectiques*. Athens: Gnosi.
(1967). The early writings of Georg Lukacs. *TriQuarterly*, *9*, 165.
(1969). The subject of cultural creation. In R. S. Cohen & M. W. Wartofsky (Eds.), *Proceedings of the Boston Colloquium for the Philosophy of Science 1966/1968* (Vol. 4, pp. 241–260). Dordrecht: Springer.
(1975). Dialectical materialism and literary history. *New Left Review*, *92*, 39–51.
(1994). *The epistemology of sociology*. Harlow, Essex: Longman.
Goldmann, L., & Boelhower, W. Q. (1980). *Essays on method in the sociology of literature*. St. Louis, MO: Telos Press.
Grever, M., & Adriaansen, R. J. (2019). Historical consciousness: The enigma of different paradigms. *Journal of Curriculum Studies*, *51*(6), 814–830.
Grever, M., & Stuurman, S. (Eds.). (2007). *Beyond the canon: History for the twenty-first century*. New York: Springer.
Hadjipavlou, M., & Mertan, E. B. (2010). Cypriot feminism: An opportunity to challenge gender inequalities and promote women's rights and a different voice. *Cyprus Review*, *22*(2), 247–268.
(2019). A multilevel intervention: The case of the Cyprus gender advisory team (GAT) – achievements and challenges. *Journal of Peacebuilding & Development*, *14*(2), 125–137.
Harwood, J. (2017). Indirect and mediated intergroup contact. *The International Encyclopedia of Intercultural Communication*, 1–9.
Henrich, J. (2015). *The secret of our success: How culture is driving human evolution, domesticating our species, and making us smarter*. Princeton, NJ: Princeton University Press.
(2020). *The weirdest people in the world: How the West became psychologically peculiar and particularly prosperous*. New York: Farrar, Straus & Giroux.
Henrich, J., & Muthukrishna, M. (2021). The origins and psychology of human cooperation. *Annual Review of Psychology*, *72*, 207–240.
Hsueh, Y. (2009). Piaget in the United States, 1925–1971. In U. Müller, J. I. M. Carpendale, & L. Smith (Eds.), *The Cambridge companion to Piaget* (pp. 344–370). Cambridge: Cambridge University Press. https://doi.org/10.1017/CCOL9780521898584.016.

Imhoff, R., Bilewicz, M., & Erb, H. P. (2012). Collective regret versus collective guilt: Different emotional reactions to historical atrocities. *European Journal of Social Psychology*, *42*(6), 729–742.

Jovchelovitch, S. (2010). From social cognition to the cognition of social life. *Papers on Social Representations*, *19*, 3.1–3.10. Retrieved from: www.psych.lse.ac.uk/psr/.

Jovchelovitch, S., & Wagoner, B. (2013). Introduction: The context and development of ideas. In S. Moscovici, S. Jovchelovitch, & B. Wagoner (Eds.), *Development as a social process: Contributions of Gerard Duveen* (pp. xv–xxiii). London: Routledge.

Kadianaki, I., & Gillespie, A. (2015). Alterity and the transformation of social representations: a sociocultural account. *Integrative Psychological and Behavioral Science*, *49*, 73–88.

Kaplan, B. (1967). Meditations on genesis. *Human Development*, *10*(2), 65–87.

Kende, J., Psaltis, C., Reiter, J., Fousiani, K., Cakal, H., & Green, E. (2021). Past and present intergroup contact and conflict among inhabitants of former mixed villages of Cyprus: The role of individual and collective experiences in predicting attitudes and trust. *Political Psychology*, *43*(4), 751–768. https://doi.org/10.1111/pops.12791.

Kitchener, R. F. (2002). Jean Piaget: The unknown sociologist? In L. Smith (Ed.), *Critical readings on Piaget* (pp. 58–80). London: Routledge.

(2009). On the concept(s) of the social in Piaget. In U. Müller, J. I. M. Carpendale, & L. Smith (Eds.), *The Cambridge companion to Piaget* (pp. 110–131). Cambridge: Cambridge University Press.

(2014). Piaget's social epistemology. In J. I. M. Carpendale & U. Müller (Eds.), *Social interaction and the development of knowledge* (pp. 45–66). New York: Psychology Press.

Kozulin, A. (1990). The concept of regression and Vygotskian developmental theory. *Developmental Review*, *10*(2), 218–238.

Lee, P. (2011). Historical literacy and transformative history. In L. Perikleous & D. Shemilt (Eds.), *The future of the past: Why history education matters* (pp. 129–168). Nicosia: Association for Historical Dialogue and Research.

Leman, P. (2010). Social psychology and developmental psychology: Conversation or collaboration? Commentary on J. A. Castorina, 'The Ontogenesis of Social Representations: A Dialectic Perspective'. *Papers on Social Representations*, *19*, 19.1–19.8. Retrieved from: www.psych.lse.ac.uk/psr/.

Leman, P. J., & Duveen, G. (1999). Representations of authority and children's moral reasoning. *European Journal of Social Psychology*, *29*, 557–575.

Leshem, O. A. (2017). What you wish for is not what you expect: Measuring hope for peace during intractable conflicts. *International Journal of Intercultural Relations*, *60*, 60–66. https://doi.org/10.1016/j.ijintrel.2017.06.005.

(2019). The pivotal role of the enemy in inducing hope for peace. *Political Studies*, *67*(3), 693–711. https://doi.org/10.1177/0032321718797920.

Liu, J. H., & Hilton, D. J. (2005). How the past weighs on the present: Social representations of history and their role in identity politics. *British Journal of Social Psychology*, *44*(4), 537–556.

Lloyd, B. (2010). Gender identities and education: Serendipity in social research. *Papers on Social Representations*, *19*(1), 7.1–7.9.

Lloyd, B., & Duveen, G. (1990). A semiotic analysis of the development of social representations of gender. In G. Duveen & B. Lloyd (Eds.), *Social representations and the development of knowledge* (pp. 27–46). Cambridge: Cambridge University Press.

(1992). *Gender identities and education*. London: Harvester Wheatsheaf.

Loizides, N., Psaltis, C., Morgan-Jones, E., Sudulich, L., Popp, R., & Baykiz, T. (2022). Citizens and peace mediations in divided societies: Identifying zones of agreement through a conjoint survey experiment. *Journal of Conflict Resolution*, *66*(9), 1619–1649.

Lowenthal, D. (1998). *The heritage crusade and the spoils of history*. Cambridge: Cambridge University Press.

Lytras, E., & Psaltis, C. (2011). *Formerly mixed-villages in Cyprus: Representations of the past, present and future*. Nicosia: UNDP-ACT.

Makriyianni, C., & Psaltis, C. (2007). History teaching and reconciliation. *Cyprus Review*, *19*, 43–69.

Marková, I. (2010). Gerard Duveen on the epistemology of social representations. *Papers on Social Representations*, *19*, 4.1–4.9. Retrieved from: www.psych.lse .ac.uk/psr/.

Miles, E., & Crisp, R. J. (2014). A meta-analytic test of the imagined contact hypothesis. *Group Processes & Intergroup Relations*, *17*(1), 3–26. https://doi .org/10.1177/1368430213510573.

Moscovici, M. (2000). *Social representations: explorations in social psychology*. Cambridge: Polity Press.

Moscovici, S. ([1961/1976] 2008). *Psychoanalysis: Its image and its public*. Cambridge: Polity Press.

(1976). *Social influence and social change*. London: Academic Press.

(1990). Social psychology and developmental psychology: Extending the conversation. In G. Duveen & B. Lloyd (Eds.), Social representations and the development of knowledge (pp. 164–185). Cambridge: Cambridge University Press.

Moscovici, S., Jovchelovitch, S., & Wagoner, B. (Eds.). (2013). *Development as a social process: Contributions of Gerard Duveen*. London: Routledge.

Nasie, M., Diamond, A. H., & Bar-Tal, D. (2016). Young children in intractable conflicts: The Israeli case. *Personality and Social Psychology Review*, *20*(4), 365–392.

Nicolopoulou, A., & Weintraub, J. (2009). Why operativity-in-context is not quite a sociocultural model. *Human Development*, *52*, 320–328.

Papadakis Y. (2008). Narrative, memory and history education in divided Cyprus: A comparison of schoolbooks on the 'history of Cyprus'. *History & Memory*, *20* (2), 128–148.

Perret-Clermont, A.-N. (1980). *Social interaction and cognitive development in children*. London: Academic Press.

Petrovic, G. (1991). Reification. In T. Bottomore, L. Harris, V. G. Kiernan, & R. Miliband (Eds.), *A dictionary of Marxist thought* (pp. 463–465). Cambridge, MA: Harvard University Press.

Pettigrew, T. F., & Tropp, L. R. (2006). A meta-analytic test of intergroup contact theory. *Journal of Personality and Social Psychology, 90*, 751–783. https://doi.org/10.1037/0022-3514.90.5.751.

Pettigrew, T. F., Tropp, L. R., Wagner, U., & Christ, O. (2011). Recent advances in intergroup contact theory. *International Journal of Intercultural Relations, 35*(3), 271–280.

Piaget, J. (1923). *The language and thought of the child*. London: Kegan Paul.

(1932). *The moral judgement of the child*. London: Routledge and Kegan Paul.

(1968). *Six psychological studies*. London: Vintage.

(1977/1995). *Sociological studies*. London: Routledge.

Piaget, J., & Weil, A. M. (1951). The development in children of the idea of the homeland and of relations with other countries. *International Social Science Bulletin, 3*, 561–578.

Psaltis, C. (2005a). Social relations and cognitive development: The influence of conversation types and representations of gender. Unpublished PhD thesis. University of Cambridge.

(2005b). Communication and the construction of knowledge or transmission of belief: The role of conversation type, behavioural style and social recognition. *Studies in Communication Science, 5*, 209–228.

(2011a). The constructive role of gender asymmetry in social interaction: Further evidence. *British Journal of Developmental Psychology, 29*(2), 305–312.

(2011b). From the epistemic to the social-psychological subject: The missing role of social identities, asymmetries of status, and social representations. *Human Development, 54*, 234–240.

(2012a). Intergroup trust and contact in transition: A social representations perspective on the Cyprus conflict. In I. Marková & A. Gillespie (Eds.), *Trust and conflict: Representations, culture and dialogue* (pp. 83–104). London: Routledge.

(2012b). Culture and social representations: A continuing dialogue in search for heterogeneity in social developmental psychology. *Culture & Psychology, 18*(3), 375–390.

(2015a). Communication and the microgenetic construction of knowledge. In G. Sammut, E. Andreouli, G. Gaskell, & J. Valsiner (Eds.), *Handbook of social representations* (pp. 113–127). Cambridge: Cambridge University Press.

(2015b). Genetic social psychology: From microgenesis to ontogenesis, sociogenesis... and back. In C. Psaltis, A. Gillespie, & A. N. Perret-Clermont (Eds.), *Social relations in human and societal development* (pp. 71–94). New York: Springer.

(2016). Collective memory, social representations of intercommunal relations and conflict transformation in divided Cyprus. *Peace and Conflict: Journal of Peace Psychology*, *22*(1), 19–27.

Psaltis, C., Beydola, T., Filippou, G., & Vrachimis, N. (2014). Contested symbols as social representations: The case of Cyprus. In P. R. Dezalia & S. Moeshcberger (Eds.), *Symbols that bind, symbols that divide: The semiotics of peace and conflict*. Cham: Springer International.

Psaltis, C., Cabrera, C., Lytra, E., Filippou, G., Cakal, H., & Makriyianni, C. (2014). Oral history accounts of the former inhabitants of mixed villages in Cyprus: A social representations perspective. In H. Briel (Ed.), *Oral history in Cyprus* (pp. 34–47). Nicosia: University of Nicosia Press.

Psaltis, C., Cakal, H., Loizides, N., & Kuşçu Bonnenfant, I. (2020). Internally displaced persons and the Cyprus peace process. *International Political Science Review*, *41*(1), 138–154.

Psaltis, C., Carretero, M., & Cehajic-Clancy (2017). *History education and conflict transformation: Dealing with the past and facing the future*. London: Palgrave Macmillan.

Psaltis, C., & Duveen, G. (2006). Social relations and cognitive development: The influence of conversation types and representations of gender. *European Journal of Social Psychology*, *36*, 407–430.

(2007). Conversation types and conservation: Forms of recognition and cognitive development. *British Journal of Developmental Psychology*, *25*, 79–102.

Psaltis, C., Duveen, C., & Perret-Clermont, A. N. (2009). The social and the psychological: Structure and context in intellectual development. *Human Development*, *52*, 291–312.

Psaltis, C., Gillespie, A., & Perret-Clermont, A. N. P. (Eds.). (2015). *Social relations in human and societal development*. London: Palgrave Macmillan.

Psaltis, C., Lytras, E., & Costache, S. (2011). *History educators in the Greek Cypriot and Turkish Cypriot community of Cyprus: Perceptions, beliefs and practices*. Nicosia: UNDP-ACT.

Psaltis, C., & Zapiti, A. (2014). *Interaction, communication and development: Psychological development as a social process*. London: Routledge.

Rüsen, J. (2004). Historical consciousness: Narrative structure, moral function, and ontogenetic development. In P. Seixas (Ed.), *Theorizing historical consciousness* (pp. 63–85). Toronto: University of Toronto Press.

Seixas, P. (2005). Collective memory, history education, and historical consciousness. *Historically Speaking*, *7*(2), 17–19.

(2017). Historical consciousness and historical thinking. In M. Carretero, S. Berger, & M. Grever (Eds.), *Palgrave handbook of research in historical culture and education* (pp. 59–72). London: Palgrave Macmillan. https://doi.org/10.1057/978-1-137-52908-4_3.

Sève, L. (2018). Where is Marx in the work and thought of Vygotsky. *Seminaire International Vygotski*, *7*. Retrieved from: www.unige.ch/SIV2018/files/6515/2880/7446/Seve_Vygotski_Marx_Engl.pdf.

Shemilt, D. (2011). The gods of the copybook headings: Why don't we learn from the past. In L. Perikleous & D. Shemilt (Eds.), *The future of the past: Why history education matters* (pp. 69–127). Nicosia: Association for Historical Dialogue and Research.

Smeekes, A., McKeown, S., & Psaltis, C. (2017). Endorsing narratives under threat: Maintaining perceived collective continuity through the protective power of ingroup narratives in Northern Ireland and Cyprus. *Journal of Social and Political Psychology*, *5*(2), 282–300. https://doi.org/10.5964/jspp.v5i2.682.

Smith, L. (2013). The social construction of rational understanding. In A. Tryphon & J. Vonèche (Eds.), *Piaget-Vygotsky: The social genesis of thought* (pp. 115–132). New York: Psychology Press.

Tausch, N., Hewstone, M., Kenworthy, J. B., Psaltis, C., Schmid, K., Popan, J. R., . . . Hughes, J. (2010). Secondary transfer effects of intergroup contact: Alternative accounts and underlying processes. *Journal of Personality and Social Psychology*, *99*, 282–302. https://doi.org/10.1037/a0018553.

Thorp, R. (2014). *Historical consciousness, historical media, and history education.* Umeå: Forskarskolan Historiska medier, Umeå universitet.

Uskul, A. K., Kirchner-Häusler, A., Vignoles, V. L., Rodriguez-Bailon, R., Castillo, V. A., Cross, S. E., ... & Uchida, Y. (2023). Neither Eastern nor Western: Patterns of independence and interdependence in Mediterranean societies. *Journal of Personality and Social Psychology*, 125(3), 471.

Valsiner, J. (2000). *Culture and human development.* London: Sage.

(2013). Introduction: The idea that will live: Genetic social psychology. In S. Moscovici, S. Jovchelovitch, & B. Wagoner (Eds.), *Development as a social process: Contributions of Gerard Duveen* (pp. ix–x). London: Routledge.

Valsiner, J., & Van der Veer, R. (2000). *The social mind: Construction of the idea.* Cambridge: Cambridge University Press.

Van Alphen, F., & Carretero, M. (2015). The construction of the relation between national past and present in the appropriation of historical master narratives. *Integrative Psychological and Behavioral Science*, *49*(3), 512–530.

Vygotsky, L. S. (1962). *Thought and language.* Cambridge, MA: MIT Press.

(1978). *Mind in society.* Cambridge, MA: Harvard University Press.

Wagner, W. (1994). Fields of research and socio-genesis of social representations: a discussion of criteria and diagnostics. *Social Science Information*, *33*(2), 199–228.

Wagoner, B. (2009). The experimental methodology of constructive microgenesis. In J. Valsiner, P. Molenaar, M. Lyra, & N. Chaudhary (Eds.), *Dynamic process methodology in the social and developmental sciences* (pp. 99–121). New York: Springer.

(2024). The organismic theory of development: Romantic roots of a vital concept. *Theory & Psychology*, *34*(1), 127–149.

Wartofsky, M. (1984). The child's construction of the world and the world's construction of the child. In F. S. Kessel & A. W. Siegel (Eds.), *The child and other cultural inventions* (pp. 188–215). New York: Praeger.

Werner, H. (1956). Microgenesis and aphasia. *Journal of Abnormal Social Psychology*, 52, 347–353.
Zhou, S., Page-Gould, E., Aron, A., Moyer, A., & Hewstone, M. (2019). The extended contact hypothesis: A meta-analysis on 20 years of research. *Personality and Social Psychology Review*, *23*(2), 132–160.
Zimmerman, M. (1978). Lucien Goldmann: From dialectical theory to genetic structuralism. *Berkeley Journal of Sociology*, 151–182.
Zittoun, T., Cornish, F., Gillespie, A., & Psaltis, C. (2007). The metaphor of the triangle in theories of human development. *Human Development*, *50*, 208–229.
Zittoun, T., Duveen, G., Gillespie, A., Ivinson, G., & Psaltis, C. (2003). The use of symbolic resources in developmental transitions. *Culture & Psychology*, *9*(4), 415–448.

CHAPTER 2

Ontogenesis of Prejudice and the Role of the Educational System

Charis Psaltis

Ontogenesis of Prejudice

Ontogenesis is the process of change of the representations of a single individual through their life course. The main influential figures in shaping our understanding of this process are Jean Piaget, Hans Furth and Gerard Duveen. This process is a process influenced by microgenetic processes but also by the cognitive developmental level of the individual, the influence of norms of the in-group, and the changing role of relations of constraint and relations of co-operation beyond any maturational or biological factors.

Various theories exist that attempt to explain the development of prejudice in childhood (Aboud, 1988, 2008; Nesdale, 2001, 2004; Bar-Tal & Teichman, 2005; Nasie et al., 2021), and they have all contributed a lot to our understanding of how prejudice develops from early childhood to adolescence. Nevertheless, the narrow focus of most of the mainstream social cognition models on the single outcome of prejudice with the exception of the rich and multilevel framework proposed by Bar-Tal (2023) and his colleagues in Israel fails to explore what lies beyond the tip of the iceberg in the representations of an interethnic conflict and its transformation in historical time as mentioned earlier. Additionally, there is an intricate tension between the emerging agency and developing potential of the human mind on the one hand to grasp complexity and avoid stereotypical thinking, and on the other to form a collective identity or follow group norms that puts on the developing child contrasting orientations and creates tensions and conflict between various norms, commitments and values that have not been totally understood until today. The genetic social psychological framework can contribute to capturing some of this complexity in a way that goes beyond just the measurement of prejudice indices.

Developmental Theories of Prejudice

Most prejudice development theory and research has concentrated on the childhood years (4–12 years of age) with a particular focus on the role of social-cognitive developmental (Aboud, 1988, 2008) and motivational processes (Nesdale, 2004), but a proper synthesis of the empirical basis of these theoretical approaches has not yet taken place.

According to Doyle and Aboud (1995), who have been influenced by Piaget's work on children's cognitive development, feelings of prejudice and biased attitudes in children, peak at the age of five to seven years and then decline as they grew up. Aboud and Amato (2003) claim that the emergence of cognitive abilities during the concrete operational stage, such as the cognitive ability of multiple classification skills, relates to the reduction of prejudice. In particular, past the age of seven years, the greater attribution of importance to individual traits and characteristics rather than collective ones when assessing other individuals allows children to start recognising that both in-group and out-group members can have both positive and negative traits. This more flexible way of thinking is less stereotypical, thus leading to a gradual reduction of prejudice in late childhood.

On the contrary the motivational social identity development theory (SIDT) (Nesdale, 2004, 2017) predicts that children before six to seven years of age usually exhibit only in-group favouritism without out-group derogation. Prejudice can emerge after this age, but its emergence depends (1) on the extent to which children identify with their social group, (2) on whether prejudice is a norm held by the members of the child's social group, and/or (3) on whether the in-group members believe that their group is threatened in some way by members of the out-group.

A meta-analysis by Raabe and Beelmann (2011) shed more light on the issue of the developmental trajectory of prejudice. It included 121 cross-sectional and 7 longitudinal studies from 18 different countries and examined age differences in racial, national and ethnic prejudice from childhood to late adolescence. They found that there was a significant mean-level increase in prejudiced attitudes from early to middle childhood, thus supporting Aboud's (2008) proposition. However, this was only true for prejudice towards low-status groups. In the case of prejudice towards national out-groups and high-status groups, this was not the case. This shows that there is indeed a cognitive developmental shift around the age six to eight years that makes possible the reduction of prejudice, as suggested by Aboud, but only if the social context contains in-group norms and social representations about the inappropriateness of the marginalisation of minorities. They also found evidence of more heterogeneity in prejudiced attitudes in adolescence, suggesting that the role of the sociocultural context and environmental factors becomes more central as children grow older. More recent research supports the same conclusion (Barret & Oppenheimer, 2011; Miklikowska, 2017; Miklikowska, Thijs & Hjerm, 2019), especially in post-conflict settings where social identity in adolescence gains a prominent role in the context of ethnic antagonisms (Bar-Tal & Teichman, 2005; Nasie et al., 2019; Teichman, 2016).

Such findings can be explained by the genetic social psychology framework in that the thought of children in early childhood could be characterised as a process of agentic internalisation of social representations of various categories (first gender and then racial, ethnic, national, etc.) and meanings attached to these categories either because children obtain personal experience of coming into contact with members of these categories or because they hear or read stories *about* these categories. By the age of two years, children start forming representations and symbols that revolve around a figurative core of simple binary oppositions as shown in the work of Duveen for the case of gender. As both Furth and Duveen show, however, behind every binary opposition there is an asymmetry of power. Clearly the social representations of each group (ethnic, national, racial, etc.) would carry their own meanings and norms that would be expected to create varied prejudice developmental paths through social influence in microgenetic processes, and one should not expect a universal process of ontogenetic increase or decrease of prejudice. The specific trajectory of a single group will always depend on the specific sociohistorical context. It is clear that militarism and nationalism are one of the ways that children do gender through commemorations and national celebrations in the school context, even starting from the kindergarten (Nasie & Bar-Tal, 2020). Therefore, gender and national identities are intertwined, and patriarchy should be seen as supporting both militarism and nationalism generally and honour culture in traditional and rural societies through religion (Hadjipavlou & Mertan, 2019).

Nevertheless, what all these theoretical frameworks failed to capture is an understanding of the role of the quality of social relations in the development of prejudice as originally proposed by Piaget (1932) as well as to explore more generally the representations about 'otherness' and historical consciousness which of course incorporates a richer set of

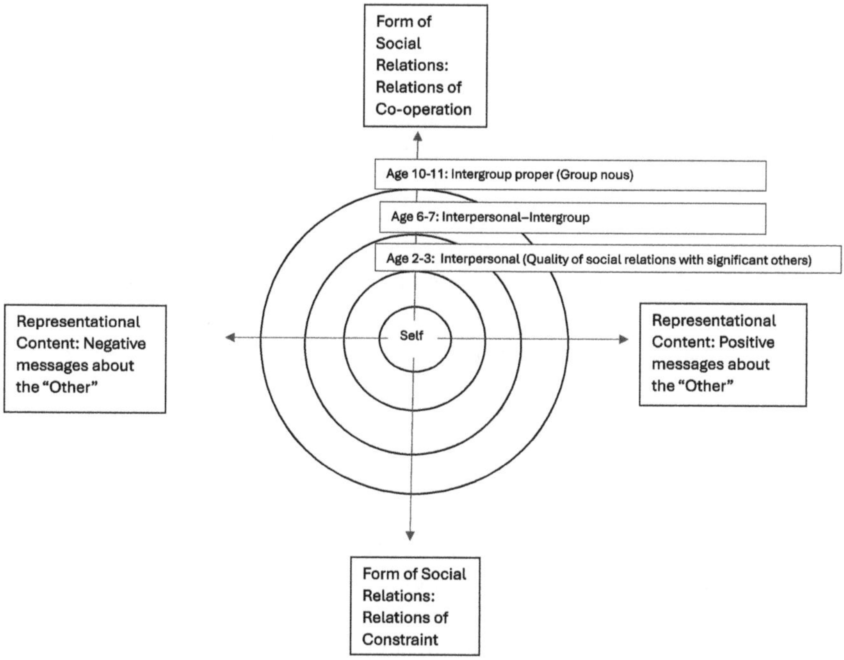

Figure 2.1 The *what* and *how* axes of family and school socialisation.

meanings than the narrow focus on prejudice and adds historical depth to the analysis. The core question then that should be studied is the following: *How do children interact with significant in-group others (parents, peers, teachers) about otherness and represent otherness itself, and how do they interact with members of various outgroups?* The two axes of this proposal are represented in Figure 2.1.

Both processes could be seen as different facets of the process of social representing the 'other'. Whether children often find themselves embedded in social relations of constraint or co-operation (Piaget, 1932) with significant others (e.g. parents, teachers) would be expected to make a difference, but changes in prejudice levels would also be expected by the *content* of what they discuss about otherness, mediated by such cultural artefacts as history texbooks or popular history, commemorations or other various symbolic resources that make reference to the outgroup. Even more impactful could be direct intergroup contact experiences with otherness, especially if what is usually being discussed within group with significant others carries negative overtones or in a context of geographical separation like Cyprus, which offers little opportunities for intergroup contact.

From our perspective, however, the effectiveness of intergroup contact would depend on children's developmental level. It would be wrong, for example, to expect children in the pre-operational level who have not yet mastered part–whole relations to generalise any positive intergroup encounters from the single case to all members of the out-group. Indeed recent reviews of the role of intergroup contact in prejudice reduction in childhood points towards this limitation for young children under six to seven years of age (Aboud & Spears-Brown, 2013). Still, it is possible for otherness related to skin colour, which is visible from early childhood and does not necessitate an understanding of part–whole relations, to still get the beneficial effects of intergroup contact in this younger age group.

In this connection, relevant to our focus on interethnic relations and the development of social representations of the Cyprus issue in Cyprus, is the notion of sociocentrism which Piaget talks about but only once explored in any detail in his work with Weil (Piaget & Weil, 1951) on the ontogenesis of the idea of homeland in children. Even though Piaget's work was written 70 years ago, it is more nuanced in capturing links between form and content than recent work and could perfectly explain the findings of a recent meta-analysis (Raabe & Beelmann, 2011), since it offers a more holistic understanding of representations than the narrow focus of prejudice reduction.

First, it helps to understand why one should not expect strong statistical relationships between intelligence and prejudice levels but only small to moderate as we would expect between intelligence and wisdom (only at about $r = 0.30$), as suggested by Demetriou et al. (2021) when they propose their own historical/developmental framework of raising Mandelas by cultivating wisdom. This is because prejudice can be sustained by various and diverse forms of thinking which depends on not only cognitive ability but also in-group norms. For example, some cognitive developmental skills in older children or adolescents make possible an understanding of part–whole relationships. However, these part–whole relations should not necessarily be inclusive of all out-groups because they might selectively or strategically keep some groups out of the definition of a superordinate in-group category depending on the sociocultural or historical context. Second, Piaget's work suggests that both cognitive structuring and the content of the representations of the group (positive or negative) can influence prejudice in childhood, and he essentially supports the idea that both prejudiced and non-prejudiced views could be sustained by in-group norms in late childhood and early adolescence. However, with every developing stage, their application would concern a wider group (or one could talk of an expanding ethical or moral horizon) that can be seen in Figure 2.1. First, there is the here and now of the egocentric child in the pre-operational stage, then the possibility of submission to family or decentration from family views and values in the concrete operational stage, and finally comes the submission or emancipation through reciprocity and decentration from wider societal views and values in the formal operational stage. The hallmark of deep and not superficial tolerant views for Piaget would be the development of reciprocity where the process of co-operative interaction and norms of mutual respect align with the positive content of representations about any 'other', thus forming a universalising attitude. Of course, given the emerging socialisation of various in-group norms that exclude otherness (religion, ethnic or gender related), this is rarely achieved indeed.

For example, positive norms about collaboration with in-group strangers (co-religionists) can be promoted by a powerful institution like religion, people in authority or the school without this necessitating acceptance of individuals from other religious or ethnic groups. In this sense the moral horizon does exclude specific others. However, in periods of positive political developments in a conflict transformation process the ethical horizon can be expanded by the will of powerful institutions. In our later chapter analysing the Cyprus case in the period from 2015 to 2017 we will see an example of this for bicommunal relations in Cyprus. In the case of conformity pressures towards a positive anti-discriminatory policy, the normative context of the in-group could be leading to lower expression of prejudice. From the perspective of genetic social psychology, this would not necessarily entail the reconstruction of knowledge but a superficial layer of beliefs ('I should not sound prejudiced') which might be enough to reduce the expression of prejudice but not the presence of prejudiced feelings (the lower right quadrant in Figure 2.1) in the mind of many individuals unless such policy shifts are accompanied by opportunities for real co-operative contact with out-group members (the upper right quadrant in Figure 2.1). Discussions between equal peers can also entail negative stereotypes about otherness. Given the increasing role of in-group peer norms in adolescence, for example, we might expect to find peer negative norms of the upper left quadrant in Figure 2.1 that might conflict with positive in-group norms at the school level represented in the lower right quadrant and lead to resistance to school positive norms. From the same perspective the lower left quadrant of Figure 2.1 is very problematic, since dominant and hierarchical institutions or authorities promote negative representations of out-groups that is usually the case in hot intergroup conflicts. Here the various forms of threats, prejudice, distrust, intergroup anxiety and lack of contact are expected at high levels, further supporting hierarchical institutions, traditional, security values and conformity largely described in the work of Bar-Tal (2023) as the "ethos of conflict."

Thus, processes relating to the quality of social relations directly relate to varieties of social influence as in the genetic model of social influence in Moscovici (1976) who discussed both majority and minority influence as two different routes to social influence with distinct qualitative characteristics. Between these two processes there seems to be a third process with somewhat ambivalent characteristics, according to Moscovici (1976), which relates to processes of normalisation and norm formation as explored originally by Muzafer Sheriff in the context of small groups. As Moscovici (1991) shows in an insightful paper where he discusses the work of Sherif and Asch in the context of Sherif's experiments, two qualitatively different reactions were observed once participants to the experiments were interviewed. There are those who, when faced with a majority, simply comply publicly, in front of others, without actually changing their internal knowledge, belief or representation of the world or reality. However, there are also those who, when faced with a majority, might actually start doubting their beliefs, knowledge or representation of the world, and in that sense it is possible that a numerical majority can also put in motion a process of deeper, real change depending on the mode of resolution of socio-cognitive conflict that will take place. This is likened by Moscovici to a process of informational influence or cognitive validation whilst the former is likened to a process of normative influence or social comparison which results in public compliance but no real internal change. From our perspective, small group settings can take both forms depending on the conversation types that evolve between subject and other in these settings and specifically whether they take the form of mutual respect (co-operation) or unilateral respect, submission or coercion (relations of constraint). Efforts to coerce can cause resistance and even reaction towards the opposite direction that the source of influence demands as we know from classic social psychological work.

The role of in-group norms in prejudice reduction in childhood has been recently explored in the context of social identity development theory (Nesdale, 2017), and a series of studies indicate that in-group norms in childhood have a powerful influence on the expression of prejudice by children, but these researchers have not really examined how deep the change is as a result of normative influences. Their findings indeed suggest that the influence of in-group peer norms becomes bigger in late childhood and early adolescence compared to adult in-group norms that influence children more in early childhood (Aboud & Spears-Brown, 2013). However, findings about in-group norms also show some interesting competing effects from group norms from smaller and larger groupings (e.g. friend's group vs school norms) with norms of larger groups being in a better position to influence older compared to younger children. This of course brings to the picture the 'ethical horizon' of the group which could expand with age and greater opportunities for intergroup contact (Allport, 1954) outside the smaller interpersonal bubble of the student.

Such an interest in the role of interpersonal social relations and part–whole relations in groups was also found in the context of western Marxism in the work of Adorno who was also largely influenced by the affective and emotive component of Freud's work and is unique in his social developmental theorisation. He suggested that punitive and strict parenting would lead to the formation of the authoritarian personality (Adorno, 1950/2019). Such parenting in Piagetian terms would be characterised by relations of constraint, as they lack the element of mutual respect and put the psychological subject in a position of passivity in relation to others (interpersonal orientation) or the group (part–whole relations). In the later work of Altemeyer (1988, 1998) there were indeed significant statistical relations identified between harsh parenting and prejudice levels.

More recently John Duckit (2001), following the steps of Altemeyer, made further distinctions within the idea of authoritarianism or within Piaget's social relations of constraint: an orientation of *submission*, likening it with social conformity; and an orientation of *domination*, likening it with Machiavellian ways of thinking about weaker others. He also brings convincing empirical evidence that the first orientation is related to the development of right-wing authoritarianism (RWA) and the second with social dominance orientation (SDO) that both predict prejudice but through different paths. Interestingly, he finds that in younger adolescents the link between RWA and SDO is less strong, but as adolescents become more politically socialised in later adolescence and especially in sociocultural contexts of strong left wing–right wing differentiation, the links become stronger. A crucial distinction between RWA and SDO seems to be the level of agency involved in the two positions. Whilst RWA minimises agency through submission to authority and tradition, SDO takes agency to the opposite end in an orientation of controlling, cold and calculating manipulation and domination of others. Very interesting social developmental research by Guidetti, Carraro and Castelli (2017) explored the links between parental RWA and SDO and their preschoolers epistemic (preference for order in stimuli), relational (conformity to peer pressure in an Asch-like task) and existential (threat sensitivity) orientations. They found that parents' RWA and SDO scores appeared to have opposite effects on children's relational needs: children's conformity increased at increasing levels of mothers' RWA and decreased at increasing levels of fathers' SDO. Also, higher mother RWA scores were related to greater sensitivity to threatening stimuli by the preschoolers. An interesting link with traditional or sexist representations of gender was noted by the authors, since the findings point to an influential path from an 'anxious' mother and a 'domineering or calculating, powerful' father influencing RWA and SDO correspondingly in their sample of preschoolers.

Toward a Triadic Model of Prejudice

From the clinical psychology point of view in terms of well-being, the development of agency away from a position of submission and helplessness is important. Piaget's relations of co-operation (Piaget, 1932) and his principle of mutual respect are again the third way between the two extremes of submission and domination. The microgenetic processes that strengthen a RWA and SDO view are obviously asymmetrical relations of constraint (unilateral respect). This relates to forms of recognition in microgenetic processes that we have identified in previous work (Psaltis & Duveen, 2006, 2007) as the defining element of the quality of social relations. On the one hand there is *instrumental recognition* which downgrades the subject to an object that serves the aims of another person or institution and diminishes agency. This was seen in our conversation type of *no resistance* where the subject passively accepted other's views or perspectives. On the other end of the spectrum of *instrumental recognition* was the *non-conserving* type where original non-conservers (less developmentally advanced children) dogmatically supported their own view without taking into consideration or ignoring the conflicting position of the other. But there was also the middle way of *recognition as a thinking subject* (Psaltis & Duveen, 2007), which is promoting the agency of the subject who is being recognised whilst at the same time recognising others as thinking subjects. In our previous work we have identified conversation types that facilitated the establishment of a social relation of co-operation as 'explicit recognition' which was the type of conversation that entailed mutual respect (Psaltis & Duveen, 2007) and, importantly, an intersubjectivity structure where both partners know that the others know what they know (Psaltis, 2005; Duveen & Psaltis, 2008).

Agency is also discussed by Gillespie (2012) as the development of the ability for distancing oneself from the immediate situation. Gillespie gives the example of the research subject in Milgram's experiment that resists the directives of an authority to harm another individual as a good example of agency. In this sense resistance to authorities and group norms would be another example of the exercise of agency as also suggested by Piaget (1932). But how does agency develop? Gillespie (2012) shows this process to be dependent on the process of position exchange that allows the integration of first- and third-order perspectives. Agency entails identification with another person's pain in Milgram's experiment and taking the perspective of others onto self as someone who is causing pain (thus the self becomes observable from another perspective), and it is this positioning that is resisted by the subject as an expression of resistance and agency. The triad of the *subject–object–other* depicted in Figure 2.1 is the significant structure to be studied; it is the unit of analysis of genetic social psychology. The triad should be conceptualised as both an activity structure and a configuration of expectations about who (in-group or out-group) should or is controlling the 'object' (property, land, power, etc.), which makes triadic expectations asymmetrical and dependent on power structures. Domestic tensions extend to regional and global through geopolitical interests of great powers.

The structure and configuration of the triad (symmetrical or asymmetrical) depend on both cognitive developmental and ideological constraints. From the cognitive developmental perspective, the triad in early childhood should be seen as undifferentiated. Subject–object and subject–other are undifferentiated before symbol formation in the child around the end of the first year of life (Furth, 1996) (see Figure 2.1), but after this age we have the emergence of the triad through a differentiation process. The process of human development can be seen as a process of gradual differentiation and coordination of perspectives. The knowledge of the child in his or her early years is constrained by the here and now and is driven by the figurative aspects of knowing. In Piagetian terms, the representations stay at the 'periphery' of subject–object interaction. Any 'prejudice' in these years of early childhood (before six to seven years old) should be seen as the result of having heard from significant others that other groups or countries 'are like that (usually negative trait)' or 'grabbed something from us' or from visible cues of difference (gender, colour, etc.). The more hierarchical the relations between subject–other (with parents or friends), the less subject–other differentiation will be observed, which will have epistemological consequences because it will hinder the movement from the periphery to the centre of knowledge and constrain the development of agency. This will facilitate a more holistic (relational) way of thinking and less analytic (abstract/categorical) way of thinking (cf. Henrich, 2020). This has a parallel in the genetic model of social influence of Serge Moscovici, where he described majority influence as setting in motion a social comparison process and conformity, whereas a minority as the source of influence was setting in motion a process of cognitive validation and a conversion process in the mind of the target of influence. Hierarchical relations of constraint supported by higher religiosity in the family will also contribute to a fixation in the periphery of knowledge and less analytical thinking. Traditional and conformity values (Schwartz, 2021) as well as honour and face values will be expected to form close links with religiosity that supports hierarchical representations of gender (sexist beliefs, machismo, etc.) and a more interdependent self-construal or understanding of self. The role of cultural values is key. For example, honor values (Uskul et al., 2023) could support both positions of submission (usually women and LGBTQI+ or minorities) and domination (machismo, bravado, retaliation, overconfidence, egocentrism, sociocentrism, assimilation over accommodation). Domination would be a position more often taken by males compared to females. This would explain, for example, why SDO is often higher in males than females.

Children, before six to seven years of age have no understanding of part–whole relations, and this would be expected to have consequences for the role of intergroup contact in the generalisation effects of prejudice reduction from an individual out-grouper to the whole out-group. Even if they have positive intergroup contact from their perspective, generalisation of positive feelings from the individual to the whole group would be difficult. At this age binary distinctions of a figurative nature would work as organising principles (gender, skin colour, etc.) and would make difficult any differentiations within groups. Children in middle and late childhood between ages of 6–7 and 10–11 years (Figure 2.1) develop their cognitive capacity to a great extent, and for them subject–object–other relations become differentiated and the move from 'periphery to centre' starts to take place. Children master part–whole relations as well as begin to make internal differentiations between out-group members on the basis of individual or trait characteristics of persons. This stereotypical thinking can be reduced but its actual reduction depends on the prevailing in-group norms and opportunities for intergroup contact whose importance increases in this period for prejudice reduction. In this period from 6–7 to 10–11 years old the role of social relations of constraint and co-operation is also important as the ethical horizon of childhood is largely exhausted in interpersonal relationships with significant others but links between the interpersonal and the intergroup sphere are beginning to emerge with children that often find themselves in positions of submission (with both peers and adults) developing a sense of threatened identity that is also projected to feelings about out-groups. In this sense this is the period that we have the beginnings of the formation of a rudimentary consciousness of RWA and SDO (Cadamuro et al., 2021), which seems to suggest a transition that entails the broadening of horizon from the interpersonal to the intergroup in a more reflective way. In this period we also have the emergence of resistance to unfair treatment as children become reflective of equality and inequality in their interpersonal relationships (Killen, 2018). Emerging agency and empathy (both emotional and cognitive) in this age period are key. Even biological or genetic factors known in the literature as primary psychopathy could play a role here. In Figure 2.1, for example, an egocentric, narcissistic or Machiavellian position, high on callous unemotional traits (Fanti & Lordos, 2022) that lack empathy, could constrain the individual into the narrower ethical horizon in terms of out-group inclusion. But even if biological factors play no role, in-group norms relating to the attitude towards out-groups will certainly play an important role here. Such a constriction or narrowing of the ethical horizon could have various consequences for not being interested in the social and political life of their community, ending up apolitical being both indifferent and negative towards out-groups by conforming to a thin layer of negative stereotypes.

Table 2.1 thus further separates the ontogenetic outcomes depending on the triadic significant structure (the submerged part of the iceberg in our metaphor) into three enduring patterns of organisation of the thought and behaviour of the social psychological subject. A relation of constraint is further subdivided into the position on either the one or the other pole of a relation of constraint (submission vs domination), although it should be recognised that children and adults depending on the 'other' they have to deal with can often take either of the two positions. The structure that makes taking the one or the other end of the relation of constraint less likely is the development of relations of co-operation (mutual respect). It should also be recognised that in the case of members of minority

Table 2.1 *Intragroup (interpersonal) and intergroup relationships and their relationships to significant structures*

Interpersonal Sphere /Part–Whole Relations	**World Views**	**Feelings towards Out-group**	**Intergroup Contact**	**Historical Consciousness**	**Ideological and Value Correlates**
Relations of Constraint (submission) Strict Parenting	Threats – Dangerous World	Prejudice, Distrust, Lack of empathy Collective Victimisation Ethos of Conflict	Low Contact	Traditional and Exemplary Historical Consciousness	High RWA High CO, TR Low AC, PO
Relations of Constraint (domination) Machiavellianism	Threats – World as a jungle – Competition Neoliberal	Prejudice, Distrust, Lack of empathy Ethos of Conflict	Low Contact	Presentism/Critical	High SDO (would not be predictive for minority groups) High AC, HE, PO Low BE, UN
Relations of Co-operation (secure attachment with parents, mutual respect)	Low threats More benevolent world view	Positive feelings, Trust, Empathy Low Ethos of Conflict	High contact	Critical or Genetic Historical Consciousness	Low RWA, Low SDO Low CO, TR, HE High UN, SD

groups, the SDO correlation structure in the middle of Table 2.1 could not actually work in the predicted direction, since legitimating inequality between groups automatically entails legitimising a structure that disfavours their in-group and self-image. An important element of the table below is *values* and their articulation with sociogenetic changes in historical time is key for genetic social psychology, and the table should be completed with the role of values (last column in Table 2.1), which is the topic of the next chapter.

REFERENCES

Aboud, F. E. (1988). *Children and prejudice*. Oxford: Blackwell.

(2008). A social-cognitive developmental theory of prejudice. In S. M. Quintana & C. McKown (Eds.), *Handbook of race, racism, and the developing child* (pp. 55–71). New York: John Wiley & Sons Inc.

Aboud, F. E., & Amato, M. (2003). Developmental and socialization influences on intergroup bias. In R. Brown & S. Gaertner (Eds.), *Blackwell handbook of social psychology: Intergroup processes* (pp. 65–85). New York: Wiley-Blackwell.

Aboud, F. E., & Spears-Brown, C. (2013). Positive and negative intergroup contact among children and its effect on attitudes. *Advances in Intergroup Contact, 80*, 176–199.

Adorno, T. (1950/2019). *The authoritarian personality*. London: Verso Books.

Allport, G. W. (1954). *The nature of prejudice*. Oxford: Addison-Wesley.

Altemeyer, B. (1988). *Enemies of freedom: Understanding right-wing authoritarianism*. San Francisco, CA: Jossey-Bass.

Altemeyer, R. A. (1998). The other 'authoritarian personality'. In M. P. Zanna (Ed.), *Advances in experimental social psychology* (Vol. 30, pp. 47–91). New York: Academic Press.

Barrett, M., & Oppenheimer, L. (2011). Findings, theories and methods in the study of children's national identifications and national attitudes. *European Journal of Developmental Psychology, 8*(1), 5–24.

Bar-Tal, D. (2023). *Sinking into the honey trap: The case of the Israeli-Palestinian conflict*. Washington, DC: Westphalia Press.

Bar-Tal, D., & Teichman, Y. (2005). *Stereotypes and prejudice in conflict: Representations of Arabs in Israeli Jewish society*. Cambridge: Cambridge University Press.

Cadamuro, A., Di Bernardo, G. A., Trifiletti, E., Bisagno, E., Shamloo, S. E., Faccini, M., & Vezzali, L. (2022). Social dominance orientation in children: The validation of the long and short version of the child SDO6 scale. *European Journal of Developmental Psychology, 19*(1), 145–157.

Demetriou, A., Liakos, A., & Kizilyürek, N. (2021). How wisdom emerges from intellectual development: A developmental/historical theory for raising Mandelas. *Journal of Intelligence, 9*(3), 47.

Doyle, A. B., & Aboud, F. E. (1995). A longitudinal study of White children's racial prejudice as a social-cognitive development. *Merrill-Palmer Quarterly*, 209–228.

Duckitt, J. (2001). A dual-process cognitive-motivational theory of ideology and prejudice. *Advances in Experimental Social Psychology*, *33*, 41–113.

Duveen, G., & Psaltis, C. (2008). The constructive role of asymmetry in social interaction. In U. Mueller, J. Carpendale, N. Budwig, & B. Sokol (Eds.), *Social life and social knowledge: Toward a process account of development* (pp. 190–211). New York: Psychology Press.

Fanti, K. A., & Lordos, A. (2022). Age patterns in psychopathic traits from age 9 to age 20: Testing unique associations with conduct disorder symptoms. *Current Psychology*, *41*(9), 6452–6463.

Furth, H. G. (1996). *Desire for society*. Boston, MA: Springer.

Gillespie, A. (2012). Position exchange: The social development of agency. *New Ideas in Psychology*, *30*(1), 32–46.

Guidetti, M., Carraro, L., & Castelli, L. (2017). An exploration of the differential effects of parents' authoritarianism dimensions on pre-school children's epistemic, existential, and relational needs. *Frontiers in Psychology*, *7*, 2079.

Hadjipavlou, M., & Mertan, E. B. (2019). A multilevel intervention: The case of the Cyprus gender advisory team (GAT) achievements and challenges. *Journal of Peacebuilding & Development*, *14*(2), 125–137.

Henrich, J. (2020). *The WEIRDest people in the world: How the West became psychologically peculiar and particularly prosperous*. New York: Farrar Straus and Giroux.

Killen, M. (2018). The origins of morality: Social equality, fairness, and justice. *Philosophical Psychology*, *31*(5), 767–803.

Miklikowska, M. (2017). Development of anti-immigrant attitudes in adolescence: The role of parents, peers, intergroup friendships, and empathy. *British Journal of Psychology*, *108*, 626–648.

Miklikowska, M., & Hurme, H. (2011). Democracy begins at home: Democratic parenting and adolescents' support for democratic values. *European Journal of Developmental Psychology*, *8*, 541–557. https://doi.org/10.1080/17405629.2011.576856.

Miklikowska, M., Thijs, J., & Hjerm, M. (2019). The impact of perceived teacher support on anti-immigrant attitudes from early to late adolescence. *Journal of Adolescence*, *48*, 1175–1189.

Moscovici, S. (1976). *Social influence and social change*. London: Academic Press.

(1991). Experiment and experience: An intermediate step from Sherif to Asch. *Journal for the Theory of Social Behaviour*, *21*, 253–268.

Nasie, M., & Bar-Tal, D. (2020). Political socialization in kindergartens: Observations of ceremonies of the Israeli Jewish holidays and memorial days. *European Journal of Social Psychology*, *50*(3), 685–700.

Nasie, M., Reifen Tagar, M., & Bar-Tal, D. (2021). Ethno-political socialization of young children in societies involved in intractable conflict: The case of Israel. *Journal of Social Issues*, *77*(4), 1257–1281.

Nesdale, D. (2001). Development of prejudice in children. In M. Augoustinos & K. J. Reynolds (Eds.), *Understanding prejudice, racism and social conflict* (pp. 57–72). London: Sage.

(2004). Social identity and ethnic prejudice. In M. Bennett & F. Sani (Eds.), *The development of the social self* (pp. 219–246). East Sussex: Psychology Press.

(2017). Children and social groups: A social identity approach. In A. Rutland, D. Nesdale, & C. S. Brown (Eds.), *The Wiley handbook of group processes in children and adolescents* (pp. 1–22). Malden, MA: John Wiley & Sons.

Piaget, J. (1932). *The moral judgement of the child.* London: Routledge and Kegan Paul.

(1977/1995). *Sociological studies.* London: Routledge.

Piaget, J., & Weil, A. M. (1951). The development in children of the idea of the homeland and of relations with other countries. *International Social Science Bulletin, 3*(3), 561–578.

Psaltis, C. (2005). Communication and the construction of knowledge or transmission of belief. *Studies in Communication Sciences, 209*, 228.

Psaltis, C., & Duveen, G. (2006). Social relations and cognitive development: The influence of conversation types and representations of gender. *European Journal of Social Psychology, 36*, 407–430.

(2007). Conversation types and conservation: Forms of recognition and cognitive development. *British Journal of Developmental Psychology, 25*, 79–102.

Raabe, T., & Beelmann, A. (2011). Development of ethnic, racial, and national prejudice in childhood and adolescence: A multinational meta-analysis of age differences. *Child Development, 82*(6), 1715–1737.

Schwartz, S. H. (2021). A repository of Schwartz value scales with instructions and an introduction. *Online Readings in Psychology and Culture, 2*(2). https://doi.org/10.9707/2307-0919.1173.

Teichman, Y. (2016). Stereotypes and prejudice in conflict: A developmental perspective. In K. Sharvit & E. Halperin (Eds.), *A social psychology perspective on the Israeli-Palestinian conflict: Celebrating the legacy of Daniel Bar-Tal* (Vol II, pp. 17–30). New York: Springer.

Uskul, A. K., Kirchner-Häusler, A., Vignoles, V. L., Rodriguez-Bailon, R., Castillo, V. A., Cross, S. E., . . . & Uchida, Y. (2023). Neither Eastern nor Western: Patterns of independence and interdependence in Mediterranean societies. *Journal of Personality and Social Psychology, 125*(3), 471.

CHAPTER 3

The Sociogenesis of Human Values
Organising Principles of Social Representations

Charis Psaltis

Values in Social Representations and in Value Theories

Values are core and definitional characteristics of social representations as a 'system of values, ideas and practices' (Moscovici, 1972), but they have rarely been given proper attention by researchers working in the social representations paradigm with the exception of some recent work that made some connections between the notion of 'worldviews', 'social axioms', 'symbolic universes', 'moral frameworks' and 'deep stories' (Misfed & Sammut, 2023). This is surprising given the burgeoning literature on human values, processes of their formation and historical change since the classic work of social psychologist Milton Rockeach. Rokeach (1973) listed 18 terminal values which refer to desirable end-states of existence (peace, family security, freedom, equality, self-respect, happiness, wisdom, national security, salvation, true friendship, accomplishment, inner harmony, comfortable life, mature love, beauty, pleasure, social recognition and exciting life) and 18 instrumental values as preferable modes of behavior, or means of achieving the terminal values (cheerfulness, ambition, love, cleanliness, self-control, capability, courage, politeness, honesty, imagination, independence, intellect, broad-mindedness, logic, obedience, helpfulness, responsibility and forgiveness).

In more recent years many social scientists turned to the study of values. Political scientists Inglehart and Welzel (Inglehard, 2018) propose two dimensions of cross-cultural variation around the world: (1) Traditional values versus secular-rational values (traditional values emphasise religiosity, national pride, respect for authority, obedience and marriage). Secular-rational values emphasize the opposite on each of these accounts). (2) Survival values versus self-expression values (survival values involve a priority of security over liberty, non-acceptance of homosexuality, abstinence from political action, distrust in outsiders and a weak sense of happiness). Based on these two axes countries (that can

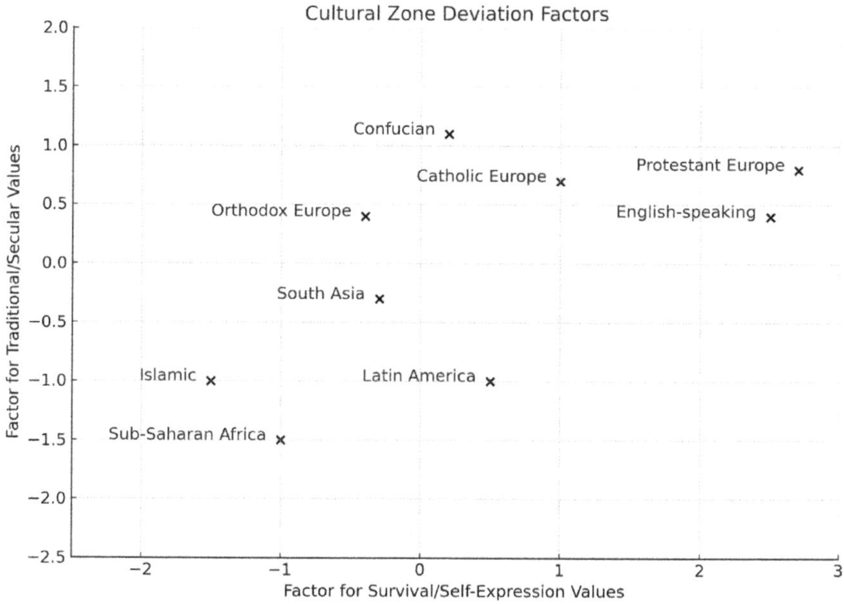

Figure 3.1 Positions of cultural groups on Values based on WVS findings. Adapted from: The Inglehart-Welzel World Cultural Map – World Values Survey 7 (2023). www.worldvaluessurvey.org/.

be grouped by religion and geographical area) can be plotted from findings of comparative world-wide research like the World Values Survey (WVS) (see Figure 3.1).

This approach emphasises national values as the unit of analysis and is rooted in a revision of the idea of modernisation in the classical works of Marx, Weber and Durkheim, which refers to the transition from agrarian-based societies to industrial and then post-industrial, knowledge-based societies. This transition is marked by economic growth, technological advancement and increased levels of education. Importantly for their revised modernisation theory, the transition from agrarian-based societies to industrial societies is expected to lead to progress on the traditional versus secular values axis, whereas transition from industrial to post-industrial and knowledge societies is expected to lead to progress on the survival vs self-expression values.

One of the most widely used theories of human values in social psychology is Shalom Schwartz's (2021) theory of basic human values. It identifies 10 basic values, which are shown to be universal across cultures, although priorities of these values change among individuals and among countries and cultures. These values represent core principles that guide human behavior, and Schwartz posits that they are rooted in one or more of three universal requirements of human existence: needs of individuals as biological organisms; requisites of coordinated social interaction; and survival and welfare needs of groups.

The 10 basic values identified by Schwartz are:

Power (PO): Emphasising social status, control or dominance over people and resources.
Achievement (AC): Valuing personal success through demonstrating competence according to social standards.
Hedonism (HE): Seeking pleasure and sensuous gratification for oneself.
Stimulation (ST): Valuing excitement, novelty and challenge in life.
Self-Direction (SD): Valuing independent thought and action – choosing, creating, exploring.
Universalism (UN): Understanding, appreciation, tolerance, and protection for the welfare of all people and for nature.
Benevolence (BE): Preserving and enhancing the welfare of those with whom one is in frequent personal contact (the 'in-group').
Tradition (TR): Respect, commitment and acceptance of the customs and ideas that traditional culture or religion provide.
Conformity (CO): Restraint of actions, inclinations,and impulses likely to upset or harm others and violate social expectations or norms.
Security (SE): Valuing safety, harmony and stability of society, of relationships and of self.

Schwartz's theory also discusses the dynamic nature of values, suggesting that they are structured in a circular manner, reflecting a continuum of related motivations (see Figure 3.2). Values that are adjacent to each other on the circle are more compatible, while values on opposite sides are in conflict. For example, the pursuit of power conflicts with the value of benevolence. This structure helps to explain individual differences in value priorities and the conflicts that arise when trying to pursue or balance different values.

The 10 values can also be grouped into higher-order values (Conservation vs Openness to change and Self-enhancement vs Self transcendence) as shown in Table 3.1.

From the perspective of genetic social psychology, the relative priority of personal values can act as organising principles of social

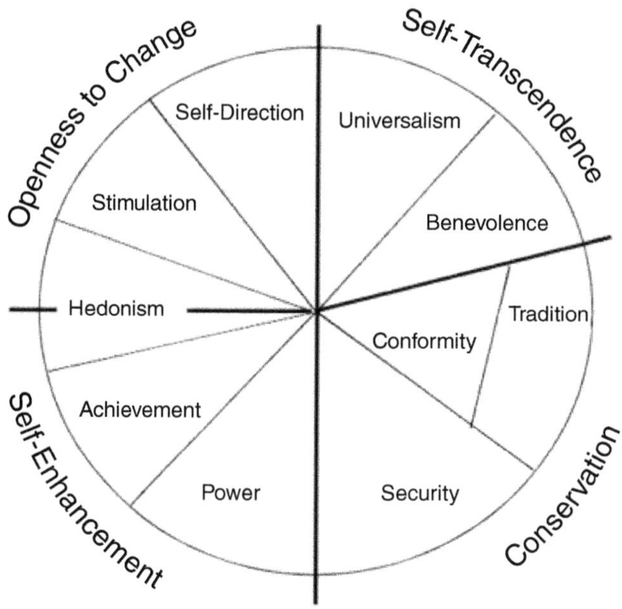

Figure 3.2 Shalom Schwartz circumplex model of values.
Source: Schwartz, S. H. (2012). An overview of the Schwartz Theory of Basic Values. *Online Readings in Psychology and Culture, 2*(1).

representations in the sense that they regulate both the process of their formation and content. For example, a representation of the opening of checkpoints in 2003 in Cyprus for an individual that gives priority to openness to change and not conservation is one that represents this opening as an opportunity for learning new things about the other community and other part of the island (stimulation), exploring new ideas beyond the controlled environment of their communally separated education along ethnic lines, and creating new friendships (self-direction). On the contrary, an individual who gives priority to Conservation values over values of Openness to change might experience the opening of the checkpoints as a threat to the in-group (security) or religious tradition becoming a source of intergroup anxiety and concern about losing one's national or religious identity. Importantly, the close relationship of tradition with conformity values suggests some important links between the form and content of representations, because traditional values are formed through social influence processes of conformity

Table 3.1 *The 21 portrait-values from Swartz's theory used in the European Values Survey (ESS)*

		Four Higher-Order Values	Personal vs Social Focus	Examples of Items Measuring Each Value
V1	Self-Direction	Openness to change	Personal	Thinking up new ideas and being creative is important to him/her. He/she likes to do things in his/her own original way.
V2	Power	Self-enhancement	Personal	It is important to him/her to be rich. He/she wants to have a lot of money and expensive things.
V3	Universalism	Self-transcendence	Social	He/she thinks it is important that every person in the world should be treated equally. He/she believes everyone should have equal opportunities in life.
V4	Achievement	Self-enhancement	Personal	It is important to him/her to show his/her abilities. He/she wants people to admire what he/she does.
V5	Security	Conservation	Social	It is important to him/her to live in secure surroundings. He/she avoids anything that might endanger his/her safety.
V6	Stimulation	Openness to change	Personal	He/she likes surprises and is always looking for new things to do. He/she thinks it is important to do lots of different things in life.
V7	Conformity	Conservation	Social	He/she believes that people should do what they're told. He/she thinks people should follow rules at all times, even when no one is watching.
V8	Universalism	Self-transcendence	Social	It is important to him/her to listen to people who are different from him/her. Even when he/she disagrees with them, he/she still wants to understand them.
V9	Tradition	Conservation	Social	It is important to him/her to be humble and modest. He/she tries not to draw attention to himself/herself.
V10	Hedonism	Openness to change	Personal	Having a good time is important to him/her. He/she likes to 'spoil' himself/herself.

Table 3.1 (*cont.*)

		Four Higher-Order Values	Personal vs Social Focus	Examples of Items Measuring Each Value
V11	Self Direction	Openness to change	Personal	It is important to him/her to make his/her own decisions about what he/she does. He/she likes to be free and not depend on others.
V12	Benevolence	Self-transcendence	Social	It's very important to him/her to help the people around him/her. He/she wants to care for their well-being.
V13	Achievement	Self-enhancement	Personal	Being very successful is important to him/her. He/she hopes people will recognise his/her achievements.
V14	Security	Conservation	Social	It is important to him/her that the government ensures his/her safety against all threats. He/she wants the state to be strong so it can defend its citizens.
V15	Stimulation	Openness to change	Personal	He/she looks for adventures and likes to take risks. He/she wants to have an exciting life.
V16	Conformity	Conservation	Social	It is important to him/her always to behave properly. He/she wants to avoid doing anything people would say is wrong.
V17	Power	Self-enhancement	Personal	It is important to him/her to get respect from others. He/she wants people to do what he/she says.
V18	Benevolence	Self-transcendence	Social	It is important to him/her to be loyal to his/her friends. He/she wants to devote himself/herself to people close to him/her.
V19	Universalism	Self-transcendence	Social	He/she strongly believes that people should care for nature. Looking after the environment is important to him/her.
V20	Tradition	Conservation	Social	Tradition is important to him/her. He/she tries to follow the customs handed down by his/her religion or his/her family.
V21	Hedonism	Openness to change	Personal	He/she seeks every chance he/she can to have fun. It is important to him/her to do things that give him/her pleasure.

to norms of values of the in-group, thus enacting relations of constraint that limit the expansion of the ethical horizon of the individual and the developing child. On the contrary, favouring intergroup contact between the two communities enacts a relation of co-operation that expands the individual's ethical horizon in a universalising direction.

The value priorities of individuals vary by geography and time, and therefore the study of the sociogenesis of social representations through historical time and cultural evolution can be greatly enhanced by an understanding of this change. Here international comparative studies that measure the 10 values mentioned earlier, such as the European Social Survey (ESS), European Values Survey (EVS) and WVS, can offer valuable insights about the direction and rate of change in various countries, revealing more general patterns in other European countries, including those culturally very different to Cyprus.

Cultural Evolution and Values

Broader discussions about cultural evolution from various disciplines at a global level can add considerable historical depth to genetic social psychology, as they offer an analysis of sociogenetic processes of changing values through millennia. In an impressive research programme Henrich (2015, 2020) has recently synthesised findings from anthropology, evolutionary biology, economics, history and social and developmental psychology into a dual inheritance theory of culture–gene co-evolution, offering ample evidence of cultural evolution patterns of change not only in values but also in cognitive and perceptual skills, morality, social cohesion and societal norms with direct implications for politics, changing democratic cultures and economic development at the country level. One of the biggest and most influential contributions of his work is the introduction of the critique of the false universalistic claims based on research with samples from a thin slice of humanity which he calls WEIRD societies.

In his historical account Henrich documents the crucial role played by religious institutions in this process of cultural evolution. First came a policy by the Roman Catholic Church that broke down large traditional kinship-based social networks through a family planning policy from around 500–1500 AD in western Europe that led to the end of polygamy and polygeny and a strengthening of the nuclear family. Belief in the Roman Catholic doctrine also facilitated trade with strangers (albeit only co-religionists) beyond the close circle of those who individual subjects knew personally. All these changes also led to more co-operation with in-groupers. Then followed the Protestant Reformation in parts of western Europe, which brought a more direct relationship with God without the mediation of church as an institution and its hierarchies with the *sola scriptura*, which brought significant increase in literacy levels, public education and a new work ethic as we know from the classic work of Weber. This long-term historical shift eventually led to more individualist values in these areas. Henrich (2020) also argues these shifts slowly changed the brains (not the genes) of people – cognitive abilities in domains of memory, facial recognition, visual processing, numerical exactness and problem solving. For Henrich, higher literacy levels of Protestantism are likened to innovative ideas and technological acceleration. During the Enlightenment new historical phenomena were added in accelerating change around the idea Henrich calls the emergence of the 'collective mind' which has to do with (1) apprenticeship institutions, (2) urbanisation and impersonal markets, (3) transregional monastic orders, (4) universities, (5) the Republic of letters (transnational scientific societies), including new religious faiths (e.g. Huguenots) that not only promoted literacy and schooling but also made industriousness, scientific insights and pragmatic achievement sacred.

Heinrich's (2020) historical account ends around that time, and he would probably state that the rest is history in how the West became successful. However, it could be argued that some crucial questions arise relating to the history of the 20th and 21st centuries having to do with the failure of the universalising potential of the enlightenment ideas, enduring racism, colonialism and post-colonialism, the rise of nationalism, fascism, Nazism, two world wars, the Holocaust and the Cold War, nuclear threat, increasing inequality and climate change that pose some pertinent questions to the social scientists interested in cultural evolution about how humanity (the successful West included) came to the brink of its own self-extinction.

In this sense, it could thus be argued that the 20th century is actually not the end but the beginning of the story for understanding how humanity can hope for any future. The contribution of genetic social psychology in rendering this conflict-ridden part of the story intelligible is key. I would argue that it is essential for social scientists to explore in depth intergroup ethnic conflicts that undo socio-economic development, and the central role of public education from its first steps in humanity until today in promoting religion and nationalism through hierarchical, ethnocentric and traditional teaching approaches in both WEIRD and non-WEIRD societies. This effort should be put at the heart of our endeavours in the pursuit for an understanding of the formation of historical consciousness and in-group norms promoted by the nation state through the articulation of microgenetic, ontogenetic and sociogenetic processes of change.

To overcome WEIRD biases, comparative work in non-WEIRD settings is of crucial importance, particularly comparisons with Christian Orthodox and Islamic settings. Henrich (2020) covers some distance in this direction when he explores pro-social behaviour, helping strangers and the difference between in-group and out-group trust from the findings of WVS. He notes that pro-social behaviour and helping strangers are higher in both Catholic and Protestant Christian countries compared to Eastern Orthodox Christian and Islamic countries. Similarly, the difference between in-group trust and out-group trust is also higher in the Orthodox Christian and Islamic countries. Further data collection from countries around the Mediterranean and the Middle East is also of great importance here because most of the cross-cultural psychological comparisons are usually comparing the West to the East, leaving the important geographical middle between them largely unexplored. In some of our recent work with colleagues we explored the existence of honour, face and dignity values in various Mediterranean countries and compared them with Asian and other Western cultures (Uskul et al., 2023). In this work we discovered that honour values are closely related to religion and traditional values in Cyprus. Given that honour values support traditional asymmetrical masculine and feminine roles, the study of adherence to honour values allows an in-depth exploration of the interanimation of social representations of conflict with social representations of gender.

Despite the impressive and very promising research programme of Henrich (2015, 2020), which in many ways is compatible with the vision of genetic social psychology for a historical psychology (Muthukrishna, Henrich & Slingerland, 2021), there seems to be great reliance on a social transmission metaphor (processes of social learning and imitation) and definition of co-operation as pro-sociality (helping, altruism, etc.) (Henrich & Muthukrishna, 2021) that comes mainly through the influence of the work of Michael Tomasello (2020). Tomasello's recent work on the emergence of obligation is certainly relevant to our discussion in the previous section about the ontogenesis of prejudice, as he discusses how at the age of about two to three years a commitment to a shared 'we' emerges from shared interpersonal intentionality. The potential of scaling up this 'we' and the expansion of the ethical horizon of the child in ontogenesis is also recognised as a possibility, but no discussion of conflicting norms, asymmetries and power can be found anywhere in his theorisation. This is probably due to the fact that his notion of cooperation is different from Piaget's (1932) definition of co-operation where it is a relation between equals in status that implies the absence of conformity towards more powerful others; It is also the presence of conflicting representations of the world that become co-ordinated into more powerful knowledge that overcomes one-sided perspectives through decentration. It is important to understand that the quality of co-operative social relations based on mutual respect can be found in adult–child relationships as well. In a similar way, relations of constraint (unilateral respect) can also be located in relations between peers. This was, in fact, one of the major findings from our first line of research with Gerard Duveen (Psaltis & Duveen, 2006, 2007). One could even extend the idea of mutual respect in very early parent–child relationships as suggested by Carpendale and Lewis (2020), thereby relating this framework with attachment styles in the sensorimotor stage of cognitive development (see the first column in Table 2.1). A lack of mutual respect – for example, of a mother towards her newborn – could be non-responding to the child's needs appropriately for whatever reason.

But in the work of Henrich (2015, 2020) there is not a single citing of either Piaget's or Vygotsky's work, which is rather strange for a social scientist who draws so much from the developmental literature. In the study of sociogenetic changes in the West in the 18th century, a period covered by Henrich, greater attention should be given to Jean-Jacques Rousseau, a prominent 18th-century philosopher well known for his contributions to political philosophy, education and literature. His ideas about the importance of the study of nature also influenced Goethe's organismic model (Wagoner, 2024). His critiques of various aspects of society and religion were influential in the Enlightenment period, shaping modern political and educational thought as well as the secularist ideals of the French Revolution. Rousseau was critical of both organised forms of Protestant religion (Lutheranism and Calvinism). He was born in Geneva, which was one of the most prominent centres of Calvinism, and he openly criticised (1) the theological Calvinist ideas of predestination (which asserts that God has already chosen who will be saved and who will be damned); (2) the authoritarian involvement of Calvinism in the political life of Geneva, advocating for a separation between church and state; and (3) social inequality, which he saw as being perpetuated by institutions, including religious ones. He believed that Calvinism, like other organised religions, could be used to justify and maintain social hierarchies. Piaget not only was the director of the Jean-Jacques Rousseau Institute in Geneva, but it could be argued that his social psychology of social relations of constraint and co-operation (Piaget, 1932) transferred the same criticisms of suppressive part–whole relations in developmental psychology and epistemology, becoming one of the most influential intellectual figures of the 20th century in the Western world. The human relationship of mutual respect and decentration that he was proposing as the ideal in promoting both cognitive and moral development was also applied in the promotion of international dialogue among educational systems of nation states and the promotion of internationalist ideals through the work of the International Bureau of Education (IBE), which later became part of UNESCO (Psaltis & Zapiti, 2014). Despite Rousseau's influence on Piaget, we can see that Piaget surpasses one of the problematic aspects of Rousseau's thinking when he created a master narrative of the history of humanity as starting from a benign nature that is corrupted by society. For Piaget, society could take the form of either social relations of constraint or co-operation, and in that sense there is nothing inherently good or bad about society. It is the way we formulate our social relations with others that could lead to benign or negative outcomes. In this sense, Piaget can thus be seen as an early critic of Rousseau, whose grand narrative of human evolution has recently been deconstructed by the work of Graeber and Wengrow (2021).

In fact, Piaget's social psychology can offer the missing mechanism in Henrich's work that forms the 'dark matter' of the significant structure of the iceberg metaphor that holds together different social representations that lead to in-group norms and the establishment of institutions. Piaget showed that analytic and dispositional thinking can only emerge through unconstrained dialogue or communication with any oppressive authority (God, teachers, parents). We believe this is a universal mechanism, and it is the failure or success of the application of these relations and norms of mutual respect that leads to cross-cultural variation. Thus, existence (or absence) of traditional kinship networks described by Henrich (2020), urbanisation and adherence to various religions are only distal predictors of the proximal causal factors which is social relational quality at an interpersonal level and part–whole relations relating to the way individuals are embedded in groups. Similarly, values are also predicted by Greenfield (2009) to have a mediating role in her theory connecting societal change (urbanisation, formal education, economic development) to human development and the development of more abstract thinking. In her approach the shift from collectivistic to more individualistic values will lead to more abstract thinking. It is important to note here that in some of her findings in Mexico where she compared children's level of cooperation in 1967 and 2017, importantly defined as a coordination game similar the one used by Doise and Mugny (1984) between children on a common goal, she found a decrease in co-operation that she attributed to rising individualist values in this period. Thus, how co-operation is defined in each study is of crucial importance, as this finding reveals that departing from collectivist values could indeed also lead to unproductive forms of individualism. The weakening of traditional, kin-based communities could entail both the reduction in conformity values, thus weakening the developmental pathway or significant structure we describe in Table 2.1, and it could mean an increase in values of rugged individualism, narcissism or Machiavellianism that we describe as the second developmental pathway. Both would make the co-operative path described by Piaget and in our Table 2.1 as the pathway in the third row less likely.

To offer clarity on this point, we believe that exploration of values attached to patterns of thinking is of crucial importance. Thus, we expect the position of submission to tradition to be related with high priority on Conformity (CO) and Tradition (TR) values but low priority on Achievement (AC), Hedonism (HE) and Power (PO) values. Given that religion can also be linked to the idea of helping others but maybe not (depending on the sociocultural context) we cannot make a prediction on Benevolence (BE) and Universalism (UN) values, since they will vary depending on the type of religion people adhere to in each context. On the contrary, we expect the domination position to be related to high Achievement (AC), Hedonism (HE) and Power (PO) Values. We also expect this position to be low on Benevolence (BE) and Universalism (UN), as it would be related to less religious adherence but overinflate the self at the expense of others (self-enhancement).

The third pathway or structure of co-operation would be expected to be related with low Conformity (CO), Tradition (TR) and Hedonism (HE) but high Universalism (UN), as it would be expected to expand the ethical horizon of the individual beyond the ingroup. It should also relate to higher Self-Direction (SD) due to an increasing sense of agency.

Protracted Conflict and Values

Perhaps, one of the most important and complicated contexts for the study of the role of values and their internalisation through social relations of co-operation or constraint and the development of prejudice is in countries where ethnic conflicts are either protracted or frozen. This could, in fact, present a significant departure from the narrow study of values and prejudice solely on its racial dimension in Western countries and mainly the United States. Coleman (2014) maintains that protracted or intractable conflicts are characterised by their persistence, a history of failed attempts to resolve the conflict and their centrality in the lives of the communities involved in the conflict influencing all aspects of social life like media, cultural production, films, school and family and peer context often captured by the notion of ethos of conflict (Bar-Tal, 2013; Bar-Tal & Teichman, 2009). Bar-Tal (2013) defines the ethos of conflict as a configuration of central, shared societal beliefs that provide a particular dominant orientation to a society and give meaning to societal life under conditions of intractable conflict. The ethos of conflict, as he found, is organised around eight themes: the justness of one's own goals, opponent delegitimisation, self-victimhood, positive self-image, security, patriotism, unity and peace. Elements of ethos of conflict have been found in various other conflicts beyond the Israel–Palestine one in which the idea was developed. For example in Cyprus, Hadjipavlou (2007) identified widespread beliefs of delegitimisation of the other group and victimisation in both communities of Cyprus. This configuration of beliefs is very similar to what we described in Table 2.1 in the first row as the significant structure of submission or victimisation closely related to traditional values and religiosity and the fact that patriotism and the goals of the group are often sacralised, becoming non-negotiable. But we would argue that there could be elements of ethos of conflict (e.g. threats or lack of empathy) that could be accompanied by a more individualist set of values as the one we describe in the second row of Table 2.1 where we could expect lower levels of ethos of conflict due to lower embeddedness in part–whole relations but still significantly lacking the co-operative potential of conflict transformation that we identify in the third row of Table 2.1.

We would claim that the major reason for this kind of variation of developmental paths relates both to different ontogenetic trajectories and historical socio-economic change. Protracted or intractable conflicts have tremendous negative consequences concerning the social and economic aspects of group life (see Coleman, 2014), but we should recognise the opposite direction of influence which raises interesting questions. How could conflict transformation evolve in a context of rugged individualism or capitalism that could be different from a context of widespread traditional values? This calls for a broader understanding of political socialisation in the broader socio-economic context of conflict. It is generally accepted that in countries where a protracted conflict is taking place, such as Cyprus and the Middle East, the development of prejudice with increasing age is increasingly influenced by political socialisation. According to Nasie et al. (2016), political socialisation is described as the ensemble of activities occurring in a social setting, thus contributing to the emergence of social representations and beliefs concerning political issues. Moreover, they claim that teenagers' political beliefs and opinions are considerably affected by significant others (parents, educators and peers) (Raabe & Beelmann, 2011). But in the case of conflict and post-conflict settings, political socialisation also involves political parties and their influence through youth organisations, which sometimes extends to actors beyond the specific country. As we will see in the case of Cyprus in the next chapter, the involvement of other countries, regional organisations, regional powers and superpowers in influencing foreign policy options often directly impacts domestic policy and the direction of the educational system. These are issues never discussed by Henrich (2020) in his recent discussion of cross-cultural variability in values and their historical development but are clearly of crucial importance for our understanding of continuity and change in the study of the articulation of processes of microgenesis, ontogenesis and sociogenesis.

Microgenetic and ontogenetic changes in prejudice should thus be seen as being embedded or canalised by institutional, socio-economic and ideological structures, material and symbolic resources in a process of overdetermination of meaning (Valsiner, 2000). Overdetermination of meaning comes from the influence of various sources such as mass-mediated processes of historical change of social representations of the other and history of the conflict itself. These are instances of a long-term sociogenetic process of change that takes various forms (e.g. intergenerational transmission of trauma, generational replacement, collective memory). In the case of the Greek Cypriot community, this overdetermination of meaning, as we will see, revolves around the cultural trauma of 1974 (Roudometof & Christou, 2015), resulting primarily from the policies of the ministry of education adopting problematic ways of extrapolating sociopolitical processes of dealing with trauma from a limited subset of personal and subjective experiences of trauma (Kansteiner, 2004). Usually ones that keep the subject in a mourning and depressing situation. For example, one political socialisation path could be a traditional-religious right-wing orientation, but another could be again a right-wing but neoliberal and individualist orientation which keeps distance from religion but is more interested in power and making money. In the case of Cyprus, like in Greece, the first would follow the triptych of sacralised values of Greek nationalism: *patris*, *thriskeia*, *oikogeneia* (homeland, religion, family) (Roudometof, 2014), but the second could only be seeing competition from Turkish Cypriots in the market for jobs and financial resources in a Machiavellian way without the full package of the ethos of conflict. Genetic social psychology can render intelligible these nuanced variations of undermining co-operative conflict transformation.

Moscovici (1990) suggested that the research strategy to understand the genesis or emergence of more complex representations from the study of simpler ones could be done either ontogenetically (Piaget and Vygotsky's way) or by a comparison of the representations of various groups (which he called Bartlett's way). He chose to do the second, although he understood the need for both in a more integrated social developmental psychology. The work of Bartlett (1932/1995) on remembering is directly relevant to this discussion, since in the case of post-conflict and divided societies like Cyprus, the past weighs on the present and future of the island through the collective memory of different cultural or chosen traumas (Volkan, 2021) in the two communities, with formal and informal education being key actors in this process.

Bartlett studied the reconstructive nature of memory in its social context (Wagoner, 2017). Whilst he agreed with sociologists like Durkheim and Halbwachs on the social nature of memory, he disagreed with them that the group itself has memories (Wagoner, 2015), hence avoiding sociological holism. His approach is compatible with the call of Moscovici for a genetic social psychology (1972, 1990), where the individual is not lost in the group but where individuality and agency itself are a function of the social relationships of the subject in the *subject–object–other* triad. Moscovici's idea of turning the unfamiliar and unfamiliarity into familiar and objectification relates directly to Bartlett's process of conventionalisation where representations get transformed as they pass from one group to another in historical time in a way that they converge with the values and orientations of the receiving group. Described as such, the study of intergroup contact could be reinterpreted through Bartlett's work: the broader process of the sociogenesis of social representations can be articulated to widen our view beyond mainstream theorising about the role of intergroup contact in prejudice reduction (Allport, 1954). This would be aligned with a methodological suggestion of Lucien Goldmann to follow the study of totality of the phenomenon, which would entail the study of not only the accompanying beliefs, ideas and practices that support the prejudicial beliefs of children but also the study of the historical change of the same structures. It is only natural that one should expect generational differences on values, and given that values function as organising principles of social representations depending on the age of the participants in our research, we should expect the emergence of different significant structures and 'splits' from previous positions into other variations in younger generations.

In post-conflict settings and deeply divided societies this suggests the need for an understanding of the societal meaning of intergroup contact itself and especially how it opens or closes opportunities for the flow of ideas between the two groups. The opportunities and outcomes of intergroup contact will be regulated and modulated by the 'prospect' of the group. In social representational terms used by Bauer and Gaskell (1999), it will depend on the representational project of the group, and in the terminology of Goldmann, it will depend on each position in the representational field as a significant structure of a group which expresses an actual and objective possibility for the future of the country.

From this perspective it is important to understand the historical evolution of the positions that are expected to be influenced by significant changes in the recent period under examination, such as the opening of the checkpoints in 2003, Cyprus joining the EU, change of administration and financial policies, financial crises, the COVID-19 pandemic, changes in technologies and the media landscape, the educational system and educational reforms, and processes of communication in social media (propaganda, propagation, diffusion) (Avraamidou & Psaltis, 2019). As we have seen earlier, individuals can take a more or less agentic position with regards to the discourse expressed by various institutions. Some teachers, parents and peers would repeat uncritically most of the expressions heard on the news or read in their echo chambers of Facebook or X (former Twitter), but others can be active agents in the effort for conflict transformation via work in local and international non-governmental organisations.

In short, from our genetic social psychological point of view, there are two types of changes: (1) changes that would take time to be effected through qualitative intergroup contact or successful semantic contact (Gillespie, 2020; Kadianaki & Gillespie, 2015) and would lead to an ideological conversion through processes described by Moscovici as cognitive validation in his theory of minority influence and (2) more superficial changes, especially for individuals, high in social conformity or authoritarianism, that could be just momentarily going with the flow through superficial normative influences and can be described as conformity or compliance through processes of social comparison in Moscovici's (1976) terms. The work of Moscovici (1961/2008) in the second part of his book on psychoanalysis, regarding mass media, where he introduces the communicative processes of propaganda, diffusion and propagation, are also relevant here, especially his use of 'semantic barriers' to the change of representations, as it evokes the microgenetic processes of resistance to change (Duveen, 2001; Gillespie, 2020).

Following the methodological suggestions of genetic structuralism, a crucial step of any scientific social analysis is the insertion of a phenomenon into a structured whole of which it is a part and where it has a function. In this case ontogenetic processes need to be understood in the context of institutional practices and activities that are there before children enter the educational system and will probably continue to be there in one form or another when they exit school and enter university. In the case of education in Cyprus they relate to management and re-production of cultural traumas (1974 for Greek Cypriots and 1963–1964 for Turkish Cypriots) that cultivate a certain historical consciousness.

Given the observed sociogenetic changes in values over generations, sometimes discussed as cohort effects in various analyses of ESS, EVS and WVS and explanations like the ones offered by Inglehard (2018) and Henrich (2020), genetic social psychology should also turn its attention to the notion of generations (see Figure 1.1).

The Problem of Generations and Its Relevance to Genetic Social Psychology

The concept of generations has been the central territory of anthropology through its study of kinship relations. It is also a focus of demography in its study of populations, of psychology in its focus on the life span and child development, and of sociology in its focus on parenthood, household and childhood. Within these disciplines and fields, there is considerable variation in the use of the term.

One of the most influential theories about generation and societal change can be found in the sociology of Mannheim (1952). Mannheim's argument is that individuals who went through their formative years during similar historical periods can be grouped into the same generation. Mannheim defined the 'formative years' as the period of youth, specifically from late adolescence to early adulthood, roughly between the ages of 17 and 25. During these years, he claims, individuals are most susceptible to the influences of their social environment and most likely to internalise the experiences of their time, which then play a significant role in shaping their world view, values and beliefs. It follows then that individuals belonging to the same generation or age group share 'a common location in the social and historical process' and are thereby limited to 'a specific range of potential experience, predisposing them for a certain characteristic mode of thought and experience' (Mannheim, 1952, p. 168).

In the words of Mannheim (1952) himself, 'Youth experiencing the same concrete historical problems may be said to be part of the same generation in actuality; while those groups within the same generation in actuality which work up the material of their common experiences in different specific ways, constitute separate generation units' (p. 184). Thus, the concept of 'generation units' was introduced to describe groups within a broader generation that share a specific collective response to the events of their formative years. These generation units are shaped by factors such as class, education and other sociocultural variables. Mannheim believes that the idea of generation units solves the problem of attributing too much unanimity to all the members of a generation, for it acknowledges different and possibly antagonistic political orientations within the broader grouping.

For example, in the United States, the political views of the Millennials (born between 1981 and 1996) and the Silent Generation (born between 1928 and 1945) vary significantly on topics such as foreign policy, immigration and same-sex marriage, among other things (Pew Research Center, 2015). However, generation units within these generations could be different depending on class, gender and other factors. In the original conceptualisation of Mannheim, a generation had to be self-conscious. Based on this definition, a 'generation' is one or more age cohorts, the members of which have in significant numbers become conscious of themselves collectively as a generation. For Cyprus, global definitions like Millennials, Baby Boomers and the like would be meaningless, since they are not used in public debates and therefore not considered relevant to the Cyprus issue. However, a pre- or post-1974 generation is sometimes discussed, and given the ominous position of this year in collective memory, it would probably make sense to explore differences between the pre- and post-1974 generations in Cyprus. Mannheim's assumptions about the power of traumatic events experienced in adolescence and young adulthood to create the sense of being a member of a generation is relevant here, as one could argue that a relevant generation that experienced the war of 1974 between the ages of about 14–25 would be individuals born between 1949 and 1960, whose age in 2024 would be between 64 and 75. In this sense, studying shorter-period cohorts might allow for a more sensitive identification of interesting cohort effects and historical shifts in values or attitudes. Even this might not be sensitive enough to capture interindividual variability and positioning in the representational field because the relevant generation units might not be defined primarily by social class or gender but rather by ways of interacting and communicating that we identified as the three enduring patterns of organisation of the thought and behaviour of the social psychological subject in Table 2.1 (submission, domination, co-operation). All these are, of course, empirical questions on which the next two chapters (Chapters 4 and 5) will shed light based on data collected from both communities of Cyprus in the period from 2003 to 2023.

The claim that adolescence and early adulthood (called the formative years) are crucial to the formation of one's values is an interesting one that needs further exploration. For example, those born in Cyprus after 1995 would be entering their formative years just when the opening of the checkpoints happened (2003) and Cyprus joined the EU (2004). This translates into opportunities for intercommunal contact through crossing to the other side of the buffer zone with their family in their early adolescence and alone in their early adulthood, assuming they did not resist such kinds of interactions due to in-group family or broader in-group norms or party allegiances. In the same historical period and during the same life stage they would be exposed in the school context to various intercultural education programs and policies that were implemented according to the alignment of Cyprus with the EU acquis and intergovernmental organisation policies like the Council of Europe (CoE). Should we expect a break in values and attitudes from 1995 onwards that could be predicted by increasing universalistic (UN) values, for example?

Some researchers claim that the same period of early 21st century and after is the time of 'global' generations as such, facilitated by transnational media flows and the internet and the appearance of Facebook in 2004 and Twitter (now X) in 2006 as uniquely interactive media platforms. Now people in radically different parts of the world can be linked through shared international experience rather than shared local experience, and thus one could also talk about the new 'internet generation' of younger people who are instantly globally connected. However, claims like these should be tested by comparing Cyprus with other countries in the same period. The extent of autonomy of a post-conflict and divided setting like Cyprus from these globalisation trends is also an empirical question to be tested.

In the next chapter we aim to show, based on empirical evidence from Cyprus collected in the last 20 years, how various sociogenetic changes relating to values, prejudice, trust and support or rejection of various possible solutions to the Cyprus issue can be conceptualised in the years after the opening of the checkpoints in Cyprus in 2003, as they directly relate to educational policy and relevant political changes, identifying points of continuity, resistance and change. Through this case study of a less WEIRD setting and the study of changes in values, attitudes and beliefs about otherness we hope to be able to situate Cyprus in the broader context of historical change in the 21st century as a deeply divided society where Muslims and Christians share a common country in a territorial conflict with internal ideological contestations around contact or no contact, unity or separation, always influenced by regional and global powers.

REFERENCES

Allport, G. W. (1954). *The nature of prejudice*. Garden City, NY: Doubleday.

Avraamidou, M, & Psaltis, C. (2019). Blocking the solution: Social representations of threats and (non)dialogue with alternative representations in Greek-Cypriot newspapers during peace negotiations. *Journal for the Theory of Social Behavior, 2019*, 1–20. https://doi.org/10.1111/jtsb.12222.

Bar-Tal, D. (2013). *Intractable conflicts: Socio-psychological foundations and dynamics*. Cambridge: Cambridge University Press.

Bar-Tal, D., & Teichman, Y. (2009). *Stereotypes and prejudice in conflict: Representations of Arabs in Israeli Jewish society*. Cambridge: Cambridge University Press.

Bartlett, F. C. (1932/1995). *Remembering: A study in experimental and social psychology*. Cambridge: Cambridge University Press.

Bauer, M. W. & Gaskell, G. (1999). Towards a paradigm for research on social representations. *Journal for the Theory of Social Behavior, 29*, 2, 163–186.

Carpendale, J. I., & Lewis, C. (2020). Tomasello's tin man of moral obligation needs a heart. *Behavioral & Brain Sciences, 43*, 19–20.

Coleman, P. T. (2014). Intractable conflict. In P. T. Coleman, M. Deutsch, & E. C. Marcus (Eds.), *The handbook of conflict resolution: Theory and practice* (3rd ed., pp. 708–744). New York: Wiley.

Doise, W., & Mugny, G. (1984). *The social development of the intellect*. Oxford: Pergamon Press.

Duveen, G. (2001). Representations, identity, resistance. In K. Deaux and G. Philogene (Eds.), *Representations of the social* (pp. 257–284). Oxford: Blackwell.

Graeber, D., & Wengrow, D. (2021). *The dawn of everything: A new history of humanity*. London: Penguin UK.

Gillespie, A. (2020). Semantic contact and semantic barriers: Reactionary responses to disruptive ideas. *Current Opinion in Psychology, 35*, 21–25.

Greenfield, P. M. (2009). Linking social change and developmental change: Shifting pathways of human development. *Developmental Psychology*, *45*(2), 401.

Hadjipavlou, M. (2007). The Cyprus conflict: Root causes and implications for peacebuilding, *Journal of Peace Research*, *44*, 349–365.

Henrich, J. (2015). The secret of our success: How culture is driving human evolution, domesticating our species, and making us smarter. Princeton, NJ: Princeton University Press.

(2020). *The weirdest people in the world: How the West became psychologically peculiar and particularly prosperous*. New York: Farrar, Straus & Giroux.

Henrich, J., & Muthukrishna, M. (2021). The origins and psychology of human cooperation. *Annual Review of Psychology*, *72*, 207–240.

Inglehart, R. (2018). *Cultural evolution*. Cambridge: Cambridge University Press.

Kadianaki, I., & Gillespie, A. (2015). Alterity and the transformation of social representations: a sociocultural account. *Integrative Psychological and Behavioral Science*, *49*, 73–88.

Kansteiner, W. (2004). Genealogy of a category mistake: A critical intellectual history of the cultural trauma metaphor. *Rethinking History*, *8*(2), 193–221.

Mannheim, K. (1952). The sociological problem of generations. *Essays on the Sociology of Knowledge*, *306*, 163–195.

Moscovici, S. (1961/2008). *Psychoanalysis: Its image and its public*. Cambridge: Polity.

(1972). Society and theory in social psychology. In J. Israel & H. Tajfel (Eds.), *The context of social psychology* (pp. 17–68). London: Academic Press.

(1976). *Social influence and social change*. London: Academic Press.

(1990). Social psychology and developmental psychology: Extending the conversation. In G. Duveen & B. Lloyd (Eds.), *Social representations and the development of knowledge* (pp. 164–185). Cambridge: Cambridge University Press.

Mifsud R., & Sammut, G. (2023). Worldviews and the role of social values that underlie them. *PLoS ONE, 18*(7), e0288451. https://doi.org/10.1371/journal.pone.0288451.

Muthukrishna, M., Henrich, J., & Slingerland, E. (2021). Psychology as a historical science. *Annual Review of Psychology*, *72*, 717–749.

Nasie, M., Diamond, A. H., & Bar-Tal, D. (2016). Young children in intractable conflicts: The Israeli case. *Personality and Social Psychology Review*, *20*(4), 365–392.

Pew Research Center. (2015). *The Whys and Hows of Generations Research*. Retrieved from www.pewresearch.org/politics/2015/09/03/the-whys-and-hows-of-generations-research/.

Piaget, J. (1932). *The moral judgment of the child*. London: Kegan-Paul.

Psaltis, C., & Duveen, G. (2006). Social relations and cognitive development: The influence of conversation type and representations of gender. *European Journal of Social Psychology*, *36*(3), 407–430.

(2007). Conservation and conversation types: Forms of recognition and cognitive development. *British Journal of Developmental Psychology*, *25*(1), 79–102.

Psaltis, C., & Zapiti, A. (2014). *Interaction, communication and development: Psychological development as a social process*. London: Routledge.

Raabe, T., & Beelmann, A. (2011). Development of ethnic, racial, and national prejudice in childhood and adolescence: A multinational meta-analysis of age differences. *Child Development, 82*(6), 1715–1737.

Rokeach, M. (1973). *The nature of human values*. New York: Free Press.

Roudometof, V. (2014). Nationalism, globalization and glocalization. *Thesis Eleven, 122*(1), 18–33.

Roudometof, V., & Christou, M. (2015). 1974 and Greek Cypriot identity: The division of Cyprus as cultural trauma. In R. Eyerman, J. Alexander, & E. Breese (Eds.), *Narrating trauma: On the impact of collective suffering* (pp. 163–187). London: Routledge.

Schwartz, S. H. (2021). A repository of Schwartz Value Scales with instructions and an introduction. *Online Readings in Psychology and Culture, 2*(2). https://doi.org/10.9707/2307-0919.1173.

Tomasello, M. (2020). The moral psychology of obligation. *Behavioral and Brain Sciences, 43*(e56), 1–58.

Uskul, A. K., Kirchner-Häusler, A., Vignoles, V. L., Rodriguez-Bailon, R., Castillo, V. A., Cross, S. E., ... & Uchida, Y. (2023). Neither Eastern nor Western: Patterns of independence and interdependence in Mediterranean societies. *Journal of Personality and Social Psychology, 125*(3), 471–495.

Valsiner, J. (2000). *Culture and human development*. London: Sage.

Volkan, V. D. (2021). Chosen traumas and their impact on current political/societal conflicts. In A. Hamburger, C. Hancheva, & V. Volkan (Eds.), *Social trauma: An interdisciplinary textbook* (pp. 17–24). Cham: Springer.

Wagoner, B. (2015). Collective remembering as a process of social representation. In G. Sammut, E. Andreouli, G. Gaskell, & J. Valsiner (Eds.), *Cambridge handbook of social representations* (pp. 143–162). Cambridge: Cambridge University Press.

(2017). *The constructive mind: Bartlett's psychology in reconstruction*. Cambridge: Cambridge University Press.

(2024). The organismic theory of development: Romantic roots of a vital concept. *Theory & Psychology, 34*(1), 127–149.

CHAPTER 4

Application of Genetic Social Psychology to the Cyprus Conflict

Charis Psaltis

The Cyprus Issue in Its Historical Perspective: Setting the Scene for Understanding Sociogenetic Processes

Cyprus history is often depicted as a long succession of different rulers: Assyrian, Persian, Alexander the Great, Ptolemy of Egypt, Roman, Byzantines, Arabs, Crusaders, Lusignans, Venetians. In 1571, Cyprus became part of the Ottoman Empire until it changed hands when administration was ceded to the British in 1878. After the First World War the British officially annexed Cyprus to the British Empire. According to the Official Census of Population of 1946 during the British colonial period, Greek Cypriots (henceforth GCs) comprised 80% of the population and Turkish Cypriots (henceforth TCs) 18%. An interesting observation about censuses is the changing identification of the two communities of Cyprus. In the 1931 census the term *Christian* and *Moslem* was used to describe the communities; in 1946 it was turned to *Greek Orthodox* and *Moslem (Turkish)*; and after the independence of 1960 it was just *Greeks* and *Turks*, pointing to the changing and socially constructed nature of national identification. The TCs were living in minority numbers in the towns, in 105 purely Turkish Cypriot villages and in many mixed villages peacefully together with GCs for hundreds of years until the ethno-nationalist projects of the 19th and 20th centuries of Greece and then Turkey were imported to Cyprus and caused the first intercommunal frictions, initially during the Ottoman period and more recently – and more pertinent to our discussion – in 1957 and 1958. This was during the 1955–1959 anti-colonial struggle of GCs organised by EOKA[1] for liberation from the British and union with Greece, and the corresponding nationalist struggle of the leadership of TCs organised

[1] Εθνική Οργάνωση Κυπρίων Αγωνιστών (National Organisation of Cypriot Fighters).

by TMT[2] for 'taksim', or the partition of Cyprus into two parts, one Greek and one Turkish (Attalides, 1979).

In 1960, the Republic of Cyprus was established as an independent bicommunal partnership state under a consociational constitution (a form of democratic power sharing between the two communities). Such a constitution was then seen by both communities as a temporary solution and the first step towards 'enosis' (union with Greece) for GCs and 'taksim' (partition of the island) for TCs. The GCs' sentiment was that the constitutional community rights accorded to the Turkish community, that was seen as a minority, were unfair and that they should only be guaranteed minority rights in the Republic of Cyprus; the Turkish Cypriots claimed that these were the just rights of a co-founding community. Soon, particular provisions relating to taxes and the autonomy of municipalities brought frictions between the two communities and a gridlock in the normal functioning of the state (Markides, 1977). In December 1963, intercommunal conflict erupted after the President of the Republic of Cyprus, Archbishop Makarios, proposed constitutional amendments to improve the functionality of the Cypriot state, that were perceived by the TC leadership as a move that removed almost all their rightful claims as co-founders of the Republic, and that was aiming at downgrading their community to the status of a minority. The armed conflicts that ensued led to the withdrawal of TC ministers from the Cabinet.

The fighting between extremists from both sides lasted throughout 1963 and 1964. TCs began retreating from isolated rural areas and villages into enclaves. After 1967, intercommunal strife ceased and Makarios started to turn away from union with Greece towards a more independent policy resisting the dictates of the Greek military junta that came to power in 1967 in Athens.

In 1974, a coup was staged by the Greek junta with the help of a local ultra-nationalist group called EOKA B, which continued its struggle for union of Cyprus with Greece against President Makarios. This was followed by a Turkish military offensive that was allegedly conducted to restore the constitutional order but actually resulted in ethnic cleansing of the northern part of Cyprus to materialise taksim (partition). As a result, 160,000 GCs living in northern Cyprus – now occupied by the Turkish military forces – were forced to flee south, and 45,000 TCs moved north to settle on land constituting 37% of island's total area, thus drastically changing the mixed demographic landscape that existed in 1960 (see Figure 4.1).

[2] Türk Mukavemet Teşkilatı (Turkish Resistance Organisation).

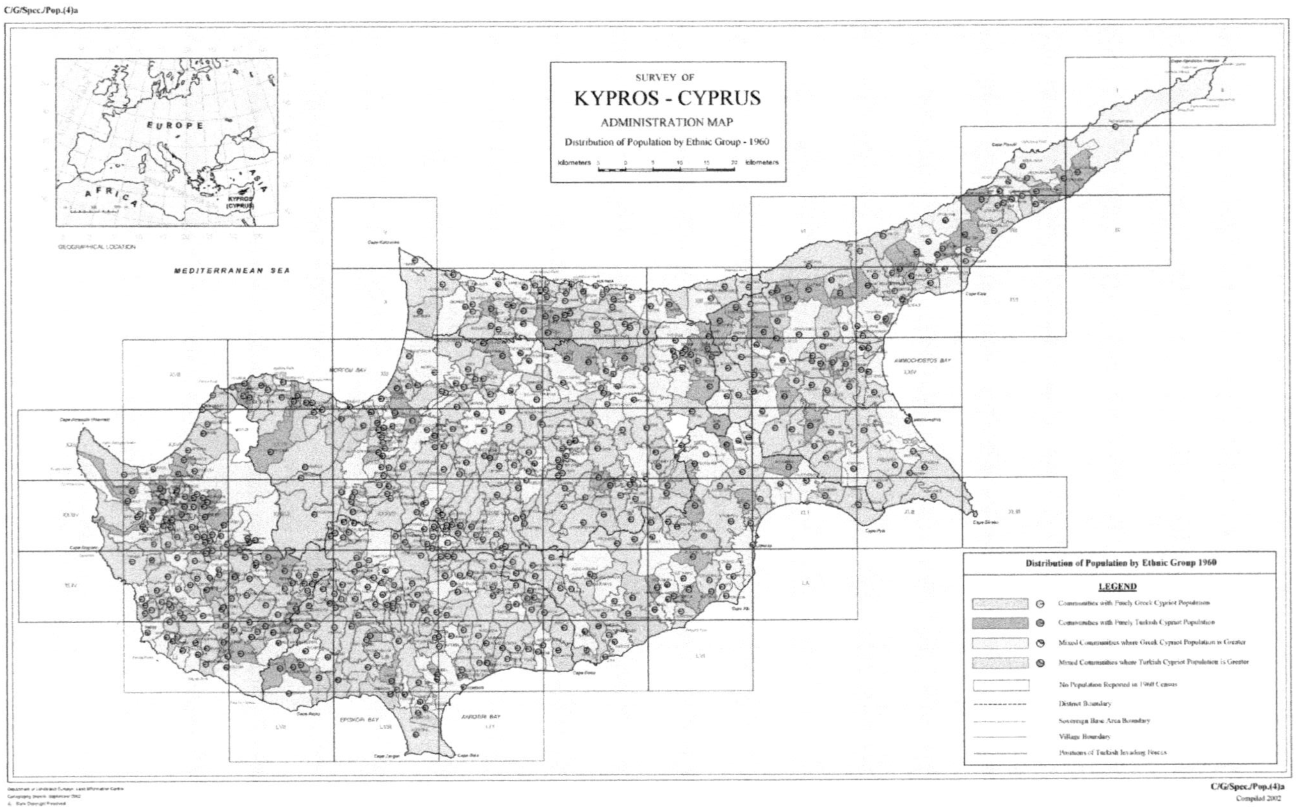

Figure 4.1 Demographic composition of Cyprus in 1960.

Table 4.1 *Direct and indirect experience of conflict in 1963–1964 and 1974 in the two communities of Cyprus*

	GCs(%)	TCs(%)
Have you ever had to move because of intimidation?	31.7	20.4
Has your home been lost (and you became a refugee)?	27.5	17.7
Have you ever been injured due to these events?	4.7	5.4
Have you ever been captured?	3.1	5.5
Has a member of your family or a close friend lost his/her home (became a refugee)?	70.7	43.3
Has a member of your family or a close friend been injured?	25.8	34.3
Has a member of your family or a close friend been captured?	29.6	31.9
Has a member of your family or a close friend been missing?	26.2	26.5
Has a member of your family or a close friend been killed?	20.4	30.6

The intercommunal conflict of 1963–1964 and the war of 1974 impacted the lives of many people in Cyprus in both direct and indirect ways, as shown in Table 4.1. The data come from a large-scale bicommunal representative survey conducted in 2007 (Psaltis, 2012), but of course it is expected that with passing time the percentage of people with direct experience of the conflict will become progressively smaller.

The two communities became geographically completely segregated in 1974. In 1983, the TC leadership established a breakaway state in the northern part of Cyprus internationally recognised only by Turkey. UN resolutions condemned the establishment as an illegal act, and the European Court of Human Rights in 1998 has described the self-styled 'Turkish Republic of Northern Cyprus' as 'a subordinate local administration of Turkey operating in Cyprus'.

The status quo on the island today is that of division, with UN forces patrolling the buffer zone between the two communities. On 23 April 2003, the TC leader announced that he would unilaterally partially lift the travel restrictions that had been enforced since the Turkish intervention/invasion of 1974,[3] and which had prevented GCs from crossing into the

[3] Certain areas, such as the city of Varosha, for example, are still partly closed to the public by the Turkish military and internally displaced GCs are not allowed to return to their homes. Varosha has a special status in the negotiations due to UN Security Council Resolutions with respect to it, in particular Resolution 550 (1984) and Resolution 789 (1992), which consider attempts to settle any part of Varosha by people other than its inhabitants as inadmissible, and which call for the transfer of that area to the administration of the UN.

northern part of Cyprus and TCs from crossing into the south. From 2003 to 2020 more checkpoints have been opened, totalling nine by 2024.

In April 2004, one year after the first opening of checkpoints, GCs rejected a UN-sponsored plan (Annan Plan) to reunite Cyprus under a Bizonal Bicommunal Federation (BBF) by 76% whilst Turkish Cypriots accepted it with 65%. Later that year Cyprus as a whole joined the EU, but the *acquis communautaire* was suspended in the north pending a solution of the Cyprus problem. After the failed UN effort in 2004, negotiations stalled for a few years, and with the election of new leadership in the GC community in 2008 (leftist Demetris Christofias), full-fledged negotiations restarted. After some progress was made, they stalled again in 2010 with the election of a nationalist leader Derviş Eroğlu in the TC community (see Figure 4.2 for a timeline of negotiations). In 2013, the presidential elections in the GC community brought to power Nicos Anastasiades who, as the leader of a right-wing party (DISY), took the risk back in 2003 to support a Yes vote on the Annan Plan under a generally negative climate for solution in the GC community engineered by the late Tassos Papadopoulos. However, little progress was achieved until 2015 when the TCs returned to the negotiating table as their leader a pro-reconciliation veteran politician Mustafa Akinci, which gave a new impetus to the negotiations, with significant progress made in the 2015–2017 period to reach a comprehensive settlement on the basis of a BBF. The two teams of negotiators led by Anastasiades and Akinci discussed the issues of (1) governance and power sharing, (2) property, (3) territory, (4) economic affairs, (5) European Union affairs and (6) security and guarantees.

In 2017, UN Secretary-General António Guterres brought all interested parties and Guarantor countries (Turkey, Greece and the United Kingdom) into a summit at Crans Montana, Switzerland. There he proposed the so-called Guterres package as a give-and-take peace plan that would essentially give political equality to TCs, end Turkish military occupation and replace the security provisions of the three Guarantor powers with an implementation agreement.

In June 2017, the effort came to its climax in a summit of the two communities, Greece, Turkey and the UK as the guarantor powers, and an EU representative taking part in the negotiations to ensure that any solution would be in line with the European *aqui*. The Conference on Cyprus in Crans Montana was widely seen as the closest the parties involved in the Cyprus issue had ever come to reaching a settlement. After a week of intensive negotiations, however, in the early morning of 7 July, Secretary-General Guterres announced to reporters that, despite

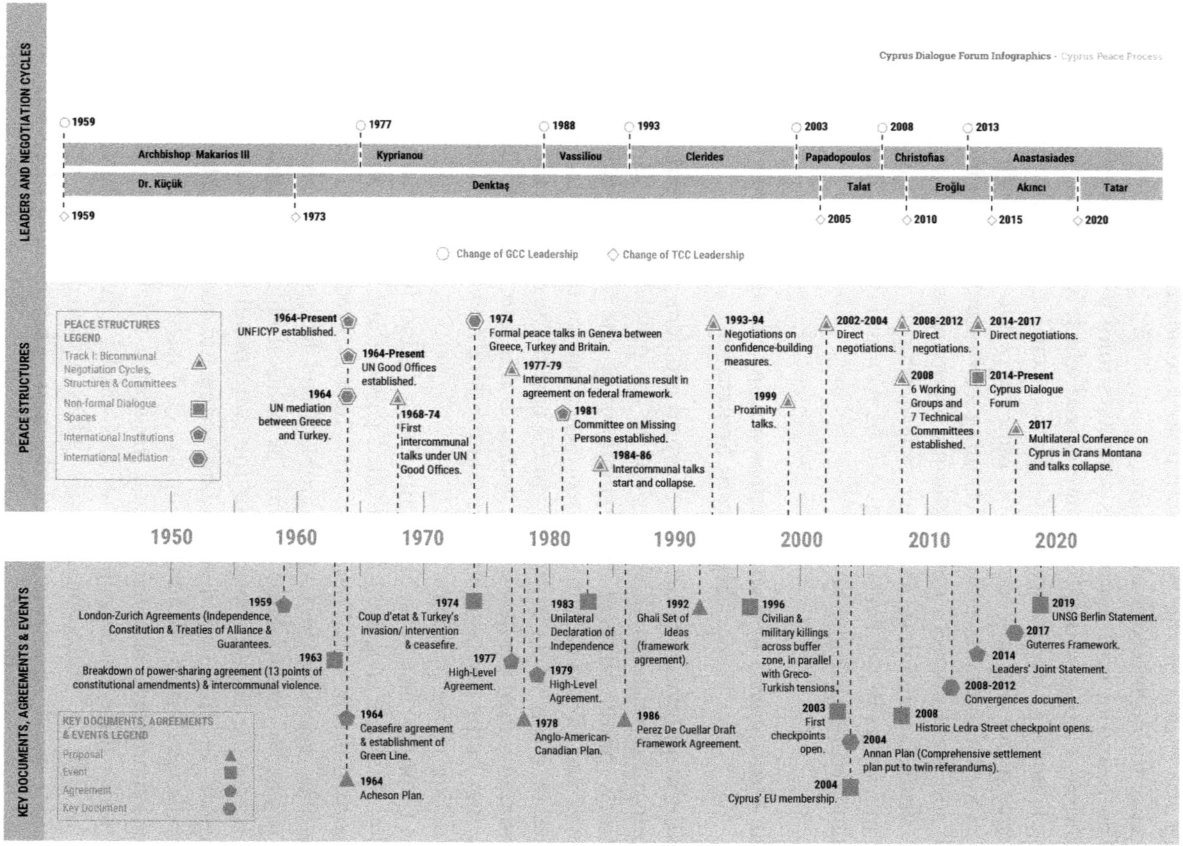

Figure 4.2 A timeline of negotiations on the Cyprus problem.

considerable efforts, the Conference was closing without an agreement. Soon after that Guterres called on all parties to take time off to reflect and asked the leaders of the two communities to jointly agree on terms of reference for negotiations to resume.

The period of no negotiations continues until today, however; in the meantime, a negative development emerged which is the claim by Turkey and the new TC leadership of Ersin Tatar, elected in 2020, that they have changed policy and now support the right for TCs to a 'sovereign equality', which for GCs is tantamount to claiming a two-state solution instead of a BBF and is considered a non-starter for negotiations.

A detailed chronology of change of leadership in the two communities and milestones in the negotiations can be seen in Figure 4.2, as produced by the Cyprus Dialogue Forum.[4]

The Ontogenesis of Social Representations of the Cyprus Issue as Significant Structures

Given the multifaced nature of the Cyprus problem, representations of the Cyprus issue relate to all dimensions of the problem, such as property, territory, power sharing, representations of the other community of Cyprus and involved countries, representations of the past and so forth. However, if one wants to understand the core of the representation in each community, then the best way to approach this is to study the educational processes in the two communities that produce new political subjectivities in relation to the problem.

In Cyprus, where two communities with distinct linguistic and religious backgrounds are geographically divided across ethnic lines for almost half a century, different social representations have evolved in each community, especially regarding the Cyprus problem and its history. Such narratives are politically manipulated by various political elites and centrally controlled by the administrations for the corresponding 'national collective struggles' in each community. The systematic use of rituals, national symbols (see Psaltis, Beydola, Filippou & Vrachimis, 2014), memorials, commemorations, national struggle museums (Makriyianni, 2006) and politically driven manipulation of the media (Avraamidou & Psaltis, 2019) and the educational system all contributed to the creation of different social representations of the past. The teaching of history in public schools reflected a specific official master narrative in both

[4] https://libguides.cydialogue.org/ld.php?content_id=31704730.

communities (Makriyianni, 2006; Makriyianni, Psaltis & Latif, 2011; Papadakis, 2008; Psaltis, 2012a) that largely contributes, as we will show below, to prejudice and distrust towards members of the other community when uncritically internalised by the individual.

According to Papadakis (2008), the central nationalistic historical narrative in the GC textbooks is one that begins with the arrival of the Greeks (14th century BC) in Cyprus that leads to its Hellenization, where the moral centre are the Greeks (of Cyprus) and the major enemy are the Turks. The plot concerns a struggle for survival by Cypriot Hellenism against foreign conquerors and the tragic end is the 'barbaric Turkish invasion' and occupation of 37% of Cyprus.

The corresponding TC narrative is one that begins with the arrival of the Turks in Cyprus (in 1571 AD), the moral self are the Turks (of Cyprus) and the major enemy are the Rums (GCs).[5] The plot concerns a struggle for survival by the Turks of Cyprus against GC domination. The war of 1974 marks a happy ending with the 'happy peace operation' by Turkey in Cyprus which saved TCs from a pending union of Cyprus with Greece following the Greek military coup.

Such official narratives clearly promote a particular form of collective remembering of victimisation by others (Psaltis, 2016). Adherence to the official narratives is not only predictive of threats (of both a realistic and symbolic form and of group esteem threat), but through these threats prejudice is increased and further distrust is created between the two communities in Cyprus. This is eventually reflected in reduced wish to co-exist with the other community in the future (Psaltis et al. 2017). The ontogenesis of the social representation of the Cyprus issue for GCs is mostly a process of internalising a feeling of one-sided victimisation which is formed quite early on. This can be mostly attributed to the educational policy of 'I do not forget and I struggle' (*Den xechno kai agonizomai*). This finding is of crucial political importance, since it reveals that the educational system in the GC community despite its proclaimed aim of reunification of Cyprus was producing dynamics that undermine the spirit of reconciliation and reunification.

[5] In 2004, the new history books for the history of Cyprus, written under the newly elected leadership of Mehmet Ali Talat, offered an alternative narrative that challenged the separatist and nationalistic narrative that was in place up to that point (see Papadakis, 2008 for an analysis of these short-lived books). However, in 2010, with the election of a new nationalist administration, these textbooks were replaced by new ones that reverted to the old nationalist narrative described here (see Makriyianni, Psaltis, & Latif, 2011 for a more updated discussion).

This policy in the case of the GCs emerged a few years after the mass displacements of 1974. It did not happen immediately after, since in the first months after the Turkish invasion internally displaced persons believed that they would soon return to their properties with a swift solution of the problem. However, after a few years they realized that this might take much longer. There was also a public discussion about the need for a long-term struggle (*makrochronios*) and the attempt to cultivate a sense of unity and patience to achieve the goal of everybody returning to their properties.

A primary objective of the GC educational system since 1974 has been to educate the new generation of GCs about the part of the island that is occupied by Turkey (Christou, 2006) and instil the desire for a reunification of the island. A major challenge for the GC educational system since 1974 has been to impart the values of 'humanism, justice, freedom and democracy' while remaining faithful to the 'preservation of our national and cultural identity' (Christou, 2006). The aims can be clearly seen in a policy brief sent to the educators by the Ministry of Education in 1994 that stated as the aims of 'I know, I do not forget and I struggle' the following:

1. To help students learn about the occupied places, to keep the memory of the occupied places alive and to cultivate the hope and will to struggle for the return;
2. To help students know and understand human rights as they have been recognised by international organisations and to work towards their implementation in Cyprus; and
3. To help students appreciate and respect all the elements (tradition, customs, manners, merits) that promoted the ethnic and physical survival of GCs and to participate in the struggle against the dangers faced by their country.

Figure 4.3 shows a billboard at an elementary school exhibiting the artefacts relating to Den Xechno ('Do not forget').

This policy has been criticised by academics in Cyprus, who see a number of problems in its rationale. According to Christou (2006), soon after 1974, the Ministry of Education, with curricular changes, directed teachers to incorporate in their courses references to the events of 1974, the plight of GC refugees and the importance of remembering the part of Cyprus that was occupied by Turkey. This is how Christou (2006) described the activities around the policy:

> At the elementary school level, three books aid teachers in creating lesson plans on these themes and integrating them in courses such as Greek

Figure 4.3 Artefacts relating to Den Xechno on a billboard at an elementary school (retrieved from https://episkopiprimaryschool-denksexno.blogspot.com/p/blog-page_20.html).

> language, history, geography, music, and the visual arts. The books are filled with pictures, personal stories and poems about life in the occupied part of the island before 1974 and the refugees' experience of displacement. Though less regularly, such references continue up to the level of the gymnasium and the lyceum. In general, however, everyday life in Greek Cypriot schools is infused with commemorations of 1974, and all school celebrations (at the primary and secondary levels) include direct references to the Cyprus Problem. (Christou, 2006, p. 289)

Whilst this bombardment of students with a one-sided victimisation narrative and 'overdetermination of meaning' is present from the genetic social psychology point of view, it should not be assumed that all children will passively internalise this master narrative in the same way. Still, as we show below, the template of victimisation that is formed in the elementary school years is present in almost all children, and variations of internalisation are premised on the same template (Wertsch, 2008, 2021) and potent enough to undermine any positive developments in the progression of historical thinking.

One early research by Chara Makriyianni (2006) shed light on this question when GC elementary school students aged 9–10 were asked to write a short 'history' of their homeland in 2002–2003. To put their narratives into a time perspective one has to be reminded that this point in time is already almost 30 years after the events of 1974; the parents of these children were probably in their early 40s or younger, so about one-third of these parents would have been personally displaced (first-generation internally displaced persons) at the age of 10 (see Makriyianni, 2006, p. 240 for more details). One child wrote the following:

> My homeland is Cyprus. Cyprus is 8000 years old. Its capital is Nicosia. The mother homeland is Greece and we are Greek-Cypriots. In 1974 there was an invasion by the Turks and we were conquered. Some people are now refugees and they long for their villages. (Girl, 4th Grader)

A shorter narrative written by a boy with no reference to Greece read like this:

> My homeland is Cyprus. Various people came and conquered us. The last enemies were the Turks. They made war against us and took half of Cyprus. (Boy, 4th Grader)

If we compare the two narratives, we can see one of the main internal ideological tensions in the GC community relating to identity politics. It is the tension between a hellenocentric and cypriocentric position (Mavratsas, 1999). The first sees Cyprus as part of Greece whilst the second suggests a more localised sense of moral centre and national identity. However, both at their core share an asymmetrical structure of small and helpless Cyprus as the unprovoked victim of a mighty and expansionist Turkey.[6]

Below are some more excerpts given by Makriyianni (2006) in her PhD thesis exploring the representations of 9–10-year-old GC students born in the 1991–1992 cohort, with data collected in 2002. These accounts are very telling for how this birth cohort constructed meaning of the Cyprus issue at a time when developmentally they start having the capacity for a more expansive horizon that could include out-groups into a more universalising morality.

The representations of the history of Cyprus extracted from these short histories reflect both messages from Den Xehno policy and indirect personal experience of internal displacement objectified in short narratives that make use of narration as traditional or exemplary types in Rusen's terms that serve memory functions of a projected future of a 'free Cyprus' but devoid of any mention of TCs and their presence in Cyprus:

> My homeland is Cyprus. In Cyprus the war between England and Cyprus took place, the Turkish invasion and now we are enslaved by the Turks. Many soldiers were killed; there were orphans, missing people, refugees, and enslaved people. I love my country very much. (Boy from urban school, Date: 10/11/2002)

> My homeland is Cyprus. I was born and have lived here for nine years. Cyprus has made loads of wars. Even today is enslaved. Turks do not allow us to go to the other half. My country is a small island. I love her a lot and I do not want to live in any other country. (Girl from urban school, no. 146, Date: 10/11/2003).

> My homeland was enslaved by the Turks because Turks came and took away from us our prettiest cities, we made a lot of war and thus we were enslaved. The war, when the Turks came, it was horrific because they took our mother from her house and forced her to leave Morfou with only the clothes she wore. (Girl from urban school, no. 512, Date: 8/3/2004)

> My homeland is Skylloura, I think it's there. It is wonderful, especially in the old times before Turks destroy it in 1974. Skylloura is one of the best villages of Cyprus. (Boy from urban school, no. 132, Date: 10/11/2002)

> My homeland is Cyprus and many years ago the Turks came and made war on us. In the end they won and now they have seized almost half of Cyprus.

[6] A collection of art by students relating to the 'Gnorizo, Den Xechno, Diekdiko' (I learn, Do not forget, I Claim) policy can be found in a 2014 publication of the Ministry of Education at: https://sch.cy/sd/333/vivlio_gnorizo_den_ksechno_08_10%202015.pdf.

> We fought with all our efforts for our country. We were very brave and courageous. I was very sad when they took Cyprus. I used to remember some of the soldiers of Cyprus but now I have forgotten about them. (Boy from urban school, no. 343, Date: 20/1/2004)

Around the same period (before the opening of the checkpoints in 2003) a study by Christou (2006) asked 15–18-year-old high school GC students to discuss what they make out of the Den Xechno slogan. Christou (2006) also notes how ideology can operate under a 'hidden curriculum', with the tacit ways in which knowledge and behaviour are constructed, outside the usual course materials and formally scheduled lessons. Christou rightly identifies a major weakness of the way the Den Xechno policy operates: 'The re-united and independent Cyprus is the professed goal, but, as I am arguing here, this goal, for the new generation, represents an official though largely empty imagination. Young Greek Cypriots reiterate "our desire to go back to our homes," but this is where their imagining of the future stops: the vision of re-united communities, which is crucial for a peaceful solution, does not exist' (p. 299). She concludes, 'The political subjectivity of the new generation of Greek Cypriots is constituted through a historical definition of struggle that oscillates between armed resistance and the silent persistence of memory.'

To sum up, the core of the significant structure of social representations is formed quite early in childhood. This can be described as an asymmetrical triadic configuration of loss of control and one-sided victimisation as shown in Figure 4.4. The shorter the distance in the other–object relationship, the stronger is control of the object by other. Such a configuration of loss of control of property depicted in Figure 4.4 in the case of the Cyprus issue is naturally – and expectedly – resisted by GCs, causing anger and resentment for the Turkish army, Turkey and the Turks.

What is most striking in the significant structure in the case of Greek Cypriots is the absence of TCs from the picture. To some extent this is due

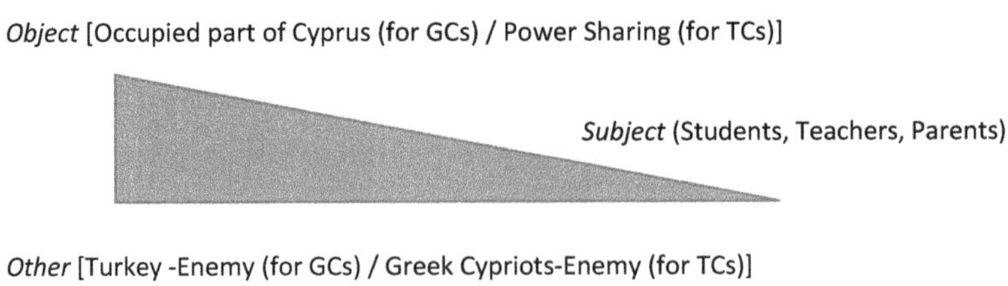

Figure 4.4 A triadic configuration of loss of control.

to the double minority syndrome nature of the Cyprus problem (Michael, 2007). TCs feel like a minority in the face of the substantial GC majority on the island; GCs feel like a threatened minority in the face of mainland Turkey 40 miles from the shores of northern Cyprus.

However, the empty imagination of GCs is very problematic, as it has no place for TCs who are not actors in the history of Cyprus. The objective possibility, in Goldmann's terms (see Chapter 1) of this representation, is exhausted into the quest for freedom for Cyprus to be achieved not by a compromise solution that will include the re-establishment of power sharing with TCs, as envisioned by the UN-supported plan since 1977 in the form of a BBF, but rather with the withdrawal of Turkish troops and the end of occupation of Cyprus. If anything becomes clear about TCs by the end of their school trajectory in public school around 17 years of age (unless they challenge this narrative) is that TCs were given too many privileges in the 1960 constitution that were unfair to the majority (GCs) and that the TCs rebelled against the legal state in 1963–1964. It thus suggests that a majoritarian unitary state that offers TCs minority rights would be all TCs could ask for. As we show in the following sections, even after a history education reform that took place in 2010 and a new curriculum written in 2016, and despite some important changes in the methodology of history teaching, the one-sided victimisation narrative remained intact with important consequences for the progression of historical thinking and orientation towards the other community.

The orientation towards otherness (the tip of the iceberg taking the form of prejudice) formed by this Den Xehno policy is clearly seen in the work of Makriyianni (2006), where the same representative sample of the 9–10-year-old students in 2002 who offered their short historical narratives of Cyprus were also asked to state their feelings towards both TCs and Turks. The results regarding feelings towards TCs were as follows: 5% stated that they like TCs a lot, 21% stated that they like TCs, most (40%) stated they neither liked nor disliked TCs, 21% stated that they do not like TCs and 12% that they do not like them at all. So, on the whole, the dominant feeling was neutral to negative, which can be explained mostly through the absence of knowledge about TCs as a community, their history in Cyprus since 1571 as well as their rightful claims to power sharing in Cyprus as the co-founding community of the 1960 constitution.

When it came to the attitude towards the Turks, the dominant feeling was significantly different: more negative to very negative, with the majority of students (54%) stating that they do not like the Turks at all and 25% stating that they do not like them. Only 16% reported neutral feelings and

5% said that they like the Turks. Only 1% said that they liked Turks a lot, which is only expected given that Turkey and the Turks occupy the position of the enemy and the Turkish state that of a barbaric occupier in the hegemonic narrative.

In the case of TCs, the asymmetrical configuration of control would concern the loss of political equality and power sharing in 1963 accompanied by a threat of marginalisation as the weaker community by GCs who would be the main enemy 'other'. These are the reasons much research undertaken just after the opening of the checkpoints and before contact started showing its positive effects that TCs showed higher levels of threats, prejudice and distrust towards the GCs compared to the levels of threats, prejudice and distrust experienced by GCs towards TCs (Psaltis, 2012) (see Appendix A and Table B.1 in Appendix B for the methodology of data collection of all studies on which the data are based of trend figures in Appendices A and B).

Opening of Crossing Checkpoints in 2003: A Historical Turning Point?[7]

This earlier brief historical framing of the Cyprus issue makes clear that the opening of crossing checkpoints on 23 April 2003 was a unique situation of rupture (Zittoun et al., 2003) of the taken-for-granted no-contact status quo that continued for 30 years since 1974.[8] Any meaningful analysis of contact in Cyprus needs to keep this historical fact in perspective. People had to face the very tangible dilemma: to cross or not to cross (see Demetriou, 2007). They had to master the unfamiliar situation of deciding whether or not they would be visiting their houses, now occupied by other people or troops, or places of highly symbolic value and nostalgia that they had left under life-threatening conditions. Crossing the checkpoints and coming into contact with people now occupying a home one left 30 years ago can be an emotionally tormenting but also ideologically laden and filled with tensions that create questions of the capacity of intergroup contact to lead to the reduction of prejudice, the promotion of trust and

[7] A detailed chronology of political developments relating to the Cyprus issue can be found at the following online project of the Cyprus Dialogue Forum, a bicommunal non-formal dialogue that aims to support and complement the formal peace process in Cyprus: https://libguides.cydialogue.org/political/chronology.

[8] One year later, in 2004, both Cyprus communities voted on a UN Secretary-General Annan Plan for a solution to the Cyprus issue, and Cyprus joined the EU with the EU *aquis* suspended in the north pending a solution to the Cyprus problem.

the reconstruction of the representations of the Cyprus problem and its hegemonic narrative under these unique conditions.

In the context of Cyprus, a meta-regression of a large number of studies (Psaltis & Ioannou, in preparation) undertaken in both communities of Cyprus since 2006 revealed that quantity of contact between GCs and TCs relates to reduced levels of prejudice in both communities. In fact, the mean effect size identified in both communities ($r = -0.37$ for GCs and $r = -0.32$ for TCs) is substantially higher than the mean effect size of $r = -0.22$ reported by Pettigrew and Tropp (2006) in their meta-analysis.

In the same year (2003), there was a change in leadership with the election of Tasos Papadopoulos in the GC community with the support of leftist party and pro-reconciliation AKEL in 2003. One year later Cyprus also joined the EU. Both of these developments as well as the opening of the checkpoints led to a reconsideration of the educational policy of 'I do not forget and I struggle' and signalled the beginning of an effort for a general educational reform that seemed, at that time, promising in revising the ethnocentric master narrative.

In a November 2003 circular issued by the Ministry of Education and Culture we find elements of attempting rapprochement with the TC community and mention of a need for a solution to the Cyprus issue that would secure GC needs:

> [S]o that all the inhabitants of our homeland live peacefully and brotherly in a new European Cyprus, under conditions of security, peace, freedom, prosperity, and justice.
>
> [A] solution that will secure the end of occupation, the withdrawal of occupying troops and settlers, the refugees' return to their homes, the disclosure of the missing people's fate, and the re-unification of our island.

With the rejection of the UN plan by the GC leadership of Papadopoulos in 2004, history education reform was put on hold until 2008. This was due to a resurgence of nationalist feelings and pressures from the church not to revise history textbooks, as it was seen by them as an effort to 'dehellenise' GCs (Makriyianni, Psaltis & Latif, 2011). However, when the leader of leftist party AKEL Dimitris Christofias was himself elected president of the Republic of Cyprus in 2008 (see Figure 4.1), the educational reform effort obtained a new impetus. In the TC community the election of a left-wing government in 2004 made some radical changes in the history teaching in terms of syllabus and methodology by promoting both multi-perspectivity and a more Cypriot-centric orientation in new history textbooks that replaced the previous nationalistic separatist teaching with clear messages of co-operation between the two communities (Papadakis, 2008; Makriyianni et al., 2011; Perikleous et al., 2021).

A New Policy by the Ministry in 2008 and Resistance to Change: New Co-operative Structures in Place

The newly elected GC leader Demetris Christofias and a leftist and pro-reconciliation ideological partner Mehmet Ali Talat met soon after the February election in March 2008 and agreed to start fully fledged negotiations. They established six working groups and seven technical committees that would work towards facilitating co-operation between the two communities in various spheres of the everyday life (health, crime, environment, cultural heritage, opening of more checkpoints, etc). They also decided to reopen Ledra Street in divided capital Nicosia as a confidence-building measure. Between May and July 2008, the leaders reaffirmed their commitment to the negotiation framework of a Bizonal Bicommunal Federation with political equality. They agreed that this partnership would have a federal government with a single international 'personality', as well as a TC constituent state and a GC constituent state of equal status. They agreed in principle on single sovereignty and citizenship. Finally, they agreed that the solution reached would be put to separate simultaneous referenda. The provision of referenda is crucial for the importance of the present book as one that explores the views of possible voters. This is the reason that all research reported in this book (with the exception of school samples) is representative of the two communities sampling people aged 18+ with voting rights. These are the people that will define the future of Cyprus in case of a new referendum in relative autonomy from their political elites.

In August 2008, before the commencement of the school year, the GC Minister of Education, Dr Andreas Demetriou, an academic and a developmental psychologist who had worked for years on developing a neo-Piagetian theory of intelligence, sent the aims of the 2008–2009 school year to all teachers. The first aim referred to the 'cultivation of a culture of peaceful co-existence, mutual respect and co-operation between Greek and Turkish Cypriots'. This was the first time in the history of Cyprus that such an aim was set by the Ministry of Education, and it was promoted whilst the Den Xechno policy was still in place. This was bound to lead to tensions given that many teachers saw the two aims as incompatible whilst others attempted to redefine the meaning of the 'I do not forget' policy in a way that the two could become compatible (Charalambous, Charalambous & Zembylas, 2014) with the spirit of reconciliation. Chistodoulou (2018) offers empirical findings about the sources of resistance to efforts for history education reform in the GC community through an analysis of interviews, policy documents, newspapers, speeches and circulars revealing a pronounced link between education and security. She identified discourses of resistance that present changes to history textbooks as a betrayal and threat to the nationalist struggle, a process that, she argues, constitutes the securitisation of history textbooks. Such resistances can be further understood by an analysis of the positions in the representational field of the Cyprus problem in Cyprus, as they form significant representational structures that, as documented below, can be largely mapped on the three significant structures described in Chapter 2, Table 2.1 of social relations of constraint (submission or domination) and co-operation.

Identity Positions in the Representational Field of the Cyprus Issue

Reactions to Demetriou's proposals ranged from enthusiastic support to vehement rejection (see Makriyianni, Psaltis & Latif, 2011). As in the case of the reception of psychoanalysis in France at the end of the 1950s, one could similarly understand the reception of this new policy depending on the ideological positions within the GC community. These reactions can be rendered intelligible by identifying the various significant structures or transindividual subjects in the representational field of the Cyprus issue. In an earlier research project in 2006–2007 we explored intergroup dynamics in Cyprus and representations of the past. There we had the chance to explore the representations of the Cyprus issue in adults 18 years old and over, in relation to the role of intergroup contact between GCs and TCs and several variables that tap the quality of intercommunal relations in Cyprus. This was a large-scale questionnaire survey with a representative sample from both communities (N = 800 GCs and N = 853 TCs) and was made possible by the partial lifting of travel restrictions across the UN buffer zone after 23 April 2003. The questionnaire in particular explored the amount and quality of contact between members of the two communities, national identification, trust, forgiveness, threats (realistic, symbolic, distinctiveness threat), intergroup anxiety, perspective taking, intergroup salience and attitudes towards the other community (see Psaltis, 2012 for details).

Attitude towards 'motherlands' (Turkey and Greece) and wish for the use of their symbols (flag, national anthem) by the corresponding community was labelled as *Helleno/Turco centrism*. On the contrary, *Cypriocentrism* (Mavratsas, 1999) was operationalised as the wish for use of Cypriot national symbols and civic identity and feelings of detachment from motherlands. Furthermore, there were questions that explored the representations of the history of the Cyprus problem and in particular the interpretation of the events of intercommunal strife in 1963–1967, the nature of the Cyprus problem and its causes and views concerning organisations like the GC EOKA and the TC TMT that fought for *enosis* (union with Greece) and *taksim* (partition), respectively. Finally, the questionnaire included questions that tried to tap the level of acceptance of a variety of possible solutions to the Cyprus issue (Bizonal Bicommunal Federation, Unitary state, Keeping the Status Quo, Two-states solution).

An analysis of this set of data from a social representations perspective (see Psaltis, 2012a) made clear that different representations of the Cyprus issue have indeed evolved between the two communities as they have been geographically divided across ethnic lines for almost half a century. Importantly, however, this research identified three different identity positions within each community: the *pro-reconciliation/co-operative*, the *communitarian* and the *ethno-nationalist* position. From the results, it appeared that in both communities, people in the pro-reconciliation clusters are people who show a very positive orientation towards members of the other community on a series of variables (trust, contact, forgiveness) and who also score lower on perceived threats and intergroup anxiety as proposed in the third row of our model in Table 2.1.

In fact, the Pro-reconciliation clusters in the two communities are almost identical in the profile of their views expressing peace activists, bicommunal non-governmental organisations (NGOs) who have the support of intergovernmental organisations such as the CoE, UN and the EU who advance a social representations project (see Bauer & Gaskell, 1999) of joint collective action for the solution of the problem. In Lucien Goldmann's terminology, the objective possibility of this significant structure was that of the vision of a reunited Cyprus. These individuals covered the political spectrum from pro-reconciliation left to cosmopolitan right and NGOs doing bicommunal work, although the majority came from leftist parties. The stronger Cypriocentric views of this position suggested that the aim was to form a superordinate political community of Cypriots that includes both GCs and TCs, a solidarity formed on either a basis of cultural similarity between the two communities or a civic form of constitutional patriotism.

The communitarian position in each community was described by more adherence to the ethno-national symbols (flag, national anthem of 'motherlands') and was related to high levels of perceived realistic and distinctiveness threats as well as lower levels of trust and contact with the other community. In the two communities these positions share structural similarities, as they represent a form of banal nationalism (Billig, 1995), where the ethical horizon of the concern of participants is constrained by the limits of their own community fed by the mundane reality of everyday living in two geographically separated communities for decades. Politically this position is related to parties of the patriotic left or the so-called centre traditionally hard-line and maximalist on the Cyprus that often express a wish for a federation with the 'right content' (not accepting political equality, or demanding both the withdrawal of Turkish troops and settlers or immigrants who came to the north of Cyprus after 1974) and sometimes veer towards an antifederalist stance altogether using the majoritarian discourse of 'one man, one vote' (Loizides, 2016, 2020).

Lastly, the ethno-nationalist position was expressed in the two communities with ideas of Greek and Turkish ethno-nationalism forming a mirror image of each other where the ethical horizon is a larger ethnic community that includes the mainland nationals but excludes the other community in Cyprus, as suggested by the low levels of intercommunal contact, trust and forgiveness and high levels of prejudice and threats. Politically this position is related to the conservative right-wing DISY and extreme right-wing parties (Allileggyi, ELAM).

To return to the reactions to the new policy of 2008, these came from the communal and the ethnonationalist stance at the grassroots level. At the institutional level it came from EOKA fighter organisations and the church who again saw an effort by the leftist government to 'dehellenise' the island. Reactions also came from officials in the ministry itself who were close to the church and the so-called maximalist centre parties against the policy of the minister, since they saw an opportunity to attract votes from the right of the political spectrum, given that in the first two years of the policy the right-wing party of Anastasiades (who supported a Yes vote during the 2004 referendum) did not resist the policies. However, after a few years, DISY started resisting the efforts for a compromise solution, and by 2010, when the TCs elected a new nationalist leader, DISY had already withdrew their support of the pro-reconciliation policies of the ruling party (both for the solution of the problem and the educational policies). Their resistance began when they realised that they started losing votes to the so-called centre maximalist parties and the newly established far-right ELAM that was the sister party of the neo-Nazi Golden Dawn in Greece. By 2010, AKEL was left on its own politically to materialise any positive changes in the educational system and then succumbed to resistance without actually achieving any substantial change in the revision of the history curriculum and textbooks or in their pro-intergroup contact policies. The fact that the newly elected TC leader Derviş Eroğlu changed the pro-reconciliation history textbooks and brought back the nationalist narrative did not help either (Perikleous, Samani & Aliusta, 2021). The only positive residue of this process was a new history curriculum in 2010 which emphasised a disciplinary understanding (the way knowledge is constructed in the discipline of history), the writing of a new history textbook for third graders in the elementary school along these lines and some production of teaching proposals and history teaching seminars. However, the ethnocentric narrative and selection of context in the curriculum stayed the same.

In fact, as it can be seen in Appendix A, 2010 was the year that most GCs showed negative feelings towards TCs. In the summer of 2011, a large amount of ammunition and military explosives self-detonated at the Mari Naval Base, killing 13 people. This development brought the Demetris Christofias government into a very difficult position and isolated AKEL more, which eventually retreated from any controversial reform efforts. Before the end of the summer, there was a reshuffle in government, and Andreas Demetriou was replaced by Giorgos Demosthenous who did not make any effort for change in history teaching. In 2013, there were presidential elections. Demetris Christofias lost power and Nicos Anastasiades from right-wing DISY was elected as the new president of Cyprus with the support of DIKO. The new minister of education came from DIKO and actively obstructed the efforts for any reform on history education, annulling secondments of educators in the ministry who were seen as a threat to the official master narrative.

Sociogenetic Change: Transformation and Continuity of Significant Structures from 2013 to 2023

On 11 February 2014, the leaders of the two communities, Nicos Anastasiades and Derviş Eroğlu, issued a joint statement expressing their willingness for fully fledged negotiations aimed at reaching a comprehensive settlement of the Cyprus problem. This led to the resignation of DIKO from the government in the south of the divide. In 2015, there were elections in the TC community that brought to power Mustafa Akinci, the pro-reconciliation veteran politician who gave a new impetus to the negotiations to resolve the Cyprus problem, with significant progress made in the 2015–2017 period. This election could have potentially resulted in significant revision of the official master narrative in the field of history teaching as well; however, the lack of support from the GC leadership of Nicos Anastasiades on this particular issue on initial proposals by Akinci and concentration on track-one negotiations by both leaders until the Crans Montana failure in July 2017 meant that history education reform was not prioritised in the end. This potential for significant change came by the establishment of the Bicommunal Technical Committee of Education by the leaders of the two communities with administrative support from the Good Offices team of the UNSG special adviser on Cyprus Espen Barth Eide, who since 22 August 2014 was appointed in this position by former UN Secretary-General Ban Ki-moon.

The Bicommunal Technical Committee on Education

On 15 November 2015, 32 years had passed since Rauf Denktaş, the TC nationalist leader, unilaterally declared the independence of a state in northern Cyprus, unrecognised internationally (TRNC). The anniversary fell on a Sunday, prompting schools in the southern part of Cyprus to permit students to hold protests the next day, 16 November. Despite ongoing peace talks improving bicommunal relations, some students affiliated with the far-right ELAM party (aligned with Greece's Golden Dawn) attacked cars with TC registration plates in central Nicosia. These incidents seemed coordinated and occurred on three different occasions.

The leaders of the two communities and the education minister in the south, Dr Costas Kadis, student unions and various political parties (excluding ELAM) condemned these actions and expressed solidarity with the victims. TC leader Mustafa Akinci called for the arrest of those responsible. By 18 November, four students from a Nicosia lyceum were detained.

Subsequent public discourse in newspapers and on social media highlighted the need for educational systems to foster reconciliation, not division. This incident catalysed a political momentum for establishing a new Bicommunal Technical Committee on issues of education. The ensuing week saw intense communication, including phone calls and emails by academics and activists, advocating for a bicommunal educational committee.

Key figures in this lobbying effort included TC Technical Committees coordinator and ex–vice president of the Association for Historical Dialogue and Research, Dr. Meltem Onurkan Samani, and people close to the bicommunal NGO, Association for Historical Dialogue and Research. They, along with associates of Andreas Pirishis, GC coordinator of the Technical Committees, pushed for this initiative.

Dr Samani was tasked by the two leaders to write a proposal outlining the committee's purpose. Given our previous co-operation with Dr Samani in the context of the intercommunal NGO Association for Historical Dialogue and research, she trusted me to write a first draft of the mandate for the committee. After feedback and revisions from Dr Samani, the final decision on the text was made during a leaders' meeting a week after the incidents, their sixth meeting in November 2015. Following this meeting, a UN representative by the end of November announced the formation of the Bicommunal Technical Committee on Education. The mandate announced was the following:

1. Review existing research and good practices in education in Cyprus and abroad and undertake new relevant research on how education can contribute to conflict transformation, peace, reconciliation and the countering of prejudice, discrimination, racism, xenophobia and extremism.
2. Work on devising a mutually acceptable mechanism for the implementation of confidence-building measures in schools of the two educational systems and promote contact and co-operation between students and educators from the two communities.
3. Recommend best policy options and course of action that will allow coordination of the two educational systems, thus contributing to a viable, sustainable and functional bicommunal, bizonal federation.

An interesting aside to the origins of the committee and its early-day workings is that a number of current and former members of the bicommunal Association for Historical Dialogue and Research (AHDR) who were appointed to this committee proposed an early study of the curriculum (including history) in the two communities supported by a number of academics in the committee and Professor Andreas Demetriou who was also appointed in the committee. Unfortunately, in the early days of the committee there was resistance from the official GC side to proceed in this direction. A few months later it looked like both official sides decided to not touch sensitive issues such as history in the context of the work of this committee, and the curriculum study component has never materialised.

Nevertheless, the Bicommunal Committee achieved several commendable successes such as establishing a mechanism, which involved co-operation with the education ministries on both sides, to address without any prejudice to the issue of official recognition of the one side by the other. It made possible the launching of the bicommunal peace education project IMAGINE praised by the UN Secretary-General in his reports on the UN operations in Cyprus.[9]

The IMAGINE programme was implemented by the Association for Historical Dialogue and Research at the 'Home for Co-operation' under the auspices and scientific guidance of the Bicommunal Technical Committee on Education. The programme was implemented between 2017 and 2022. The activities of the IMAGINE programme were successfully implemented with the participation of approximately 6,000 pupils and 800 teachers from all communities in Cyprus. During the programme, pupils engaged in pedagogical activities in which GC pupils came into contact with TC pupils of the same age, accompanied by their teachers. Activities were held in the UN-controlled area of Ledra Palace during school time. The programme's pillars included an anti-racist workshop in schools and contact preparation (before the meeting with pupils from the two communities). IMAGINE trainers would visit classrooms and engage children in experiential activities discussing issues of stereotyping, discrimination and racism as components of a culture of violence and preparing the conditions for a bicommunal meeting at the Home for Cooperation. Then the pupils would participate in bicommunal activities that took place in three languages (Greek, Turkish, English), with the option of repetition.

The committee also produced a report (*Final Report of the Technical Committee for Education: An Evaluation of the Current State of Affairs in Education, Challenges, Good Practices and Suggestions, October 2017*) of the state of affairs in education (on racism, xenophobia, history teaching, intergroup contact between the two communities in and out of schools, anti-racist education and intercultural education). The report also put forward suggestions about the production of educational material, establishment of contact schemes and a coordinating body for educational standards of the two educational systems. The second part of the report also provided a summary of recorded good practices in the two educational systems, and the third part outlined good practices and policies in the international arena that can be applicable for Cyprus.

However, these proposals were not taken up by the two leaderships when these lines were written in early 2024, despite calls by the UNSG to do so. The Committee is yet to make further progress on the issue of history textbooks also, and no substantial suggestion or delivery from the Committee on history education has yet taken place. Some have argued

[9] All reports are available at: www.securitycouncilreport.org/un_documents_type/secretary-generals-reports/?ctype=Cyprus&cbtype=cyprus.

that the absence of history education work is due to 'concerns about possible reactions caused by changes that could be considered as threatening to the official narratives' (Perikleous et al., 2021, 133). This is therefore another example of how the dominance of the two conflicting ethnocentric narratives does not allow changes in the teaching of history. After the 2020 election of TC leader Ersin Tatar and his consequential policy shift away from the pursuit of BBF, the Bicommunal Technical Committee's work is almost frozen and the IMAGINE project was unilaterally stopped by the TC leadership in late March 2022. It is worth noting that a few days before this unilateral freezing of the programme, several ultra-nationalist newspapers in Turkey published front-page articles against the IMAGINE project, depicting it as a GC propaganda mechanism to promote BBF in Cyprus.

It should be recognised, nevertheless, that some minor changes in the methodology of history teaching seem to have taken place in the TC community more recently. In 2013, the TC educational system, under the aegis of the TC educational authorities and funded by the Turkish embassy, initiated the Basic Education Curriculum Development Project (TEPGEP) (Perikleous et al., 2021). This project was managed by a TC university and marked the first development of a basic education curriculum for Cyprus history within the TC educational framework. The curriculum, titled 'Cypriot and Turkish Cypriot History Curriculum' for lower secondary education, was designed to be student centred, drawing on 'Progressivism and Reconstructionism' as its guiding educational philosophies, with the goal of enhancing historical thinking. A team comprising Turkish and TC academic historians and history teachers authored three colourfully illustrated school textbooks, but the island's periods of intercommunal conflict are depicted from the TC viewpoint still.

As Perikelous et al. (2021) state, despite the curriculum's stated objective of fostering historical thinking, the textbooks primarily deliver factual knowledge and offer limited scope for students to engage in constructing their own understanding or developing critical, historical and reflective thinking skills.

History teachers in Cyprus and beyond are thus correct in noting that what history education is able to deliver 'may be limited by more culturally powerful representations of a past variously preserved in folk traditions and memorials, perpetuated by the heritage lobby, or invented by the media and entertainment industries' (Perikleous & Shemilt, 2011, pp. 12–13). And the argument is correct in more than one way: not only because representations of the Cyprus issue and its history raise resistance in efforts to reform the curriculum as we have seen before, but also in how history teaching is done in the classroom. In a PhD project completed recently by Georgiou (2020) at the Institute of Education at University College London under the supervision of Professor Arthur Chapman, it was clear that 17–18-year-old GC students assimilated conflicting historical accounts into the official and practical past they know, since the educational system is such that it does not encourage the distinction between collective memory and history. Georgiou notes that 'the past is mythologised, fetishized and eternalised, and consequently reproduced as history through curricula, textbooks and the hidden curriculum'. In her work she shows, for example (with data collected in the years 2014–2015), how the interpretation of two conflicting accounts (a key historical thinking skill) about the events of 1974 in Cyprus is assimilated into the official master narrative and textbook narratives students have already internalised in the earlier years of their school career.

Positions in the Representational Field in 2017

Given all these ups and downs in political developments after 2013, the positive climate of 2015–2017 but also the failure of Crans Montana in July 2017, the blame game that followed and the parallel positive but slow movement in the educational systems, one might wonder if the positions in the representational field discussed earlier changed in any way the three positions presented earlier in this chapter (ethnonationalist, communitarian and pro-reconciliation/co-operative) in the representational field of the Cyprus issue in the GC community. To explore this topic, in 2017 we collected data a few months after the Crans Montana failure and proceeded with a similar mapping of the positions in the representational field to the one that was conducted 10 years earlier in 2007. The corresponding two-step cluster analysis in the GC community was interesting because – compared to the similar analysis of 2007 (Psaltis, 2012) – a new position was detected that was absent a decade earlier.

The new position was a partitionist position, surprising for GCs given that this was historically equivalent to the Turkish and TC nationalists claim to taksim. But given the apparent increasing acceptance of the idea of partition by some right-wing circles around the GC leader or at least scepticism towards BBF at that time,[10] this fact might have freed some

[10] Charis Georgiades, one of the ministers in Nicos Anastasiades's cabinet, a few years after the Crans Montana failure also expressed a veiled acceptance of partitionist views, calling for a new realism in

people from the guilt of expressing an anti-normative view. One might wonder why, if this position was present since 2007 (see Figure A.5 of Appendix A), it was not revealed in the 2007 cluster analysis. This is probably due to the fact that the communitarian position in 2007 already included the seeds of an emerging alienation from TCs in the younger generation, but the correlations between the variables that we identified in Table 2.1 were not articulated clearly enough to form a distinct position in cluster analysis. But most importantly, self-enhancing values related to the golden passport bonanza were not widespread either.

Thus, it is possible that back in 2007 some younger members of the communitarian position without emotional bonds to the north, when asked whether they would accept a two-state solution, answered in the affirmative – without, however, formulating a structured set of beliefs, values and attitudes that would support this position. However, 10 years later, delegitimisation of the previous leftist government and the following financial benefits from development of the real estate sector by a right-wing government flooded by millions from the golden passport scheme (mostly in Limassol and Paphos districts), a more machiavellian and cold-minded neo-liberal stance was already crystalising, freed from the master narrative but motivated by self-enhancing values of power, stimulation and hedonism as described in the second row of Table 2.1 and captured by an expression allegedly used by Anastasiades during this period when he was asked about the solution of the Cyprus issue: '*I Lemesos peta tziai eseis milate mou gia to kypriako*' ('Limassol is flying, and you are talking to me about the Cyprus issue'). The fact that a publication by Gregoris Ioannou (2020) suggested that many of the GC elites and laypeople normalised partition in their consciousness in this period made the importance of exploring the existence and 'epidemiology' of this view in public opinion more urgent.

The four positions that emerged in 2017 were:

1. Pro-reconciliation/Pro-BBF – federalist mentality
2. Neutral towards TCs – favouring a unitary state / BBF as a solution of necessity / against partition
3. Ambivalent/Polarised attitude towards TCs – partitionist
4. Xenophobic/Hellenocentric – anti-federation

2021. The article in which he expressed his views was published in *Kathimerini* on 3 January 2021. It can be accessed at: www.kathimerini.com.cy/gr/apopseis/arthrografia/xaris-georgiadis/1-neos-realismos.

It must be stated from the outset that all four groups in their majority agree that the Cyprus problem should be solved through compromise and reject the idea of armed struggle. There is a very small percentage of extremists who do not reject armed confrontation; these constitute the hard core of the xenophobic/Hellenocentric/anti-federal bloc, most of whom bear a grudge about the military defeat in 1974. Moreover, it should be noted that 58% of the entire sample would accept BBF either as a satisfactory solution or as a solution of necessity, while about 70% clearly reject a two-state solution.

Analysis of the first position (18.8%), those clearly in favour of the UN-supported BBF and reconciliation and involved in bicommunal work and NGOs working for reconciliation, reveals the following characteristics: very positive attitude towards the other community, high level of trust, quality contact with the TC community, and low levels of perceived realistic and/or symbolic threats. Identity issues are distinguished by a more Cypriot-centric approach, and this position sees federation and the single state as satisfactory solutions and rejects both the two-state solution and the status quo. The majority believe that the church should not interfere in educational matters. The majority are educated, male and believe firmly in the need for reconciliation and forgiveness. Compared to the other three groups, this group has the least anxiety about the functionality of a future BBF state, Turkey's intervention in a federal Cyprus and Turkish settlers acquiring citizenship in the new state. Together with the second group, they express the lowest levels of fear that GCs are not ready to co-exist with TCs. On the contrary, they have the highest degree of hope that, in the event of a solution, relations with Turkey will be normalised and economic development and free movement will take place throughout Cyprus. In terms of historical consciousness, one could find both the critical and the genetic types in this position, the hallmark being the future-oriented imaginary of a united Cyprus that overcomes division through co-operation between the two communities.

The second group (Neutral towards TCs), which is also the most numerous (43.1%), maintains a neutral attitude towards TCs and has neutral levels of qualitative contact and trust towards TCs but has a particularly negative attitude towards Turkey and Turkish settlers. Although they express high levels of perception of realistic and symbolic threats, and view the single state as an ideal solution to the Cyprus problem, they are ready to accept federation as a compromise and explicitly reject the two-state solution (90% of the group). About one-third of this group accept the status quo, but the rest reject it. Considering the hopes and fears relating to a possible solution on the basis of BBF, this group profile is very similar to that of the rapprochement group but reveals significantly higher fears for the functionality of the state, Turkey's possible intervention in the future federation and a significantly lower degree of hope that, in the event of a solution, relations with Turkey will be normalised and economic growth will take place. Another subdivision within this group is those who support federation either as a satisfactory solution or as a solution of necessity (about 63%). This group is estimated to be between 18% and 23% of the general electorate, and they also seem to be influenced by the prevailing climate (optimism or pessimism) in Cyprus at any given time, thus being more susceptible to changing in-group norms compared to the first group. In terms of historical consciousness, it has not completely made a break with the traumatic past, as there is still the fear of Turkish 'expansionist' plans, since the reading of history is mostly exemplary. They see Turkey as always being a lurking threat, despite their more neutral disposition towards TCs and their wish for reunification of Cyprus. For them, ideally, TCs would one day demand the end of occupation of Cyprus together with GCs. This would be the condition of full acceptance of TCs as partners in overthrowing Turkish occupation. At the same time, those who see BBF as a painful compromise and not a satisfactory solution find it difficult to accept political equality with the smaller community and share power.

The third group (Mixed attitude to TCs) (18.6%) is comprised by an increased number of youth, and their profile reflects the decades-long geographical separation of the two communities. Thus, this position is expressed by primarily younger, more educated, female and those with few emotional ties to the occupied part of Cyprus. In one sense they have become emancipated from the Den Xechno policy of 'all refugees should return to their homes' but not from the idea of 'expansionist Turkey'. Thus, in the absence of contacts with TCs and increased symbolic threats, stereotypes for the present state of the north of Cyprus and political apathy, they fail to see the usefulness of reunification, which could be a risk to some educated young professionals who are competing for jobs in a shrinking job market.

Although this group has, on average, neutral feelings towards the TCs, and their support comes from the big two parties (AKEL and DISY, who lost hope on the return of refugees or a solution), there is also a minor part (coming from the extreme right-wing party ELAM) with extreme negative emotions towards TCs. The group shows significant distrust and expresses feelings of symbolic threat as they feel different to the TCs; they prefer the two-state solution or maintenance of the status quo to federation or the unitary state. However, about 50% said they could accept the BBF mainly if it were necessary (one may assume if it took the form of a decentralized or 'loose' federation as proposed by some centre-right politicians and later in 2019–2021 by GC leader Nicos Anastasiades).

It is important to note the age of this group and consider how the educational curriculum may have contributed to their positions. A series of surveys in the GC community have shown a positive correlation between age and the quality of bicommunal relations / readiness to live together with TCs. Specifically, the older the participant, the higher the wish for a solution – and vice versa (Psaltis et al., 2021). This relationship is largely due to the youth never having lived with the other community, and therefore not knowing TCs (unless they have established contacts or friensdships after the opening of the checkpoints). Indeed, in another research with inhabitants of formerly mixed villages we found that those who had contacts before 1974 or came from villages with higher intergroup contact and less conflict were, in 2010, less likely to show prejudice and distrust towards members of the other community (Kende et al., 2022).

Although there is a sense of Cypriotness in the historical narrative of this partitionist position which indicates some distance from the Hellenocentric orientation of the narrative, it does not go beyond the official narrative of 'Turkey has always wanted to conquer the whole of Cyprus' and shows great ignorance of the mistakes or atrocities committed by the GC community against the TC community. Those who do recognise these atrocities might approach them with a cynical attitude of 'things like that unfortunately happen in wars, the Turkish army did the same', making perspective-taking a part of a Machiavellian sociocentric approach. Through these moral disengagement strategies (Psaltis et al., 2017) the sense of victimisation remains unchanged, due in large part to the educational stance of 'I Know, I Do not Forget, I Claim' that is taught from primary school onwards. Cyprus history is taught in a way that encourages perceptions of realistic and symbolic threats, bias and lack of trust (Makryianni & Psaltis, 2007; Psaltis et al., 2017). Regarding the hopes and fears in relation to a scenario of a solution on the basis of BBF, this group expresses considerably more concern about the functionality of the state, the intervention of Turkey in the future federation and/or problems with Turkish settlers who will acquire citizenship in the new state. They also present, together with the fourth group, the least hope that, in the event of a solution, relations with Turkey will be normalised and economic development and free movement will take place throughout

Cyprus. It is worth noting that this group has the greatest fear of living together, declaring that 'we are unprepared as a society', 'we did not grow up to live peacefully together' and 'nationalists will mess things up'.

The emergence of this position should be read as age related and partly a longer-term cohort effect and not a recent period effect. It expresses the view of some people from the post-1974 generation that were raised in a partitioned geographical space who have normalised in their mind the partition of the island, mostly due to significant gaps in the cultivation of relationships with the TC community in their educational system for years (with the exception of the recent post-2003 opening of the checkpoints and the IMAGINE years).

The fourth and final group (Xenophobic/Hellenocentric) (19.5%) believes in the continuation of traditional Greek nationalism in Cyprus, characterised particularly by anti-Turkish and negative feelings towards the TCs (whom they often equate with Turks); shows the greatest mistrust, very high perceptions of symbolic and realistic threat arising from difference, and feelings of superiority arising from a generalized ethnocentric, Hellenocentric and xenophobic ethos (also against immigrants). This group is strongly opposed to federation as a solution to the Cyprus problem and sees the ideal solution to the Cyprus problem as the unitary state or 'liberation', while a small extreme right-wing nationalist fraction still seeks union with Greece (enosis). However, almost half of this group sees the maintenance of the status quo or even the two-state solution as the second-best solution to avoid federation (about 40% of this group). It should be noted that despite the general anti-federal feelings in this group, one-third reported they could accept the federation as a solution of necessity.

Most in this group are middle-aged, and therefore, apart from their traditional Hellenocentric roots, they are also influencing many in the younger generation through extreme nationalist groups and various 'right-wing' football clubs. This group also identifies as the most religious and the most frequent churchgoers, so they may also be influenced by church preachings. Regarding the possible solution of the Cyprus problem on the basis of BBF, this group does not differ significantly from the previous partitionist group, since it is also characterised by a high degree of fear that there will be problems with the Turkish settlers who will acquire citizenship in the new state. They also have a lower degree of hope that, in the event of a solution, relations with Turkey will be normalised and economic development and free movement will take place throughout Cyprus. Moreover, this group believes most strongly in the lack of functionality of the federal state, due to possible interventions by Turkey.

The Role of Ontogenetic and Sociogenetic Changes in Values in the Greek Cypriot Community

Expanded analysis of sociogenetic changes of values in Cyprus further supports the claim that the detection of the fourth partitionist position in the 2017 data could be attributed to age and partly cohort-generational change of values given their crucial role as the organising principles of representations. In Appendix C an analysis of the Round 9 ESS data (collected in 2018) on Shwartz 10 values from the GC community can be found, along with their relationship with various sociodemographic characteristics. The relationships are what one would expect from findings in other parts of the world (Shwartz, 2021). The social vs personal higher-order focus has a clear relationship with age. The younger the people, the more they prioritise personal (Achievement [AC], Power [PO], Hedonism [HE], Stimulation [ST], Self-Direction [SD]) over social (Universalism [UN], Benevolence [BE], Security [SE], Tradition [TR], Conformity [CO]) values.

Modelling of Age–Period–Cohort effects in our lab using ESS Round 9 data for Cyprus (Nicolaou, in preparation) reveals that for some of the values the relationship of values with age can be attributed more clearly to an age effect. Cohort effects, however, are also present (more on this distinction in the next chapter), having to do with increasing individualism over decades in Cyprus with the exception of cohorts born after 1995, for which a reversal of the trend is noted. In particular, after 1995, a unique pattern related to Cyprus is observed where social values start gaining importance. There is, of course, variation in social values, and not all could be seen as conducive to co-operative relations. Self-transcendence values (BE and UN), for example, are related to more benevolence to in-groupers and out-groupers. The increase in these values that we find in those born after 1995 and in the period of the last decade could be related to generations who in their school and formative years experienced Cyprus as an EU member state. However, in the same cohorts and period there is an increase in the importance of tradition and security values, which could be related to a more threatening Turkey after the Crans Montana failure and the financial crisis of 2012. Self-enhancement values in the same cohorts and period follow the opposite trend of losing importance. Given these general trends in the recent period, the partitionist position identified in the cluster analysis of 2017 should be read as either (a) expressing a minority of people around the golden passport bonanza and not the wider public or (b) a time-lagged expression of increased individualism that mostly affected younger cohorts but not the too young ones born after 1995, following a U-shaped curvilinear relationship with age. This hypothesis will be further explored later in this chapter and the next one.

We also see in Appendix C that the health status of the individual significantly relates to almost all values, with poorer health relating to more social values. This is clearly related to a life stage change of values as an age effect. There is also a similar pattern in relation to gender where females seem to be more oriented towards social values (e.g. Security and Benevolence) compared to men. Women also score significantly lower than men on Self-Determination, Stimulation and Hedonism. These three values probably relate to the influence of religion on women, since there are significantly more religious women than men in the GC community. There is also a clear pattern of findings relating to education of the participant as well as maternal and paternal educational levels, with higher education leading to higher personal focus values at the expense of social focus values, especially conservation values. The pattern of correlations for income is also similar to the education findings, suggesting that higher socio-economic status plays the predicted role of promoting individualist values as in Inglehard and Welzel (2010) as well as in the work of Henrich (2020).

Interestingly, political orientation on the left–right spectrum is largely unrelated to values, with the only exception being the value of Benevolence with the left being higher in benevolence compared to the right. On the contrary, religiosity is clearly related to specific social values, with conservation values being higher in more religious people. Interestingly, Universalism is unrelated to religiosity in the GC community, which is different from findings in other European countries. Xenophobic attitudes relate to higher conservation values and lower self-transcendence values. Intergroup contact with TCs relates to higher Openness to Change values and lower self-enhancement and conservation values, which supports our proposal for the relationship between the co-operative significant structure and self-transcendence values in Table 2.1 of Chapter 2.

The findings presented in Appendix C also shed light on the role of communication technologies. The more participants watch, read or listen to news related to politics, the higher they score on social values (especially conservation values). This is probably reflecting youth alienation from politics in Cyprus. On the contrary, the more hours spent on the internet, the more they prioritise personal (especially stimulation and hedonism) over social values. This is an important finding, as it suggests high internet use is related to more individualist values. The findings are suggestive of a negative impact of excessive social media use to the extent that it constricts the ethical horizon of the youth into self-enhancement rather than self-transcendent values, unless of course they use social media to interact with the other community. Indeed, we found evidence that people of Cyprus who have Facebook friends from the other community had lower prejudice levels (Zezelj et al., 2017).

In some of our work in progress (Psaltis & Georgiou, in preparation) we found evidence of linkages between values and various social psychological variables relating to intercommunal relations in Cyprus. Specifically, we run hierarchical regression models to predict prejudice levels towards TCs, trust and stance on various forms of solution (BBF, Two States, Unitary state, Continuation of Status Quo) from various demographic variables and all 10 values of Appendix C. It was revealed that age, paternal and maternal educational level, position on the ideological spectrum, contact, rejection of immigrants and health status predicted prejudice levels. Interestingly, the direction of maternal and paternal educational levels was in opposite directions when predicting prejudice and trust, with those having more educated mothers showing more prejudice and less trust towards TCs compared to those with less educated mothers. On the contrary, those with more educated fathers showed less prejudice and more trust compared to those with less educated fathers.

Universalist values predicted less prejudice over and above the demographic variables. The findings for predicting trust were similar, with the only exception that two values predicted prejudice. One was again universalism in the expected direction and the other was security. The higher the score for security values, the higher were the distrust levels. Similarly, higher universalism increased support for BBF and lowered support for Two States and continuation of the Status Quo.

The age-related effects, however, are not clear-cut, as we show below and in the next chapter. Sometimes they are non-linear, taking a U shape, with very young people and older people who lived in a united Cyprus before 1974 being more similar to each other on some measures than compared to people aged between 35 and 55, at least in the GC community. So, the legitimacy of the idea of partition seems to be restricted in the minds of a minority of some younger or middle-aged GCs and political elites who became complacent with the spoils of power irrespective of age. Sometime this position is expressed with the words 'a wall in the middle and that's it' (*toicho mes tis mesi tziai kanei*), but the present findings clearly show that we cannot talk about normalisation of partition (cf. Ioannou, 2020) in the GC community as a whole, since this view represents only about 20% of the population and seems to be contained in a young professional's middle-aged group who are probably already in well-paid jobs, largely unpolitical, narcissistic and individualist usually in the right wing of the ideological spectrum. This position in the representational field is closer to what we described in Chapter 2, Table 2.1 as a significant structure of Machiavellian domination.

Youth and the Cyprus Issue in 2020

The consequences of the empty imagination of GC youth that we identified in 9–10-year-old GC students studied in 2002 by Makriyianni (2006) (the 1991–1992 cohort) can be captured 17 years later when this cohort is about 26–27 years old in a research just published that compared the views of 18–35-year-olds with the views of 36–54-year-olds and those aged 55+ on the Cyprus issue in 2020 (Psaltis et al., 2021), as well as another research by Dizdaroglu (2020) who explored the views of the younger generation of the two communities about the Cyprus issue.

This recent research has pointed to certain generational differences about representations of the Cyprus problem, the feeling of hope and wish for solution, political culture and intergroup relations in research participants of the age group 18–35 in both communities (Dizdaroglou, 2020; Psaltis et al. 2021). In both communities there is an increased sense of alienation and low participation in politics and election processes in this age group, which seems to be related to a feeling of distrust for political parties, the government and even the parliament. This seems to be because the youth feel non-recognised as active citizens by the parties but also, as we know from the findings of the European Social Survey (ESSR9) data collected in 2018–2019, the GC youth in their vast majority do not feel confident in contributing to politics. In the GC community this has to do with the low levels of agency that institutional structures in Cyprus support (educational system, the church and some traditional family values that keep the youth at the parental house sometimes until they get married).

On bicommunal relations, there is more recognition by TC youth than GC youth of the importance of the opening of checkpoints and more frequent crossing to the south (about 50% of TCs cross regularly) for shopping or excursions. GC youth cross much less often and are not so keen on the opening of more checkpoints. This is probably because they are trapped into the discourse of some GC 'centre' political parties (EDEK, DIKO) but maximalist on the Cyprus issue who claim that 'crossings normalise partition' or 'offer moral recognition and financial support to the non-recognised state in the north', whereas the reality of social psychological findings is that the opposite of this discourse is true. On a more optimistic note, half of the youth in both communities state as a reason for not visiting the other side that 'it just didn't happen', thus not evoking hatred or ideological resistance to the idea of having intergroup contact (Dizdaroglu, 2020). Similarly, the majority (around 60–70% in both communities) approve of socialisation of members of the two communities under various conditions, even when some of them assume member of other communities being in positions or roles of higher status (e.g. boss at work) (Dizdaroglu, 2020). This shows that GC youth would support contact and relationships between the two communities but not crossings of GCs to the other side, which they see as having negative consequences for the collective struggle of not allowing the recognition of the illegal state in the north of Cyprus. At the same time, the lack of a federalist mentality in the youth is also present, as there is a low acceptance of the idea of a president of the country from the other community (Dizdaroglu, 2020), which can be explained by the content transmitted through the educational system as discussed earlier. This is probably related to educational content of the last years of the lyceum, since in the research of Kyriakides (2020), as students moved from the gymnasium to the lyceum, the percentage of those who disagreed with the idea that GCs and TCs can govern Cyprus together increased.

In Psaltis et al. (2021) we found that the GC youth (aged 18–35) compared to older people are less likely to wish for peace, less likely to expect that peace will be achieved and less likely to support peace-promoting steps. Importantly, however, this is not because they are more prejudiced or distrustful than older people. In fact, they score significantly lower on the ethos of conflict scale compared to the older age groups (Psaltis et al., 2021). So, their weakened willingness to take positive steps should be interpreted more as the result of alienation and apathy than fanaticism. This is supported by another finding that they are less likely, compared to older people, to attend events where the Cyprus issue is discussed. The youth are also more uncompromising compared to older people, although the majority is still in favour of the idea that the solution to the Cyprus issue should satisfy the needs of both communities (around 70% compared to around 85% in older people).

There is also less enthusiasm in the youth about taking steps to promote BBF compared to older people. The less appetite for BBF is seen in another question where they are asked if they wish for a mutually agreed-upon solution on the basis of BBF. On this question 47.8%

expressed no wish and 52.2% expressed a wish for a solution on the basis of BBF. In older age groups the wish to solve the issue by going the BBF route was much higher at close to 70%.

Overview of the Impact of Political Developments on Public Opinion and Students Views in the Period 2003–2023

In the GC community there were a few periods since 2003 when most of the people expressed negative feelings towards TCs (2005–2010) and other times when they were positive (2015–2017) (see Appendix A), particularly when the leaders of the two communities exhibited willingness to negotiate in good faith to resolve the Cyprus problem, made public appearances together and publicly showed trust in each other (Karayianni & Psaltis, 2023). It is hard to believe that such a big portion of the population shifted their views in such a short period of time due to a deep ideological conversion. A more likely candidate is to attribute the change to a change in norms that mostly reduced people's readiness to express prejudiced views during this period. Long-term positive changes are, however, still noticeable (Yucel & Psaltis, 2020a, 2020b) and mostly have to do with continuing contact and an increasing number of people from both communities that established intergroup friendships – a condition that, according to Pettigrew, satisfies the optimal conditions of intergroup contact. For example, by 2020, about 50% of TCs and 30% of GCs stated that they had at least one friend from the other community.

An additional factor contributing to this significant improvement, given that it was also accompanied by improvement of attitudes of students towards other out-groups (e.g. immigrants) compared to older research, could be related to the impact of EU and CoE policies after Cyprus joining the EU in 2004. Indeed, since 2008, the Ministry of Education, Sport and Youth (MOESY) in Cyprus has been actively promoting peace education more generally, anti-racist education and human rights education. These initiatives, even if they did not often directly relate to the Cyprus problem, included revising curricula and textbooks, altering education policies and participating in European programmes focused on human rights and peace education. For example, the MOESY has integrated human rights, anti-racist and intercultural education into the health education curriculum since 2011. This curriculum, applicable at all educational levels, includes success indicators addressing issues like bullying, violence, social identity, respect for diversity and peaceful co-existence. Teacher manuals, such as 'Discovering the Elephant' and Compasito (Council of Europe), support the implementation of these themes. The ministry in the south also gave a lot of attention to teacher training through policies at the Cyprus Pedagogical Institute (CPI) that provided training for teachers to work effectively in multicultural environments. In 2022, various in-service seminars were offered, covering topics like anti-racist policy, managing bullying and school violence, and empowering teachers in these areas. An anti-racist policy was also implemented since 2014–2015 that conceptualises racism broadly (sexism, homophobia, ethnic-related prejudice) and includes steps for schools to handle racist incidents. Additionally, an upgraded educational policy focused on the smooth integration of pupils with migrant backgrounds, emphasising intercultural approaches and teaching Greek as a second language. Finally, the MOESY and CPI have been involved in European projects like the 'EU/CoE Pilot Projects Scheme on Human Rights and Democracy in Action'. These projects provided resources and training for teachers to address controversial issues holistically. The CPI also participated in implementing the Council of Europe's Descriptors of Competences for Democratic Culture (CDC), adapting these to the Cypriot context. The ministry in the south of the divide also collaborated with other organizations on human rights education related to antisemitism and refugees. For example, MOESY organised educational visits in collaboration with the Vad Yashem International School of Holocaust Studies for teachers and students once a year and a special conference for teachers on the pedagogical practices of the Holocaust, and a specialised educator gives in-service seminars on the subject for students and teachers. Finally, since 2017, the CPI, in collaboration with the UNHCR Cyprus Office, has organised three teacher-training conferences on issues of racism, nationalism, migration and asylum in education.

The broader picture in both communities is one of a positive shift in the period 2007–2017 in both prejudice reduction, trust building (Yucel & Psaltis, 2020a) and the acceptance of BBF as a compromise solution (see Appendices A and B). One cannot stress enough the positive effects of intergroup contact after the opening of the checkpoints that could be seen as a mechanism reversing the negative impact of alienation of the two communities through passing time.

In the recent years there are also a number of findings from TC students and youth and their attitudes towards GCs from the work of Shenel Husnu and her collaborators. Despite the fact that for TC children the GCs fit the picture of the enemy image (Mertan & Husnu, 2014), they still found that imagined contact (Husnu & Crisp, 2010) with university students and indirect contact interventions through storytelling at the elementary school can decrease prejudice levels towards GCs (Husnu et al., 2018). They also found that contact and positive in-group norms about contact can predict forgiveness in youth (Stathi et al., 2017).

The working of various bicommunal technical committees and the positive climate between the two leaders in the period 2015–2017 also played a positive role in the formation of positive in-group norms. The positive climate was also transferred in education of the GC community as revealed by the study of Kyriakides who collected data in 2017 from public schools for ages 7 to 17. In his findings 44% of GC students expressed positive feelings towards TCs, 33% were neutral and 23% showed negative feelings towards TCs. Regarding feelings towards Turks, there was also an impressive improvement compared to the findings reported in 2003 by Makriyianni (2006): 32% expressed positive feelings, 28% showed neutral feelings and 40% showed negative feelings. This was probably also due to changing in-group norms by a positive policy introduced in 2015 and 2016 in the GC community that connected peace education in relation to the TC community with general anti-racist educational policies announced by a circular to educators at the beginning of the school year as one of the general goals. An anti-racist policy could more easily facilitate a universalising expansion of the ethical horizon of students as described in Chapter 1, Figure 1.2.

In the same work (Kyriakides & Psaltis, 2023) exploring the views of GC students between 7 and 17 years old we also explored the role of Piagetian relations of constraint and co-operation with significant others (peers, family and teachers). We found low correlations between prejudice and social relations of constraint and co-operation in the interpersonal sphere in middle childhood but not adolescence, and additionally the increasing influence of both positive and negative norms in the expression of prejudice in early and late adolescence. The other interesting finding from this research is the emergence of resistance in early adolescence against positive norms, which is moderated by the strength of subgroup identification (proud of being GC). Early adolescents who have very high level of identification with the GC identity are not influenced by positive in-group norms by significant others, suggesting friendships with TCs, but they are influenced by negative norms. In contrast, in middle childhood, when interpersonal relations of constraint and co-operation play a stronger role in predicting prejudice, subgroup identification moderates the link in the opposite direction by enhancing the role of positive in-group norms in predicting prejudice reduction. As predicted by Piaget and Weil (1951) and proposed in Chapter 1, Figure 1.2, older children start relating to

Table 4.2 *National identification of Greek Cypriot students aged 7–17 from Kyriakides (2020)*

	7–8 years old	10–11 years old	13–14 years old	16–17 years old
Cypriot	57%	55.9%	55.6%	40.2%
Cypriot Greek	9.3%	11%	8.5%	8.5%
Greek Cypriot	16.3%	21.3%	29.5%	36.8%
Greek of Cyprus	12.8%	1.6%	1.3%	4.3%
Greek	4.7%	10.2%	5.1%	10.3%

ideals and political views or even world views that free themselves from the here and now. In the case of GCs, due to the Hellenocentric orientation of the education system, they create elective affinities, imaginary fraternal links with Greeks and Greece, or see Cyprus as part of wider Hellenism. Unfortunately, the historical ideological baggage of this 'imagined community' (Anderson, 1991) is often linked with ultra-nationalist views of the 'Cyprus is Greek' kind, which manifests as resistance in accepting normative suggestions to be friendly towards TCs in the context of relationships with the other community of Cyprus, and their strength of identification as simply Cypriot diminishes through their time in the public school system (see Table 4.2 based on Kyriakides, 2020). It is important to note that this is not criticism of positive feelings towards any out-group members. It is only when love for Greece translates to exclusive territorial claims of collective psychological ownership (Storz et al., 2020), as we discovered in recent research, that repercussions towards reconciliation in Cyprus take their toll.

Ontogenetic Considerations

From an ontogenetic point of view, it could be hypothesised that as children develop from childhood to adolescence, relations at the interpersonal level of social constraint will diminish and relations of co-operation will increase as their agency develops. However, the actual content of the representations they are surrounded by will be mediated by in-group norms. In this transition the role of intergroup contact will be crucial, as it can define the limits of their ethical horizon beyond any cognitive developmental effect of widening of perspectives. The role of semiotic means the content of various symbolic resources (history textbooks, films, etc.) and school rituals in the orientation of the widening ethical horizon seems crucial. The mastery of part–whole relationships and multiple classification is in fact a prerequisite of an understanding of these more complex part–whole relationships. Dual identities also become more comprehensible. For example, in the research by Makriyianni, 9–10-year-olds had difficulty understanding what a Greek Cypriot and a Turkish Cypriot is. Most often, definitions were 'people born in Cyprus but who came from Greece' or speak Greek for GCs and 'people who live in Cyprus but came from Turkey or speak Turkish' for TCs. GC children have a difficulty understanding when exactly TCs came to Cyprus. Some mistake TCs with Turkish people from mainland Turkey that came to Cyprus after 1974, called settlers by the RoC, which is expected given that they are never taught anything about the history of the TC community except some cursory mentions of the 'rebellion' of TCs in 1963–1964 who did not accept the 'just' claims of President Makarios to change the constitution that was not functioning and gave TCs 'over-privileges'. This kind of content is usually taught in late adolescence (lyceum) just before male students get prepared to enlist for military service.

From Marios Kyriakides's PhD thesis we have some important empirical evidence about the importance of the transition period of 10–11 years old. This is the same age that Piaget identified as the transition to formal operational thinking. On the one hand, progressively fewer children around this age act trapped within the immediate situation and adults' directions. Similarly, increasingly more children doubt and challenge authority while strengthening relations of co-operation. This suggests that influence from parents and teachers becomes less pronounced but influence from peers becomes more important. Also, individual intergroup experiences are expected to become a more significant source of information compared to earlier years. Indeed, this was verified by Kyriakides (2020) who found that the effects of contact in the period of 10–14 years of age were more pronounced compared to younger children and older adolescents. In a longitudinal study by Hjerm, Eger and Danell (2018) of 13- and 16-year-olds that were followed for five consecutive years in Sweden showed that the mean level of prejudice in peer groups in both ages predicts their later individual prejudice levels. Additionally, popular students at the centre of social networks were found to be less influenced by the group having lower prejudice levels. Similar effects for parental attitudes were found. Interestingly, political discussions (irrespective of their content) were also found to have a prejudice reduction effect. This suggests that beyond the importance of the content there is also an important role played by the type of social interaction enacted if it takes the form of skills in democratic processes of open dialogue, which in the terms of genetic social psychology is the significant structure of co-operation.

This again would be predicted by Piaget in his idea of social relations of co-operation (open dialogue where all views can be expressed and new knowledge can be synthesised). The role of the formation of historical consciousness, as discussed earlier, is also crucial, and in contexts of protracted conflict, the misuse of history by politicians and the state is a well-known phenomenon that goes hand in hand with the political socialisation in the educational system (Psaltis, Carretero & Cehajic-Clancy, 2017).

The role of constraints to developing agency by infrastructures of a traditional historical culture even in a period of positive bicommunal developments became clear in the work of Eleni Kotzamani (2020), who studied the representations of childhood and children's rights in Cyprus. Through qualitative analysis she found that in the circulars of the Christian Orthodox Church sent to schools by the Archbishop, minimal agency was extended to students through a patronising attitude that allowed children to take initiatives only to the extent that they satisfied the aims of the church to cultivate religious subjects or become willing participants in the collective struggle for the liberation of Cyprus from Turkish occupation. And although most 16-year-old students would resist any effort by the family, church or state to impose on them organised nationalist or religious rituals, there was about 20% of the sample that had internalised a position of social conformity and who had no problem whatsoever with the curtailment of their rights as long as the national cause or religion was served. This position of submission in our proposal (see Chapter 2, Table 2.1) was related in a sample of both 16-year-old students and their educators with a conservative view of childhood relating to diminished agency, higher religiosity, realistic and symbolic threats as well as patriotism and nationalism.

Developments after 2017

This shift towards conflict transformation became more difficult after November 2016 with a break in trust between the two leaders, when the GC leader Anastasiades showed cold feet to proceed to a solution on a few occasions. Around the same period the Greek Minister of Foreign Affairs

Nikos Kotzias promoted publicly and through leaks in the GC press that Greece would not agree to any solution that would not annul the securities by Turkey, Greece and the UK and entail the withdrawal of all Turkish troops from Cyprus (see Avraamidou & Psaltis, 2019). This was accompanied by a provocative move by the extreme right-wing party ELAM when it requested in February 2017 in parliament that schools commemorate the plebiscite of 1950 for Union of Cyprus with Greece (a request which was not resisted by right-wing ruling party DISY). This created mistrust between the leaders of the two communities. The negotiations nevertheless proceeded with an international summit in June 2017 at Crans Montana in Switzerland to reach a package agreement. The negotiations collapsed in July 2017 amidst both sides accusing one another of not making the necessary final steps to lock a mutually agreed-upon solution. The 2018–2020 period was quite stagnant in terms of bicommunal negotiations, although very active, and filled with tensions, at the regional level. Foremost, Turkey carried out exploration and drilling for natural gas in parts of the Mediterranean that the Republic of Cyprus had delimited, in agreement with other countries, as their own Exclusive Economic Zone (EEZ). Turkey also undertook explorations in contested parts of the Mediterranean where Greece was laying claims, which led the two countries to the brink of a military confrontation in August 2020. At the same time, Turkey, in collaboration with nationalist TC party leaders, threatened to open Varosha under TC administration – a direct violation of the UN Security Council resolutions that demanded the return of Varosha to their rightful GC owners under UN administration. That threat was partly carried out in the days just prior to the elections for a new TC leadership, when Tayip Erdogan with Ersin Tatar, who eventually won the 2020 elections for the TC leadership with Turkey's heavy backing, announced the opening of a stretch of beach in Varosha for visits without a change in its administration status, going against UN Security Council resolutions.

Research undertaken in 2019 and 2020 showed that the positive sentiments of GCs towards TCs and a BBF solution registered in 2015 and 2016 showed a lot of resilience, as the aforementioned negative developments after 2017 were not reflected as a turn against the wish for a solution and did not lead to worsening of the views towards TCs. This is probably because these events have made it clear to GCs how dangerous for their communal interests is the continuation of the status quo. Confirming this is the fact that from 2019 to 2020 there was a significant increase in the percentage of those who reject the status quo, from 50.8% to 79.4% (see

Appendix A). At the same time, the option of a two-state solution also became less acceptable, with the rejection of it growing from 72.4% in 2019 to 80% in 2020, thus shrinking the appeal of the newly identified significant structure of partitionists.

These latest developments would suggest that the bridging social capital built with TCs in the period 2003–2017 formed a certain resilience in GC attitudes towards the other community. Given that these post-2017 provocations are mostly seen as emanating from Turkey and not TCs, one would not expect a deterioration of relations with the other community.

On the other hand, the relationship with Turkey in the minds of GCs is different. Tensions with Turkey about the EEZ are expected to be read by most GCs as fitting into the representation of an expansionist Turkey. At the same time, worsening relations with an emerging regional power like Turkey would probably lead some GCs into a more pragmatic attitude. The real options for them are not a choice between their ideal solution of a unitary state and the compromise solution of a BBF, but the choice between a compromise BBF and a costly permanent partition with no United Nations Peacekeeping Force in Cyprus patrolling the buffer zone, constant tensions with Turkey over gas exploitation and a complete demographic change in the north. At least some people faced with a dilemma of this nature would choose the compromise solution in order to avoid the costs of permanent partition. In the years after Crans Montana, for example, there was a steady increase in those who could either tolerate the BBF as a solution of necessity or accept it as a satisfactory solution (58.1% in 2018, 65% in 2019, 76% in 2020 and 80.5% in 2023). This finding makes the case that support for BBF is regulated by regional developments beyond the quality of intercommunal relations in Cyprus.

REFERENCES

Anderson, B. (1991). *Imagined communities: Reflections on the origin and spread of nationalism*. London: Verso.

Attalides, M. (1979). *Cyprus: Nationalism and international politics*. Edinburgh: Q Press.

Avraamidou, M., & Psaltis, C. (2019). Blocking the solution: Social representations of threats and (non)dialogue with alternative representations in Greek-Cypriot newspapers during peace negotiations. *Journal for the Theory of Social Behavior, 2019*, 1–20. https://doi.org/10.1111/jtsb.12222.

Bauer, M. W., & Gaskell, G. (1999). Towards a paradigm for research on social representations. *Journal for the Theory of Social Behaviour*, *29*(2), 163–186.

Billig, M. (1995). *Banal nationalism*. Thousands Oaks, CA: Sage.

Charalambous, P., Charalambous, C., & Zembylas, M. (2014). Old and new policies in dialogue: Greek-Cypriot teachers' interpretations of a peace-related initiative through existing policy discourses. *British Educational Research Journal*, *40*, 79–101. https://doi.org/10.1002/berj.3030.

Christodoulou, E. (2018). Deconstructing resistance towards textbook revisions: The securitisation of history textbooks and the Cyprus conflict. *Global Change, Peace & Security*, *30*(3), 373–393.

Christou, M. (2006). A double imagination: Memory and education in Cyprus. *Journal of Modern Greek Studies*, *24*(2), 285–306.

Demetriou, O. (2007). To cross or not to cross? Subjectivization and the absent state in Cyprus. *Journal of the Royal Anthropological Institute*, *13*, 987–1006. https://doi.org/10.1111/j.1467-9655.2007.00468.x.

Dizdaroglu, C. (2020). *The perceptions of Cypriot youth matter: FES briefing*. Nicosia: FES Cyprus.

Geogriou, M. (2020). 17–18 year-old Greek-Cypriot students' understandings of differing historical accounts: an exploratory study of how students engage with history in the Republic of Cyprus. Unpublished PhD thesis. Institute of Education, London.

Henrich, J. (2020). *The weirdest people in the world: How the West became psychologically peculiar and particularly prosperous*. New York: Farrar, Straus & Giroux.

Hjerm, M., Eger, M. A., & Danell, R. (2018). Peer attitudes and the development of prejudice in adolescence. *Socius*. https://doi.org/10.1177/2378023118763187.

Husnu, S., & Crisp, R. J. (2010). Imagined intergroup contact: A new technique for encouraging greater inter-ethnic contact in Cyprus. *Peace and Conflict: Journal of Peace Psychology*, *16*, 97–108. http://dx.doi.org/10.1080/10781910903484776.

Husnu, S., Mertan, B., & Cicek, O. (2016). Reducing Turkish Cypriot children's prejudice toward Greek Cypriots: Vicarious and extended intergroup contact through storytelling. *Group Processes & Intergroup Relations*, *14*, 193–206.

(2018). Reducing Turkish Cypriot children's prejudice toward Greek Cypriots: Vicarious and extended intergroup contact through storytelling. *Group Processes & Intergroup Relations*, *21*(1), 178–192.

Inglehart, R., & Welzel, C. (2010). Changing mass priorities: The link between modernization and democracy. *Perspectives on Politics*, *8*(2), 551–567.

Ioannou, G. (2020). *The normalisation of Cyprus' partition among Greek Cypriots: Political economy and political culture in a divided society*. Cham: Springer.

Ioannou, M., Hewstone, M., & Al Ramiah, A. (2017). Inducing similarities and differences in imagined contact: A mutual intergroup differentiation approach. *Group Processes & Intergroup Relations*, *20*(4), 427–446.

Karayianni, C., & Psaltis, C. (2023). Tweet for peace: Twitter as a medium for developing a peace discourse in the hands of the Greek-Cypriot and Turkish-Cypriot leaders. *Online Information Review*, *47*(5), 925–943.

Kende, J., Psaltis, C., Reiter, J., Fousiani, K., Cakal, H., & Green, E. (2022). Past and present intergroup contact and conflict among inhabitants of former mixed villages of Cyprus: The role of individual and collective experiences in predicting attitudes and trust. *Political Psychology*, *43*(4), 751–768.

Kotziamani, E. (2020). Universality and inalienability of children's rights: The impact of social beliefs about childhood and intergroup conflict on social representations of children's rights. Unpublished PhD thesis, University of Cyprus.

Kyriakides, M. (2020). Formation of prejudice and national identity: The role of cognitive development and in-group and inter-group relations in children and adolescents. Unpublished PhD thesis, University of Cyprus.

Kyriakides, M., & Psaltis, C. (2023). Suppressing the expression of prejudice and prejudice reduction from childhood to adolescence: The view of genetic social psychology. *European Journal of Psychology of Education*, *38*(1), 179–202.

Loizides, N. (2016). *Designing peace: Cyprus and institutional innovations in divided societies*. Philadelphia: University of Pennsylvania Press.

(2020). *The politics of majority nationalism*. Stanford, CA: Stanford University Press.

Makriyianni, C. (2006). History, museums and national identity in a divided country: Children's experience of museum education in Cyprus. Unpublished PhD thesis, University of Cambridge.

Makriyianni, C., & Psaltis, C. (2007). *History teaching and reconciliation. Cyprus Review*, *19*, 43–69.

Makriyianni, C., Psaltis, C., & Latif, D. (2011). History teaching in Cyprus. In E. Erdmann & W. Hasberg (Eds.), Facing mapping, bridging diversity: Foundations of a European discourse on history education, part 1 (pp. 91–138). Frankfurt: Wochen Schau Wissenschaft.

Markides, K. (1977). *The rise and fall of the Cyprus Republic*. New Haven, CT: Yale University Press.

Mavratsas, C. V. (1999). National identity and consciousness in everyday life: Towards a sociology of knowledge of Greek-Cypriot nationalism. *Nations and Nationalism*, *5*(1), 91–104.

Mertan, B. E., & Husnu, S. (2014). Understanding of 'enemy' in Turkish Cypriot children. *Peace and Conflict: Journal of Peace Psychology*, *20*(4), 465–473.

Michael, M. S. (2007). The Cyprus peace talks: A critical appraisal. *Journal of Peace Research*, *44*(5), 587–604.

Papadakis, Y. (2008). A comparison of schoolbooks on the 'history of Cyprus'. *History & Memory*, *20*(2), 128–148.

Perikleous, L., Onurkan-Samani, M., & Onurkan-Aliusta, G. (2021). Those who control the narrative control the future: The teaching of History in Greek Cypriot and Turkish Cypriot schools. *Historical Encounters*, *8*(2), 124–139.

Perikleous, L., & Shemilt, D. (Eds.). (2011). *The future of the past: Why history education matters*. Nicosia: Association for Historical Dialogue and Research.

Pettigrew, T. F., & Tropp, L. R. (2006). A meta-analytic test of intergroup contact theory. *Journal of Personality and Social Psychology*, 90(5), 751–783.

Piaget, J., & Weil, A. M. (1951). The development in children of the idea of the homeland and of relations with other countries. *International Social Science Bulletin*, *3*, 561–578.

Psaltis, C. (2012). Intergroup trust and contact in transition: A social representations perspective on the Cyprus conflict. In I. Marková & A. Gillespie (Ed.), *Trust and conflict: Representations, culture and dialogue* (pp. 83–104), London: Routledge.

(2016). Collective memory, social representations of intercommunal relations and conflict transformation in divided Cyprus. *Peace and Conflict: Journal of Peace Psychology*, *22*(1), 19–27.

Psaltis, C., Beydola, C., Filippou, G., & Vrachimis, N. (2014). Contested symbols as social representations: The case of Cyprus. In P. R. Dezalia & S. Moeshcberger (Eds.), *Symbols that bind, symbols that divide: The semiotics of peace and conflict* (61–89). Cham: Springer.

Psaltis, C., Carretero, M., & Čehajić-Clancy, S. (2017). *History education and conflict transformation: Social psychological theories, history teaching and reconciliation*. Berlin: Springer Nature.

Psaltis, C., Franc, R., Smeekes, A., Ioannou, M., & Žeželj, I. (2017). Social representations of the past in post-conflict societies: Adherence to official historical narratives and distrust through heightened threats. In C. Psaltis, M. Carretero, & S. Čehajić-Clancy (Eds.), *History education and conflict transformation: Social psychological theories, history teaching and reconciliation* (pp. 97–122). Berlin: Springer Nature.

Psaltis, C., Halperin, E., Loizides, N., Stefanovic, D. Leshem, A., & Cakal, H. (2021). Youth and politics in protracted conflicts: A comparative approach on hope for a settlement and return of IDPs. Final report of research project funded by the LSE Hellenic Observatory. Available at: www.lse.ac.uk/Hellenic-Observatory/Assets/Documents/Research/Cyprus/Projects-2019-20/Youth-and-Politics-in-Protracted-Conflicts-Project-Report.pdf.

Schwartz, S. H. (2021). A repository of Schwartz Value Scales with instructions and an introduction. *Online Readings in Psychology and Culture*, *2*(2). https://doi.org/10.9707/2307-0919.1173.

Stathi, S., Husnu, S., & Pendleton, S. (2017). Intergroup contact and contact norms as predictors of postconflict forgiveness. *Group Dynamics: Theory, Research, and Practice*, *21*(1), 20.

Storz, N., Martinović, B., Verkuyten, M., Žeželj, I., Psaltis, C., & Roccas, S. (2020). Collective psychological ownership and reconciliation in territorial conflicts. *Journal of Social and Political Psychology*, *8*(1), 404–425.

Wertsch, J. V. (2008). Collective memory and narrative templates. *Social Research: An International Quarterly*, *75*(1), 133–156.

(2021). *How nations remember: A narrative approach*. New York: Oxford University Press.

Yucel, D., & Psaltis, C. (2020a). The effects of direct and indirect contact on prejudice: 2007 and 2017 results among Greek Cypriots and Turkish Cypriots. *European Societies, 22*(5), 610–635.

(2020b). Intergroup contact and willingness for renewed cohabitation in Cyprus: Exploring the mediating and moderating mechanisms. *Group Processes & Intergroup Relations, 23*(4), 578–597.

Zezelj, I., Ioannou, M., Franc, R., Psaltis, C., & Martinovic, B. (2017). The role of inter-ethnic online friendships in prejudice reduction in post-conflict societies: Evidence from Cyprus, Serbia and Croatia. *Computers in Human Behavior, 76*, 386–395.

Zittoun, T., Duveen, G., Gillespie, A., Ivinson, G., & Psaltis, C. (2003). The use of symbolic resources in developmental transitions. *Culture & Psychology, 9*(4), 415–448.

CHAPTER 5

Single-Case Generalisation through Mixed Methods

Charis Psaltis

Articulating Change at Different Timescales and Levels of Analysis

Genetic social psychology stands in a privileged position to render intelligible both continuity and change in the process of conflict transformation in post-conflict settings and beyond. Observing change in various timescales can render intelligible mechanisms of microgenetic, ontogenetic and sociogenetic change (Duveen & Lloyd, 1990) and possible openings for change. However, it can also identify regressive forces that undermine this potential for change.

Given the complexity of articulating change in these various timescales from a methodological point of view – what Moscovici called 'methodological polytheism' – social psychological imagination is necessary. Under the broad umbrella of mixed methodologies, more specific methods look particularly promising. Autobiographical and diary methods (Zittoun & Gillespie, 2017) can help interweave significant social interactions, social relations and social influences in a person's life trajectory with particular turning points in one's lifespan development whilst at the same time not losing sight of significant historical and technological developments as they unfold in historical time. The analysis of autobiographical narratives has been recently proposed in the context of the Vygotskian tradition as a powerful method for understanding the subjectivity of research subjects and the articulation of microgenetic and ontogenetic processes in their cultural historical context (Ferreira et al., 2023; Rego, 2022). What one participant selects to narrate as an important point in a life trajectory is important not only for one's narrative construction of an identity but also because important social relationships in the ontogenetic construction of consciousness and experiences can be located without etic presuppositions. From the perspective of genetic social psychology, we are also interested in how participants change positions in the representational field, as well as instances of significant turning points in one's life trajectory. In what follows I expose personal details of my own life trajectory to make visible the experience of an internally displaced person from the events of 1974 and maximise the potential of extraction of theoretical insights given that the narration is at the same time an expression of what the theoretical perspective I am developing allows me to make visible. Of course, collecting multiple autobiographical narratives from various research participants can also allow generalisations beyond single-case studies. Such accounts can also be combined with quantitative approaches where meanings behind numbers and correlations can be made transparent. Recently Fonseca and Jovchelovitch (2024) applied some of our theoretical ideas in the study of the microgenesis of social representations relating to the reconciliation process in Colombia. The method they used is very promising, since it is a longitudinal qualitative analysis of change with observations, interviews and diaries before, during and after an 11-day visit programme of urban university students to rural communities of ex-guerillas.

Quantitative methods can also help to disentangle age from period and cohort effects provided that there are available datasets, like the European Social Survey (ESS) or World Values Survey (WVS), that afford such analysis. Ethnographic data from the family and educational context that focus on social interactions between peers and students with educators can shed light on the social construction of relations of co-operation and constraint around various objects of representation. Researchers sensitive to the need for interdisciplinary research have recently added important methodological innovations in similar explorations with the use of big data from the internet. For example, Patricia Greenfield used Google's ngram viewer of Google Books (Michel et al., 2011) (https://books.google.com/ngrams/) to locate value change in China over the last 40 years (Zeng & Greenfield, 2015). If, for example, one runs a comparison of the words 'co-operation' and 'competition' in the English language edition of books until 2019, it is interesting to note that competition was discussed more than co-operation in the period from 1800 to 1938. With the beginning of the Second World War, co-operation overtakes competition, but then after 1953, with the exception of the period 1968–1979, competition retakes the lead (Figure 5.1).

Findings like the one above suggest there are changing trends of representations and significant structures that could be relating to long-term socio-demographic changes but also more abrupt changes that depend on significant historical turning points (war, fall of Berlin Wall, global financial crisis, COVID-19 pandemic, etc.) that capture the attention of the academic community and writers and make some themes more important for discussion and others less so in specific periods.

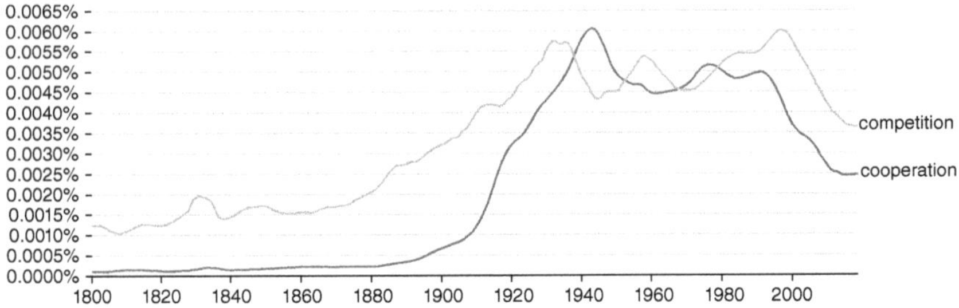

Figure 5.1 Comparison of frequency of words 'co-operation' and 'competition' in the English edition of books until 2019 in ngram viewer.

Disentangling and articulating changes relating to economic and socio-political changes in different timescales and different levels of analysis (Doise, 1986; Doise, 2011; Doise & Valentim, 2015) is a real methodological challenge. As we have seen in the previous chapter, value changes that follow predictable patterns given certain socio-demographic changes in each sociocultural context can lead to the emergence of new social representations of the Cyprus problem and its solution. How are other levels of explanation in Doise and Valentim's (2015) recent theorisation of six levels of analysis articulated in this example?

How does one move from the intersocietal level to the ideological/social representational level, the intergroup/positional, the interpersonal and the intrapersonal down to the neurological level? In the case of Cyprus and the Greek Cypriot (GC) community, we have seen in the previous chapter that there is a portion of the younger GCs who have internalised (intrapsychological level) more individualist or personal values related with the values of stimulation, hedonism and power while they feel alienated not only from the other community but also from political processes and decision-making in their own community. Due to their self-centred, egocentric and apolitical stance, they either fall prey to an uncritical internalisation of the hegemonic representation of the Cyprus issue or take a Machiavellian and cynical stance on the existence of multiple interpretations of the Cyprus issue that could also be described as a relativist stance. With colleagues from Israel we have recently discovered that in Israel, Palestine and the two communities of Cyprus the youth is characteristic for showing lower levels of hope for a settlement of their conflicts (Hasler et al., 2023). The mechanism behind this finding appeared to be that older people have a longer perspective on the conflict and its fluctuations whilst younger people have a more static perception of the conflict, which resonates with our suggestion about the role of historical consciousness in Table 2.1.

The time-limited view extends to interpersonal relationships among the youth in Cyprus, who tend to be limited to relationships within the limits and ethical horizons of their own communal group (intragroup level), forming a stance of indifference towards the other community or even avoidance of crossing to the other side of Cyprus, having lower intergroup contact or friendships and distancing themselves from the idea of renewed cohabitation with the other group (intergroup level). This individualist turn (which, in any case, does not represent the majority of the youth) was favoured by neo-liberal policies in the government amid serious financial scandals and geopolitical influences from Russia, whose own national interests were not served by a Cyprus settlement (Drousiotis, 2022), despite the best efforts of the EU to support the reunification of Cyprus (intersocietal level). It is interesting to note how Russia uses financial leverage through its oligarchs and the Christian Orthodoxy as the prevailing religion in Cyprus, as well as its connections with Mount Athos in Greece, to expand its soft power over Cypriot laypeople and politics. Religion, traditional values (see Stronski, 2021; Varnava, 2023), magical thinking full of miracles and prophecies about the demise of Turkey and support of extreme right-wing parties in countries of the EU all become a vehicle of Russian geopolitical strategy as they contribute to the formation of a consciousness that undermines co-operative significant structures in Cyprus.

In this book I do not touch on the neurological level of analysis added more recently by Doise and Valentim (2015). I would argue, however, that if one wanted to understand the complexity of intergroup relations at the neurological level, the aim would be to understand how the brain forms functional networks to accommodate the articulation of these levels of analysis in the process of social represention of various forms of significant structures of *subject–object–other*, like the three basic ones proposed in Chapter 1 (submission, domination, co-operation) that weave together emotions, beliefs and values, extending in time through forms of historical consciousness.

To return to our proposal of the three significant structures (submission, domination, co-operation) of Table 2.1, the struggle for the reunification of Cyprus in the recent period after the opening of the checkpoints has to compete not only with this newly emerging dominance-egocentric structure but also with the older traditional-submissive one premised on the uncritical internalisation of a reified and polarised master narrative of one-sided collective victimisation narratives. This latter one curtails the agency that young people might otherwise cultivate if they were helped to hone their critical skills instead of internalising myths and dogmas of the state and church.

Increased intergroup contact with the other community is key in Cyprus, since its value is now proven empirically, but it does not touch the lives of the majority in both communities. If the youth were to massively and systematically come in contact with the other community, Cyprus could be a different place. They would be emancipated to make meaning of the social world in the past–present–future nexus in a transformative and genetic historical consciousness through a co-operative decentring of their master narratives. As things currently stand in public education, the nonsense of conflict gains meaning by situating oneself in a community whose collective trauma is anchored in a common narrative of trauma (Bekerman & Zembylas, 2017) as well as a feeling of perceived collective victimisation (Psaltis et al., 2017; Bar-Tal et al., 2009) that leads to the formation of a fragile and fearful collective ego that is backward instead of forward looking.

The direction of potential positive change is facilitated in Cyprus by intergovernmental organisations like the EU, the Council of Europe (CoE) and the UN. In the case of the GC community, a major driver forward is the opening of the checkpoints in 2003 and the joining of the EU in 2004, which put in motion a number of changes relating to the institutionalisa tion of diversity management towards more inclusion in both the legal and educational landscapes of Cyprus relating to alterity (gender equality, immigration, ethnic minorities, Roma, LGBTQ+). Methodologically, rendering intelligible developments at lower levels of analysis can be complemented by institutional analysis and collection of statistical information relating to alterity.

For example, the opening of the checkpoints created millions of opportunities for contact and trade via the 'Green Line Regulation'.[1] This EU regulation states that the whole of Cyprus is part of the European Union; however, in the northern part of the island, where the government of the Republic of Cyprus does not exercise effective control, EU legislation is suspended in line with Protocol 10 to the 2003 Act of Accession. The Green line is not considered by the EU as an external border of the EU. Council Regulation 866/2004 ('Green Line Regulation') sets out the terms

[1] A description of this regulation can be found at: https://commission.europa.eu/about-european-commission/departments-and-executive-agencies/structural-reform-support/green-line-regulation_en.

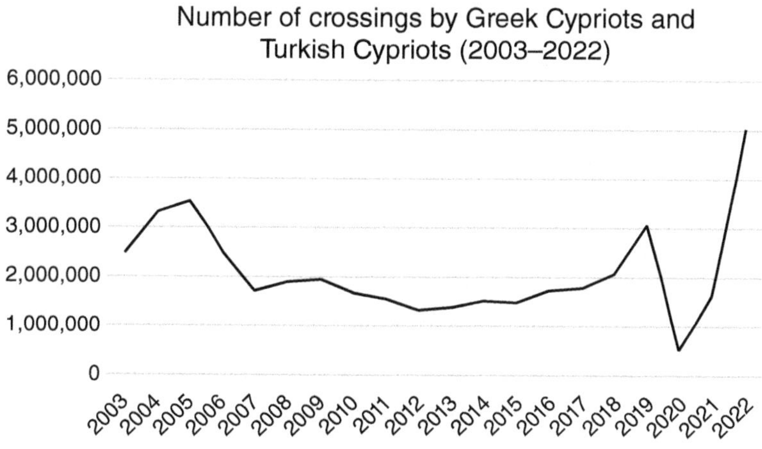

Figure 5.2 Number of crossings through the checkpoints in the period 2003–2022 (according to data published by authorities on both sides of the divide).

under which persons and goods can cross this line from the non-government-controlled areas into the government-controlled areas. The non-government-controlled areas are outside the EU's customs and fiscal territory, but this does not affect the personal rights of TCs as EU citizens.

Despite the trade part of the regulation not working optimally due to 'psychological barriers' (Ersözer, 2019) relating to non-recognition of the north, each year millions of people are crossing, thus creating opportunities for intergroup contact between the two communities. Figure 5.2 suggests that an increasing number of crossings, especially after the COVID-19–period closings, is taking place. This is partly due to the recent depreciation of the Turkish lira used in the north, but it is also indicative of a decreasing stigmatisation of crossings in the eyes of GC public despite efforts by nationalist parties and economic lobby groups to close the checkpoints. How one goes from opportunities for contact into the study of the impact of contacts on individual prejudice levels, trust, acceptance of Bizonal Bicommunal Federation or renewed cohabitation is an issue of empirical examination that we will tackle later in this chapter.

Promising change is not without its own challenges, however. Recent migration flows to Cyprus due to the war in Syria and other international conflicts brought to Cyprus a record number of immigrants and asylum seekers, which led to a new rising tide of xenophobic attitudes in 2022 (UNHCR-Cyprus, 2023), which followed the previous one of the period 2010–2012, largely as the direct outcome of a governmental policy of securitisation by the Anastasiades government. On the positive side of things there is also regular public discussion about issues of gender equality and discrimination, disability and LGBTQ+ rights in both communities of Cyprus, which shows that change that strengthens self-transcendence values can be supported by various aligned groups acting in solidarity.

Financial downturns also indirectly relate to attitudes towards alterity, as they create a fertile ground for xenophobic media to play on feelings of realistic threat (well-being or financial status of the community). Cyprus was one of the main victims of the financial crisis of 2012–2013 that also deepened some social class divisions as it underwent austerity measures, spending cuts and limitations on the renewal of the public service personnel. The 2012–2013 Cypriot financial crisis involved the exposure of Cypriot banks to overleveraged local property companies, the Greek government debt crisis, the downgrading of the Cypriot government's bond credit rating to junk status by international credit rating agencies, the consequential inability to refund its state expenses from the international markets and the reluctance of the government to restructure the troubled Cypriot financial sector.

On 25 March 2013, a €10 billion international bailout by the Eurogroup, European Commission (EC), European Central Bank (ECB) and International Monetary Fund (IMF) was announced in return for Cyprus agreeing to close the country's second-largest bank, the Cyprus Popular Bank (also known as Laiki Bank), imposing a one-time bank deposit levy on all uninsured deposits there, and seizing around 48% of uninsured deposits in the Bank of Cyprus (the island's largest commercial bank).

In regards to the pursuit of the values of a co-operative society, it is clear that one of the main obstacles is Cyprus is the unresolved Cyprus issue that is draining the resources of people for more trusting approaches to the 'others', as one of the usual mottos of various bodies and political actors is that 'the Cyprus issue is our priority', and other issues such as violations of human rights and discrimination are not actively addressed with the same sensitivity in the public sphere or are seen through the Cyprus issue perspective. A good example of this is the issue of immigration where, after the failure of Crans Montana, a securitisation discourse was promoted by the GC authorities with claims of Turkey instrumentalising immigration flows to the south of Cyprus through the checkpoints, leading to pushbacks on both land and sea and a very strict asylum regime (Trimikliniotis, 2019).

The almost 50-year geographic separation also allowed corruption in the two communities to run rampant as financial interests from the separation of Cyprus became more vocal in both communities in the past few years, mainly around the real estate sector in both communities and, in the GC community, also around the Golden Passport scheme, tourism, supermarkets, petrol stations and pharmaceuticals. These find their financial interests challenged by crossings made possible after 2003 and the possibility of reunification of Cyprus on the basis of BBF.

On the whole, despite the fact that Cyprus has adopted a significant number of laws in most policy areas that aim at creating a more co-operative society, especially after its joining the EU in 2004, there is a discrepancy between the existence of clear and positive legal framework and its implementation on issues of discrimination. Cyprus has ratified nearly all of the core international human rights treaties. Equality and non-discrimination are extensively regulated in Cyprus, and legislation has been in place for several years, but Cyprus suffers severely on the implementation part. When it comes to the functioning of the judicial system, there are some critical structural weaknesses that need amendment to tackle corruption more efficiently. The recently published Rule of Law report for 2023 is very telling: its recommendations point to some important deficits around issues of tackling corruption and transparency of financing relating to political parties and of media ownership.[2] Increasing individualism, the financial crisis and the recent scandals around the golden passport scheme have shaken the public trust in all institutions in Cyprus (except universities) as well as what is called generalised trust according to a recent analysis of Round 10 (2020) data of the European Values Survey (ESS) in the GC community.

Articulating Microgenesis, Ontogenesis and Sociogenesis

Articulating microgenesis, ontogenesis and sociogenesis involves understanding the interplay among these processes and recognising their complementary nature in shaping human development. Each of these processes provides a unique perspective on development, and they are interconnected in various ways. It is possible to suggest the following ways of articulating them:

1. Multi-layered perspective: Recognise that human development is a complex and multi-layered process that incorporates moment-to-moment changes (microgenesis), long-term individual development (ontogenesis) and the influence of social and cultural factors in

[2] https://commission.europa.eu/system/files/2023-07/31_1_52612_coun_chap_cyprus_en.pdf.

historical time (sociogenesis) at various levels of analysis (Doise & Valentim, 2015). Adopting a comprehensive approach that acknowledges the interactions between these processes and articulation of the various levels of analysis can provide a more complex but accurate and nuanced understanding of human development.

2. Integration of timescales: Understand that these processes operate on different timescales, with microgenesis focusing on immediate changes, ontogenesis on life-long development and sociogenesis on historical and cultural changes. By integrating these timescales we can render intelligible the influence of short-term events on long-term development and how social and cultural factors impact individual growth over time.
3. Interdisciplinary approach: Since these processes involve various aspects of human development, it is essential to adopt an interdisciplinary approach that draws on insights and methodology from psychology, sociology, history, politics, anthropology and other related fields. This enables researchers to explore the interconnections between individual, social and cultural factors and understand how they jointly contribute to human development.
4. Contextualising development: Acknowledge that individual development is shaped by the specific social, cultural and historical contexts in which it occurs. By examining the sociogenesis of psychological phenomena, researchers can better understand how individual development is influenced by broader social and cultural factors, and how these factors change over time.
5. Mutual influence: Recognise that microgenesis, ontogenesis and sociogenesis do not occur in isolation but are mutually influential processes. For example, moment-to-moment experiences (microgenesis) can shape long-term development (ontogenesis) and are influenced by historical changes (sociogenesis). Sociogenetic changes can also lead to the setting up of new institutions and infrastructures that support new significant structures (e.g. the Home for Co-operation in Cyprus). Understanding the dynamic interactions between these processes in both directions of change (Psaltis, 2015) can help researchers to develop more comprehensive models of human development.

To make this articulation possible in the case of the study of these processes in Cyprus, we need to apply a mixed-methods approach that would entail: (1) the collection of representative samples from both communities of Cyprus in different periods of time and of people covering a wide age range; (2) qualitative data from focus groups discussions, interviews collection and analysis of policy documents from different periods and different age groups at different points in time; 3) identifying new ways to understand complex phenomena of change and transformation such as agent-based modelling and hierarchical age-period-cohort (HAPC) analysis.

In the rest of this final empirical chapter I will show how two methodological approaches, one qualitative and one quantitative, can be applied in the Cyprus case to facilitate disentangling and articulating microgenesis, ontogenesis and sociogenesis.

A Case Example: Some Autobiographical Notes

I was born in 1973 in Varosha, the new city next to historic Famagusta, now occupied by the Turkish army, which has been turned into a military zone. Given that nobody has been allowed to inhabit the town after 1974, it turned into a 'ghost city' filled with derelict buildings. I was one of the 160,000 internally displaced persons. My mother and father, after months of temporary refuge at various relatives' homes, settled down in rented accommodations, in Derynia, a village next to old Famagusta and Varosha, that also happened to be my father's birthplace. Up to the fifth grade of the elementary school, I attended the village school. I still remember some of the financial hardships of the early years after 1974, and I remember my teachers promulgating the discourse of the barbaric Turkish invasion and its consequences, with our duty being to join the in-group collective struggle for justice. I still remember my father waiting by the radio to hear news of the outcomes of the negotiations to solve the Cyprus problem, and the key to our apartment in Varosha that my mother kept in the drawer next to her bed – experiences very common to many internally displaced GCs, as we know from other research (Loizos, 1981; Zetter, 1998).

One of my first memories from living in Derynia is the image in Figure 5.3 that I would see day in and day out for the first 12 years of my life from the balcony of our rented house, sometimes accompanied by my parents' commentary: 'You see this building? This is our house.' 'We were living in that apartment.'

This image was often accompanied by a feeling of loss and sorrow, mixed with resentment towards the Turkish army that occupied my house

Figure 5.3 A view of Varosha from Derynia.
Source: Famagusta. View Point from Deryneia. Photographer: Evgeniy Isaev, https://flickrcom/photos/43257267@N08/14083634076.

and a strong will to return. In the work of Ernst Boesch (2001) and his symbolic action theory we find the distinction between 'myths and fantasms' which is relevant here. Myths are the widely held and shared beliefs in a community. In my case, the widely shared myth would be that of the 'barbaric invasion of expansionist Turkey' and the duty of a collective struggle 'for return' and 'not forgetting'. Fantasms are the individualised versions of myths that make sense to one particular individual. The image in Figure 5.3 seems to have for me the importance of a 'fantasm' that haunts my life since my early childhood, giving orientation and a goal towards striving to return to Varosha. So, this is a fantasm yearning for a fantasm/ghost town. The image in Figure 5.4 captures the sentiment completely. In one of the visits to Varosha a GC internally displaced person left this note on the fence: 'I LEFT MY SOUL INSIDE. OPEN UP!'

The sign next to the note on the fence states (in Greek, so the GCs would definitely get the meaning): 'PROHIBITED AREA, ENTRANCE PROHIBITED', which is an example of what Jaan Valsiner (2021) refers to as a hypergeneralised sign. The image is interesting for its contrast of the two signs. Both are hypergeneralised forms that point to different futures

Figure 5.4 A written note left on the fence of Varosha by a Greek Cypriot Varoshiotis.

for the town. The handwritten one on the left points towards return and the revival of the city while the one on the right points towards the negation of this return in a fine example of what Valsiner described as a demonogenetic representation. It creates the demon of the enemy that scares away GC internally displaced persons from Famagusta, like the scarecrow put in place to keep the birds away. Another variation of this can be found in Figure 5.5, in which the scare function is even clearer.

Another of my first memories was visits to my grandparents' house in Strovilia, a very small 'enclaved' village, mostly comprised of a few families, relatives of my father, situated between Varosha and the UK military base of Ayios Nikolaos. Incidentally, this small village figures in the UN Secretary-General (UNSG) reports on the Cyprus issue, every six months, since 2000 when the Turkish troops moved their control a short distance from Varosha up to the UK bases.[3] This action violated a unique status quo, a no man's land; before that, a small strip of land in Strovilia was patrolled by two soldiers (a UN peacekeeper and a TC soldier), and my relatives would be obliged every Sunday to confirm, in writing, their presence in the village. My first few visits to this place were a source of

[3] The UN Security Council resolution 685 in 2020 (which can be accessed at: www.securitycouncilreport.org/atf/cf/%7B65BFCF9B-6D27-4E9C-8CD3-CF6E4FF96FF9%7D/s_2020_685.pdf) noted, 'Particular reference should be made to the violations in the Strovilia enclave which characteristically manifest the Turkish policy to flagrantly disregard repeated calls of the UN Security Council to lift the continuous military status quo violation, in place since 2000. These violations not only persist but they have been exacerbated with additional ones, including through actions aimed at undermining the ability of UNFICYP to exercise its tasks.'

Figure 5.5 A military sign by the Turkish army on the fence of Varosha. (Photo taken by Gerard Duveen on a visit to Cyprus in 2007.)

horror: I was terrified of the Turkish soldier who patrolled there and resided in a small house, that belonged to my aunt, together with the UN soldier. I remember, years later, to have repeating nightmares until my early adulthood: me being chased by Turkish soldiers in that strip of land and/or the Turkish army moving further forward to kill the whole family, myself included.

A year after 1974, my father was offered a job as a secondary school art teacher. From then on, things started improving financially for our family. My mother stayed at home looking after my sister (born in 1977) and myself. In 1983, my father asked for a transfer to the divided capital, Nicosia, thinking that my sister and I would get better educational opportunities. He was instead transferred to Larnaca, a smaller town; we stayed there for three years. In 1986, the whole family finally moved to Nicosia. Both my sister and I excelled in school.

Just before the end of my studies at the lyceum there were big anti-occupation rallies organised by students, and I remember myself taking part. A student who had lowered a Turkish flag from a poll in Nicosia was celebrated in the press as a new hero from our youth and attracted the admiration of many students.

Becoming an educator back then was considered an excellent career for 'good students', as it was a well -paid, secure, civil servant's job. Hence, I focused on successfully passing the prestigious entry exams that secured me a position at the Pedagogical Academy of Cyprus (a three-year teacher training college). My studies there did not lead to any change of views regarding the bad Turks and certainly did not fill my ignorance gaps regarding TCs, as we never discussed different perspectives nor were able to meet any TCs. Nevertheless, I did start developing an interest in psychology in my studies there.

In terms of my political views, I supported the left-wing patriotic party EDEK (socialists), as I was influenced by my father who was a very active member of the central committee of the party until 1990 and a bold trade-unionist for the same party in his work sphere; his strong involvement meant my attendance of the party's rallies and anti-occupation marches from a young age. If anything, my political stance, whilst a student at that Pedagogical Academy, had become even more negative towards any solution other than that of a unitary state, with Turkish troops out of Cyprus. I do recall an essay of mine (thought at that time to be a valid research piece, even though my only source of reference was an encyclopedia that I had found on my father's bookshelf), 'evidencing' that federation as a political system did not work in any country, therefore it would be catastrophic if applied to the Cyprus context. In hindsight, the literature review I had provided would have been unacceptable by any academic standard. In my defence, the library of the Pedagogical Academy was an outdated one (called Severios, it also served the historical school Pankyprion, a centre of Hellenic education in Cyprus and with a history of participation in the struggle of EOKA for reunification with Greece) that mainly had old books coming from Greece and not much in terms of current literature.[4] We also did not have the internet back then. However, I got a very good grade for this 'research piece' and warm, public congratulations by our geography teacher, who had made it clear, throughout his teachings, that he was against BBF. I was a thorough opponent of any bicommunal efforts to solve the Cyprus problem. I recollect lashing out at a colleague who revealed that he had contacts with TCs; I accused him of undermining the patriotic fighting spirit that was needed for the anti-

[4] My first encounter with current English-language psychology literature was when I took a summer job with a good friend during my studies at the Pedagogical Academy at the newly established University of Cyprus unpacking the crates of books newly bought by the library. I recall with embarrassment that once, some good people working at the library at the time – who are my colleagues today – found me sleeping, exhausted, in a pile of books.

occupation struggle. It is now obvious that I was then trapped in a mindset that considered contacts with the 'other' as signs of treason and obstructive to the collective struggle that 'we' GCs had to sustain to end occupation by Turkey. Back then, I was convinced that the Cyprus problem was 'solely an issue of invasion and occupation by Turkey', an oft-cited mantra of the then-EDEK leader, Vassos Lyssarides.

In 1993, I was in my 20s, a graduate of the Cyprus Pedagogical Academy and a qualified primary school teacher. Immediately, I went to complete my military service that I have left unfinished in 1990. During the two years of my military service, I would, every morning, listen to an ultra-nationalist radio show, feeling exhilarated by the radio producer's militaristic language, extremely nationalistic comments, accusations against expansionist Turkey and his full support of the Kurdish resistance, that last one on the basis of a rationale that 'the enemy of my enemy is my friend'.

I also applied to become a military officer. I passed the written exams (IQ test and essay writing) and athletic performance with flying colours. I also had to go through an oral examination/interview, during which the strength of my patriotic feelings was evaluated by (1) how hard I hit my foot down when saluting the officers and (2) my capacity to recite from memory a poem about the Greek revolution of 1821. Having passed all tests, I was sent to Sparta, Greece, to train as a cadet.

The Greek military officers treated us Cypriots as Greeks from the periphery of Greece. A particular officer who got the impression that I was not religious enough turned my time there into a living nightmare, with hazing and bullying. The reason? I laughed and said that I am not a real 'psaltis' when, after reading my surname, the officer wanted to assign me to sing psalms in the church every Sunday (*psaltis* is the Greek word for a chanter of religious hymns).

I finished my military service in 1995 with a sense of revulsion for the army and the military mindset, which I considered a degrading experience of wasted human potential and misspent youth. Entering a new chapter in my life, that of a teacher, was a step I anticipated with great joy and relief.

My transition to working as an elementary school teacher could be described as being turned into an active agent of the advancement of the Den Xechno philosophy. I now remember the one-sided kind of history and religious education I taught my students. I was usually following the textbook for each new course and rarely looked for other sources with which to teach my students. I was not even reflective on the propagandistic nature of it. At rare moments of actual reflection I would explain it away by reasoning that we needed to defend ourselves from all-powerful Turkey, so patriotic feelings had to be created in children as a form of resistance to Turkey.

In 1996, I was fortunate enough to take some extra courses for a year at the Pedagogical Institute of Cyprus by academics of the newly founded University of Cyprus as part of a special course that would equalize the three-year pedagogical academy degree with a four-year BA in Education. The influence of Professor Andreas Demetriou, a developmental psychologist (and later colleague and minister in President Demetris Christofias's cabinet in 2008), was decisive as it furthered my interest in psychology and helped me to grasp what academic rigour and proper research should be. He also sparked my interest in Piaget and cognitive development to the extent that I decided to obtain a second BA in psychology. I prepared again for the national entry exams. Interestingly, my grade in history in the entry exams in 1996 was much lower than in my entry exam in 1990. The reason for this probably was that this time I did not just recite the pages of the textbook and instead tried to elaborate and deepen my thinking. Despite lower scores, I was able to gain admission at the psychology department of Panteion University in Athens. This department had a strong orientation towards social psychology, and in one of my courses I discovered the work of Serge Moscovici and the social Genevans (Doise & Mugny, 1984) in a Greek translation in a central bookstore in Athens. Having read that book, I knew that this line of research was what I wanted to study for my BA thesis, which I completed in 1999 by reviewing this tradition of research on social interaction and cognitive development.

As soon as I returned to Cyprus, I was seconded for a year at the Educational Psychology Service of the Ministry of Education and Culture, and in the same year I applied for an MSc in Educational Psychology at University College London (UCL). In the spring of 2000, I was invited to interview at UCL as part of their MSc entry processes. Given my plans to visit London, I thought of exploring other possibilities with universities that could accommodate my research interest in the role of social interaction in cognitive development. Searching the internet (dial-up connection just recently made its appearance in Cyprus at that point), I came across the work of Duveen at University of Cambridge, who seemed to be one of the few academics in the United Kingdom who was studying social representations and cognitive development that were my main research interests. I sent him an email, saying I would be traveling to the UK soon and asking for a meeting to discuss a possible collaboration.

Being the generous soul that he always was, Duveen replied that he would be happy for us to meet and arranged a meeting at his Corpus Christi College office. When we met, we discussed his work with Patrick Leman, and he said he would be interested to expand that line of research. Upon my professing an enthusiastit interest in this kind of work, Duveen said he would be happy for us to work together if I wanted to apply for an MPhil at Cambridge, which I did. Some months later I was accepted at both UCL and Cambridge and ultimately decided to go to Cambridge for an MPhil in Social and Developmental Psychology. While in the programme, I worked on an empirical investigation of the representations of gender in social interaction around the Piagetian task of the conservation of liquids, which was later published as Psaltis and Duveen (2006), and overall did well enough to have decided to continue towards a PhD.

Turning Points in Life

Around that time my friendship with Chara Makriyianni, a classmate from the Pedagogical Academy, has turned into a love affair. I was 27 years old. Chara already completed a Master in History Education with Peter Lee at the Institute of Education in London, and she was quite critical of the propagandistic nature of our history teaching in Cyprus. I remember in our first discussions we had disagreements about what the aims of history teaching should be, but once I started reading materials she suggested (and especially the connections of the work of Peter Lee with Piaget that made the epistemological foundations of new history much clearer in my eyes), I started revising my old views.

In the same year I had my first contact with TCs. My best friend arranged for me and Chara to go to a bicommunal workshop in Pyla/Pile, the only mixed village of Cyprus in the Larnaca district, facilitated by Nicos Anastasiou. There we completed an exercise of positioning landmark historical events on a 'history ladder' that represented the history of Cyprus. I remember how surprised I was to see how different points were important in the narrations of the two communities and how different a meaning we attributed to events that we all identified on the timeline.

My studies in social developmental psychology at Cambridge helped me to become more critical of our situation in Cyprus and of our educational system. I remember spending many hours in the Cambridge Library locating books on Cyprus history from Turkish, TC and UK perspectives that I never knew existed. In 2002, Chara joined me at Cambridge when she was accepted into a PhD programme at the Department of Education with Professor Peter Cunningham, an expert on oral history. Cohabitation with Chara in Cambridge became a constant source of new readings and discussions for me about nationalism and history, the use and abuse of history and opportunities to attend conferences of the NGO EuroClio where the abuse of history in other parts of the world became very clear in my mind. At one of these meetings Chara discussed with Joke van der Leeuw-Roord, then president of EUROCLIO, the idea of setting up a bicommunal NGO about history teaching in Cyprus, something that would be made possible by the recent opening of the checkpoints in Cyprus. A few months after the opening of the checkpoints in April 2023 we, along with other educator friends, located TC teachers who were interested in the idea. This was not difficult, since TC teachers, along with other trade unionists, had a reputation of always being at the forefront of collective action to reunite Cyprus. This led to the birth of the Association for Historical Dialogue and Research (AHDR), the first bicommunal NGO dealing with the sensitive issue of history teaching in a post-conflict and divided Cyprus. AHDR soon became the local partner of the CoE, and with their support, a number of training seminars for teachers from both communities on history teaching were organised every year. Nationalist press, the media and some right-wing and so-called centre parties trade unionists attacked the work of AHDR from the beginning, and although I understood why they did it, the organised nature of these attacks also made me want to study more institutionalised propaganda in the Cypriot press, which I recently was able to do with a colleague from media studies (Avraamidou & Psaltis, 2019).

Given my new reflective stance on nationalism and my study of intergroup relations, once I finished my PhD in 2005, I looked for a way to work in the United Kingdom in a relevant field until my partner would also finish her studies. The perfect opportunity appeared after a discussion with Miles Hewstone at Oxford when he organised a European Association of Social Psychology (EASP) meeting on minority influence in 2003 that I attended; we were approved, for a research grant to study intergroup contact between GCs and TCs in Cyprus, so I started working at the Oxford Centre for the Study of Intergroup Contact with Miles.

Since 2006, I got involved in the study of intergroup relations between GCs and TCs from a social psychological perspective. I remember how many of my stereotypes for TCs and Turks were deconstructed along the way. I now have many TC friends and research partners. A year later I was appointed as a lecturer of social psychology at the University of Cyprus.

I was the first GC social psychologist to work in an academic institution in Cyprus. In 2007, I took the initiative to establish the first Association of Social Psychologists in Cyprus on an intercommunal basis, and in 2008 it was officially registered.

That same year we had presidential elections that brought leftist Dimitris Christofias to power, and my colleague Professor Andreas Demetriou was appointed Minister of Education. Demetriou attempted a positive pro-reconciliation educational reform that promoted a culture of co-operation and a policy of contact between students and teachers from both communities. As we were colleagues with Andreas, I had communicated to him several of my research findings about the positive role of contact in prejudice reduction and suggestions by AHDR about history teaching. Members of AHDR during his term in the ministry were seconded in the Pedagogical Institute for the writing of new history textbooks. AHDR also had the support of the government in the establishment of the Home for Co-operation in the UN buffer zone in Nicosia, a bicommunal educational centre for NGOs supported by the European Economic Area (EEA) and Norway Grants financial mechanism. The Home for Co-operation opened its doors on 6 May 2011, with an opening ceremony bringing together the leaders of the GC and TC communities, representatives of civil society and dignitaries from around Europe, including the CoE, Norway, Sweden, Switzerland and the Netherlands, who supported its establishment. As part of a four-day celebration marking the inauguration of the Home, I organised a scientific symposium with the title 'Human and Societal Development: The role of Social Relationships' on 9 May 2011. In my talk I explained how Piagetian ideas on social relations of co-operation inspired the establishment and naming of the Home for Co-operation. The talks of the symposium were later published as an edited volume with Alex Gillespie and Anne-Nelly Perret Clermont (Psaltis et al., 2017). The photo in Figure 5.6 is from the conference.

Unfortunately, Demetriou's positive policy proposals failed to be fully implemented due to resistance from the church, organised teacher trade unions and teachers in the classroom, but they were nevertheless the first seeds of some positive ideas around contact that would materialise later. AHDR and the Home for Co-operation flourished and became internationally recognised. A testament to this is the three prestigious international awards received: Europa Nostra 2014 Conservation Award, celebrating and aiming to promote excellence in cultural heritage work; Max Van der Stoel Award in 2016 in recognition of extraordinary achievements aimed at improving the position of national minorities in the area of

Figure 5.6 The speakers at the inauguration symposium at the Home for Co-operation.

the Organization for Security and Co-operation in Europe (OSCE); and the 2018 Seán MacBride Peace Prize in recognition of its outstanding work for peace, disarmament and human rights. The short documentary produced by OSCE about AHDR and the Home for Co-operation provides a nice summary of this story.[5]

In 2009, Chara and I were married and our son was born. In the same year I was invited to join the Greek Turkish Forum (GTF),[6] which is a 1.5-track[7] diplomacy initiative to discuss informally bilateral political issues (e.g. the Aegean contestation), established in 1998 right after Greece and Turkey came to the brink of war (see Ker-Lindsay, 2016 for the history of GTF), in order to facilitate dialogue between Greece and

[5] www.youtube.com/watch?v=bak_7zkdyXs.

[6] Several accounts of the history of GTF establishment can be found at: https://greekturkishforum.com/.

[7] Track II diplomacy is the practice of non-state actors using conflict resolution tactics (such as workshops and conversations) to create non-governmental, informal and unofficial contacts in order to improve communication and understanding between citizens. Track 1.5 denotes communication with decision-makers and leaders of the conflicting sides in addition to Track II processes.

Turkey and promote confidence-building measures (CBMs). The GTF brought together politicians who did not hold a formal position in the administration, retired senior diplomats and military officers, business leaders and other figures from the media and academia. After 2002, GTF took more interest in the Cyprus issue as one of the main issues poisoning Greek–Turkish relations, and in 2006 there was a Cyprus chapter established with a GC and a TC team. I was one of the first GC members invited as an academic in 2008, and in 2014 I became the coordinator of the GC team of the Cyprus chapter of GTF. We had many meetings since 2008 in Athens, Istanbul, Ankara and Nicosia, many times with the acting ministers of foreign affairs of the two countries (Greece and Turkey) and the leaders of the two communities in Cyprus. In this context I was fortunate to understand the core issues of the tensions between Greece and Turkey and the core political underpinnings of the Cyprus issue. Above all, I understood the regional dynamics of the Cyprus issue and the way political developments, election cycles and economic developments influence the agenda of discussions. I also realised that trust at the interpersonal level and co-operative relations can facilitate the production of valuable ideas for confidence-building measures that can be implemented by politicians if they are convinced of their value when they have the support of both communities of Cyprus as well as of Greece and Turkey.

My son is 15 years old when these words are written in 2024. I rarely discuss my home in Varosha with him, but whenever we find ourselves in the southern part of Famagusta during a summer holiday, I do point out that somewhere in the buildings of the 'ghost town' is the apartment we left in 1974. I remember my surprise when my son came up to me when he was four years old and said: 'Dad, Turks are bad.' I asked, 'Why do you say that, son?' 'Because my grandmother said that Turks came and took our houses back in 1974,' was the reply. That incident made me realise how early in life children internalise that sense of loss described as the figurative nucleus of the representation of the Cyprus problem discussed in Chapter 3.

When we had the chance to visit Varoshia as a family with my parents and located our apartment in 2022 after the opening of a small part of Varosha to visits, my son found the experience distressing and said he did not want to do it again. He did, however, visit the Home for Co-operation many times with me and Chara from his early childhood and had the chance to meet many of our TC friends and their children. He also took part in a bicommunal meeting at the Home for Co-operation in the UN buffer zone in Nicosia organised specifically for children. This was done with the support of the Ministry of Education. A more permanent contact scheme during school time in the mornings was made possible later in 2017 as an initiative by the newly established Bicommmunal Technical Committee of education as part of the IMAGINE programme which by 2020 had touched the lives of more than 5,000 students.[8]

In the past few years, the work of the committee has been slowed by a number of developments: the Crans Montana failure in July 2017; the COVID-19 pandemic in 2020 that led to the closing of a number of checkpoints; and in the same year a change of leadership in the north that brought nationalist Ersin Tatar as head of government for the TC community, with a subsequent change in TC policy from supporting BBF by Akinci to support of a two-state solution in Cyprus and a change in the number of the TC members of the committee (former members of AHDR and other pro-reconciliation academics and supporters of BBF). The committee nevertheless still functions, but the TC side unilaterally decided to end the IMAGINE programme. One does not need a lot of imagination to understand that this programme goes against the separatist views of those in power in the TC community.

This autobiographical analysis could be used both as a window into personal experience and the way personal meanings and fantasms (Boesch, 2001) orient people to certain actions. They are also invaluable in rendering intelligible intergenerational influences and the slow but crucial process of ideological conversion. In the story told in the previous sections one can identify various meetings with alterity that introduced doubt in my subjectivity as suggested by Duveen (2002). As suggested by Kadianaki and Gillespie (2015), the meeting with alterity can take various forms: (1) rupture with the physical world (alterity in action), (2) social contact (alterity in other), (3) movement between contexts (alterity in self) and (4) semiotic dialogicality (alterity in the structure of knowledge). In my case the feeling of loss of our house in Varosha was formed early on through processes of intergenerational transmission and was reinforced by the educational policy of Den Xechno. Until my attendance of my first bicommunal workshop in Pyla and the exercise on the history line I had developed good defensive mechanisms (semantic barriers) to downplay alternative representations of the Cyprus issue as unpatriotic, still under the spell of an ethos of conflict. Meeting TCs for the first time and encountering their own perspective (alterity in other) were the beginning

[8] www.ahdr.info/peace-education/58-education-for-a-culture-of-peace-imagine.

of a life-changing experience. Then came meetings with other alterities (my wife, professors, colleagues, etc.). Moving abroad to study further changed the social context for me by introducing me to networks of people with an outsider's perspective on the Cyprus problem. Changing my role from student to university teacher also allowed me to meet alterity in self. My readings about the Cyprus problem from various perspectives increased my multiperspectivity and introduced alterity in my structure of knowledge. Finally, my visits to the other side of the island after 2003 offered plenty of opportunities for rupture with the physical world (alterity in action) that made me deconstruct many misconceptions about the everyday life of the other community.

This narrative analysis can also help in transitioning into a more quantitative analysis that more systematically examines the interaction of age with historical events. Going back in time, compared to my autobiographical note, let us take, for example, the birth cohort of my parents to understand at what age they experienced some important historical turning points. For the quantitative analysis that will follow in this chapter I have created 5-year-band birth cohorts as shown in Table 5.1. Following this

Table 5.1 *The 14 cohorts available in data collected in 2007, 2010 and 2017 in the two communities of Cyprus.*

14	Born 1995–1999
13	Born1990–1994
12	Born 1985–1989
11	Born 1980–1984
10	Born 1975–1979
9	Born 1970–1974
8	Born 1965–1969
7	Born 1960–1964
6	Born 1955–1959
5	Born 1950–1954
4	Born 1945–1949
3	Born 1940–1944
2	Born 1935–1939
1	Born 1930–1934

NB. Shades connect to Table 5.2 in page 176

categorisation, I fall into cohort 9 and my parents fall into cohort 3, as they were born in 1944.

A Reconstruction of Important Historical Events for the Cohort Born 1940–1944

According to renowned anthropologist Peter Loizos, the first half of the 20th century in Cyprus was a period of rapid sociodemographic and structural changes (Loizos, 1975, 2001). Whilst in 1878, 9 out of every 10 Cypriots was a villager, in 1955 this figure was closer to 6 out of every 10. In the same period the population increased two and a half times, from 186,000 to more than 450,000. In the meantime, while 18.6% of Cypriots aged 15–24 were illiterate in 1931, this figure fell to just 5.9% by 1946. In his reflection on this period Loizos is especially concerned with transformation of relations of authority, which, according to him, are to be found 'embedded in central political, economic, religious and social ideas about relations of all kinds-relations between people and their gods, between men and women, between parents and children, masters and servants, employers and employees, rich and poor, between racial and cultural groups, ideas about justice, property and marriage' (Loizos, 2001, p. 128). His words describe this period eloquently:

> So a series of challenges take place within our period. The British displaced the Ottomans and challenged the church. Sons challenge fathers. Workers, challenge employers. Communism and socialism challenge the church and its traditional leadership in both ethical and political life. Women challenge men, at first by their educational and occupational achievements, then by direct confrontation. But later as militant Greek Cypriots came to challenge the legitimacy of the British colonial rule, then those schoolgirls mobilized by EOKA came to confront men of the British security forces. (Loizos, 2001, p. 138)

Of course, these indications of challenging authority were only the first signs of challenging a traditional culture of honour and shame characteristic of Mediterranean societies described through ethnographic work in the Greek Cypriot Pitsilia Highland village of Alona in 1954 by Peristiany (1966). This work was foundational in the field, as it was among the first to systematically examine how honour and shame function as central social values that shape interpersonal relationships, gender roles, social structure and community dynamics in these societies.

To return to significant historical periods in the life of the cohort born 1940–1944, their childhood would coincide with the Second World War.

Growing up under the British colonial rule, the sociopolitical atmosphere of the island would be charged, with the undercurrents of nationalistic sentiments for enosis (union of Cyprus with Greece) growing stronger. The left–right ideological polarisation would be a defining period in their childhood years, charting trajectories and networks of social interactions of socialisation that could involve closer or more distant relationships with members of the other community. Leftists organised under AKEL and youth or worker organisations in the GC community would be often persecuted or threatened by EOKA members in their teen years, although they would tend to have closer and better relations with TCs. Youth of more centrist and leftist political views (although not AKEL members) would tend to have more ambivalent feelings towards the EOKA struggle given the dominant position of the church and the overwhelming majority of GCs taking active part in religious practices at the time. On the whole, the GC perspective towards TCs during this time would be of a marginal minority and financially worse-off community that should have no say in what GCs as the majority considered their legitimate national aspirations. Another defining experience of these years would be for those who lived in mixed villages who had the chance to establish co-operative and everyday relationships with members of the other community versus areas with no mixed population where opportunities for intergroup contact and co-operation would be much more rare.

Adolescence (1950s): Their teenage years would be marked by the armed struggle of EOKA for the union of Cyprus with Greece. This period would shape their understanding of nationalistic aspirations and the reactions from the British colonial power. Right-wing EOKA supporters would have the chance to be actively involved in the enosis struggle of GCs, but leftists would not. In the TC community there was a much wider acceptance of the TC resistance organisation Türk Mukavemet Teşkilatı (TMT) as a legitimate resistance organisation that could block GC efforts for enosis (Ktoris, 2013).

Early Adulthood (1960s): The establishment of the Republic of Cyprus in 1960 would be a significant milestone. The subsequent intercommunal clashes would further shape their perceptions and experiences. The propaganda on both sides generated an intense enmity between the members of the two communities and encouraged a number of violent acts across the island. In coffee shops around the island, both GCs and TCs used exaggerated talk, echoing the extremist language and propaganda used in most of the press of both communities (Packard, 2008). Children in the mixed villages who had once played together now fought, taunted and threw stones at each other if they met by chance in the street (Patrick, 1976a). The educational systems of the two communities in the period continued to be separate, since the 1960 constitution gave responsibility for education to the two communal chambers. The orientation of both systems in the period 1960–1974 continued to be towards their corresponding and opposed national aims of enosis and taksim (Pavlou, 2015), respectively, with most textbooks imported by the so-called motherlands (Greece and Turkey) that were seen as the 'national centre'.

However, not all of the population was polarised, nor did the entirety of it blindly followed the extremist groups. Some accounts report that GC villagers were often suspicious and wary of the old EOKA network, as it was claimed that they had connections with the criminal underclass (Packard, 2008, p. 90). Similarly, not all TCs blindly followed TMT, as some accounts report that TC leaders in some villages forbade any friendly relations with the GCs, and any TCs caught being friendly with GCs or walking or enjoying themselves in Greek areas were penalised with heavy fines, imprisonment or even whipping (see also Patrick, 1976a, p. 133; Drousiotis, 2005). There are also accounts that report that TCs in mixed villages were not allowed by their leaders to use the postal services of the government, as this was considered not only to promote fraternisation with the other community but also to be a sign of recognition (Patrick, 1976a, p. 112) of the GC-run state. Lastly, there is evidence that in some cases in late 1964, local paramilitary commanders resorted to armed threats, and even to murder, in order to keep TC refugees from moving into areas controlled by the Cyprus government (Patrick, 1976b, p. 345).

As a result of the intercommunal violence, many TCs were forced (either by TMT members or simply due to insecurity) to leave their homes in mixed villages and sought refuge in enclaves. These enclaves were predominantly TC areas where they could seek protection from the violence and live in relative safety. The creation of enclaves essentially led to a physical division of the island along ethnic lines, which would later be solidified by the Turkish invasion in 1974. There were many enclaves across the island, ranging in size from small villages to large urban centers. Some of the larger enclaves included Famagusta, Lefka and the Bogaz area between Kyrenia and Nicosia. The number and size of enclaves changed over time as the situation on the ground evolved. These enclaves functioned as states within states for about 10 years until the war of 1974, with internal organisation and economy supported by Turkey and minimal to no contact between members of the two communities, since they were guarded by TC fighters and GCs could not enter these areas. Many of the TCs who spent their early adulthood in enclaves would be deprived of opportunities to study, as they took fighter duties with TMT, although some would get the chance after 1968 to study in Turkey – an important socialisation experience, since many of them would be socialised in the leftist circles of Istanbul in the period around 1968 (Moudouros, 2020), a period of progressive student activism that was even more strongly felt in other European countries at the same time. GC students who went to study abroad usually report the 1968 events as important political socialisation years, especially in the United Kingdom and Czechoslovakia (where leftist students would also often go to study supported by AKEL in Cyprus). The youth from AKEL families would also often go to study in the USSR on scholarships, but the experience of the USSR was different, to say the least, from the student movement in Western Europe.

Middle Age (1970s–1980s): The 1974 Turkish invasion/intervention would occur when they were 30–34 years old. Like the previous cohort, many would likely have participated in the conflict, and about 30% would experience displacement. This would be a challenging period, especially for those with young families or those who had recently settled into their homes. The 1974 events would be collectively experienced by GCs as a collective trauma but by TCs with an elation of almost apocalyptic proportions because it ended the more difficult 10 years of their lives in enclaves (Bryant, 2010).

Later Life (1990s–2000s): As they transitioned into their older age, the unresolved nature of the Cyprus issue and a history of repeated failures to solve the problem that was becoming protracted would be a significant concern. The opening of the checkpoints in 2003 and Cyprus's EU accession in 2004 are the events they would witness with a lifetime of experience and understanding. Most GCs and TCs of this birth cohort would take advantage of the newfound opportunity in 2003 to revisit their properties and homes that they left during their early 30s. Those that used to live in mixed villages would get the chance to see childhood and adolescent friends from the other community with whom they probably lost contact since 1963 when they were 19–23 years old. At the same time it was reported that some people with direct involvement in paramilitary organisations and intercommunal conflict would avoid crossing to the other side due to fear of retaliations more than 40 years after the 'troubles'.

Articulating Microgenesis, Ontogenesis and Sociogenesis through Disentangling Age, Period and Cohort Effects

Three possible effects are at play when data are collected from participants of different age cohorts at different points in time: age, period and cohort. The three variables relate to one another in an exact linear fashion. For example, for each age and calendar year there is a unique birth cohort. This causes the well-known identification problem in modelling. However, the HAPC modelling framework does not incur the identification problem because the three effects are not assumed to be linear and additive at the same level of analysis. HAPC models can capture the contextual effects of periods and cohorts and thus stimulate new conceptualisations of processes of change.

The repeated cross-sectional design (representative sample surveys taking place in different periods with different participants but with same questionnaire such as ESS or WVS) is in fact a multilevel design in which individual-level observations are nested in, and cross-classified simultaneously by, the two higher-level social contexts defined by time period of data collection and birth cohort. Global descriptions of generations and cohorts like, for example, the Millennials, Baby Boomers and the Silent Generation make no sense in the context of Cyprus, since generations are never discussed publicly in this context. However, the original discussion by Mannheim that we covered in Chapter 3 on generations is certainly relevant in this context, especially his insight that big events like war can be a defining moment of rapture that could create groupings of people that self-identify with these categories (e.g. born before or after 1974). A more detailed analysis that would allow for the detection of aggregate generational differences between the various cohorts described in Table 5.1, and specifically comparisons of all other cohorts with the one described in detail earlier (1940–1944), follows below. The data used for the analysis that follows come from three large-N bicommunal representative sample surveys of data collected in 2007, 2010 and 2017. The method was multistage stratified sampling, and more details on the methodology can be found in published work (Psaltis, 2012a), OSF (open-source cloud-based project management platform)[9] and Appendix B, Table B.1.

[9] Both methodology and data from 2017 can be found at OSF at: https://osf.io/5rj3u/wiki/home/.

Disentangling Age, Period and Cohort Effects

The analytical strategy followed here was to test various HAPC models predicting in turn: Prejudice, Trust, Acceptance of Bizonal Bicommunal Federation as the position agreed by leaders since 1977 and Readiness for renewed Cohabitation. Each cohort (different shades in Table 5.1 above) can be located in the accounting model below shown in Table 5.2. The table below presents the mean level of prejudice towards the other community measured with the feeling thermometer ranging from 0 (cold/very negative) to 100 (warm/very positive). A score of 50 indicates neutral feelings.

For each dependent variable six models in total were tested. The first one was a basic model including as predictors only the following demographic variables: Age, Age Squared, Education, Living in Urban or Rural area, IDP status (either first or later generation IDP), Gender, Period of Data Collection (2007, 2010 or 2017) and Recoded Birth

Table 5.2 *An account model of the scores of feelings towards the other community by different birth cohorts in the two communities of Cyprus from data collected in 2007, 2010 and 2017*

	GCs			TCs		
			Period			
Age	2007	2010	2017	2007	2010	2017
18–22	38.55	28.06	40.45	40	40.48	40.81
23–27	36.25	35.67	46.12	26.94	35.96	41.79
28–32	43.66	32.60	44.67	35.98	38.19	39.70
33–37	40.00	34.50	38.16	25.35	37.08	44.71
38–42	43.95	39.90	43.80	28.91	41.78	39.71
43–47	38.89	38.30	45.88	30.46	34.16	40.48
48–52	47.78	41.20	42.93	27.50	42.75	38.27
53–57	50.79	43.76	48.48	25.21	36.76	38.03
58–62	54.00	39.83	45.60	22.34	35.67	35.89
63–67	57.44	49.01	49.89	20.44	25.24	31.14
68–72		50.31	50.13	27.22	23.13	26.21
73–77		54.69	51.75	15.45	27.50	24.55

Cohorts. A subset of the 14 cohorts presented in the Table 5.2 that satisfied the criterion of having measurements in all three periods was used, excluding cohorts 1, 2 and 12, 13 from the analysis due to the incompleteness of data.

The second was a variation of testing the same variables with period as a fixed factor and recoded cohort as a random factor. The third was a model with the same variables but treating both period and recoded cohort as random factors as suggested by Yang and Lund (2013) in chapter 7 of their authoritative book on age, period and cohort analysis using mixed lineal models.

The fourth, fifth and sixth models tested followed the rationale of a hierarchical regression model and included all the demographic variables tested in the first three models but additionally several social psychological variables that were expected to significantly predict the outcomes. For the models predicting feelings towards the other community and intergroup trust, these were the social psychological predictors: Quantity of Contact with members of the other community, Number of Outgroup friendships, Strength of Communal Identification, Threats (Realistic and Symbolic) and Importance of Religion in their life. Contact and friendships are a good indication of what is happening at the interpersonal level of analysis, and microgenetic processes, strength of communal identification and religiosity capture to some extent the embedding of self in the collectivity and part–whole relationships and affinity to tradition, honour, and shame values and threats that are a good indicator of intergroup dynamics at the intergroup level of analysis.

For the models predicting Acceptance of BBF and Readiness for Cohabitation, two additional predictors were added: Feelings towards the other community, Trust for ordinary people from the other community. This strategy would allow the comparison of basic demographic HAPC models with the more comprehensive models so that we could establish whether any of possible Age, Period or Cohort Effects would still be significant after the inclusion of this set of social psychological variables as predictors, given our hypothesis that political decisions that could influence the restructuring of institutions would be at least partly mediated by the quality of intergroup relations.

Predicting Positive Feelings towards the Other Community

Greek Cypriot Community

From the basic model (see Table 5.3) we see that education, area of residency (urban or rural), gender, period and cohort are significant

Table 5.3 *Linear regression predicting positive feelings towards Turkish Cypriots by Greek Cypriots*

Feelings towards TCs	Coef.	St. Err.	t-value	p-value	[95% Conf	Interval]	Sig
Age	.009	.38	0.02	.981	–.74	.76	
Age squared	–.007	.01	–1.56	.120	–.016	.01	
Education: base Reads and writes	0	.	.	.	.	.	
Elementary	12.26	6.84	1.79	.073	–1.15	25.67	*
Gymnasium	13.18	6.94	1.90	.058	–.43	26.80	*
Lyceum	14.87	6.83	2.18	.030	1.47	28.26	**
College	13.75	6.98	1.97	.049	.06	27.45	**
University	18.06	6.93	2.60	.009	4.46	31.66	***
Postgraduate (master/PhD)	20.01	7.21	2.77	.006	5.86	34.17	***
Urban	3.00	1.18	2.53	.011	.67	5.32	**
IDP	.65	1.16	0.56	.575	–1.62	2.92	
Male	2.89	1.08	2.68	.007	.77	5.01	***
Period: base 2007	0	.	.	.	.	.	
2010	–5.45	1.77	-3.08	.002	–8.92	–1.98	***
2017	1.27	4.04	0.31	.753	–6.66	9.20	
Cohort: base 1940–1944:	0	.	.	.	.	.	
1945–1949	–7.81	3.03	–2.57	.010	–13.77	–1.86	**
1950–1954	–10.50	4.51	–2.33	.020	–19.37	–1.64	**
1955–1959	–12.64	6.26	–2.02	.044	–24.93	–.35	**
1960–1964	–17.97	7.97	–2.25	.024	–33.61	–2.33	**
1965–1969	–17.94	9.79	–1.83	.067	–37.14	1.25	*
1970–1974	–19.37	11.55	–1.68	.094	–42.02	3.28	*
1975–1979	–19.70	13.35	–1.48	.140	–45.88	6.48	
1980–1984	–23.41	15.23	–1.54	.124	–53.29	6.45	
1985–1989	–19.54	17.09	–1.14	.253	–53.07	13.98	
Constant	43.05	10.61	4.06	.001	22.24	63.86	***

Mean dependent var	43.888	SD dependent var	26.535
R^2	.064	Number of obs	2361
F-test	7.213	Prob > F	.000
Akaike crit. (AIC)	22071.117	Bayesian crit. (BIC)	22203.754

*** $p < .01$, ** $p < .05$, * $p < .1$

predictors of positive feelings (reduced prejudice) towards TCs. The higher the education, the more positive the feelings towards TCs. Living in an urban area and being male are also related to more positive feelings towards the other community. There is a linear trend of cohorts so that the older the cohort, the more positive the feelings towards TCs In 2010, there was a significant negative dip in feelings towards TCs that by 2017 has recovered in levels comparable to 2007. The total variance explained by this model was adj $R^2 = 0.06$.

When the social psychological variables were entered in the model (see Table 5.4), the total variance explained by the model was significantly increased (adj $R^2 = 0.30$). Interestingly, all significant predictors in Table 5.3 except period became non-significant, which suggests that area of residency, education and cohort are having their effects on the outcome (Positive Feelings towards TCs) through the social psychological variables that are significant predictors in this model. These are out-group friendships and threats. There was also a trend for those who are more religious to be more prejudiced towards TCs.

Turkish Cypriot Community

From the basic model (see Table 5.5) we see that age squared, education and IDP status are significant predictors of feelings towards GCs. The age squared significant findings suggest that older generations of TCs were especially negative towards GCs The period effect was significant, indicating higher scores for years 2010 and 2017 compared to 2007 The total variance explained by this model was adj $R^2 = 0.06$.

When the social psychological variables were entered in the model (see Table 5.6), the total variance explained by the model was significantly increased (adj $R^2 = 0.26$). Interestingly, the effect of education became non-significant, which suggests that having a master or PhD probably makes people more resistant to succumbing to the ethos of conflict (captured by the social psychological variables). Similarly, the effect of IDP status became non-significant, which probably also suggests some mediation by social psychological variables. The effect of age squared remained close to significance and an age trend was also present. Some demographic variables also became significant, specifically Area of residency and gender. Males were more prejudiced compared to females and those living in urban areas were more prejudiced compared to those living

Table 5.4 *Linear regression predicting positive feelings towards Turkish Cypriots by Greek Cypriots (social psychological variables included)*

ThermoOG	Coef.	St. Err.	t-value	p-value	[95% Conf	Interval]	Sig
Age	.43	.33	1.31	.19	–.22	1.09	
Age squared	–.01	.01	–.96	.33	–.012	.01	
Education: base Reads and writes	0	.	.	.	.	.	
Elementary	8.04	5.93	1.36	.17	–3.58	19.67	
Gymnasium	9.46	6.01	1.57	.11	–2.33	21.26	
Lyceum	10.61	5.92	1.79	.07	–.99	22.22	*
College	9.87	6.05	1.63	.10	–1.99	21.74	
University	11.10	6.02	1.84	.06	–.70	22.90	*
Postgraduate (master/ PhD)	5.37	6.28	0.86	.39	–6.94	17.69	
Urban	.99	1.04	.95	.34	–1.05	3.03	
IDP	–.57	1.02	–.56	.57	–2.57	1.42	
Male	.07	.97	.08	.93	–1.82	1.97	
Quantity of Contact	.35	1.10	.32	.75	–1.82	2.52	
Friendships	6.68	.75	8.89	.01	5.20	8.15	***
Communal ID	–.15	.64	–.25	.80	–1.41	1.09	
Threats	–13.32	.65	–20.33	.00	–14.61	–12.04	***
Religiosity	–.87	.51	–1.71	.08	–1.88	.12	*
Period: base 2007	0	.	.	.	.	.	
2010	–8.56	1.55	–5.52	.01	–11.60	–5.52	***
2017	–4.16	3.57	–1.17	.24	–11.17	2.84	
Cohort base: 1940–1944	0	.	.	.	.	.	
1945–1949	–2.58	2.66	–.97	.33	–7.81	2.64	
1950–1954	–2.30	3.96	–.58	.56	–10.07	5.4	
1955–1959	–2.54	5.49	–.46	.64	–13.30	8.22	
1960–1964	–5.03	6.98	–.72	.47	–18.72	8.66	
1965–1969	–2.68	8.57	–.31	.75	–19.49	14.12	
1970–1974	–.29	10.11	–.03	.97	–20.12	19.53	
1975–1979	1.18	11.68	.10	.91	–21.71	24.09	
1980–1984	1.24	13.32	.09	.92	–24.88	27.37	
1985–1989	3.77	14.94	.25	.80	–25.52	33.07	
Constant	86.67	10.03	8.63	0	66.99	106.36	***
Mean dependent var	43.87		SD dependent var		26.51		
R^2	.30		Number of obs		2326		
F-test	36.28		Prob > F		.000		
Akaike crit. (AIC)	21077.03		Bayesian crit. (BIC)		21238.09		

**** $p < .01$, ** $p < .05$, * $p < .1$*

Table 5.5 *Linear regression predicting positive feelings towards Greek Cypriots by Turkish Cypriots*

ThermoOG	Coef.	St. Err.	t-value	p-value	[95% Conf	Interval]	Sig
Age	−.59	.37	−1.59	.11	−1.32	.13	
Age squared	−.010	.01	−1.93	.05	−.019	.01	*
Education: base Reads and writes	0	.	.	.	.	.	
Elementary	−2.91	4.15	−.70	.48	−11.06	5.24	
Gymnasium	−5.43	4.07	−1.33	.18	−13.43	2.56	
Lyceum	−3.42	3.99	−.86	.39	−11.24	4.40	
College	−3.72	4.24	−.88	.38	−12.04	4.59	
University	−.042	4.07	−.01	.99	−8.04	7.95	
Postgraduate (master/ PhD)	10.37	5.13	2.02	.04	.29	20.44	**
Urban	−1.05	1.08	−.98	.33	−3.17	1.06	
IDP	2.90	1.23	2.36	.01	.48	5.31	**
Male	−1.67	1.05	−.59	.11	−3.73	.39	
2007b	0	.	.	.	.	.	
2010	7.21	1.83	3.94	.01	3.62	10.80	***
2017	13.83	3.90	3.54	.01	6.17	21.50	***
Cohort base: 1940–1944	0	.	.	.	.	.	
1945–1949	−5.20	4.20	−1.24	.21	−13.45	3.04	
1950–1954	−4.63	5.43	−.85	.39	−15.30	6.02	
1955–1959	−4.30	6.93	−.62	.53	−17.91	9.30	
1960–1964	−7.35	8.67	−.85	.39	−24.36	9.65	
1965–1969	−11.16	10.39	−1.07	.28	−31.55	9.21	
1970–1974	−13.73	12.10	−1.14	.25	−37.46	9.99	
1975–1979	−12.74	13.73	−.93	.35	−39.67	14.18	
1980–1984	−17.03	15.34	−1.11	.26	−47.12	13.05	
1985–1989	−18.14	17.08	−1.06	.28	−51.65	15.36	
Constant	42.65	9.75	4.37	.01	23.52	61.77	***

Mean dependent var	34.388	SD dependent var	25.05
R^2	.06	Number of obs	2224
F-test	6.73	Prob > F	.000
Akaike crit. (AIC)	20537.95	Bayesian crit. (BIC)	20669.21

*** $p < .01$, ** $p < .05$, * $p < .1$

Table 5.6 *Linear regression predicting positive feelings towards Greek Cypriots by Turkish Cypriots (social psychological variables included)*

ThermoOG	Coef.	St. Err.	t-value	p-value	[95% Conf	Interval]	Sig
Age	–.63	.35	–1.81	.07	–1.31	.053	*
Age squared	–.01	.01	–1.92	.05	–.018	0	*
Education: base Reads and writes	0	.	.	.	.	.	
Elementary	2.95	3.93	.75	.45	–4.75	10.66	
Gymnasium	1.06	3.85	.28	.78	–6.50	8.63	
Lyceum	2.09	3.77	.55	.57	–5.30	9.49	
College	–.42	4.02	–.10	.91	–8.30	7.46	
University	3.94	3.86	1.02	.30	–3.63	11.50	
Postgraduate (master/ PhD)	6.31	4.83	1.31	.19	–3.17	15.80	
Urban	–2.00	1.01	–1.98	.04	–3.99	–.017	**
IDP	.97	1.15	.85	.39	–1.28	3.23	
Male	–2.00	.98	–2.04	.04	–3.93	–.073	**
Quantity of Contact	4.61	.73	6.31	.01	3.18	6.04	***
Friendships	5.63	.50	11.19	.01	4.64	6.61	***
Communal ID	.12	.61	.20	.84	–1.07	1.32	
Threats	–4.96	.58	–8.52	.01	–6.10	–3.82	***
Religiosity	–2.83	.44	–6.30	.01	–3.71	–1.94	***
Period: base 2007	0	.	.	.	.	.	
2010	.32	1.80	.18	.85	–3.21	3.85	
2017	4.96	3.71	1.34	.18	–2.32	12.25	
Cohort base: 1940–1944	0	.	.	.	.	.	
1945–1949	–2.85	4.03	–.71	.47	–10.76	5.05	
1950–1954	–3.10	5.14	–.60	.54	–13.18	6.98	
1955–1959	–4.66	6.54	–.71	.47	–17.49	8.16	
1960–1964	–5.90	8.17	–.72	.47	–21.94	10.13	
1965–1969	–10.56	9.78	–1.08	.28	–29.76	8.628	
1970–1974	–12.01	11.39	–1.05	.29	–34.36	10.34	
1975–1979	–12.86	12.90	–1.00	.31	–38.17	12.43	
1980–1984	–17.28	14.40	–1.20	.23	–45.53	10.96	
1985–1989	–19.46	16.04	–1.21	.22	–50.92	11.99	
Constant	54.32	10.08	5.39	.01	34.53	74.10	***

Mean dependent var	34.34	SD dependent var	25.03
R^2	.26	Number of obs	2006
F-test	26.20	Prob > F	.000
Akaike crit. (AIC)	18053.80	Bayesian crit. (BIC)	18210.71

*** $p < .01$, ** $p < .05$, * $p < .1$

in rural areas. The social psychological variables that are significant predictors in this model are quantity of contact, outgroup friendships and threats, all in the predicted direction. There was also a significant effect for religiosity, suggesting that TCs who are more religious are more prejudiced towards GCs. Finally, running an HAPC model with period and cohort as random effects revealed that age, age squared, period and cohort significant effects were present, with younger TCs and younger cohorts being related to more positive feelings towards GCs and 2010 and 2017 feelings being more positive than the 2007 feelings.

Predicting Intergroup Trust, Support for Bizonal Bicommunal Federation and Renewed Cohabitation

Applying the same analytical strategy with three additional outcome variables, the findings are generally in the same direction as the findings about feelings towards the other community reported in the previous section (Table 5.7).

Table 5.7 *Summary of findings from HAPC analysis*

	Trust (GCs)	Trust (TCs)	BBF (GCs)	BBF (TCs)	Cohab. (GCs)	Cohab. (TCs)
Age	√	ns	ns	Ns	√	ns
Age Squared	Ns	√	ns	Ns	√	√
Period	√	√	√	√	√	ns
Cohort	√	√	ns	ns	√	√
Education	ns	Ns	ns	ns	Ns	√
Urbanisation	ns	Ns	ns	√	√	ns
IDP status	ns	Ns	√	ns	Ns	ns
Male	ns	Ns	√	√	√	ns
Quantity of Contact	ns	√	ns	√	√	√
Friendships	√	√	ns	ns	Ns	ns
Communal ID	ns	Ns	ns	ns	Ns	ns
Threats	√	√	√	√	√	√
Feelings	-	-	√	√	√	√
Trust	-	-	√	√	√	√
Religiosity	√	√	ns	√	Ns	√
Adj. R^2	.22	.19	.19	.20	.49	.27

√: Significant ns: Non Significant

Predicting Trust towards TCs in the Greek Cypriot Community

From the basic model testing only the demographic variables as predictors and treating period and cohort as fixed effects, a significant finding is revealed only for education and gender. Those with a master or PhD are more trustful of TC ordinary people compared to the uneducated. Male participants are more likely to exhibit trust compared to women. The total variance explained by this model was adj $R^2 = .04$.

When the social psychological variables were entered in the model, the total variance explained by the model was significantly increased (adj $R^2 = .22$). Interestingly, age and cohort became significant with older people and those of older cohort showing significantly higher levels of trust compared to younger participants and generations. Indeed, HAPC analysis treating both period and cohort as random effects revealed that there were significant random effects for both variables and a significant effect for age. The social psychological variables that are significant predictors in this model were outgroup friendships and threats in the expected direction. Religiosity was also significant, indicating that those who considered religion important in their life were more likely to show less trust towards TCs.

Predicting Trust towards GCs in the Turkish Cypriot Community

From the basic model testing only the demographic variables as predictors and treating period and cohort as fixed effects, a significant finding is revealed for age squared, area of residency and period. Those living in urban areas showed more trust compared to those living in rural areas. The mean score for data collected in 2010 on the dependent variable was significantly higher compared to the same in 2007. The total variance explained by this model was adj $R^2 = .08$.

When the social psychological variables were entered in the model, the total variance explained by the model was significantly increased (adj $R^2 = .19$). Interestingly, age squared remained significant, but area of residence became non-significant. An HAPC analysis treating both period and cohort as random effects revealed that there were significant random effects for both whilst the age squared effect was still significant. The predicted values of intergroup trust indicated an increased trust in the younger compared to the older cohorts, with a higher rate of increase for cohorts 3–6. Predicted values of intergroup trust were also higher in both the 2010 and 2017 period compared to the same in 2007. The social psychological variables that are significant predictors in this model were quantity of contact and outgroup friendships and threats all in the expected direction. There was also a significant finding for religiosity with those who were more religious being less trustful of members of the other community.

Predicting Acceptance of BBF in the Greek Cypriot Community

From the basic model we see that education, IDP status, gender and period are significant predictors. Higher education (and especially having a master or PhD) increases the odds of acceptance of BBF compared to the odds of no support for BBF. For example, the odds for acceptance of BBF by a master or PhD holder is almost three times (2.89) the odds of somebody who only reads and writes. The male's odds of accepting BBF are 1.5 times compared to females. The odds of accepting BBF being IDP is 1.19 times the odds of supporting BBF when not being IDP. The findings from this model are significant because, when controlling for period, there is neither an age nor a cohort effect that would show diminishing possibilities for support for BBF in the younger generations as one might expect from our discussion in the previous chapter, and that a partitionist mentality in the Greek Cypriot community seems to be more closely linked with the younger generation and the findings in this chapter about a generational gap in prejudice and trust levels in the GC community. All these go to suggest that the model of BBF is a versatile model of governance that accommodates both centrifugal and centripetal ways of thinking about the future institutional governance of Cyprus.

The effects of period were, however, significant given that acceptance of BBF increased steadily in the period 2007–2017. This increasing trend is in fact continuing after the year 2017 according to more recent research findings (Psaltis et al., 2021). In fact, the increasing support in recent years is clearly linear (58.1% in 2018, 65% in 2019, 76% in 2020 and 80.5% in 2023) (see also Appendix A), which suggests large dependence on recent political developments.

When the social psychological variables were entered in the models, the total variance explained by the model was significantly increased (pseudo $R^2 = .137$). Interestingly, the IDP status, gender and period effects remained significant, but education became non-significant, which suggests that probably education is having its effects on the outcome (acceptance of BBF) through the social psychological variables that are significant predictors in this model. These are feelings towards the other community (prejudice), intergroup trust and threats.

Predicting Acceptance of BBF in the Turkish Cypriot Community

From the basic model we see that gender, area of living (urban or rural) and period are significant predictors. Living in an urban area increases the odds of acceptance of BBF compared to the odds for those living in rural areas. For example, the odds for acceptance of urban dwellers are 1.32 times the odds for somebody who lives in rural areas. The male's odds of accepting BBF are 1.22 times compared to females. In the period 2007–2017 there is, as in the case of GCs, a significant increase in the percentage of people who would accept BBF.

The period effect was significant and its effect of big magnitude with a significant linear improvement in the period 2007–2017. Data from the later period (2020–2023) (see Appendix A) suggest that there was a decrease in acceptance levels of BFF at 71.2%, which might relate to the policy turn of newly elected Ersin Tatar, backed by Turkey, away from BBF and towards recognition of separate sovereignty for TCs or two states but the acceptance bounced back (79.8%) in 2023.

When the social psychological variables were entered in the model, the total variance explained by the model was significantly increased (pseudo $R^2 = 0.19$). Interestingly, the area of residency, gender and period effects remained significant. The social psychological variables that are significant predictors in this model are quantity of contact and intergroup trust in the expected direction. There was also a significant finding for religious importance with more religious people being less likely to support BBF.

Predicting Willingness for Renewed Cohabitation in the Greek Cypriot Community

From the basic model testing only the demographic variables as predictors and treating period and cohort as fixed effects, a significant finding is revealed for age and age squared, gender, place of residence (urban or rural) and period. Male participants, those living in urban areas and older GCs are more likely to support renewed cohabitation. Also, the mean score for data collected in 2010 on the dependent variable was significantly lower compared to the same in 2007. The total variance explained by this model was adj $R^2 = .08$.

When the social psychological variables were entered in the model, the total variance explained by the model was significantly increased (adj $R^2 = .49$). Interestingly, age and age squared, gender, place of residence (urban or rural) and period effects remained significant. Additionally, a significant cohort effect was revealed. Indeed, HAPC analysis treating both period and cohort as random effects revealed that there were significant random effects for both variables, with older participants being more ready for renewed cohabitation compared to younger. The social psychological variables that are significant predictors in this model were quantity of contact, feelings towards the other community (prejudice), intergroup trust and threats all in the expected direction.

Predicting Willingness for Renewed Cohabitation in the Turkish Cypriot Community

From the basic model testing only the demographic variables as predictors and treating period and cohort as fixed effects, a significant finding is revealed for age squared, education and period. More educated and younger TCs are more likely to support renewed cohabitation. Also, the mean score for data collected in 2010 and 2017 on the dependent variable was significantly higher compared to the same in 2007, exhibiting an increasing linear trend of support for cohabitation in time. The total variance explained by this model was adj $R^2 = .04$).

When the social psychological variables were entered in the model, the total variance explained by the model was significantly increased (adj $R^2 = .27$). Interestingly, age squared and education effects remained significant, but period effects became non-significant. An HAPC analysis treating both period and cohort as random effects revealed that there were significant random effects only for cohort, whilst the age squared effect became non-significant. The predicted values of cohabitation indicated an increased appetite for renewed cohabitation in the younger compared to the older cohorts. The social psychological variables that are significant predictors in this model were feelings towards the other community (prejudice), intergroup trust and threats all in the expected direction. There was also a trend for those having more contact to be more ready for renewed cohabitation, whilst those who were more religious tended to be less ready for cohabitation.

Summary of Findings and Policy Implications for CBMs, BBF Design and Referendums

All in all, the findings suggest that the social psychological variables of prejudice, trust, threats and contact play a crucial role in regulating the wish for renewed cohabitation and, to a lesser extent, the acceptance of BBF that appears to depend also on political developments and IDP status for GCs (on IDPs and their stance, see Psaltis et al., 2020). As the negative role of prejudice and distrust is important, policymakers need to realise that there are two major routes for prejudice reduction, intergroup contact and threat reduction, and they both depend on mood in public debate in the media (Avraamidou & Psaltis, 2020; Karayianni & Psaltis, 2023) and, in the longer term, on good-quality education mostly at the post-graduate level and probably study experiences abroad. Despite the presence of ethnocentric narratives in both communities, education has a positive impact on prejudice reduction. The fact that the effects are more pronounced at the higher levels of education is suggestive of the greater potential of higher education to become critical and reflective of master narratives of conflict compared to the elementary and secondary schools that are still hostages to the propaganda of master narratives.

Cohort effects can be located in the GC community for both prejudice, trust towards TCs and wish for renewed cohabitation showing an increasing alienation of the younger generation of GCs from the other community. On the contrary, the older generation of TCs is more alienated from GCs. Alienation from the other community in terms of trusting relations is higher in rural compared to urban areas where more traditional and conservative values (religiosity included) create a heightened sense of difference through symbolic threats.

Positive period effects relating to decreasing prejudice and distrust since 2007 have been clearly present in the TC community and seem to be related to more contact opportunities with the GC community, thus deconstructing the enemy image that existed since intercommunal strife in the 1960s and the following separatist Rauf Denktas narrative that 'we cannot live with Greek Cypriots'. Here it is interesting to note that after the Crans Montana failure in two measurements in 2020 and 2023, a majority of TCs for the first time stated that they could accept a unitary state, which also puts in question the policy followed by Ersin Tatar and Turkey recently. Of course, this is a policy not supported by the UN security council resolution on Cyprus, but it is indicative of a trend in the public that goes against the followed policy.

In the GC community there was a temporary worsening of prejudice in the year 2010, which probably relates to the isolation of the ruling leftist party which actively supported rapprochement efforts and the consequent reactionary backlash against the left (Trimikliniotis & Bozkurt, 2012). Also, one year earlier, in 2009, saw the rise of nationalist Derviş Eroğlu as prime minister in the north, which could have also influenced the GC view about the wish of TCs for a solution. The period 2010–2012 was also marred by financial hardships and heightened xenophobic attitudes towards immigrants in the GC press (see Kadianaki et al., 2018), which might have spilled over to bicommunal attitudes also. The election of Mustafa Akinci in 2015, however, completely reversed this picture with an impressive improvement of attitudes that still holds until today, even after the Crans Montana failure. These findings point to an important regulator of prejudice levels in each community which has to do with the outcome of elections, beyond any effects of contact well documented already. When a pro-reconciliation leader is elected in one community on a clear mandate for a compromise solution like BBF, there seems to be a positive impact on the public opinion of the other community, since they probably read the positive outcome of the elections as a collective will for peace within the out-group, thus reducing threats. It is interesting to note here that the election of nationalist Ersin Tatar in 2020 did not seem to negatively influence the emotions of GCs towards TCs, which is probably due to the fact that Mustafa Akinci lost the election by fewer than 5,000 votes and only after significant intervention from Ankara in favour of Tatar, which was interpreted by GCs as not a significant change of the will of the TC laypeople for peace.

Attitude towards BBF mostly depends on two factors. The first is social psychological relating to contact and reduced prejudice, threats and distrust. The second is political developments in the last 20 years that increased the federalist mentality of the two communities, even partly through pragmatic concerns relating to regional tensions or the legitimate wish to return to lost homes among older GC IDPs for whom the emotional connection with their lost home is still alive (see Psaltis et al., 2020). The increasing alienation of the younger generations of GCs from TCs registered in this and the previous chapter seems to leave unchanged the increasing support for BBF in the past few years. One could legitimately hypothesise, given the versatility of interpretations BBF can accommodate, that a more decentralised form of BBF and bizonality would not be particularly repulsive to the younger generation of GCs compared to the older generation of the same community, given their higher alienation levels from TCs. A decentralised federation might be more acceptable if there were a referendum tomorrow, but of course this does not mean it will be the best model in the long term for the sustainability of the future of reunited Cyprus. What is certain from the current findings in Appendices A and B is that the only model supported by the UN resolution and that could be accepted by a clear majority in both communities is that of BBF.

When it comes to referendums, the dynamics of the voters' decisions will naturally depend on prejudice levels, trust, stance on renewed cohabitation and BBF, but there are additional factors that will need to be taken into account like the Yes and No campaigns organisation and content, their funding and dynamic, the stance of political parties, not to mention interference by foreign states, influence from political leaders and, of course, the final content of the peace package (Loizides, 2014). In some of our research we asked people of the two communities about their general stance on a possible referendum scenario at various points in time (see Appendices A and B, Figures A.7 and B.7). Despite the variability observed, which partially depends on the state of public debate about the negotiations at a given point, some observations are noteworthy. For example, there was a negative turn around January 2017 (Avraamidou & Psaltis, 2020) in the GC press compared to a much more positive climate in 2015 and 2016 (see Karayianni & Psaltis, 2023), which is reflected in Figure A.7 of Appendix A. However, by April 2017, and only three months before Crans Montana, those trending to Yes in the GC community were almost double those trending to No. Beyond the aforementioned fluctuation, it is worthwhile noting that in the GC community the dominant trend was for those trending to Yes to outnumber those who trended to No by a 2:1 ratio.[10] In the TC community the picture was generally not so hopeful, which, compared to the results of the referendum in 2004, was suggestive of a reversal that might have given Akinci a hard time if there was eventually a referendum. Given lower prejudice levels towards GCs in the TC community recently compared to 2007, we have to conclude that the negative stance of TCs on referendum had to do with some provisions in the Guterres framework that they found difficult to accept, and not the quality of their intercommunal relations.

However, beyond speculation, what is more important in the case of exploring referendum intentions is to specify as concretely as possible the content of the peace package before asking people to position themselves with a Yes or a No. In our most recent research we applied the method of conjoint analysis to do exactly that in specifying varieties of all dimensions of the Guterres framework, and we were in a position to identify at least two variations in the framework that could garner a majority vote in both communities simultaneously (see Loizides et al., 2022). Online dialogues that are now made possible by AI-facilitated platforms can also offer quick

[10] This is a finding that raises suspicions about the motives of the public relations manager of Anastasiades who, according to Drousiotis, stated with conviction to some high-level cadres of the ruling party DISY in February 2017, 'Let me put it to you bluntly. This solution will not pass a referendum!' (Drousiotis, 2021, p. 286).

and valuable feedback to policymakers about the wish of the two communities and the formulation of a peace package that will be accepted by both communities in a referendum.[11]

Immediate and long-term CBMs with direct impact on the core mediating variables of our findings (e.g. threats) are of crucial importance, as they will facilitate reconciliation prefiguring a reunited Cyprus. The implementation of microgenetic processes through intergroup contact and the revision of one-sided victimisation narratives need to take priority. Our ideas of intergroup contact as microgenesis were recently applied in post-settlement Colombia (Fonseca & Jovchelovitch, 2024), where urban university students lived for 11 days with former guerillas in rural areas, with impressive transformations of the representations of students about their identities as peacemakers, deconstructing the enemy image of the other and the representation of peace and reconciliation itself. A similar programme of hospitality in houses of the other community on a mass scale can be designed in Cyprus in the pre-settlement period, which is expected to bring the positive effects of contact at massive levels in a short time through direct and indirect forms of contact (Yucel & Psaltis, 2020; Donno et al., 2021).

Such CBMs are needed not only to prepare the ground for renewed negotiations and a successful outcome but also for the longer sustainability of living together and co-operating in a BBF. In this sense it is very unfortunate that the IMAGINE programme was halted and that the two communities did not find the way to promote history teaching on both sides of the divide free from nationalistic and one-sided victimisation narratives. One idea that is gaining support in both communities of Cyprus[12] is the writing of school history textbooks by a group of historians and educators from both communities. About 70% of respondents from the GC community and 82% from the TC community accepted this idea in 2023. These high levels of acceptance were another indicator of the positive transformation that took place after the opening of the checkpoints in terms of bicommunal relations and the work of the AHDR in civil society that started more than 20 years prior.

The current statistics about the frequency of checkpoint crossings can also be significantly improved. In the same bicommunal research completed in 2023 (see Appendix B, Table B.1 for its methodology)

[11] One such platform can be found at www.remesh.ai/.

[12] The finding was published in newspaper *Politis* on 20 August 2023. Available at https://politis.com.cy/670958/article.

mentioned in the previous paragraph we also asked two questions relating to crossings. The first was if they visited the other side after the opening of checkpoints in 2003 and, if yes, how many times. In the GC community 31% never crossed to the north of the divide. Those who have crossed only once accounted for 18.9% of the group, 22.7% crossed two to three times, 9.4% crossed four to six times and 18% crossed seven or more times. In the TC community, 19.5% never crossed, 8.1% crossed once, 8.8% crossed two to three times, 6.9% crossed four to six times and 56.6% crossed seven or more times.

Table 5.8 suggests that the stigmatisation of crossing to the north still holds for the majority of the GC community, who either never crossed or crossed only once and did not intend to cross again. Only about 30% of GCs cross at least a few times a year with some regularity. In the TC community the situation is much different, with less than 20% having never crossed, and among those who do, 84% cross at least a few times a year. This translates into about 68% of the overall population crossing regularly. There is even a small percentage (1.4%) of TCs who work in the south and cross on a daily basis.

Clearly there is much more to be done in the GC community to facilitate contacts between the two communities and de-stigmatise crossing to the north.

In terms of the demographic variables, the youth and women need to significantly increase their participation in discussions about the Cyprus problem and bicommunal activities, as well as people living in rural areas and people of lower socio-economic status. IDPs who have 'skin in the game' also need to be included in the negotiations. Obviously the educational systems can do much more in not only promoting contact and revising history textbooks or promoting multiperspectivity but also promoting civic education of students and increasing their knowledge about federal systems in the world and basic rules of their functioning. Given

Table 5.8 *Frequency of crossing to the other side in 2023*

	GCs (%)	TCs (%)
I visited only once and I will not visit again	24.7	4.2
I visited a few times and I will not visit again	30.8	11.8
I visit a few times a year	35.4	40.4
I visit once or twice a month	7.2	26.4
I visit a few times a week	1.0	11.6
I visit almost every day	0.9	4.2
I work there (I visit every day)	0	1.4

some spillover effects from the migration issue to the Cyprus issue, if negotiations are to restart, the xenophobic climate against migration that was purposefully cultivated by the previous government in the south through a securitisation discourse (Trimikliniotis, 2019; UNHCR-Cyprus, 2023) will need to be defused and alternative narratives of cultural enrichment through diversity and financial benefits will need to be promoted. A national strategy for integration of immigrants could go a long way in helping in this direction. The role of the media is crucial in reducing realistic and symbolic threats towards alterity more generally. Drastic measures in the media landscape in the direction of peace journalism are also urgently needed.

REFERENCES

Avraamidou, M., & Psaltis, C. (2019). Blocking the solution: Social representations of threats and (non) dialogue with alternative representations in Greek-Cypriot newspapers during peace negotiations. *Journal for the Theory of Social Behaviour, 49*(4), 460–479.

Bar-Tal, D., Chernyak-Hai, L., Schori, N., & Gundar, A. (2009). A sense of self-perceived collective victimhood in intractable conflicts. *International Review of the Red Cross, 91*(874), 229–258.

Bekerman, Z., & Zembylas, M. (2017). Mediating collective memories and official histories in conflict-affected societies: Pedagogical responses to 'individual' memories. In R. Parkes, A. Clark, H. Elmersjö, & M. Vinterek (Eds.), *Teaching rival histories: Pedagogical responses to the history and culture wars* (pp. 133–154). Basingstoke: Palgrave Macmillan.

Boesch, E. E. (2001). Symbolic action theory in cultural psychology. *Culture & Psychology, 7*(4), 479–483.

Bryant, R. (2010). The state of Cypriot silences. *Cyprus Review, 22*(2), 113–122.

Doise, W. (1986). *Levels of explanation in social psychology: European monographs in social psychology*. Cambridge: Cambridge University Press.

(2011). The homecoming of society in social psychology. In J. P. Valentim (Ed.), *Societal approaches in social psychology* (pp. 9–34). Berne: Peter Lang.

Doise, W., & Mugny, G. (1984). *The social development of the intellect*. Oxford: Pergamon Press.

Doise, W., & Valentim, J. P. (2015). Levels of analysis in social psychology. In J. D. Wright (Ed.), *International encyclopedia of the social & behavioral sciences* (2nd ed., pp. 900–904). Amsterdam: Elsevier.

Donno, D., Psaltis, C., & Zarpli, O. (2021). Extended intergroup contact in frozen conflicts: Experimental evidence from Cyprus. *Conflict Management and Peace Science, 38*(4), 411–433.

Drousiotis, M. (2005). *The first partition of Cyprus 1963–1964*. Nicosia: Alfadi. [in Greek]

(2022). *Crime in Crans Montana: How and why the gang thwarted the Cyprus solution* [in Greek]. Nicosia: Alfadi Publications.

Duveen, G. (2002). Construction, belief, doubt. *Psychologie et Societe, 3*, 139–155.

Duveen, G., & Lloyd, B. B. (Eds.). (1990). *Social representations and the development of knowledge*. Cambridge: Cambridge University Press.

Ersözer, F. (2019). The Green Line regulation and its potential for cooperation in Cyprus. PRIO Cyprus Centre Report No. 9. Nicosia: PRIO Cyprus Centre.

Ferreira, L. R., Aléssio, R. L. dos S., & Pedrosa, M. I. (2023). Autobiographical narrative as a methodological instrument of the network of meanings. *Paidéia (ribeirão Preto), 33*, e3326. https://doi.org/10.1590/1982-4327e3326.

Fonseca, L., & Jovchelovitch, S. (2024). The long hard road of reconciliation: Prefiguring cultures of peace through the transformation of representations of former combatants and identities of urban youth in Colombia. *European Journal of Social Psychology, 54*, 1–16. https://doi.org/10.1002/ejsp.2967.

Hasler, B. S., Leshem, O. A., Hasson, Y., Landau, D. H., Krayem, Y., Blatansky, C., Cakal, H., Psaltis, C., & Halperin, E. (2023). Young generations' hopelessness perpetuates long-term conflicts. *Scientific Reports, 13*(1), 4926.

Kadianaki, I., Avraamidou, M., Ioannou, M., & Panagiotou, E. (2018). Understanding media debate around migration: The relation between favorable and unfavorable representations of migration in the Greek Cypriot press. *Peace and Conflict: Journal of Peace Psychology, 24*(4), 407–415. https://doi.org/10.1037/pac0000285.

Kadianaki, I., & Gillespie, A. (2015). Alterity and the transformation of social representations: A sociocultural account. *Integrative Psychological and Behavioral Science, 49*, 73–88.

Karayianni, C., & Psaltis, C. (2023). Tweet for peace: Twitter as a medium for developing a peace discourse in the hands of the Greek-Cypriot and Turkish-Cypriot leaders. *Online Information Review, 47*(5), 925–943.

Ker-Lindsay, J. (2016). The Greek-Turkish forum: A portrait of a track 1.5 peace support initiative. Global Strategy Forum and the British Council, London.

Ktoris, S. (2013). AKEL and the Turkish Cypriots (1941–1955). *Cyprus Review, 25*(2), 15–38.

Loizides, N. (2014). Negotiated settlements and peace referendums. *European Journal of Political Research, 53*(2), 234–249.

Loizides, N., Psaltis, C., Morgan-Jones, E., Sudulich, L., Popp, R., & Baykiz, T. (2022). Citizens and peace mediations in divided societies: Identifying zones of agreement through a conjoint survey experiment. *Journal of Conflict Resolution, 66*(9), 1619–1649.

Loizos, P. (1975). Changes in property transfer among Greek Cypriot villagers. *Man, 10*, 503–523.

(1981). *The heart grown bitter: A chronicle of Cypriot War refugees*. Cambridge: Cambridge University Press.

(2001). *Unofficial views: Cyprus: Society and politics*. Nicosia: Intercollege Press.

Michel, J. B., Shen, Y. K., Aiden, A. P., Veres, A., Gray, M. K., Google Books Team, ... & Aiden, E. L. (2011). Quantitative analysis of culture using millions of digitized books. *Science, 331*(6014), 176–182.

Moudouros, N. (2020). *State of exception in the Mediterranean: Turkey and the Turkish Cypriot community*. Berlin: Springer Nature.

Packard, M. (2008). *Getting it wrong: Fragments from a Cyprus diary 1964*. Milton Keynes: Authorhouse.

Patrick, R. (1976a). A general system theory approach to geopolitical aspects of conflict between communities with particular reference to Cyprus since 1960. In J. H. Bater & R. Preston (Eds.), *Political geography and the Cyprus conflict: 1963-1971* (pp. 1–323). Ontario: Department of Geography, University of Waterloo Publication Series.

(1976b). Inter-communal conflict in Cyprus: Some demographic and geopolitical consequences. In J. H. Bater & R. Preston (Eds.), *Political geography and the Cyprus conflict: 1963-1971* (pp. 339–352). Ontario: Department of Geography, University of Waterloo Publication Series.

Pavlou, P. (2015). *State, ideology, politics and education in Cyprus 1959-1974*. Athens: Papazisi. [in Greek]

Peristiany J. G. (Ed.). (1966). *Honour and shame: The values of Mediterranean society*. Chicago: University of Chicago Press.

Psaltis, C. (2012). Intergroup trust and contact in transition: A social representations perspective on the Cyprus conflict. In I. Marková & A. Gillespie (Eds.), *Trust and conflict: Representations, culture and dialogue* (pp. 83–104). London: Routledge.

(2015). Genetic social psychology: From microgenesis to ontogenesis, sociogenesis. . . and back. In C. Psaltis, A. Gillespie, & A. N. P. Perret-Clermont (Eds.), *Social relations in human and societal development* (pp. 71–94). London: Palgrave McMillan.

Psaltis, C., Cakal, H., Loizides, N., & Kuşçu Bonnenfant, I. (2020). Internally displaced persons and the Cyprus peace process. *International Political Science Review, 41*(1), 138–154. https://doi.org/10.1177/0192512119872057.

Psaltis, C., & Duveen, G. (2006). Social relations and cognitive development: The influence of conversation type and representations of gender. *European Journal of Social Psychology, 36*(3), 407–430.

Psaltis, C., Franc, R., Smeekes, A., Ioannou, M., & Žeželj, I. (2017). Social representations of the past in post-conflict societies: Adherence to official historical narratives and distrust through heightened threats. In C. Psaltis, M. Carretero, & S. Čehajić-Clancy (Eds.), *History education and conflict transformation: Social psychological theories, history teaching and reconciliation* (pp. 97–122). Berlin: Springer Nature.

Psaltis, C., Halperin, E., Loizides, N., Stefanovic, D., Leshem, A., & Cakal, H. (2021). Youth and politics in protracted conflicts: A comparative approach on hope for a settlement and return of IDPs. Final report of research project funded by the LSE Hellenic Observatory. Retrieved from: www.lse.ac.uk/

Hellenic-Observatory/Assets/Documents/Research/Cyprus/Projects-2019-20/Youth-and-Politics-in-Protracted-Conflicts-Project-Report.pdf.
Rego, T. C. (2022). Autobiographical narratives and research on the constitution of subjectivity in the Vygostkian perspective. *Paidéia (ribeirão Preto)*, *32*, e3224. https://doi.org/10.1590/1982-4327e3224.
Stronski, P. (2021). *A difficult balancing act: Russia's role in the Eastern Mediterranean*. Carnegie Endowment for International Peace. Available at https://carnegieendowment.org/files/Stronski_RussiaEastMed_final1.pdf.
Trimikliniotis, N. (2019). *Migration and the refugee dissensus in Europe: Borders, security and austerity*. London: Routledge.
Trimikliniotis, N., & Bozkurt, U. (Eds.). (2012). *Beyond a divided Cyprus: A state and society in transformation*. New York: Palgrave Macmillan.
UNHCR-Cyprus (2023). Perceptions of Cypriots about refugees, asylum-seekers and migrants: An opinion poll conducted by the University Center for Field Studies (UCFS), University of Cyprus on behalf of UNHCR, the UN Refugee Agency, in Cyprus. Nicosia. Available at www.unhcr.org/cy/wp-content/uploads/sites/41/2023/03/UNHCR-Opinion-Poll_Full-Report_March-2023.pdf.
Valsiner, J. (2021). *Hyper-generalization by the human mind*. Giessen: Psychosozial-Verlag.
Varnava, G. (2023). Russian soft power under Putin: The case of Cyprus. PhD thesis, Dept. of Sociology, Karlov University, Prague.
Yang, Y., & Land, K. C. (2013). *Age-period-cohort analysis: New models, methods, and empirical applications*. New York: Taylor & Francis.
Yucel, D., & Psaltis, C. (2020). The effects of direct and indirect contact on prejudice: 2007 and 2017 results among Greek Cypriots and Turkish Cypriots. *European Societies*, *22*(5), 610–635.
Zeng, R., & Greenfield, P. M. (2015). Cultural evolution over the last 40 years in China: Using the Google Ngram Viewer to study implications of social and political change for cultural values. *International Journal of Psychology*, *50*(1), 47–55.
Zetter, R. (1998). We are strangers here: Continuity, transition and the impact of protracted exile on the Greek Cypriot refugees. In V. Calotychos (Ed.), Cyprus and its people: Nation, identity and experience in an unimagined community 1955–1997 (pp. 69–84). Boulder, CO: Westview Press.
Zittoun, T., & Gillespie, A. (2017). Using diaries and self-writings as data in psychological research. In E. Abbey & S. Surgan (Eds.), *Emerging methods in psychology* (Vol. 1, pp. 1–26). London: Routledge.

APPENDIX A

Trends in the Greek Cypriot Community, 2007–2023

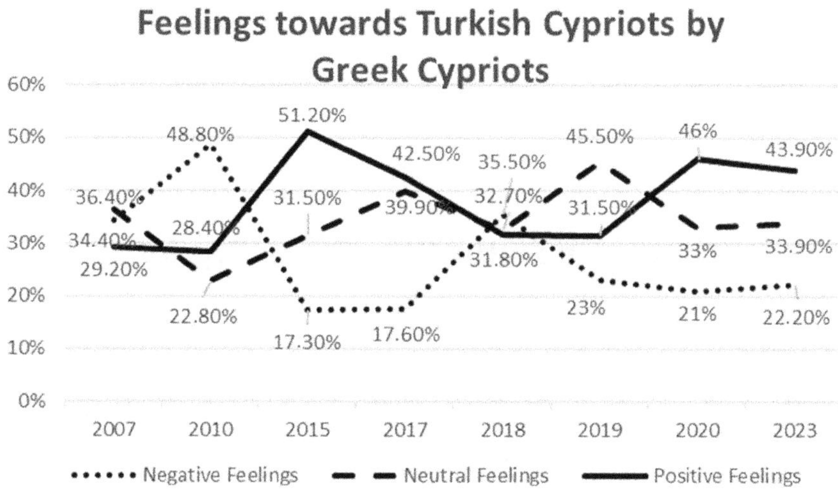

Figure A.1 Feelings towards Turkish Cypriots by Greek Cypriots in the period 2007–2023.

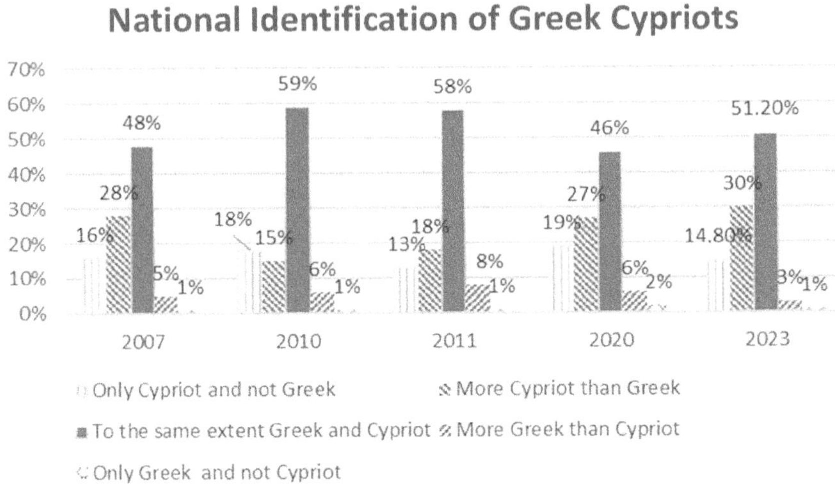

Figure A.2 National identification of Greek Cypriots in the period 2007–2023.

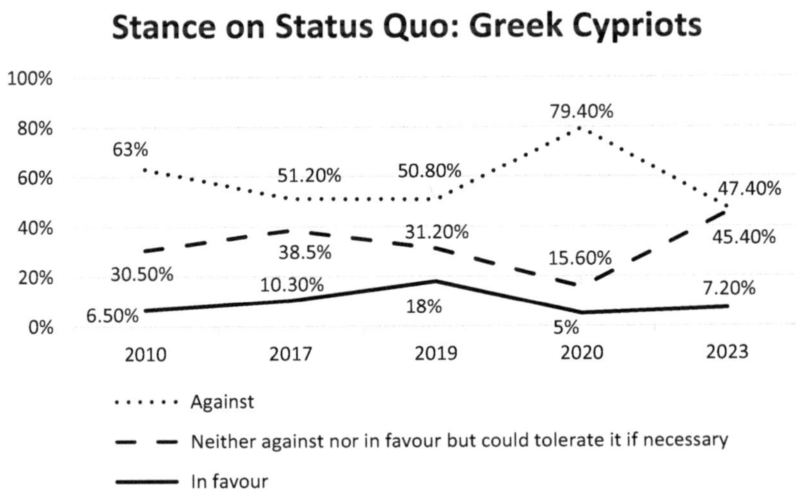

Figure A.3 Stance towards keeping the current situation (status quo) in the period 2010–2023.

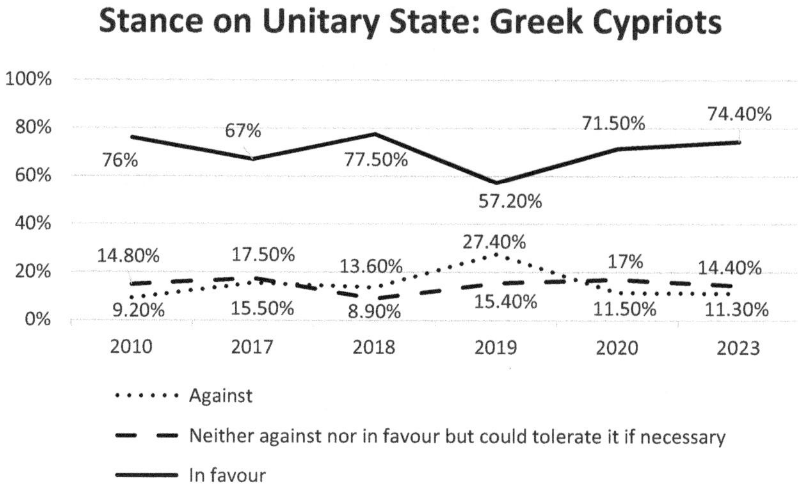

Figure A.4 Stance of Greek Cypriots towards unitary state in the period 2010–2023.

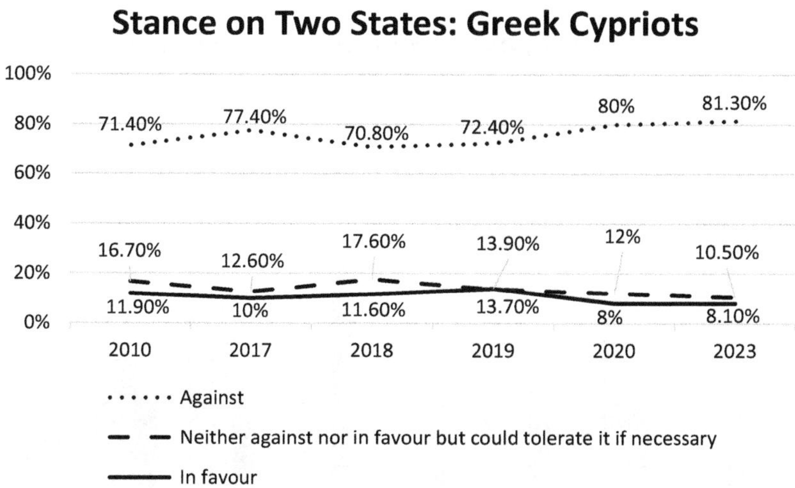

Figure A.5 Stance of Greek Cypriots towards two states in the period 2010–2023.

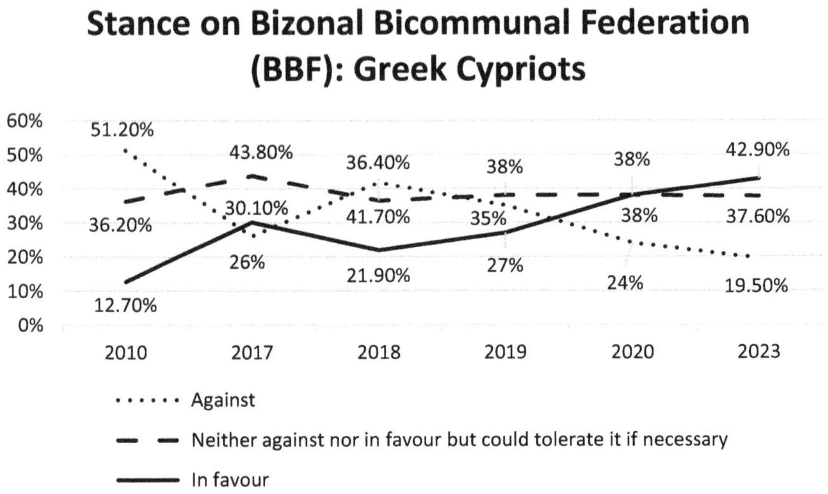

Figure A.6 Stance of Greek Cypriots towards Bizonal Bicommunal Federation (BBF) in the period 2010–2023.

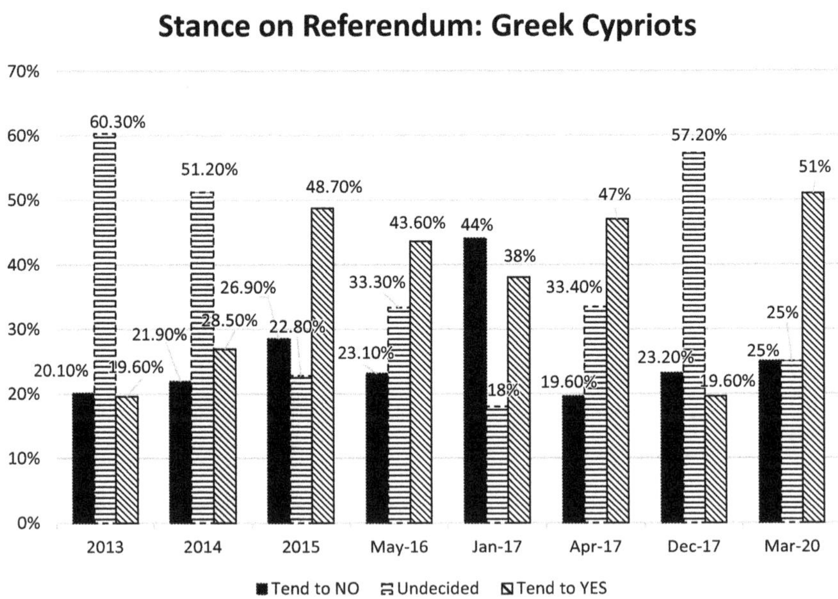

Figure A.7 Stance of Greek Cypriots towards referendum scenario in the period 2013–2020.

APPENDIX B

Trends in the Turkish Cypriot Community, 2007–2023

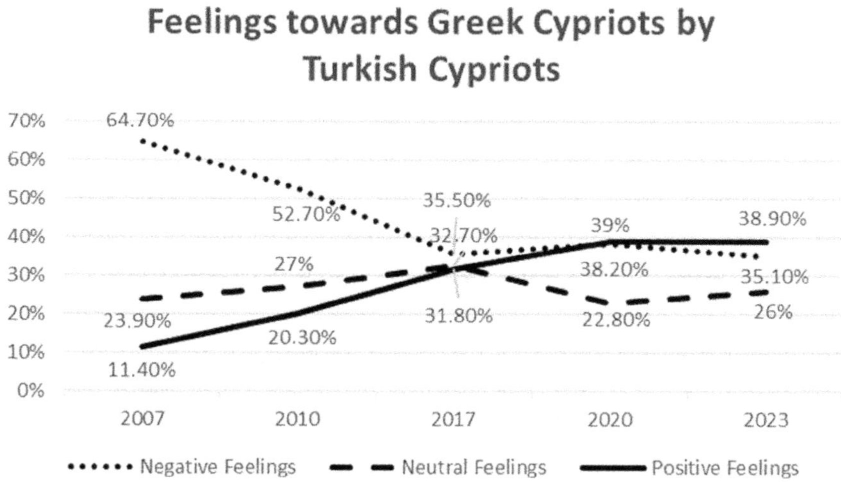

Figure B.1 Prejudice levels of Turkish Cypriots towards Greek Cypriots in the period 2007–2023.

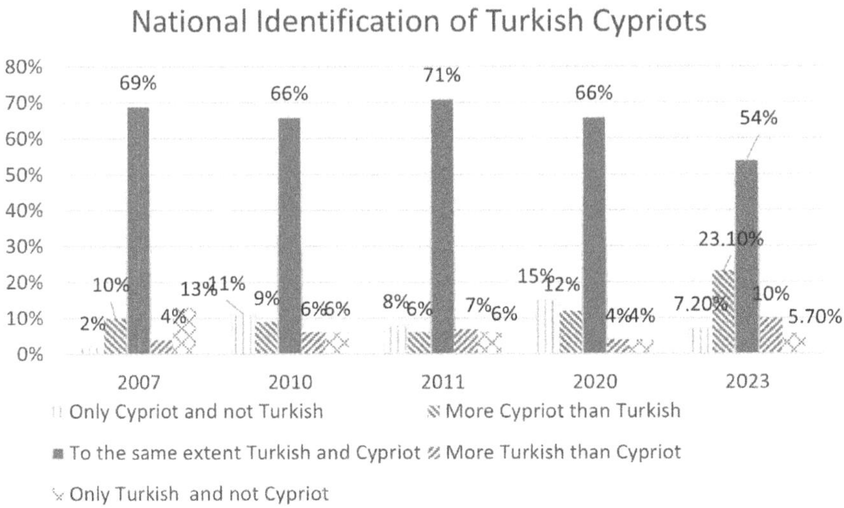

Figure B.2 National identification of Turkish Cypriots in the period 2007–2023.

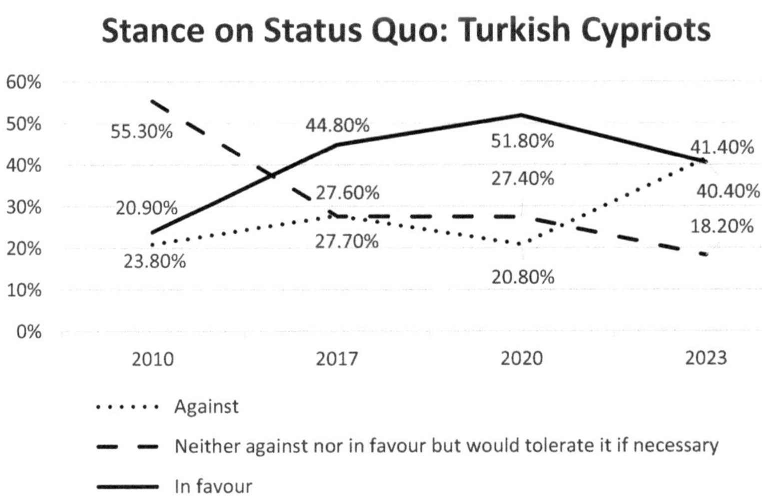

Figure B.3 Stance of Turkish Cypriots towards keeping the current situation (status quo) in the period 2010–2023.

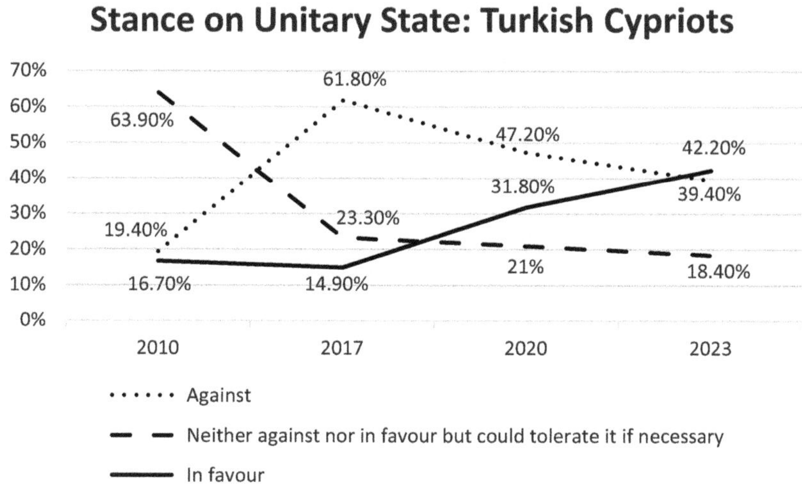

Figure B.4 Stance of Turkish Cypriots towards unitary state in the period 2010–2023.

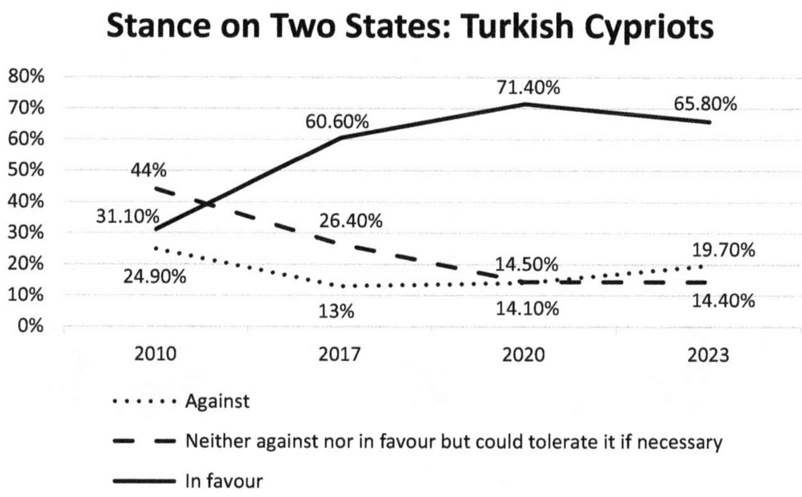

Figure B.5 Stance of Turkish Cypriots towards two states in the period 2010–2023.

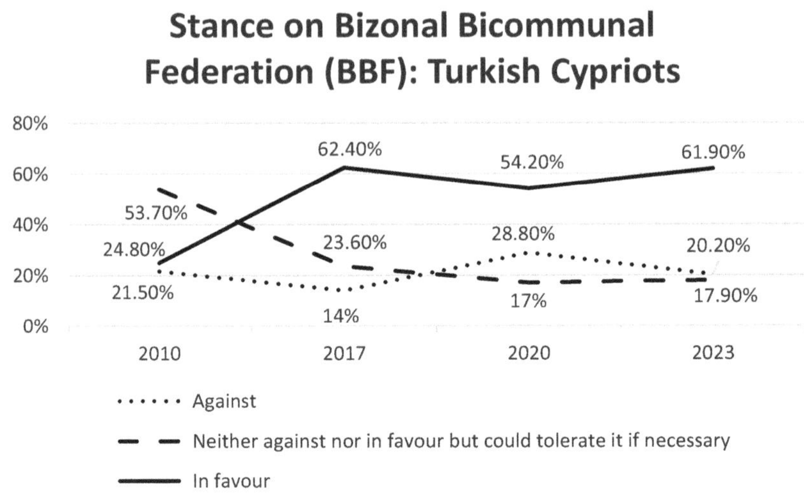

Figure B.6 Stance of Turkish Cypriots towards Bizonal Bicommunal Federation (BBF) in the period 2010–2023.

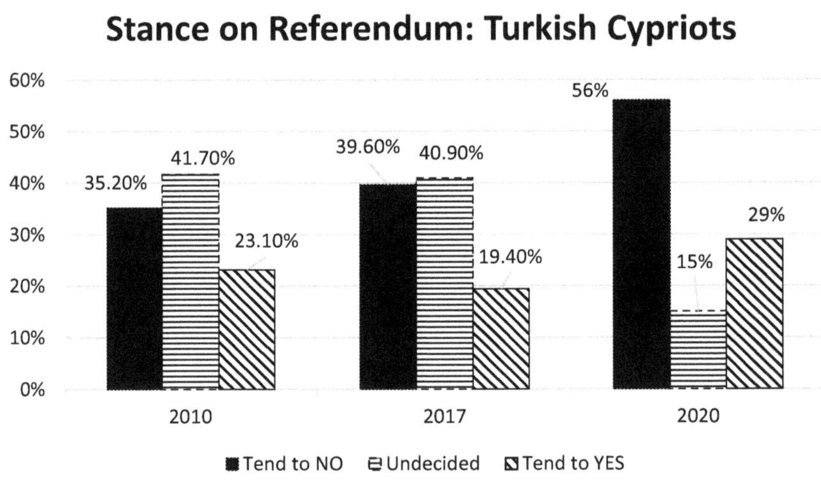

Figure B.7 Stance of Turkish Cypriots towards referendum scenario in the period 2013–2020.

Table B.1 *The representative large N surveys reported in the trends in Appendices A and B, methodology, research teams and funding bodies*

	Survey year	GCs	TCs	Methodology	Research team	Funded by (Grant)
1	2007	RAI	KADEM	F2F, Multistage Stratified Sampling, N = 800 GCs, 853 TCs	Psaltis, C., Hewstone, M.	Nuffield Foundation (New Career Development Fellowship Intergroup contact between Greek-Cypriots and Turkish-Cypriots)
2	2010	CYMAR	KADEM	F2F, Multistage Stratified Sampling 3-wave Longitudinal First wave N = 1,000 GCs, 1,000 TCs	Psaltis, C., Lytra, E., (AHDR) Hewstone, M.	UNDP-ACT EU Civil Society in action Programme (Representations of History and Intergroup Relations in Cyprus)
3	2015	UCFS		CATI Random Digit Calling with post-stratification weights N = 512 GCs	Donno, D., Psaltis, C.	The European Studies Center at the University of Pittsburgh to Donno, D.
4	2016	UCFS		CATI Random Digit Calling N = 1,605 GCs	Loizides, N., Psaltis, C., Stefanovic, D., Cakal, H.	ESRC and Leverhulme Trust RF-2014-401
5	2017	UCFS	PROLOGUE	CATI Random Digit Calling with post-stratification weights N = 505 GCs, 600 TCs	Psaltis, C., Yucel, D.	UCY Research funds of Psaltis Grow Civic Programme financed by the European Union
6	2017–2018	UCFS	PROLOGUE	F2F, Multistage Stratified Sampling N = 811 GCs, 801 TCs	Psaltis, C., Loizides, N., Cakal, H., Stefanovic, D., Hewstone, M.	A.G. Leventis DOI 10.17605/OSF.IO/5RJ3U (The Internally Displaced in Cyprus and Return Intentions: Social Psychological, Sociological and Political Determinants)

Table B.1 (*cont.*)

	Survey year	GCs	TCs	Methodology	Research team	Funded by (Grant)
7	2018–2019	UCFS		F2F, Multistage Stratified Sampling	Vryonides, M., Psaltis, C., Nicolaou, A., Georgiou, E.	ESS Round 9, Republic of Cyprus https://ess.sikt.no/en/?tab=overview
8	2020	UCFS	LIPA	CATI Random Digit Calling with post-stratification weights N = 536 GCs, 550 TCs	Psaltis, C., Halperin, E., Leshem, O., Cakal, H., Loizides, N.	LSE Hellenic Observatory (Youth and Politics in Protracted Conflicts: A comparative approach on hope for a settlement and return of IDPs)
9	2023	UCFS	LIPA	F2F, Multistage Stratified Sampling N = 717 GCs, 731 TCs	Psaltis, C., Michael, A., Soros, N., Nicolaou, A., Loizides, N., Kovras, I., Constantinides, A., Dagli, I., Cakal, H.	Internal Funding UCY (Justification mechanisms of the status quo, perceptions of transitional justice and forms of solving the Cyprus problem: A bicommunal research in the Cypriot context)

Note: F2F: Face to Face Data Collection. More information on the ESS methodology can be found at: www.europeansocialsurvey.org/methodology/methodology-overview.
Various publications with our research team also include more details on the methods. They are all included in the reference lists of the chapters in Part I of this book.

APPENDIX C

Associations between Human Value Scales (Centered) with Sociodemographic Characteristics and Various Sociopolitical Predictors (GCs-2018)

Table C.1

	BE	UN	SD	ST	HE	AC	PO	SE	CO	TR
Sociodemographics	Mean ± SD	Mean ± SD	Mean ± SD	Mean ± SD	Mean ± SD	Mean ± SD	Mean ± SD	Mean ± SD	Mean ± SD	Mean ± SD
Age (years), *r*	**0.237**	**0.197**	**−0.096**	**−0.452**	**−0.362**	**−0.181**	−0.010	**0.261**	**0.309**	**0.380**
Gender										
Male	**0.75 ± 0.6**	0.66 ± 0.6	**0.42 ± 0.6**	**−0.88 ± 1.0**	**−0.50 ± 0.9**	−0.65 ± 0.9	−1.02 ± 0.8	**0.76 ± 0.6**	−0.34 ± 0.8	0.48 ± 0.8
Female	**0.87 ± 0.6**	0.73 ± 0.5	**0.30 ± 0.7**	**−1.10 ± 1.0**	**−0.68 ± 1.0**	−0.60 ± 0.9	-1.08 ± 0.8	**0.89 ± 0.6**	−0.24 ± 0.9	0.52 ± 0.8
Years of education, *r*	**−0.160**	**−0.131**	**0.122**	**0.341**	**0.270**	**0.204**	−0.012	**−0.222**	**−0.339**	**−0.273**
Paternal educational level										
Low	**0.91 ± 0.5**	**0.78 ± 0.5**	0.35 ± 0.6	**−1.25 ± 1.0**	**−0.79 ± 0.9**	**−0.74 ± 0.9**	−1.07 ± 0.8	**0.92 ± 0.6**	**−0.18 ± 0.9**	**0.67 ± 0.8**
Medium	**0.63 ± 0.7**	**0.49 ± 0.5**	0.41 ± 0.6	**−0.49 ± 0.9**	**−0.24 ± 0.8**	**−0.34 ± 0.8**	−1.04 ± 0.8	**0.67 ± 0.6**	**−0.48 ± 0.8**	**0.17 ± 0.8**
High	**0.57 ± 0.6**	**0.60 ± 0.5**	0.32 ± 0.7	**−0.38 ± 0.8**	**−0.10 ± 0.7**	**−0.44 ± 0.9**	−1.02 ± 0.8	**0.60 ± 0.6**	**−0.57 ± 0.8**	**0.13 ± 0.8**
Maternal educational level										
Low	**0.90 ± 0.5**	**0.77 ± 0.5**	0.33 ± 0.6	**−1.23 ± 1.0**	**−0.74 ± 1.0**	**−0.74 ± 0.9**	−1.06 ± 0.8	**0.92 ± 0.6**	**−0.18 ± 0.9**	**0.65 ± 0.8**
Medium	**0.58 ± 0.6**	**0.48 ± 0.5**	0.42 ± 0.7	**−0.38 ± 1.0**	**−0.26 ± 0.9**	**−0.27 ± 0.8**	−1.02 ± 0.9	**0.63 ± 0.5**	**−0.54 ± 0.8**	**0.13 ± 0.7**
High	**0.62 ± 0.6**	**0.64 ± 0.5**	0.43 ± 0.6	**−0.46 ± 0.7**	**−0.21 ± 0.6**	**−0.50 ± 0.9**	−1.05 ± 0.8	**0.63 ± 0.6**	**−0.59 ± 0.8**	**0.17 ± 0.8**
Number of people in household, *r*	**−0.079**	−0.017	0.002	**0.132**	**0.094**	0.031	−0.034	**−0.085**	−0.069	−0.064
Predictors										
Placement on right/left scale, *r*	**−0.109**	−0.068	−0.079	−0.033	0.037	0.054	−0.028	0.059	0.067	0.063
How religious are you, *r*	**0.120**	0.029	**−0.176**	**−0.240**	**−0.171**	−0.054	−0.073	**0.166**	**0.214**	**0.305**
Contact score, *r*	0.000	0.032	**0.104**	**0.105**	**0.166**	**−0.076**	**−0.098**	**−0.082**	**−0.134**	−0.053
Watching, listening or reading political news (hours/day)										
Never	0.75 ± 0.6	**0.68 ± 0.4**	0.31 ± 0.6	**−0.44 ± 0.9**	**−0.13 ± 0.8**	−0.46 ± 0.9	−1.19 ± 0.7	**0.63 ± 0.7**	**−0.71 ± 0.9**	**0.23 ± 0.9**

Up to half an hour	0.78 ± 0.6	**0.75 ± 0.5**	0.31 ± 0.7	**−0.98 ± 1.0**	**−0.54 ± 0.9**	−0.66 ± 0.9	−1.01 ± 0.7	**0.91 ± 0.6**	**−0.35 ± 0.9**	**0.42 ± 0.8**
Half to one hour	0.86 ± 0.6	**0.73 ± 0.5**	0.44 ± 0.7	**−1.13 ± 1.0**	**−0.63 ± 1.0**	−0.65 ± 0.9	−1.13 ± 0.9	**0.81 ± 0.6**	**−0.28 ± 0.8**	**0.61 ± 0.8**
Over an hour	0.82 ± 0.6	**0.60 ± 0.6**	0.34 ± 0.6	**−1.03 ± 1.1**	**−0.74 ± 1.0**	−0.58 ± 0.9	−0.99 ± 0.9	**0.80 ± 0.6**	**−0.10 ± 0.8**	**0.57 ± 0.8**
Internet use (hours/day)										
Never	**0.97 ± 0.5**	**0.84 ± 0.5**	**0.28 ± 0.6**	**−1.55 ± 1.0**	**−1.04 ± 0.9**	**−0.88 ± 0.9**	−1.05 ± 0.8	**1.05 ± 0.6**	**0.10 ± 0.7**	**0.87 ± 0.7**
Up to an hour and half	**0.78 ± 0.5**	**0.62 ± 0.5**	**0.32 ± 0.7**	**−0.85 ± 0.9**	**−0.42 ± 0.9**	**−0.55 ± 0.9**	−1.08 ± 0.8	**0.80 ± 0.6**	**−0.36 ± 0.8**	**0.48 ± 0.7**
From an hour and half to three hours	**0.68 ± 0.7**	**0.63 ± 0.6**	**0.46 ± 0.6**	**−0.73 ± 1.0**	**−0.45 ± 0.9**	**−0.44 ± 0.8**	−0.94 ± 0.7	**0.68 ± 0.6**	**−0.45 ± 0.9**	**0.25 ± 0.9**
Over three hours	**0.71 ± 0.6**	**0.65 ± 0.5**	**0.46 ± 0.6**	**−0.47 ± 0.9**	**−0.16 ± 0.7**	**−0.45 ± 0.9**	−1.13 ± 0.9	**0.83 ± 0.6**	**−0.71 ± 0.9**	**0.16 ± 0.8**
Happiness score, ***r***	−0.018	−0.040	−0.037	0.053	**0.106**	0.057	0.001	**−0.083**	−0.046	−0.058
Rejection of immigrants, ***r***	**−0.125**	**−0.174**	−0.074	**−0.092**	−0.020	0.042	0.043	**0.085**	**0.155**	**0.147**
Health status										
Very good/good	**0.74 ± 0.6**	**0.65 ± 0.5**	**0.41 ± 0.6**	**−0.84 ± 1.0**	**−0.40 ± 0.8**	**−0.55 ± 0.9**	−1.06 ± 0.8	**0.75 ± 0.6**	**−0.40 ± 0.8**	**0.37 ± 0.8**
Fair	**0.96 ± 0.6**	**0.78 ± 0.6**	**0.21 ± 0.8**	**−1.29 ± 1.1**	**−0.95 ± 1.0**	**−0.74 ± 0.9**	−1.10 ± 0.9	**1.00 ± 0.6**	**−0.06 ± 0.9**	**0.82 ± 0.8**
Very bad/bad	**1.03 ± 0.5**	**0.94 ± 0.5**	**0.24 ± 0.5**	**−1.70 ± 0.9**	**−1.40 ± 0.9**	**−0.98 ± 0.9**	−0.84 ± 0.7	**1.10 ± 0.6**	**0.15 ± 0.6**	**0.98 ± 0.6**
Household's total net income, all sources (EURO/month)										
Less than 1,000	**0.90 ± 0.6**	0.75 ± 0.6	0.29 ± 0.7	**−1.23 ± 1.1**	**−0.78 ± 1.1**	**−0.75 ± 1.0**	−1.03 ± 0.8	**0.91 ± 0.7**	**−0.13 ± 0.9**	**0.72 ± 0.8**
1,001–1,500	**1.00 ± 0.5**	0.84 ± 0.6	0.27 ± 0.7	**−1.21 ± 1.1**	**−0.89 ± 0.9**	**−0.81 ± 0.8**	−1.21 ± 0.9	**1.03 ± 0.6**	**−0.10 ± 1.0**	**0.64 ± 0.81**

Table C.1 (*cont.*)

	BE	UN	SD	ST	HE	AC	PO	SE	CO	TR
1,501–2,200	**0.86 ± 0.5**	0.69 ± 0.5	0.41 ± 0.6	**−1.12 ± 1.0**	**−0.60 ± 0.8**	**−0.51 ± 0.9**	−1.01 ± 0.8	**0.80 ± 0.6**	**−0.36 ± 0.8**	**0.52 ± 0.7**
2,201–3,200	**0.77 ± 0.6**	0.71 ± 0.5	0.44 ± 0.5	**−0.85 ± 0.9**	**−0.41 ± 0.8**	**0.71 ± 1.0**	−1.10 ± 0.7	**0.76 ± 0.6**	**−0.46 ± 0.8**	**0.48 ± 0.7**
More than 3,200	**0.73 ± 0.6**	0.75 ± 0.5	0.34 ± 0.7	**−0.74 ± 0.9**	**−0.27 ± 0.8**	**−0.38 ± 0.8**	−1.14 ± 0.8	**0.71 ± 0.5**	**−0.55 ± 0.9**	**0.20 ± 0.9**

* Bold indicates statistically significant differences ($p < 0.05$); t-tests for two independent samples; ANOVA tests for more than two independent samples; Pearson's r correlation coefficient (*r*).

PART II

Commentaries and Rejoinder

CHAPTER 6

Dialectics of Genesis and Structure

Ivana Marková

In Part I of this volume Charis Psaltis states that the direct predecessors of the theoretical framework of genetic psychology he is developing can be found in Piaget's genetic epistemology, Lucien Goldmann's genetic structuralism, and Serge Moscovici's genetic model of social influence. The ideas of these scholars were further elaborated in Gerard Duveen's contributions directed towards the advancement of genetic social psychology. Psaltis states that common threads binding these approaches together were the concepts of the dialectics of genesis and structure, part–whole relations and temporality. Psaltis emphasises that these common threads were linked with the fundamental epistemological questions that had already preoccupied philosophers such as Immanuel Kant, Georg W. F. Hegel and Karl Marx. In this commentary I shall suggest that while the questions about the nature of knowledge bind these philosophers together, their proposed answers surpass their common links because, depending on their epistemological presuppositions, their answers are based on diverse concepts concerning the nature of knowledge. Consequently, these answers were reflected in different ways in the contributions of Piaget, Goldmann, Moscovici and Duveen in their studies of the dialectics of genesis and structure.

Epistemological questions of Kant, Hegel and Marx about the nature and possibility of knowledge necessarily bring into focus the relations between the knower and the object to be known – that is, between the individuals' minds and their outside world. The objects to be known in the outside world encompass physical, biological, social and symbolic phenomena and, therefore, entail different modes of understanding. In posing questions about the nature of knowledge, Piaget and Goldmann approached them in terms of relations between the individual (or transindividual) and object, while Moscovici and Duveen approached them as the triadic self–other–object relation. Epistemological issues these different kinds of relations imply are fundamental for answering the questions about the dialectics of genesis and structure. However, as we shall see in this commentary, answers to these questions are determined in specific ways in concrete instances of the problem these researchers attempt to solve.

There are several concepts that, in my view, distinguish Piaget's genetic epistemology from interactional (or genetic) epistemology of Moscovici. Among these, I shall choose three of Piaget's concepts that exemplify theoretical distinctions between Piaget and Moscovici, namely the epistemic subject, equilibrium and a linear or continuous development. These concepts of Piaget are of course well known to all developmental psychologists, but I shall briefly remind the reader of them in the first part of my comment; they also apply to Goldmann's interpretation of Piaget's theories. In the second part of my comment, I shall discuss oppositions to these three concepts in Moscovici's and Duveen's genetic epistemologies.

Genetic Epistemology of Piaget and Its Interpretation by Goldmann

Epistemic Subject

In his *Critique of Pure Reason,* Immanuel Kant (1781/1929) stated that despite enormous efforts of rationalists and empiricists, their attempts to answer the question of how knowledge is possible have failed. Both rationalists and empiricists assumed the existence of two separate realities: the knower and the object to be known. Rationalists presupposed that the mind logically deduces the truth from self-evident universal principles and applies them to reality. Empiricists presupposed the existence of the physically structured reality which humans acquire in daily experience by inductive reasoning. Rationalists and empiricists, such as Descartes and Locke, thought that ideas, either innate or acquired in experience, respectively, merge together and resemble objects in the outside world. For example, Locke stated that an object that signifies a *swan* is composed of simple ideas such as white colour, long neck, red beak and so on. These simple ideas, when connected, resemble a *swan* (Locke, 1690/1961, II, xxiii) existing in the outside world.

In contrast, Kant postulated that the ideas of humans do not resemble objects as Descartes and Locke thought. Having been critical of the duality between the knower and the object to be known, Kant introduced the concept of a 'phenomenon' (appearance) that explained how objects *appeared* to individuals. He assumed that structural elements of knowledge which organise human experience are mental structures. The 'phenomenon' or an 'appearance' of an object results from interaction between the knower's (subject) mental structures and the object of knowledge. Kant argued that objects (appearances) must conform to human concepts (Kant, 1781/1929, B xvi–xviii). He proposed that the knower (subject) is equipped with a priori mental structures or categories such as time, space, number, quantity, and causality and others. Categories impose themselves on the knower's experience of objects, and so they construct their appearances. Therefore, Kant viewed the knower as an agent in the construction of knowledge. This Kant's idea was a vital innovation in philosophy. However, Kant conceived a priori categories of knowledge as atemporal and fixed universals, thus following the Platonic concept that true knowledge was atemporal and universal.

Just like Kant, Piaget was critical of rationalism and empiricism, and he suggested that the major determinants of the individual's knowledge were mental structures. However, in contrast to Kant, he believed that mental structures produce knowledge in the process of the structuration of biological tendencies of the human mind in their living environment. These processes, to which Piaget referred as 'genetic epistemology', take place during the child's development, and are the proper solution to the problem of knowledge. New structures are progressively elaborated by the child as an epistemic subject (Piaget, 1970, p. 728) in the dialectical process of development and transformation. This process is rational, and it logically evolves in the epistemic subject due to autoregulation and equilibration. The epistemic subject, which became the centre of genetic epistemology, was an analytical abstraction conceived as an ideal knower cognising physical objects or persons. The epistemic subject was concerned with the forms of knowledge rather than with concrete contents of the individual's knowledge. These forms were common to all children who are at the same level of development of cognitive structures. Piaget distinguished the so conceived epistemic subject from the psychological subject, which included non-cognitive activities of the individual.

Duveen (1984/2013, p. 73) drew attention to the difference between the epistemic and psychological subject already in his early writings and continued to refer to it throughout his career. He did not use the concept of Piaget's epistemic subject in his own work but was concerned with a holistically conceived psychological person including cognitive and non-cognitive activities in his/her interactions with others. Although he was critical of Piaget's view of the epistemic subject as being 'transindividual' (see later discussion), Duveen emphasised that it was essential for Piaget's theory to conceptualise the epistemic subject as an abstract concept in order to bring into focus the point of view that *the epistemic subject was not an individuated subject.* Nevertheless, Duveen kept emphasising that one of the limitations of Piaget's genetic epistemology was that it did not pay attention to the holistic psychological subject.

Piaget's concept of epistemic subject was related to his approach to language. Elkind (1967) pointed out that the Piaget essay on 'Language and thought from the genetic point of view' is one of few attempts of Piaget to deal systematically with the relation between thought and language. Piaget's position was that language and thought have different origins: thought is derived from the abstraction of the child's acting upon things, while language arises from imitations provided by adults and, therefore, is not the product of the child's proper activity. While thought precedes language, once language emerges, language and thought become linked in a genetic circle, in which they 'both depend on intelligence itself, which antedates language and is independent of it' (Piaget, 1967, p. 98). When language emerges, it starts to interact with and becomes a tool for further transformation of thinking, and for the attainment of more advanced forms of equilibrium. Having explored language in concrete operations and propositional logic, Piaget concluded that language is necessary but not sufficient to construct logical operations, because these are rooted in actions of thinking and in sensorimotor mechanisms, and these, Piaget emphasised, are deeper than linguistics.

Equilibrium

In his essay on 'Genesis and Structure in the Psychology of Intelligence', Piaget (1967) explained what he meant by 'structure' and 'genesis'. He defined 'structure' very broadly, as a system which has laws and properties as a totality. It holds true for human species; as forms of knowledge are progressively constructed, their emergence is explained by assimilation and accommodation as the two poles of an interaction between the organism and the environment (Piaget, 1954, p. 353). Development is an active process of progressive equilibration (e.g. Piaget, 1967, p. 104) through the transformation of disequilibrium and re-equilibration of cognitive structures. Equilibration is achieved when new contents and newly formed kinds of knowledge are integrated into the existing cognitive mathematical and logical structures through a succession of stages. While equilibrium is characterised by stability, it does not mean immobility. Equilibrium is both mobile and stable. Its stability is achieved by movements in opposite directions. Its specific role is to compensate for the intrusion coming from the external world by the actions of the subject: 'Equilibrium, thus defined, is not something passive but, on the contrary, something essentially active; the greater the equilibrium, the more activity is required . . . Equilibrium is synonymous with activity. . . . A structure is in equilibrium to the extent that an individual is sufficiently active to be able to counter all intrusions with external compensations' (Piaget, 1967, p. 151).

Linear or Continuous Development

Piaget's theory of the child cognitive development postulated the stages in which knowledge becomes progressively more complex. This development is hierarchical, in which lower stages form a necessary grounding for the higher stages. Each stage is characterised by equilibrium, and its disturbance forms the basis for a restructuring that leads to a higher stage. The stage development presupposes a hierarchical development conceived as a progressive continuity and as a path towards the development of logical thinking. The stage development is a fundamental Piagetian perspective in which the child, by means of assimilation and accommodation, acquires progressively higher forms of knowledge. Such linear and continuous process was also incorporated in Durkheim's perspective, by means of which, in a historical process, religious representations are gradually transformed into scientific representations.

Lucien Goldmann[1]

Piaget's 'genetic epistemology' attracted the Romanian humanist, philosopher and sociologist Lucien Goldmann (1913–1970). A deeply convinced Marxist, Goldmann migrated through several European countries, and during the Second World War he came to Switzerland to work with Piaget whom he viewed as 'the most authentic dialectician, at least in the West' (Cohen, 1994, p. 57). Goldmann was a prominent critic of static forms of structuralism in literature and arts, to which he applied his method of genetic structuralism. As a part of his critique, he attempted to synthesise György Lukács's Marxist philosophy and genetic epistemology of Piaget.

[1] I am discussing the relation between Goldmann and Piaget in some detail because, as Psaltis (Part I of this volume) states,

1. Goldmann's genetic structuralism was one of the direct predecessors building a theoretical framework of genetic social psychology; and
2. It was crucial for understanding basic theoretical, methodological and epistemological questions that preoccupied Duveen throughout his career as the problems of Western Marxist thought.

Although Duveen and Psaltis often refer to the importance of the relation between Piaget and Goldmann in the context of the dialectic of structure and genesis, I shall attempt to complement their references by raising some issues about Goldmann's contributions to genetic epistemology.

Goldmann (1959) was convinced that there was a strong correspondence between Piaget's genetic epistemology and Marx's dialectical method. He believed that Piaget's ideas concerning the epistemic subject's construction of knowledge as a universal process corresponded to Marx's position according to which the individual must be conceived as a transindividual subject – that is, as a subject who, in basic respects, is the same as other subjects. Goldmanm adopted the credo of young Marx: 'Man's individual and species-life are not *different* . . . In his *consciousness of species* man confirms his real *social life* and simply repeats his real existence in thought, just as conversely the being of the species confirms itself in the species-consciousness and exists for itself in its generality as a thinking being' (Marx, 1959, p. 46, emphasis in the original). In this context Goldmann quoted Piaget saying that 'it is necessary for sociology to envisage society as a whole, even though this whole, which is quite distinct from the sum of individuals composing it, is only the totality of relations or interactions between these individuals' (Piaget, 1947/2001, p. 171). These references show why Goldmann viewed Piaget's genetic epistemology as a parallel to the Marxist dialectic method. As a psychologist, Piaget was concerned with the development of equilibrium between the individual's cognition and natural environment, and this process was the same for all subjects at the same developmental stage. As a sociologist, Goldmann argued that every social group – that is, the transindividual subject – looks for equilibrium in developing a coherent response to problems that are common to all members, in their social and natural environment. Goldmann's transindividual subject creates history, generates world views and makes possible societal changes (Boelhower, 1980). World views have concrete historical and cultural contents. They cannot be developed by individuals; they are forms of collective consciousness. Collective consciousness of social classes is linked with their actions. As social classes make up fundamental sections of society, they can achieve societal changes that individuals could never make,[2] by understanding the relations of

[2] Goldmann (1959) dedicated his book on *Recherches dialectiques* to Piaget as his master and friend. He devoted two chapters fully to Piaget. One chapter is concerned with the method of Piaget's psychology, and the other chapter is concerned with Piaget's dialectics. Goldmann analysed in detail the philosophical similarities between Marx and Piaget. He claimed that the concerns about the role of nature, matter and object were identical in the historical materialism of Marx and in psychology of Piaget. He also saw analogies between the adaptive nature of intelligence and historical materialism and between Marx's idea of superstructures developing in productive forces and Piaget's assimilation and accommodation. Goldmann also found similarities between Piaget's logic and the dialectical logic of Marxism. He analysed in detail Piaget's ideas on intelligence, thinking and perception.

production and the development of productive forces.[3] Goldmann emphasised that his concept of collective consciousness had nothing to do with Durkheim's 'collective consciousness' because Durkheim's concept was external to subjects existing as affixed reality (Goldmann, 1980).[4]

Subject–Object in Piaget's and Goldmann's Genetic Epistemologies

To the extent that Piaget and Goldmann conceived the question of knowledge in terms of the relation between the subject and object, they both followed Kant's solution, according to which the knower (subject) is equipped with the structural elements of knowledge. In contrast to Kant, the active epistemic subject of Piaget and of Goldmann constructs knowledge from these mental structures during his/her experience in interacting with biological and social environment, explained as 'genetic epistemology' and 'genetic structuralism', respectively. According to both scholars, the subject's mental structures were the same for everybody in human species. I suggest that this presupposition implied that to explain the nature of knowledge, it was not necessary to postulate the concept of the other because in cognitive terms, the other was the multiplied single subject. 'Others' existed, of course, in non-cognitive terms as psychological and social individuals, but with respect to generating knowledge, 'others' were no more than mental structures that were the same for everybody.

Goldmann, however, as a sociologist, went beyond this point of view. He emphasised cultural and historical changes in societies in which groups were dependent on other groups and linked to class consciousness. The Marxist notion of class consciousness was inseparable from social practices by means of which proletariat would achieve its historical goal of uniting working people, developing a new world view and substituting the capitalist system[5] by socialism.

Commenting on Piaget's (1942) study on perception in his book on *Classes, relations et nombres*, Goldmann (1980, p. 140) argued that 'le rapprochement between Marx and Piaget is inevitable'.

[3] In addition to Piaget, Goldmann was strongly influenced by the Hungarian Marxist philosopher György Lukács. He argued that Piaget's work enabled him to reinterpret Lukács's categories in a more coherent manner by giving them a more anthropological basis (Boelhower, 1980). In *Recherches dialectiques* Goldmann (1959) emphasised again and again that Piaget, who did not refer either to Hegel or to Marx, nevertheless completely confirmed their claims.

[4] Durkheim, as a non-Marxist, postulated his concept of 'collective consciousness' as a historical transformation of less adequate forms of 'collective consciousness' into more adequate forms. Later in his career Durkheim substituted the notion of 'collective consciousness' with 'collective representations'.

[5] During 1950s and 1960s, and during after the Soviet invasion of Czechoslovakia in 1968, Goldmann became critical of Marxism as practised in the USSR. He also became critical of some Marxist theoreticians, including Lukács. He thought that Marxism became outdated and should be

I suggest that the most important issues that attracted Duveen to Goldmann were (1) Goldmann's social, historical and cultural approach and (2) the concept of identity. Concerning the former, Goldmann's dialectics went far beyond Piaget's epistemic subject with its emphasis on the links between collective action and collective consciousness. Duveen suggests that in child development, the external coordination of the child's action with others is important for the child's construction of internal coordinations of actions – that is, for the construction of operations. These operations are products of collective actions, and Duveen (1984/2013, p. 71) refers again to Goldmann's transindividual subject. According to Goldmann's perspective, both the epistemic subject and the transindividual subject are active and collective agents. Their functions in social events are defined as activities of the social subjects who are adapting or transcending their natural and social environment (Mayrl, 1978).

For Duveen, Goldmann's approach offered a historically and culturally based social perspective on child development and the acquisition of identity. Without going into complex arguments about the separation of the subject and the object of knowledge (see earlier discussion) and about the identity of subject and object in Marx, Hegel and Lukács, Goldmann postulated the concept of partial (or possible) identity, linking it to culture or world views.[6] Identities are constructed in cultures, which for Duveen meant that they were constructed in social representations. Duveen acknowledged Goldmann's ideas that stabilities and changes in identities are linked to stabilities and changes of representations and social influences as cultural phenomena. Identities are not fixed forms of consciousness, but they are possible forms of consciousness because they develop in the changing world views. Identities constrain representations in the sense that they determine what forms of consciousness individuals or groups might find acceptable and what they might resist. Goldmann thought that potential (possible) consciousness was the most important contribution to the dialectical method (Mayrl, 1978). Duveen also appreciated that Goldmann linked identity to communication by drawing attention to what is possible to communicate and what is incommunicable. In problematic communication, cultural identities become particularly visible (Duveen, 2001/2013).

radically rethought, including the view of the role and identity of the proletariat. He expressed these altered views in his last book on *Lukács and Heidegger* (Goldmann, 2009).

[6] Details of these philosophical discussions can be found in Goldmann (1976, 1980, 2009) and in Cohen (1994), among others.

In conclusion, let us remind ourselves that the question of 'genesis' or 'development' was a feature of not only 'genetic epistemology' but all social and humanistic approaches that rejected non-developmental positions of rationalism and empiricism since the late 17th century (e.g. Vico) through to the 20th century (e.g. Mead, Levinas, Bakhtin and many others). Some of these scholars also emphasised structures of thought, or were sympathetic to structural approaches (e.g. Marx, Husserl, Luckmann, Berger, Schutz, Cassirer). The uniqueness of Piaget and Goldmann was to place 'genesis' and 'structure' at the centre of their approaches. Concerning Goldmann's interest in Piaget's genetic epistemology, I suggest that although it was motivated intellectually, it was primarily inspired politically. As a convinced Marxist, Goldmann viewed and interpreted all genetic ideas of Piaget in terms of Marxist dialectic, disregarding any other possibilities.

In discussing the psychology of intelligence, and the structure and genesis in psychology, Piaget (1967) commented that psychology, in contrast to sociology, did not stem from systems such as those of Hegel and Marx. In the history of psychology and biology, Piaget argued, although the concepts of structure and genesis have been used, they were not conceived as dialectically related: genesis was conceived without structure or structure without genesis. According to Piaget, genesis originates from a structure and culminates in another structure. All structures presuppose a construction, and therefore, structure and genesis are indissociable. In psychology and biology, dialectics of structure and genesis was developed by Piaget, Vygotsky, Moscovici and Duveen (see Psaltis, Part I of this volume).

Piaget was sympathetic to Goldmann's efforts to develop genetic structuralism in human and social sciences. He appreciated Goldmann as 'a creator of ideas as one rarely meets in a lifetime' and 'the inventor of a new form of symbolic thoughts' (Cohen, 1994, p. 4), and he arranged in Switzerland a studentship for Goldmann's PhD project on Kant. Goldmann made Piaget read Marx, but it is not clear to what extent Piaget adopted Goldmann's ideas in his genetic epistemology.

Genesis and Structure in Moscovici's and Duveen's Approaches

In his article on 'Genesis and structure' Duveen (2001/2013) posed the question: In what ways did Piaget inspire Moscovici? He responded to his query by referring to Moscovici's concern with the study of structures and social change: 'most characteristic of Moscovici's socio-psychological imagination is the attempt to thematise change', or even better, 'it is the way in which change is thematized in Moscovici's social psychology which is distinctive' (Duveen, 2001/2013, p. 61). Yet despite this, while adopting Piaget's constructivist epistemology in general terms as an opposition to static approaches to the acquisition of knowledge, Moscovici conceived 'structure' and 'genesis' as being embedded in the triangular relation of the self–other–object. This signified several vital epistemological differences between him and Piaget. First, in contrast to Piaget, who studied logical and mathematical constructions in child development, Moscovici studied transformations in social knowledge not only in terms of relations between thought and action but, vitally, as a process of communication. Second, and following from the first, in contrast to Piaget, for Moscovici language was not just a tool expanding thought but the defining feature of social knowledge and of social influence. Therefore, the relation between self and other was characterised not only by cooperation and constraint in terms of action and interaction; rather, these were language- and communication-based activities.

Duveen (2001/2013), who adopted the triangular model in his studies, emphasised that to understand transformations of social knowledge, following Moscovici, we must focus not only on dynamics of cognitive processes but also on transformations of values, ideas and practices. These developmental processes are always embedded in communication, whether interpersonal or mass mediated, and this implies that 'the structure of any social representation is a construction and thus the outcome of some developmental process' (Duveen & Lloyd, 1990, p. 5). This sociogenetic perspective was the feature of the three above-mentioned concepts that distinguished Piaget's genetic epistemology from Moscovici's epistemology, as will now be shown.

Epistemic Subject versus Psychological Subject

Duveen and Psaltis (2008/2013) pointed out that even in his most sociological writings Piaget did not appreciate the constitutive importance of social interaction in the genesis of structures. In contrast, social interaction is the leading force in Duveen's sociogenesis, and particularly in microgenesis. Rather than adopting Piaget's model of the epistemic subject in the form subject–object in the child's development of knowledge, Duveen embraced the triangular ego–alter–object relation (Moscovici, 1972), making the constructivist position inherently social. The child does not acquire knowledge solely through his or her own reasoning, but he/she constructs knowledge in the dynamics of social life which involves values and ideas that are embedded in communication and social practices. The child–child–task/object is a fundamental unit of analysis in the studies of interaction and knowledge and an excellent example portraying the ego–alter–object triangular model of the epistemology of social representations. This epistemology assumes the totality of living experience embedded in, and accumulated through, history and culture.

The epistemology of living experience implies that in one sense, relations between the ego–alter are those of constraint and force, leading to compliance due to the authority of the other. In another sense, relations between the ego–alter capture trust and communication rather than in the constraint due to asymmetric relations and authority. Developmental, situational, cultural and societal constraints carry the symbolic value in social representations.

Equilibrium versus Development through Conflict

One of Moscovici's early influences was Wiener (1948) who, in his studies of cybernetics, explored logical relations between the individual and social groups. He showed that individuals do not create a group or community to achieve homeostasis, but that a society is created by numerous kinds of interactions among members and their modes of communication involving patterns, gestalts and configurations. The concepts of 'structuredness' and 'formness' in cybernetics thus fundamentally contrasted with concepts of 'elements' or 'stimuli' and with their aggregates that prevailed in positivistic and behaviouristic approaches at the time. Equally, these concepts contrasted with many kinds of interaction in social psychology that were characterised by the tendency for symmetry, homeostasis, reciprocity and equilibrium, all searching to establish or restore balanced states. For example, Kurt Lewin's group dynamics is underlain by the idea of homeostasis and equilibrium among interacting agents and driving forces encouraging social change and restraining forces that resist change (Lewin, 1947/1951). The driving and restraining forces both contribute to creating equilibrium. Piaget's concept of interaction, just like Lewin's interaction, places emphasis on equilibration of cognitive structures through accommodation and assimilation (Piaget, 1954).

In a series of articles published in the 1990s, rather than building on psychological and sociological concepts of interaction, Galam and Moscovici (1991, 1994, 1995) took as their point of departure *thermodynamics and statistical physics*, specifically the concept of *spontaneous symmetry breaking*. Drawing on electrodynamics, they discussed the breaking of symmetry as a more general phenomenon that is 'evidenced at several levels of reality from cosmology to biology' (Galam & Moscovici, 1994, p. 481). Both physical and biological systems emerge from spontaneous movements of matter, from its symmetrical to asymmetrical states – that is, from static to dynamic states. The concept of *symmetry* in modern physics retains its importance with reference to laws of invariance, and it still dominates certain fields in physics, for example, the theory of relativity (Einstein rejected the concept of asymmetry as being too complex). Nevertheless, *spontaneous symmetry breaking* has become one of the most important concepts in accounting for dynamic physical effects and has become widely discussed and researched. Interaction breaks invariances; when humans interact and become interdependent, homeostasis and symmetry change into asymmetric and diverse forms of interaction. Individuals have a capacity to switch from asymmetry to symmetry, from equilibrium to disequilibrium, from conformity to innovation, and vice versa. It is the breakdown of symmetry that initiates a dynamic order, an order that is evolving, encouraging innovative ways of thinking, differentiating and generating new patterns of knowledge, beliefs, images and activities (Galam & Moscovici, 1994).

Interactions in social representations are directed towards both symmetries and asymmetries. Symmetries lead to compromise and a relative stability of social representations and recall Durkheim's collective representations. Some forms of communication, such as rumours or information provided by the media, may seem to encourage the metaphor of the spread by contagion (Sperber, 1990) and relative inactivity. In contrast, asymmetries of knowledge and of perspectives in which humans are actively involved are likely to create conflict and tension, instigate communication and motivate innovation.

Pre-established Stages versus Dynamic and Open Systems

Finally, Moscovici rejected Piaget's perspective that mental structures are determined by pre-established stages. Instead, he was attracted by two kinds of new developments that were taking place during the 1950s and 1960s. One was the phenomenological perspective of Merleau-Ponty (1964) who understood child's development as a dynamic and open system in a holistic manner. Merleau-Ponty (1964) did not view the child's representations as being initially inadequate or irrational and only gradually, through the passage of cognitive stages, reaching mature and logical adult thinking. Instead, Merleau-Ponty emphasised that children's mental processes and activities are adequate to their 'lived experience' in which these processes and activities take place. The other development concerned newly emerging fields such as cybernetics, system theories and communications. Among these, Moscovici was attracted to the study of intricate interactions between humans and nature. Exploring the interdependence between nature and culture, humanity and animality, as well as nature as historical and humans as natural, Moscovici (1974/2012) postulated the concept of *biunique societies as a new episteme.* 'Biunique' implied the one-to-one relationship between each society or community and its specific natural environment. Both humans and nature transform one another in the dynamic and historical process that for Moscovici defined the ecological movement in the 1960s and 1970s. Just like Moscovici, the French philosopher Edgar Morin adopted this perspective in the ecological movement. Morin's epistemology of dialogical thinking and Moscovici's new episteme were motivated by the Hegelian/Marxian ideas of dynamic and historical interdependencies of antagonistic processes. The dialogical principle regards antagonistic processes as being united in a complementary way in a single reality, and so indissociable from one another. Whilst the classic scientific thinking strictly separated order from disorder, organised from disorganised states, and rationality from irrationality, Morin (2008, p. 19) does not view opposites as excluding one another. Instead, the logical core of dialogical complexity is to treat 'separability-inseparability, whole-parts, effect-cause, product-producer, life-death, homo sapiens-homo demens' as complementary in the Hegelian manner. Moscovici subscribed to an open logic based on living experience without any predetermined stages. The structure transforms itself in dependence on the newly selected, de-selected and re-selected features based on the oppositional nature of human thinking, such as hidden/apparent, involuntary/voluntary, inner/outer.

Moscovici and Morin reject 'hierarchy' as an organising principle of the system. For Moscovici, the alternative to 'hierarchy' is not anarchy, promiscuity or randomness, but 'heterarchy', which means that the tasks between individuals and groups are distributed to coordinate their actions in cooperation. Heterarchy presupposes a decentralised organisation which safeguards a degree of freedom and establishes a reflexive relationship between parts. As an example of heterarchy, let us recall an extreme event showing multiple self–other relations that followed the catastrophe of the Grenfell Tower fire in London on 14 June 2017 in which 72 people tragically died. Flora Cornish (2021), who has undertaken an ethnographic study of this catastrophe, showed multiple heterarchical relations between the self and members of the community and between the self, community and institutions. Cornish explained that while much literature focuses on 'collective actions' as being successful, the experience of activism after Grenfell has been characterised by frustrating partial wins, inertia, delays and setbacks, or what she calls 'activism beyond hope and despair'. She described how the affected individuals transformed into activists demanding changes in public policies to ensure that such a tragedy would never happen again. Collective actions of survivors of the catastrophe and their struggle with institutions implicated by this event showed that activism is not modelled on a linear and hierarchical journey to succeed or fail, but is a frustrating heterarchical journey in which setbacks, glimpses of hope, delays and short steps forward all take pace simultaneously.

Conclusion

Although the constructivist epistemologies of Piaget, Goldmann, Moscovici and Duveen are linked by questions about the nature knowledge, I have tried to show in this commentary that these epistemologies are not 'the same'. Their responses concerning the construction of knowledge are based on different concepts of rationality which, in one case, are answered in 'cognitive' terms and in the other case include both 'cognitive' and 'non-cognitive' characteristics. Such a broad distinction between constructivist epistemologies, however, requires further stipulations, because specific research and professional problems demand different epistemological arguments. Let us consider two examples which show that what is meant by the 'same' or 'different' epistemology depends on the problem with which the researcher is concerned in the concrete here-and-now.

In one context, Duveen (1997/2013) stated that Moscovici and Piaget shared the same epistemological stance. He made this claim in the context of Piaget's and Moscovici's defences and elaborations of their constructivist positions, arguing against empiricism or a priori rationalistic approaches: both Piaget and Moscovici insisted that human world is constructed from interactions between the individual and environment, and the term 'genetic' expressed the constructivist epistemological positions that they both held. To that extent it was meaningful to state that Piaget and Moscovici shared the same epistemological stance.

In another context, when Duveen was exploring (e.g. Duveen, 1984/2013; Duveen and Psaltis, 2008/2013) the epistemology of social representations *within* in the context of constructivism, he expressed doubts about genetic epistemology as formulated by Piaget. Piaget's constructivist epistemology was concerned only with the epistemic subject and not with the psychological subject, and this seriously reduced the relevance of genetic epistemology for social representations. Duveen kept raising the perspective of Piaget's differentiation between the epistemic subject and the psychological subject throughout his career, both defending and critiquing Piaget's perspective (see also Psaltis, Part I in this volume).

In this commentary I chose this latter case in order to contrast constructivist epistemologies of Piaget/Goldmann (based on the subject–object interaction) and Moscovici/ Duveen (based on the subject–other–object interdependence). I focused on their diverse perspectives in relation to three concepts, namely epistemic *versus* psychological subject, equilibration *versus* the development through conflict, and linear or continuous development *versus* discontinuity. Both kinds of epistemology refer to themselves as dialectic. Piaget and Goldmann conceive their epistemologies as dialectic because they emphasise evolution and the transformation of knowledge. Just like the dialectic of Marx or Hegel, they assume the hierarchical development of less advanced into more progressive stages. These kinds of dialectic are based on the idea that evolutions and histories strive towards predetermined goals (for details of 'histories' with a goal, see Marková, 2003, pp. 21–23). For Piaget, the dialectic hierarchical progression is completed when the child achieves formal operations.

Moscovici rejected dialectics based on the development in stages and hierarchies. He and Morin (see earlier discussion) argued that hierarchies are not organising principles of living systems. Instead, processes between individuals and groups are organised as 'heterarchies' – that is, decentralised organisations which safeguard a degree of freedom and establish reflexive relationships among components of the system. Moreover, the triadic self–other–object relation presupposes a communicative interdependence. Communication and dialogue are open processes that cannot be organised into hierarchies, and one cannot predict where the development will lead. This is one of the most important features that distinguish dialectics with a predetermined goal from dialogicality as an open system leading to undetermined events. As Michael Bakhtin insisted, the last word has not yet been spoken. Social representations, as Moscovici and Duveen showed, develop in and through dialogue.

REFERENCES

Boelhower, W. Q. (1980). Introduction. In L. Goldmann (Ed.), *Essays on method in the sociology of literature* (pp. 5–34). Transl. W. Q. Boelhower. St. Louis, MO: Telos Press.

Cohen, M. (1994). *The wager of Lucien Goldmann*. Princeton, NJ: Princeton University Press.

Cornish, F. (2021). 'Grenfell changes everything?' Activism beyond hope and despair, *Critical Public Health*, *31*, 293–305.

Duveen, G. (1984/2013). Social life and the epistemic subject. In S. Moscovici, S. Jovchelovitch, & B. Wagoner (Eds.), *Development as a social process: Contributions of Gerard Duveen* (pp. 67–89). London: Routledge.

(1997a/2013). Psychological development as a social process. In S. Moscovici, S. Jovchelovitch, & B. Wagoner (Eds.), *Development as a social process: Contributions of Gerard Duveen* (pp. 90–111). London: Routledge.

(1997b/2013). Construction, belief, doubt. In S. Moscovici, S. Jovchelovitch, & B. Wagoner (Eds.), *Development as a social process: Contributions of Gerard Duveen* (pp. 112–123). London: Routledge.

(2001). Representations, identities, resistance. In K. Deaux & G. Philogène (Eds.), *Representations of the social* (pp. 257–270). Oxford: Blackwell.

(2001/2013). Genesis and structure: Piaget and Moscovici. In S. Moscovici, S. Jovchelovitch, & B. Wagoner (Eds.), *Development as a social process: Contributions of Gerard Duveen* (pp. 56–64). London: Routledge.

Duveen, G., & Lloyd, B. (Eds.). (1990). *Social representations and the development of knowledge*. Cambridge: Cambridge University Press.

Duveen, G., & Psaltis, C. (2008/2013). The constructive role of asymmetries in social interaction. In S. Moscovici, S. Jovchelovitch, & B. Wagoner, B. (Eds.), *Development as a Social Process: Contributions of Gerard Duveen* (pp. 13–153). London: Routledge.

Elkind, D. (1967). Editor's introduction. In Piaget, J. *Six psychological studies* (pp. v–xviii). Transl. A. Tenzer. New York: Random House.

Galam, S., & Moscovici, S. (1991). Towards a theory of collective phenomena: consensus and attitude changes in group. *European Journal of Social Psychology*, *21*, 49–74.

(1994). Towards a theory of collective phenomena. II: Conformity and power. *European Journal of Social Psychology*, *24*, 481–495.

(1995). Towards a theory of collective phenomena: III: Conflicts and forms of power. *European Journal of Social Psychology*, *25*, 217–229.

Goldmann, L. (1959). *Recherches dialectiques*. Paris: Les Editions Gallimard.

(1976). *Cultural creation in modern society*. St Louis, MO: Telos Press.

(1980). *Essays on method in the sociology of literature*. Transl. and Ed. W. Q. Boelhower. St. Louis, MO: Telos Press.

(2009). *Lukács and Heidegger: Towards a new philosophy*. Transl. W. Q. Boelhower. London: Routledge.

Kant, I. (1781/1929). *Critique of pure reason*. Transl. N. K. Smith. London; New York: Macmillan; St Martin's Press.

(1788/1873). *Critique of practical reason*. Transl. T. K. Abbott. London: Longsman, Green.

Lewin, K. (1947/1951). Frontiers in group dynamics. In D. Cartwright (Ed.), *Field theory in social science: Selected theoretical papers by Kurt Lewin* (pp. 188–237). New York: Harper.

Locke, J. (1690/1961). *An essay concerning human understanding*. Two volumes. Ed. J. W. Yolton. London; New York: Dent; Dutton.
Marková, I. (1982). *Paradigms, thought and language*. Chichester: Wiley.
(2003). *Dialogicality and social representations*. Cambridge: Cambridge University Press.
Marx, K. (1959). *Economic and philosophical manuscripts of 1944*. Transl. M. Milligan. Moscow: Progress Publishers.
Mayrl, W. W. (1978). Genetic structuralism and the analysis of social consciousness. *Theory and Society*, 5(1), 19–44.
Merleau-Ponty, M. (1964). Méthode en psychologie de l'enfant. *Bulletin de Psychologie*, *18*, 109–140.
Morin, E. (1959). *Autocritique*. Paris: Editions de Seuil.
(2008). Restricted complexity, general complexity. arXiv:cs/0610049v1[csCC] 10 Oct 2006.
Moscovici, S. (1972). Society and theory in social psychology. In J. Israel & H. Tajfel (Eds.), *The context of social psychology: A critical assessment* (pp. 17–68). London: Academic Press.
(1974/2012). Nos sociétés biuniques. *Revue Communications*, *22*, 135–150.
Moscovici, S., & Marková, I. (2000). Ideas and their development: A dialogue between Serge Moscovici and Ivana Marková. In G. Duveen (Ed.), *Social representations* (pp. 224–286). London: Polity Press.
Piaget, J. (1942). *Classes, relations and nombres*. Paris: Vrin.
(1947/2001). *The psychology of intelligence*. Transl. M. Piercy & D. E. Berlyne. London: Routledge.
(1954). *The construction of reality in the child*. Abington: Routledge and Kegan Paul.
(1967). *Six psychological studies*. Transl. A. Tenzer. New York: Random House.
(1970). Piaget's theory. In P. H. Mussen (Ed.), *Carmichael's manual of child psychology* (Vol. I, pp. 703–732). Transl. G. Cellérier & J. Langer. New York: John Wiley.
(1971). *Biology and knowledge*. Edinburgh: Edinburgh University Press.
Sperber, D. (1990). The epidemiology of beliefs. In C. Fraser & G. Gaskell (Eds.), *The social psychological study of widespread beliefs* (pp. 25–44). Oxford: Oxford University Press.
Wiener, N. (1948). *Cybernetics, or control and communication in the animal and the machine*. New York: Wiley.

CHAPTER 7

Towards a Future-Oriented Psychology

Creating Human Development

Alex Gillespie

Introduction

Psaltis (Part I in this volume) invites us to rethink the aims of social and developmental psychology to address our contemporary challenges better. We currently face a 'polycrisis' – that is, interacting crises that feedback on themselves, catalysing themselves. This term originated in the 1990s (Kern & Morin, 1993) and has recently gained traction in characterising how several crises are compounding one another (Derbyshire, 2023). Climate change, inequality, infectious diseases, inflation and war are mutually reinforcing crises. This escalation creates uncertainty. What should individuals and societies do? The aim of science, Dewey (1929) argued, is to reduce uncertainty.

One source of certainty in our unfolding polycrisis concerns our role in it. We can take hope and despair, in equal measure, from the fact that human behaviour is implicated in each crisis. While it is tragic that we are grappling with problems of our own making, it should also give us courage because in so far as we have made these problems, we also have the potential to address them. It is not just the polycrisis but specifically our role in either exacerbating or attenuating these crises that necessitates a rethink of social and developmental psychology.

Given our central role in the polycrisis, is it still sufficient for social and developmental psychology to describe people as they are? Questions about how people develop and interact, in a timeless sense, seem quaint. Surely, our current conditions call for more radical questions. How could we develop? What could we become? The question is not whether humans can agree a plan to address our various crises, but rather how we can make it so that humans can address these crises.

The Aims of the Research

While there is some debate about the extent to which the scientific method is independent of social and political concerns (Beland & Cox, 2010), there can be no debate about the fact that what we choose to direct the scientific method at is inherently guided by social and political concerns. The problems that we choose to address with science reflect the concerns of our time (Mead, 1936; Rorty, 1998). The scientific method can address an infinite number of questions, but the vast majority have no apparent theoretical or practical interest. For example, measuring the distance from each grain of sand on a beach to every other grain of sand would be a herculean task, dwarfing the resource investment of any scientific study to date. But we choose (quite sensibly) not to pursue it. The questions we choose to pursue tend to benefit someone – and not always the people being studied (e.g. research on advertising, persuasion and manipulation). The point is that there is no neutral scientific question because every scientific study entails a choice not to study something else. The choice of what to study is always social and political.

Social and developmental psychology have amassed mountains of empirical data – hundreds of thousands of studies. But Psaltis (2023) asks: What for? Beyond the cynical answer to this question – that it is 'for' career advancement – Habermas (1968) has identified three broad interests guiding knowledge construction, namely technocratic, hermeneutic and emancipatory interests.

Technocratic interests seek knowledge that predicts, guides interventions and can influence the world and especially other people. For example, political parties use big and small data to make strategic choices on policy issues to increase the chances of being elected. Governments research the impact of remote working, lockdowns and citizen incomes to manage and guide societal changes. Technocratic interests do not require understanding, merely prediction and control. In the social sciences, technocratic interests often entail one group (e.g. companies, governments, health services) creating knowledge to predict the behaviour of another group (e.g. consumers, citizens, patients).

Hermeneutic interests seek knowledge that provides understanding, explanation and tells a good story. This interest leads to knowledge that provides insight into the world, history and the human condition. From a hermeneutic standpoint, technocratic knowledge (e.g. prediction) is unsatisfying because it does not explain the 'why' of human behaviour. Knowledge answering to hermeneutic interests does not need to predict or control anything; it only aims to explain, using narratives and metaphors, to help us make sense of our predicaments.

Emancipatory interests seek knowledge that empowers people to act on the world or themselves. Habermas (1968) argues that this entails reflective reason grasping itself as interested and attempting to transcend those interests. Habermas gives the example of psychoanalysis, which provides people with concepts they can use to liberate themselves from their unconscious. Emancipation often begins with understanding the causes of behaviour, but then, through this understanding, humans can manipulate these causes to produce different outcomes. Thus, ironically, understanding these so-called causes of human behaviour can liberate humans from these causes, turning them into choices (e.g. choices about genetic modification, socialisation and education).

Psaltis's (2023) proposal for genetic social and developmental psychology is emancipatory. He aims to offer a theory of social change as a road map that will enable humans to think critically and subsequently guide themselves into the future. Specifically, he seeks to build on the work of Piaget (1977) and Duveen (2008) to construct a theory that captures the dynamics of social change that foregrounds heterogeneity, identity and asymmetries. This aim is laudable and deserves our support. But does it go far enough to address our current polycrisis?

Using a road map entails a desired destination. Most maps can lead to many destinations. How should one choose? And how do tourists decide to travel to a destination that they have never been to before? They choose based on pre-imagined potential destinations. Before arrival, there is an expectation. Indeed, much of popular culture (films, novels, internet stories) scaffold our imagination of distant destinations, enabling us to imagine a wide range of destinations. These imaginations empower tourists to choose their destinations (Gillespie, 2007). Similarly, we can conceptualise human development as a journey. From this standpoint, we need to begin with an understanding of the possible destinations of human development. Thus, it is not enough to have a theory of social change based on what is (as if our knowledge is a mirror of nature; Rorty, 1981). Instead, we must refocus on what could be (Gergen, 2015; Rorty, 1999). We need to create possibilities through which people become emancipated to make choices about their development. That is to say, in addition to creating road maps, social and developmental researchers also need to help people imagine the possible destinations of human and societal development. And more narrowly, researchers need to become more explicit about their role in the social change process. Even ignoring researchers' role in social change is a choice.

To rethink the future of social and developmental psychology, I argue two assumptions need to be adopted. First, human social and societal development is open-ended. Second, research should aim not merely to describe what is but also to imagine what could be.

Open-ended Development

Despite many profound insights, neither Piaget nor Vygotsky fully appreciated the diversity of possible outcomes for human or societal development. Their work was foundational for understanding how social relations drive human and societal development through scaffolding (Berk & Winsler, 1995; Gillespie & Hald, 2017; Vygotsky, 1978) and relations of cooperation and constraint (Psaltis & Duveen, 2006, 2007). Their ideas form the basis for a sociocultural understanding of how humans shape their own material and social environments, which in turn feed back and shape human and societal development. But they both assumed that individuals (and, to a lesser extent, societies) were teleologically developing towards an endpoint. However, since their pioneering work, the assumption of linear development has been increasingly challenged. The metaphor of human development as linear should be replaced with less normative and prescriptive metaphors (Zittoun & Gillespie, 2020). Research on people with autism that attempts to give up on neurotypical assumptions and study autistic people on their own terms has found increasingly subtle forms of sociality (Heasman & Gillespie, 2017, 2019). Research on animals continues to surprise not only in terms of how advanced they are relative to humans but especially in terms of how advanced they are on their own terms (Wynne & Udell, 2020). And research on plants increasingly reveals communication and coordination capabilities that are simply incomparable to any human ability (Bonfante & Anca, 2009). The metaphor of the 'tree of life' adequately captures the innumerably diverse development endpoints, both between and within species. We need to become more attuned to the diversity of potential developments both between and within species. This sensitivity logically entails a new research question. The question is not how individuals or societies develop. The question becomes: What type of individuals or societies do we want?

There is a paradigmatic difference between dialectical and dialogical development (Wegerif, 2008). Piaget and Vygotsky, influenced by Marx and Hegel, had teleological or dialectical models of development. They assumed that development was towards a singular and known point. In contrast, consider Bakhtin's (1981, 1986) ideas about dialogical development. Novels, like dialogues, Bakhtin argued, can have multiple endings: they do not teleologically progress toward a predefined endpoint. Instead, they are fundamentally open-ended. Participants in a dialogue make history; the sequence of words in context and the emerging nuances will be unique (assuming it is more than a formulaic interaction). There are so many degrees of freedom in a dialogue, with multiple parties contributing, that the development is fundamentally creative and emergent. Similarly, novels have an infinity of possible endings because of the infinite degrees of freedom being laid down, word by word, by the author. The key point is that although the outcome of dialogues, novels and, by extension, human life is unpredictable and creative, it does not mean we should give up studying development. It means we should examine the agency and responsibility of all participants to make their future. It means we should investigate the extent to which the participants can critically reflect on the future that they are making, and whether they are aware of alternative futures.

Like Psaltis (2023), I believe that social and developmental psychology needs a strong future orientation. Some may see this as optimistic, but it is also the basis for pessimism. Without humans on the planet, I would be much more optimistic about the future of all terrestrial plants and species. Humans have growing agency; we are increasingly responsible for the fate of ourselves, other species, and even the earth's ecology. In each case, our individual and collective behaviour could lead to diverse outcomes.

However, human agency cannot be taken for granted. As Psaltis (2023) argues, agency can be cultivated or curtailed. Certain institutions, patterns of education and societal norms can conceal the choices that people could make individually and collectively. The mere awareness of alternative possibilities has been enough to change individuals' life trajectories and alter the course of entire societies (Power, 2020; Wagoner et al., 2018; Zittoun & Gillespie, 2018). This is why alternatives are so destabilising (Gillespie, 2008). Revolutions, for example, begin not with what is, but with ideas about what could be (Zittoun & Gillespie, 2015).

Research that aims only to describe the world as it is, rather than what it could be, is complicit in naturalising our current polycrisis. By naturalising I'm referring to the tendency to see human-made crises as a product of nature rather than a product of human activity (Berger & Luckmann, 1967). To study what is, to only make predictions about what will be, as if the present inevitably leads to the future, is to conceal humans' role in constructing the future. Such research is, arguably, dangerous because it obscures our responsibility for the crises we face and the future we will create. Thus, from the idea of open-ended development, we must recover a sense of personal and collective responsibility for our individual and societal trajectories. We must acknowledge that whatever happens, the outcome could have been different depending on our actions.

Creating Possibilities

Choosing the goals of human and societal development is not a scientific question. Social scientists should not seek to solve our contemporary crises. Instead, researchers can play a critical role in helping people to imagine possible futures and provide rigorous speculation about possible pathways. It is not for researchers to tell people which possible future to strive for. Instead, they should help people to envision their individual and collective possible futures. This has already happened in climate change simulations that show the impact of various policies and the models that were used during the COVID-19 pandemic to project mortality rates under various interventions. I propose to extrapolate this basic idea into the core business of social science in general and social and developmental psychology in particular.

Assuming that social and developmental psychology has an emancipatory aim, the question becomes: How should we best achieve that aim? Given the infinity of possible research questions, which research questions should we pursue? What research projects are most likely to emancipate and empower people? Research already examines the factors that lead to our current state of human and societal development. What is lacking is more abductive and creative research on alternative trajectories of human and societal development. What pathways of ontological development are possible? What are the possible near, medium and far goals for human societal development? And, for any developmental trajectory, what are the most useful resources to empower people and societies on their journey (Gillespie & Zittoun, 2010)?

As a case study in development, Psaltis's (2023) account of moving from a nationalist to a reflective and sceptical position is instructive. It reveals the many sociocultural layers that hold the Cypriot conflict in place: politics and education are obvious barriers, but also grandparents, family history, classroom practices and students' dreams for the future (e.g. in education or the military). Psaltis's account, beyond showing the forces of stasis, also provides insight into how social change, at least at the level of an individual, can occur and how a perspective-transcending viewpoint can emerge. How does this happen? In Psaltis's case, leaving Cyprus (first for military training in Greece, and then for higher-level studies in the United Kingdom) seems particularly important. This physical distance from Cyprus arguably enabled psychological distancing (Gillespie & Martin, 2014) and self-reflection (Gillespie, 2018). It also put Psaltis in contact with other people who think differently, who saw the conflict from the outside, and who provided new discourses about conflict, nationalism and the infrastructure that is needed to imagine a community and prolong a conflict. These encounters with people and ideas enabled Psaltis to see the Cyrus issue in a new light; to see possibilities for the future that had been obscured. But such cognitive distanciation and self-reflection is insufficient. Creating the future requires conviction and a sense of responsibility to act upon such insights, to cease being determined by history, and instead to try and create history – as Psaltis did with his colleagues when they established the Home for Co-operation.

When analysing a conflict situation such as Cyprus, current social psychological theory turns to the contact hypothesis (Allport, 1954). Hundreds of studies have refined the conditions for positive contact, including institutional support, the prototypicality of interactants, successful outcomes, clear role division and interacting on the basis of group rather than individual identities (Paluck et al., 2019; Zhou et al., 2019). Studies have examined the frequency of contact, whether the contact is voluntary, whether the observed behaviour confirms or disconfirms expectations, whether the contact is superficial or intimate, face-to-face or mediated and so on. And yet, despite so many studies, with so many variables, our capacity to overcome group conflict remains minimal. The problem is that the so-called theory is, more accurately, a 'laundry list' of variables (Gillespie, 2015; Pettigrew, 1998). Each time the theory fails, another condition is added to the list. But maybe no one set of conditions will inevitably yield conflict reduction. Perhaps it is necessary to go beyond generic factors to consider specific factors. Perhaps it is necessary to go beyond the push from the past to consider the potential full for the future. Thus, the focus should be less on what caused the conflict and more on what can be done to construct a future that sufficiently addresses peoples' specific concerns. The aim is not for a perfect 'solution' or 'resolution' but rather to create in incremental improvement upon the present (Lederach, 2005).

Psaltis (2023) correctly focuses on the 'prospect' of the group: that is, what the representational project of the group is (Bauer & Gaskell, 1999). I suggest building on this insight. The aim of contact should not be to resolve the past but to transform the future (Mitchell, 2002). The communities should be helped to envision various scenarios out of the multitude of possible futures, for example, a continuation of the status quo, conflict escalation or living together. An alternative future becomes possible once the participants have agreed upon it and believe they have the power to institute it. As Psaltis points out, such progress will likely require substantial material changes to education, media and communication.

These challenges are real and should not be underestimated. My point is that such changes are impossible unless communities desire a new future and believe they have the agency to make it a reality. Thus, the aim is not to resolve or rewrite the irreversible events of the past, but rather to create tomorrow's history by seizing today (Lederach, 2015).

Making a new future is challenging. There are many barriers and forces of stasis that must be overcome. To overcome these obstacles, research can be helpful. Psaltis (2023) shows how education in Cyprus prevents the creation of a future in which both Turkish and Greek Cypriots live together. Instead, education emphasises the events of 1974 and implies that a return to the past is the only fair and natural outcome. The problem is that such narratives can be 'semantic barriers' (Gillespie, 2020; Psaltis, 2012) that block engagement with alternative futures. A return to the past is not realistic for either side. The current starting point is not in the past but in the present. The question becomes: What changes might improve what is rather than what was? But engaging in such future-making requires openness. And researchers can promote such openness by critically examining the ideas that block the exploration of possible futures (Zittoun & Gillespie, 2015).

Conclusion

It can seem naïve to write about creating possibilities in a time of crisis (Glăveanu, 2022). But we must keep in mind that we have created, or at least contributed to, our current crises. Creating possibilities is not just about the upside. Humans have shown, time and again, that we are tragically able to create downside possibilities. The crises we face are, in large part, human creations. Yet, despite causing them, we have not fully taken responsibility for them. The point is that we need to appreciate that our future will be, in part, our collective creation. With the increasing power of technologies (both material and social), we are increasingly shaping our future. Only by acknowledging this can we become sufficiently empowered to choose our future. Conversely, not acknowledging this, and continuing to study human development as we find it, risks perpetuating our current crises. Given our polycrisis, the real naïvete is naturalising the future, assuming that it happens to us independently of human choices.

REFERENCES

Allport, G. (1954). *The nature of prejudice*. Boston, MA: Addison-Wesley.
Bakhtin, M. (1981). *The dialogic imagination: Four essays*. Austin: University of Texas Press.

(1986). *Speech genres & other late essays*. Austin: University of Texas Press.
Bauer, M. W., & Gaskell, G. (1999). Towards a paradigm for research on social representations. *Journal for the Theory of Social Behaviour, 29*(2), 163–186.
Beland, D., & Cox, R. H. (2010). *Ideas and politics in social science research*. Oxford: Oxford University Press.
Berger, P. L., & Luckmann, T. (1967). *The social construction of reality*. New York: Doubleday.
Berk, L. E., & Winsler, A. (1995). *Scaffolding children's learning: Vygotsky and early childhood education*. Washington, DC: National Association for the Young Children.
Bonfante, P., & Anca, I.-A. (2009). Plants, mycorrhizal fungi, and bacteria: A network of interactions. *Annual Review of Microbiology, 63*(1), 363–383. https://doi.org/10.1146/annurev.micro.091208.073504.
Derbyshire, J. (2023, January 1). *Year in a word: Polycrisis*. Financial Times. Available at www.ft.com/content/f6c4f63c-aa71-46f0-a0a7-c2a4c4a3c0f1.
Dewey, J. (1929). *The quest for certainty*. New York: Minton, Balch & Company.
Duveen, G. (2008). Social actors and social groups: A return to heterogeneity in social psychology. *Journal for the Theory of Social Behaviour, 38*(4), 369–374. https://doi.org/10.1111/j.1468-5914.2008.00385.x.
Gergen, K. J. (2015). From mirroring to world-making: Research as future forming. *Journal for the Theory of Social Behaviour, 45*(3), 287–310. https://doi.org/10.1111/jtsb.12075.
Gillespie, A. (2007). Time, self and the other: The striving tourist in Ladakh, north India. In L. Simao & J. Valsiner (Eds.), *Otherness in question: Development of the self* (pp. 163–186). Charlotte, NC: Information Age Publishing.
(2008). Social representations, alternative representations and semantic barriers. *Journal for the Theory of Social Behaviour, 38*(4), 375–391. https://doi.org/10.1111/j.1468-5914.2008.00376.x.
(2015). Non-transformative social interaction. In C. Psaltis, A. Gillespie, & A. N. Perret-Clermont (Eds.), *Social relations in human and societal development* (pp. 97–113). London: Palgrave Macmillan.
(2018). Distinguishing two processes of self-reflection. In J. Valsiner & A. Rosa (Eds.), *The Cambridge handbook of sociocultural psychology* (pp. 245–259). Cambridge: Cambridge University Press.
(2020). Semantic contact and semantic barriers: Reactionary responses to disruptive ideas. *Current Opinion in Psychology, 35*, 21–25. https://doi.org/10.1016/j.copsyc.2020.02.010.
Gillespie, A., & Hald, J. (2017). The paradox of helping: Contradictory effects of scaffolding people with aphasia to communicate. *PLoS ONE, 12*(8), e0180708. https://doi.org/10.1371/journal.pone.0180708.
Gillespie, A., & Martin, J. (2014). Position Exchange Theory: A socio-material basis for discursive and psychological positioning. *New Ideas in Psychology, 32*, 73–79.
Gillespie, A., & Zittoun, T. (2010). Using resources: Conceptualizing the mediation and reflective use of tools and signs. *Culture & Psychology, 16*(1), 37–62. https://doi.org/10.1177/1354067X09344888.

Glăveanu, V. P. (2022). Possibility studies: A manifesto. *Possibility Studies & Society*, 27538699221127580. https://doi.org/10.1177/27538699221127580.
Habermas, J. (1968). *Knowledge and human interests*. Cambridge: Polity Press.
Heasman, B., & Gillespie, A. (2017). Perspective-taking is two-sided: Misunderstandings between people with Asperger's syndrome and their family members. *Autism*, *22*(6), 740–750. https://doi.org/10.1177/1362361317708287.
(2019). Neurodivergent intersubjectivity: Distinctive features of how autistic people create shared understanding. *Autism*, *23*(4), 910–921. https://doi.org/10.1177/1362361318785172.
Kern, A.-B., & Morin, E. (1993). *Terre-patrie*. Paris: Média Diffusion.
Lederach, J. (2005). *The moral imagination: The art and soul of building peace*. Oxford: Oxford University Press.
(2015). *Little book of conflict transformation: Clear articulation of the guiding principles by a pioneer in the field*. New York: Simon and Schuster.
Mead, G. H. (1936). *Movements of thought in the nineteenth century* (M. H. Moore, Ed.). Chicago: University of Chicago Press.
Mitchell, C. (2002). Beyond resolution: What does conflict transformation actually transform? *Peace and Conflict Studies*, *9*(1), 1–23. https://doi.org/10.46743/1082-7307/2002.1020.
Paluck, E. L., Green, S. A., & Green, D. P. (2019). The contact hypothesis re-evaluated. *Behavioural Public Policy*, *3*(2), 129–158. https://doi.org/10.1017/bpp.2018.25.
Pettigrew, T. F. (1998). Intergroup contact theory. *Annual Review of Psychology*, *49*(1), 65–85. https://doi.org/10.1146/annurev.psych.49.1.65.
Piaget, J. (1977). *Sociological studies* (L. Smith, Ed.). London: Psychology Press.
Power, S. A. (2020). Editorial overview: The psychology of rallies, riots, and revolutions. *Current Opinion in Psychology*, *35*, v–x. https://doi.org/10.1016/j.copsyc.2020.08.018.
Psaltis, C. (2012). Culture and social representations: A continuing dialogue in search for heterogeneity in social developmental psychology. *Culture & Psychology*, *18*(3), 375–390. https://doi.org/10.1177/1354067X12446233.
Psaltis, C., & Duveen, G. (2006). Social relations and cognitive development: The influence of conversation type and representations of gender. *European Journal of Social Psychology*, *36*(3), 407–430.
(2007). Conservation and conversation types: Forms of recognition and cognitive development. *British Journal of Developmental Psychology*, *25*(1), 79–102.
Rorty, R. (1981). *Philosophy and the mirror of nature*. Princeton, NJ: Princeton University Press.
(1998). *Truth and progress: Philosophical papers*. Cambridge: Cambridge University Press.
(1999). *Philosophy and social hope*. New York: Penguin.
Vygotsky, L. S. (1978). *Mind in society: The development of higher psychological processes*. Cambridge, MA: Harvard University Press.
Wagoner, B., Moghaddam, F. M., & Valsiner, J. (2018). *The psychology of radical social change: From rage to revolution*. Cambridge: Cambridge University Press.

Wegerif, R. (2008). Dialogic or dialectic? The significance of ontological assumptions in research on educational dialogue. *British Educational Research Journal, 34*(3), 347–361. https://doi.org/10.1080/01411920701532228.

Wynne, C. D. L., & Udell, M. A. R. (2020). *Animal cognition: Evolution, behavior and cognition*. London: Bloomsbury Publishing.

Zhou, S., Page-Gould, E., Aron, A., Moyer, A., & Hewstone, M. (2019). The extended contact hypothesis: A meta-analysis on 20 years of research. *Personality and Social Psychology Review, 23*(2), 132–160. https://doi.org/10.1177/1088868318762647.

Zittoun, T., & Gillespie, A. (2015). *Imagination in human and cultural development*. London: Routledge.

(2018). Imagining the collective future: A sociocultural perspective. In C. de Saint-Laurent, S. Obradovic, & K. R. Carriere (Eds.), *Imagining Collective Futures* (pp. 15–37). London: Palgrave. https://doi.org/10.1007/978-3-319-76051-3_2.

(2020). Metaphors of development and the development of metaphors. *Theory & Psychology, 30*(6), 827–841. https://doi.org/10.1177/0959354320939194.

CHAPTER 8

Affects and the Person in Integrative Developmental Psychologies

Tania Zittoun

Introduction

When one is a developmental psychologist, how is it possible to study a phenomenon as complex as the historical transformation of an island together with the experience of its inhabitants? How can we both try to understand the history of the division of Cyprus and at the same time how it affects the everyday lives of people? And how, then, can we conceive that these persons whose lives are deeply shaped by the conflict may imagine new possible futures?

To address such difficult questions, Charis Psaltis proposes a research program, or rather a theoretical approach, that he refers to as genetic social psychology. In his words, 'It is the grasp of the totality of an object of study through an investigation of its development through time' (see Part I of this volume). The core question raised by such an approach is: How to conceptualise a complex phenomenon, made of components of different sorts (institution, ideologies, walls, people), that obey different forms of processes and yet interact? Various meta-theories have proposed ways to conceptualise complex systems in psychology, based on various ontologies and epistemologies (Bronfenbrenner, 1995; Doise & Valentim, 2015; Engeström & Sannino, 2010; L. B. Smith & Thelen, 2003). One criterion for the choice of such models is how well they respect the requirements of the type of explanation to be given to a phenomenon under study. Here, Psaltis wants to address development (of the child, the person, intergroup dynamics, the country) and how these various actors conceive the others – both in terms of cognitive understanding and meaning-making. This thus requires a model that captures the temporality – the historicity, or the genesis of the phenomena at hand – and its complexity at different scales (Lemke, 2000). In his project of a genetic social psychology, Psaltis proposes to integrate various strands of psychology along the tripartite concepts of sociogenesis, microgenesis and ontogenesis. He applies it to the case study of

Cyprus and its long-standing division. His analysis aims at integrating the sociogenesis of the social representations of the out-group – Greek Cypriots vs Turkish Cypriots, the microgenesis of intergroup contacts and the ontogenetic narrative of his own biographical trajectory

In this chapter, I first propose to retrace three conceptual variations of the tripartite model, and I highlight conceptual ambiguities they maintain around the issues of affects, and their model of the subject. Second, drawing on these two points, I emphasise the role of affects in the case study reported by Psaltis, and I argue that it needs an adequate model of the person. Third, as an opening, I propose to engage a dialogue with sociocultural psychological approaches; a dialogue across case studies may bring us to develop a more integrative understanding of how humans develop in a changing world.

Articulating Sociogenesis, Microgenesis and Ontogenesis: A Triple Genealogy of Concepts

For his project of a genetic social psychology, Psaltis draws on the work of Gerard Duveen, who precisely devised a simple system to address the genesis of social representations in people, in interactions and in the social world with the notions of sociogenesis, microgenesis and ontogenesis. This tripartite concept has a great heuristic power, but it also has some limits. Looking closer at their genealogy, it appears that similar conceptualisation came to be in the 1990s, but with different roots. Although they partially overlap, they also differ – and interestingly, it is in their divergences that lay the weaker points of the proposal.

A First Genealogy of a Tripartite Concept

As carefully retraced by Psaltis (Part I in this volume), in the early 1990s, Duveen proposed to articulate the contributions of social psychology, especially Serge Moscovici's social representations (Moscovici, 2000, 2008), and of developmental psychology in the double lineage of Jean Piaget and Lev Vygotsky. He defined the project of a 'genetic social psychology' by which he meant that both cognitive schemes à la Piaget and social representations could be seen as structures 'as a particular moment in development': 'a structure is the relative enduring organisation of a function, while the realisation of a function implies its organisation in a structure' (Duveen & Lloyd, 1990, p. 5). Looking at the genesis of these structures, Duveen and Lloyd identified

> *Sociogenesis*, which concerns the construction and transformation of social groups about specific objects, *ontogenesis*, which concerns the development of individuals in relation to social representations, and *microgenesis*, which concerns the evocation of social representations in social interactions. (Duveen & Lloyd, 1990, p. 6)

In this tripartite analysis, the authors focus on the construction of social representations. Sociogenesis demands a diachronic analysis, they underline, to examine how diverse groups meet social representations and transform them, and how these evolve historically. In ontogenesis, the authors propose to examine how a child constructs a given representations, or how people meet them as part of certain groups; it is about 'how social representations become psychologically active for individuals' (Duveen & Lloyd, 1990, p. 7), and how these participate to the construction of social identities. Finally, 'there is a genetic process in all social interaction in which particular social identities and the social representations on which they are based are elaborated and negotiated' (Duveen & Lloyd, 1990, p. 8); this is microgenesis, and it may involve conflicts of perspectives, new coordination and occurs through language.

For Duveen and his colleagues, the three forms of genesis are always related. Note that if some of their examples are about social representations – for instance, how a child gets to consider gender – other transformations concern knowledge in general. For instance, they suggest:

> Let us assume that we are dealing with an Einstein or Freud proposing a radical new interpretation of the human situation or human experience. Through various forms of social interaction (publications or lectures) the scientist tries to communicate his theory to colleagues. The communication will have been successful to the extent that other scientists will have understood the concepts proposed and also accepted that these concepts are well founded and not in error. The outcome will be ontogenetic transformations in the representations held by these scientists as individuals, as well as sociogenetic transformation in the representations held by the scientific community as a social group. (Duveen & Lloyd, 1990, p. 9)

Finally, they suggest that 'microgenesis constitutes a motor, as it were, for the genetic transformation of social representations' (Duveen & Lloyd, 1990, p. 9), an idea that has then been taken on by others (Duveen & de Rosa, 1992; Gillespie & Cornish, 2010; Kadianaki & Gillespie, 2015).

Thus, if the tripartite concepts proposed by Duveen were meant to encompass the development of knowledge in the child, à la Piaget, and of social knowledge, as in Moscovici, it could potentially include any form of formal or informal knowledge, scientific or social – as long as it can somehow be described in terms of a structure, or at least of a form of system, held by a group, unfolding in an interaction or organising a person's thought.

Duveen's tripartite organisation has been inspirational; it has become a methodological standard in the studies of social representations (Flick et al., 2015) and a theoretical guidance in social and cultural psychology (Gillespie & Cornish, 2010; Zittoun et al., 2008).

An Alternative Genealogy of a Tripartite Concept

The research of a complex analysis of developmental process was of course also conducted by others. Before Duveen's proposal, it was the case of Lev Vygotsky, who was aiming at combining an analysis of historical development and ontogeny. By ontogeny, a term used many times in his *Notebooks* (Zavershneva & Van der Veer, 2018), Vygotsky meant both the development of specific functions and the development of the child, as the study of ontogeny meant 'the problem of the child's thinking; the problem of instruction and development' (Vygotsky, 1932, in Zavershneva & Van der Veer, 2018, p. 279). According to Vygotsky, ontogeny is related to 'the development of ideology' (Vygotsky, 1929, in Zavershneva & Van der Veer, 2018, p. 122); in that sense, it seems closer to what Duveen would call sociogenesis.

In their long-standing analysis of Vygotsky's contributions (Valsiner & Van der Veer, 2000; Van der Veer & Valsiner, 1988, 1993, 1994), Jaan Valsiner and René Van der Veer mention the three forms of processes also in the early 1990s. Ontogenesis – a term used by Vygotsky – thus designates the development of the child via the mastery of sign systems inherited from previous generations – that is, culture (Van der Veer & Valsiner, 1993). The study of ontogenesis is linked to actual occurrences of problem solving or interactions. Thus 'Vygotsky's consistent emphasis on taking a developmental perspective of psychological phenomena, be they those of child development (ontogenesis) or adults' and apes' problem-solving (microgenesis), is an approach well worth continuing today' (Van der Veer & Valsiner, 1993, p. 398). Hence, Van der Veer and Valsiner connect ontogeny to microgenesis, but it is not clear whether the latter term exists in Vygotsky (as indicated by Psaltis, the term can be found in Werner & Kaplan [1963] and others).

Finally, historical or 'ideological' development itself is not called sociogenesis in Vygotsky. According to Van der Veer and Valsiner, sociogenesis designates in his work what has often been called the first law of social development, that 'higher psychological functions emerge first in the collective behavior of the child, in the form of cooperation with others, and only subsequently become internalized as the child's internal functions' (Van der Veer & Valsiner, 1993, p. 317) – an idea they trace back to the work of Mark Baldwin and Pierre Janet (Van der Veer & Valsiner, 1988):

> We now are in the position to summarize Vygotsky's concept of sociogenesis. All higher psychological processes (thinking, volition) rest on the application of social means to the self. These means are mastered in a social relationship between two people (Vygotsky, 1986, p. 53)[1] and afterward will become internalized by the individual child. They were first used to influence others and afterward to influence the self. Words are by far the most powerful social means. "Sociogenesis is the key to higher behavior" (Vygotsky, 1986, p. 57). (Van der Veer & Valsiner, 1988, p. 55)

Hence, in this reading of Vygotsky, sociogenesis has a very different meaning than in Duveen's integration of Moscovici and Piaget. Of course, not reading the Russian original, it is difficult to know if Vygotsky was actually using the term 'sociogenesis' or a term that has been thus translated later.

A Third Origin of the Tripartite Concept

Interestingly, there is a third line of tripartite concepts, which are rarely brought in the discussions in social and cultural psychology. It is the one pursued by Geoffrey Saxe, a developmental psychologist that studies mathematical cognition in diverse countries and within contrasting cultural systems. His work, initially anchored in Piagetian scholarship, was developed in dialogue with North American cultural psychology and their early reading of Vygotsky (Cole, 1996; Scribner & Cole, 1986; Wertsch, 1998). In his obituary to Piaget, Saxe emphasised the author's double interests in sociogenetic processes, as sociohistorical development of ideas, and ontogenesis (Saxe, 1983).[2] Although he had long studied children's mathematics (Saxe, 1981, 1982), he started to present his work along three levels of genesis only in the late 1990s, where he presented his approach as developmental as follows:

[1] Van der Veer and Vygotsky refer here to a text inaccessible to me: Vygotsky, L. S. (1986). *Konkretnaya psikhologiya cheloveka [A concrete psychology of man]*. Vestnik Moskovskogo Universiteta. Seriya 14. Psikhologiya (pp. 52–65). [In Russian]

[2] Piaget himself used the terms 'psychogenesis' to designate the formation of knowledge at the individual level and 'biogenesis' to discuss its biological basis (Piaget, 1970).

> A core assumption is that novel cognitive developments emerge in individuals' efforts to structure and accomplish goals in practices. The focus is on three levels of analysis, each of which concerns the interplay between cultural forms, such as number systems, and cognitive functions, the purposes for which forms are used as individual structure and accomplish practice-linked goals. The analyses concern processes of (1) microgenesis, or cognitive changes that occur as individuals transform cultural forms into cognitive means for representing and accomplishing goals in practices; (2) ontogenesis, or shifting relations between individuals' uses of particular forms and functions in practices as they grow older; and (3) sociogenesis, or changes that occur in cultural forms as individuals' representational and strategic accomplishments become valued by other members of a community and spread to serve variant functions in individuals' practice-related goals. (Saxe, 1999, p. 20)

Here, the tripartite concept is applied to functions, recreated by individuals in culture, thus transforming that cultural environment. Microgenesis is used in reference to Vygotsky (1986) and Werner and Kaplan (1963) 'to refer to a process by which forms – with the cognitive functions they afford – are transformed into means for accomplishing emerging goals in the activity' (Saxe, 2012, p. 19 n. 11). Sociogenesis applies to the transformation of a skill or an operation; it 'involves the microgenetic activities of multiple sites that, collectively, constitute a process in which representational forms and functions and reproduced and altered in a community over time' (Saxe, 2012, p. 29). Sociogenesis is thus understood as a form of diachronically and synchronically distributed activity, also defined as 'the reproduction and alteration of collective forms of representation in community networks through historical time' (Saxe, 2015, pp. 477–478).

Hence, in his own synthesis of the Piagetian tradition and Vygotskian-inspired cultural psychology, Saxe comes to a proposition very close to that of Duveen; as neither of the two authors quotes the other (to my knowledge), it is impossible to know if they were aware of each other's work.

On Three Possible Confusions

These three lines of readings of the complex social and cultural development of the person and their minds have many overlaps, among which are a fundamental developmental take and a sense that human psyche and knowledge can only be understood as a social process, in time. However, these three lines of thinking have also used some notions with partly or fully conflicting meanings, which is important to underline here. I will highlight three possible confusions, some more important than others, and with different implications.

First, ontogenesis seems to designate at times the development of the child, and at other times the development of a specific function, or of a form of knowledge. Eventually, what should be studied: the genesis of social representations (Barreiro & Castorina, 2017), of cognitive function or perations, or of social knowledge, identities, and scientific knowledge? These slight divergences are not a deep problem; they relate to the long-standing question of 'what it is that develops' (Perret-Clermont, 1993). They also demand a reflection on the types of knowledge that are considered socially and culturally cultivated, and on how these are differentiated and categorised (Zittoun, 2022, 2023). And there, for instance, one may wonder why scientific knowledge and social representations are always emphasised while ignoring other modes of more literary, artistic or affective knowledge. It is important to underline that these modes of knowledge were at the heart of the Vygotskian enterprise (Vygotsky, 1931, 1971, 2004; Zittoun & Stenner, 2021); they are still only rarely addressed in this line of research (but see Sánchez et al., 2022). Here, the knowledge Psaltis addresses is of a different kind; it is historical knowledge, anchored also in daily narratives and fictions. Although history can be constituted as formal, secondarised knowledge (Rochex, 1998), it does not obey the logic of mathematical sciences. This will need to be further examined.

Second, if this first concept of ontogeny applies not to skills or knowledge but to a person, then who is the subject of psychology? As it is well documented, Jean Piaget turned to the study of the 'epistemic child', which implies that his studies considered interpersonal variations and idiosyncrasies – even of his own children – as negligible (Morgado, 1998). To this, various authors have tried to oppose a socio-psychological child (Psaltis, 2011), a clinical child (de Ribaupierre, 1976) or a more global subject (Inhelder & de Caprona, 1997). In contrast, Vygotsky was clearly leaning in favour of a psychology of the person as a whole. He thus proposed in 1927, 'Psychology is the science of mental life. But what is mental life? The answer is psychology as a whole' (Zavershneva & Van der Veer, 2018, p. 109). He would come back to this point as he was further defining 'Psychology as the science of mental life' around 1933:

> Life not in the biological sense, but in the sense of a biography, a life description. After all, it is not breathing and blood circulation that form the topic of a biography, of one's existence, of a drama, of a novel, but the events of a human life, i.e., the problem of the psychologie concrète comes first. (Vygotsky, 1933, in Zavershneva & Van der Veer, 2018, p. 368)

This is an attempt that seems to be worth pursuing (Brinkmann, 2020; Zittoun, 2019) and to which I will also return.

The third confusion is the most problematic. Sociogenesis at times designates the development of the competence of the person via social mediation, as read by Valsiner and van der Veer (1993), or the development of knowledge or competences across persons in a given society (Duveen & Lloyd, 1990; Saxe, 2012, 2015), a confusion identified and discussed by Duveen (1996), or the historical development of a society as a whole (Psaltis, Part I in this volume). Clearly the same term is being used here to designate different phenomena. I believe Duveen's, Saxe's, and Psaltis's views are compatible as they apply to collective transformation, and so I will align with their positions and will reserve sociogenesis to speak about the development of the social world.

Hence, this first exploration of the concepts constituting the project of a genetic social psychology brought us to clarify one use of the notion of sociogenesis, and to highlight two under-theorised issues: the role of affects in knowledge; and definition of the person, or the subject of such a psychology. Going deeper into Psaltis's case study of Cyprus, I propose to highlight their importance.

Affects and the Person in Complex Case Studies

Psaltis proposes to apply the tripartite genetic reading to Cyprus: at the sociogenetic level, he retraces the history of the division of Cyprus in a Greek Cypriot and a Turkish Cypriot part, retracing the rupturing events in 1963–1964, leading to the war of 1974 (a 'historical trauma'), with the recent opening of checkpoints 2003, until the present situation. With it, he shows the development of two conflicting social representations of the island, and of the other group (via historical consciousness, narratives, remembering, projects, etc.). He finally shows the progressive transformation of an 'ethical (imaginative) horizon' associated to the change of leadership, the implementation of new educational programs (2008), the initiatives toward bicommunal committees, etc. At a microgenetic level, he recalls the intergroup reconciliation process that took place through intergroup contact or reconciliation history teaching. He thus shows the difference between superficial compliance to the other's perspective and the long-term transformation of representations. Finally, at the ontogenetic level, he presents his autobiographical trajectory and the development of his ideas, from his early experiences as a child of a displaced family to the progressive transformation of his representation of the past and the other groups, thanks to interpersonal relations, dialogues and the use of various knowledge as resources, before he himself took an active role in an initiative towards a reconciliation between the two communities.

The overall analysis is courageous and inspiring and demonstrates the relevance of the analytical proposition. Given his theoretical background, Psaltis sees knowledge as way to overcome the conflict: reconciliation should be achieved through an acknowledgement of historical facts, as well as the other group's perspectives. It should thus be a work on the cognitive understanding of history, as a culturally constructed body of knowledge, and a reduction of social representations that polarise the relation to the out-group.

The history retraced by Psaltis is a dramatic one; it is that of a close war on an island, translated into forced mobility, people losing their houses and properties, confrontation between armed forces and intergroup tensions. Reading both children testimonies and Psaltis's autobiographic narratives, one cannot help but notice the strong impact these experiences had on families – on the generation that experienced the war and expropriation, and on their children that grew up with the sense of loss. It is of course not a surprise that these experiences are associated with negative social representations of the out-group; and it is of course a fundamental work undertaken by Psaltis and his colleagues to bring people to be able to reconstruct these representations in the hope of a reconciliation. In addition, the situations brought to the fore by Psaltis strike me for their strong emotional and embodied aspects; yet these aspects are absent of his theoretical exploration. Interestingly, this unquestioned aspect also corresponds to the two questions we raised: the role of affects and the model of the person that can be integrated in a tripartite reading of development. In what remains of this chapter, I will quickly address them; I will argue that a full sociocultural psychology, or social genetic theory, ought to address them.

Affects in Complex Case Studies

First, let us consider affects. People experiencing situations, interpersonal encounters, and social and political discourses are not only cognitively treating the information; they actively make sense of the situations they meet, the conduct of people they interact with, and the discourses they are confronted by. Primarily these encounters are always and also affective: we 'feel into' situations as much, or perhaps more, than we grasp them (Fonagy et al., 2005; Valsiner, 2020). Importantly, potentially affective meanings circulate at all levels – socio-, micro- and ontogenetic. Think, nowadays, at the impact of news about the pandemic situation, or the war in Ukraine; they provoke affects in the audience, which are discussed and lead to actions. The affective nature of the semiosphere has recently been demonstrated by various authors in cultural psychology (Neuman, 2014; Neuman et al., 2017; Salvatore et al., 2021; Valsiner, 2019, 2020). The affectivisation of the semiosphere is not detached from the affective life of people. Single persons have emotionally loaded experiences, and these may find echoes in the experiences of other persons; in addition, social discourses may feed into these affective experiences, as well as be nourished by them (Zittoun, 1996). Affects circulate at onto-, micro- and sociogenetic levels and among them.

Let us go back to some of the elements mentioned by Psaltis. At the ontogenetic level, he mentions in his autobiographical narrative that he was aged one year when the 1974 war took place, and his Greek Cypriot family had to abandon their house and properties. He may not remember that forced movement, yet he remembers his father's anxiety when listening to the radio, and his visits to relatives in a zone patrolled by soldiers:

> I was terrified of the Turkish soldier who patrolled there and resided in one small house, that belonged to my aunt, with the UN soldier. I remember, years later, to have repeating nightmares until my early adulthood: me being chased by a Turkish soldier in that strip of land and/or the Turkish army moving further forward to kill the whole family and myself. (Psaltis, Part I in this volume)

Experiences of terror for a child – that is, overwhelming experiences of fear that a child cannot contain or elaborate – are traumatic and likely to appear as repetitive dreams (Abraham & Torok, 1972; Kaës, 1993; Tisseron, 1995). In a family, parents have experienced the same events but with their own perspective, life history and capacities to make sense of them, and possibly contain them. These experiences – intense fear oriented towards a soldier of the out-group – can also be amplified in everyday encounters; Psaltis thus reports the teacher's hateful discourse against the Turkish Cypriots, as they met his early life experiences. These can also be amplified by social discourses, historical narratives and the media – and here note that Psaltis speaks of a 'cultural trauma'. Hence, the children Psaltis interviews 30 years later still report some aspects of this affective load, which, we can hypothesise, was transmitted in families and the semiosphere. For example,

> My homeland was enslaved by the Turks because Turks came and took away from us our prettiest cities, we made a lot of war and thus we were

> enslaved. The war, when the Turks came, it was horrific because they took our mother from her house and forced her to leave Morfou with only the clothes she wore. (Girl from urban school, no. 512, Date: 8/3/2004) (Psaltis, Part I in this volume)

It is beyond the scope of this chapter to explore this systematically; what I wish to underline is the core role of affective dynamics in human development. Psaltis identifies them as part of the attitude toward the out-group in terms of prejudice vs positive attitude, distrust vs trust or lack of empathy vs empathy. In contrast, I wish to say that these are more than attitudes or valences of social representations; they are associated with vital memories (Brown & Reavey, 2015), are structuring for the person, infuse the people's encounters with others and can be amplified, guided or constrained by social discourses. As an ontogenetic process, it takes a lot of time to unpack, deploy, elaborate and transform such experiences, as Psaltis himself retraces (also see Zittoun, 2020). The implication of this is, I believe, that complex case studies built at three levels need to account for these affects and their circulation, as they play a pivotal role not only in people's lives but in interpersonal encounters, intergroup dynamics and social transformation – and backwards, in all dialogical possible directions.

The Person in Complex Case Studies

If affects have to be taken seriously in complex case studies analysed from a social genetic or sociocultural perspective, then one has to hold a consistent theory of the person. If the subject of psychology is a purely epistemic or cognisant one, it is impossible to account for these affective dynamics, and the fact that they play a key role in actual thinking and representing. Vygotsky's plea for a science of the living person with their biography, evoked earlier in this chapter, is more convincing here. Let us again turn to the case described by Psaltis. In Cyprus, anyone arriving on the island from the airport and driving to Nicosia, the capital, can see a beautiful landscape unfolding, with the city and the forest and hills beyond. Only on the hill, a giant Turkish flag has been embedded in the landscape; one can thus immediately, quasi-physically experience the national conflict. Nicosia, an old and majestic city, is cut in two by a wall, and one can cross to the other side only by passing through a military-guarded checkpoint and crossing a buffer zone patrolled by UN soldiers. The buffer zone, and so probably the 'ghost towns' mentioned by Psaltis, is a disquieting experience for anyone coming from a European region at peace.[3] Living in a divided city and island can thus be physically experienced in one's daily life. In other words, the subject of a psychology that aims to account for the interplay between socio-, micro- and ontogenetic process needs to be a person with an embodied mind, who feels, acts, remembers, imagines as well as makes sense and reasons. Hence, when Psaltis recalls that 'there is no place in genetic social psychology for individuation' (see Part I in this volume), I would respond: the genetic social psychology can only account for human development if it accounts for both the development of knowledge and the development of person who builds, experiences, feels and lives through that knowledge.

Opening: Integrative Developmental Psychologies

Genetic social psychology is a scientific project which positions itself in a genealogy of approaches articulating studies of cognitive development with social dynamics (Carugati & Perret-Clermont, 2015; Duveen, 1997, 1998; Perret-Clermont, Carugati, et al., 2004; Perret-Clermont, Pontecorvo, et al., 2004; Perret-Clermont, 2015; Psaltis et al., 2015). Rooted in the same sources, sociocultural developmental psychology has, over the past 20 years, addressed a comparable question: How does the person develop in their changing sociocultural environment (Valsiner, 2021; Zittoun et al., 2003; Zittoun & Gillespie, 2022)? Sociocultural psychology of the life-course has many similarities with the project of genetic social psychology; foremost, it also analyses developmental dynamics at the scale of socio-, micro- and ontogenesis (Brinkmann & Kofod, 2017; Gillespie, 2021; Power et al., 2023; Valsiner, 2021; Wagoner, 2017; Zittoun, 2016; Zittoun et al., 2013). In contrast to genetic social psychology, though, it emphasises semiotic dynamics, the circulation of signs, at all levels of individual and collective experiences, rather than simply cognition; doing so, it opens the space for the primacy of affects in human experience, as well as for a diversity of modes if sense-making and imagining (Zittoun et al., 2013). However, comparably to genetic social psychology, sociocultural psychology has recently privileged case studies to progress both empirically and theoretically (Demuth, 2018; Molenaar & Valsiner, 2008; Salvatore & Valsiner, 2010).

[3] I thank Charis Psaltis for the repeated invitations to Cyprus, for Freud's 150th anniversary in 2006, at the Home for Co-operation in 2011, and as a host of our annual CUPSYNET meeting in 2016, 2023 and 2024.

In our own work, like Psaltis, we tried to apply such understanding at the scale of case studies, with regional case studies – studies at the scale of a hill, an island or a canton (for instance, Pedersen, 2022; Zittoun, 2019; Zittoun et al., 2022). We consider in sociogenesis any historical or sociological transformations that enable us to understand the constitution of the phenomena we study and that guide people's experiences. In microgenesis, we analyse situated activities, interactions, negotiations, meaning-making occurrences, etc. And through ontogenesis, we reconstruct the development of the person, usually bringing to the fore the transformations of their understanding or activities through time – sense-making, imagination, relationship to the past, etc. In order to account for the circulation of meaning and power across these temporal scales, we proposed a dialogical framing (Cornish, 2020; Marková, 2017; Marková et al., 2020). For instance, we currently work on a regional, dialogical case study of the transformation of the landscape of care at the scale of a Swiss canton. We thus study the sociogenesis of a new policy regarding housing modes for older persons, the microgenetic negotiations as people inhabit their homes, explore their environment or are engaged in shared activities in daily lives or in institutions, and, more longitudinally, the ontogenetic transformation of the person (Cabra & Zittoun, 2022; Grossen et al., 2022; Zittoun et al., 2024). Working on the experience of older persons in a highly politicised debate, affects become central – both at the collective and the individual level; and when we study the trajectories of older person, we must account for the whole complexity of their embodied, affective and biographical experience. We are thus faced with the same challenges as Psaltis: to account for affects and the person from an integrative perspective.

To conclude with an opening, then, I believe that complex, integrative approaches to developmental psychology are necessary to understand lives in complex and changing societies. In that sense, complex endeavours such as genetic social psychology, or sociocultural psychology, will best progress by engaging in a dialogue, possibly around case studies, and on crucial concepts, for it is reasoning through case studies – that is, theorising in dialogue with the world – that remains one of the most powerful ways to advance our understanding of human development in changing worlds.

REFERENCES

Abraham, N., & Torok, M. (1972). Mourning or melancholia: Introjection versus incorporation. In N. T. Rand (Ed.), *The Shell and the kernel. Renewals of psychoanalysis* (pp. 125–138). Chicago: The University of Chicago Press.

Barreiro, A., & Castorina, J. A. (2017). Dialectical inferences in the ontogenesis of social representations. *Theory & Psychology*, *27*(1), 34–49. https://doi.org/10.1177/0959354316681863.

Brinkmann, S. (2020). Psychology as a science of life. *Theory & Psychology*, *30*(1), 3–17. https://doi.org/10.1177/0959354319889186.

Brinkmann, S., & Kofod, E. H. (2017). Grief as an extended emotion. *Culture & Psychology*, 1354067X17723328. https://doi.org/10.1177/1354067X17723328.

Bronfenbrenner, U. (1995). Developmental ecology through space and time: A future perspective. In P. Moen, G. H. J. Elder, & K. Luscher (Eds.), *Examining lives in context: Perspectives on the ecology of human development* (pp. 619–647). Washigton, DC: American Psychological Association.

Brown, S. D., & Reavey, P. (2015). *Vital Memory and Affect: Living with a difficult past*. London: Routledge.

Cabra, M., & Zittoun, T. (2022). *Thematic Engagements: Affects and Learning in Older Age*. SSRN Scholarly Paper No. 4272357. https://doi.org/10.2139/ssrn.4272357.

Carugati, F., & Perret-Clermont, A.-N. (2015). Learning and instruction: Social-cognitive perspectives A2 – Wright, James D. In *International Encyclopedia of the Social & Behavioral Sciences* (2nd ed., pp. 670–676). Philadelphia, PA: Elsevier. www.sciencedirect.com/science/article/pii/B978008097086892035X.

Cole, M. (1996). *Cultural psychology: A once and future discipline*. Cambridge, MA: The Belknap Press of Harvard University Press.

Cornish, F. (2020). Communicative generalisation: Dialogical means of advancing knowledge through a case study of an 'unprecedented' disaster. *Culture & Psychology*, *26*(1), 78–95. https://doi.org/10.1177/1354067X19894930.

de Ribaupierre, A. (1976). Du sujet épistémique au sujet clinique. *Archives de Psychologie*, *44*, 145.

Demuth, C. (2018). Generalization from single cases and the concept of double dialogicality. *Integrative Psychological and Behavioral Science*, *52*(1), 77–93. https://doi.org/10.1007/s12124-017-9399-1.

Doise, W., & Valentim, J. P. (2015). Levels of analysis in social psychology. In J. D. Wright (Ed.), *International encyclopedia of the social & behavioral sciences* (2nd ed., pp. 900–904). Philadelphia, PA: Elsevier. https://doi.org/10.1016/B978-0-08-097086-8.24032-4.

Duveen, G. (1996). The development of social representations of gender. *The Japanese Journal of Experimental Social Psychology*, *35*(3), 256–262. https://doi.org/10.2130/jjesp.35.256.

(1997). Psychological development as social process. In L. Smith, J. Bockrell, & P. Tomlinson (Eds.), *Piaget, Vygotsky and beyond* (pp. 67–90). London: Routledge.

(1998). The psychosocial production of ideas: Social representations and psychologic. *Culture & Psychology*, *4*(4), 455–472.

Duveen, G., & de Rosa, A. (1992). Social representations and the genesis of social knowledge. *Ongoing Production on Social Representations*, *1*, 94–108.

Duveen, G., & Lloyd, B. (1990). Introduction. In B. Lloyd & G. Duveen (Eds.), *Social representations and the development of knowledge* (pp. 1–10). Cambridge: Cambridge University Press. https://doi.org/10.1017/CBO9780511659874.001.

Engeström, Y., & Sannino, A. (2010). Studies of expansive learning: Foundations, findings and future challenges. *Educational Research Review*, *5*(1), 1–24. https://doi.org/10.1016/j.edurev.2009.12.002.

Flick, U., Foster, J., & Caillaud, S. (2015). Researching social representations. In E. Andreouli, G. Gaskell, G. Sammut, & J. Valsiner (Eds.), *The Cambridge handbook of social representations* (pp. 64–80). Cambridge: Cambridge University Press. https://doi.org/10.1017/CBO9781107323650.007.

Fonagy, P., Gergely, G., Jurist, E., & Target, M. (2005). *Affect regulation, mentalization, and the development of self.* New York: Other Press.

Gillespie, A. (2021). From social positions to psychological perspectives: The social creation of possibility. *Theory & Psychology*, 0959354321995559. https://doi.org/10.1177/0959354321995559.

Gillespie, A., & Cornish, F. (2010). What can be said? Identity as a constraint on knowledge production. *Papers on Social Representations*, *19*, 5.1–5.13.

Grossen, M., Gfeller, F., Cabra, M., & Zittoun, T. (2022). Bien plus qu'un simple décor. Déménager dans un appartement avec encadrement: Une occasion de développement psychologique? *Psychoscope*, *1*, 26–29.

Inhelder, B., & de Caprona, D. (1997). What subject for psychology? *The Genetic Epistemologist*, *25*(2), 1–5.

Kadianaki, I., & Gillespie, A. (2015). Alterity and the transformation of social representations: A sociocultural account. *Integrative Psychological and Behavioral Science*, *49*(1), 73–88. https://doi.org/10.1007/s12124-014-9285-z.

Kaës, R. (1993). *Transmission de la vie psychique entre les générations.* Paris: Dunod.

Lemke, J. L. (2000). Across the scales of time: Artifacts, activities, and meanings in ecosocial systems. *Mind, Culture, and Activity*, *7*(4), 273–290. https://doi.org/10.1207/S15327884MCA0704_03.

Marková, I. (2017). Case studies and dialogicality. *Journal of Deafblind Studies on Communication*, *3*(1), 28–45.

Marková, I., Zadeh, S., & Zittoun, T. (2020). Introduction to the special issue on generalisation from dialogical single case studies. *Culture & Psychology*, *26*(1), 3–24. https://doi.org/10.1177/1354067X19888193.

Molenaar, P. C. M., & Valsiner, J. (2008). How generalization works through the single case: A simple idiographic process analysis of an individual psychotherapy. In S. Salvatore, J. Valsiner, S. Strout-Yagodzynski, & J. Clegg (Eds.), *Yearbook of ideographic science* (pp. 23–38). Rome: Firera Publishing.

Morgado, L. (1998). The epistemic subject and the psychological subject: A different methodological appoach. In A. C. Quelhas & F. Pereira (Eds.), *Cognition and context* (pp. 97–111). Lisbon: Instituto Superior de Psicologia Aplicada.

Moscovici, S. (2000). *Social representations: Studies in social psychology* (G. Duveen, Ed.). Cambridge: Polity Press.

(2008). *Psychoanalysis: Its image and its public* (G. Duveen, Ed.; D. Macey, Trans.). Cambridge: Polity Press.

Neuman, Y. (2014). *Introduction to computational cultural psychology*. Cambridge: Cambridge University Press.

Neuman, Y., Hames, H., & Cohen, Y. (2017). An information-based procedure for measuring semantic change in historical data. *Measurement, 105*, 130–135. https://doi.org/10.1016/j.measurement.2017.04.017.

Pedersen, O. C. (2022). Imagining the future: A sociocultural psychological study of im/mobility in and around Suðuroy. PhD Dissertation, Neuchâtel.

Perret-Clermont, A.-N. (1993). What it is that develops? *Cognition and Instruction, 11*(3 & 4), 197–205.

(2015). The architecture of social relationships and thinking spaces for growth. In C. Psaltis, A. Gillespie, & A.-N. Perret-Clermont (Eds.), *Social relations in human and societal development* (pp. 51–70). New York: Cambridge University Press.

Perret-Clermont, A.-N., Carugati, F., & Oates, J. (2004). A socio-cognitive perspective on learning and cognitive development. In J. Oates & A. Grayson (Eds.), *Cognitive and language development in children* (pp. 305–332). Hoboken, NJ: Blackwell Publishing.

Perret-Clermont, A.-N., Pontecorvo, C., Resnick, L., Zittoun, T., & Burge, B. (2004). *Joining society: Learning and development in adolescence and youth*. Cambridge: Cambridge University Press.

Pettigrew, T. F., & Tropp, L. R. (2011). *When groups meet: The dynamics of intergroup contact*. New York: Psychology Press.

Piaget, J. (1970). *L'épistémologie génétique* (2nd ed.). Paris: Presses Universitaires de France.

Power, S. A., Zittoun, T., Akkerman, S., Wagoner, B., Cabra, M., Cornish, F., Hawlina, H., Heasman, B., Mahendran, K., Psaltis, C., Rajala, A., Veale, A., & Gillespie, A. (2023). Social psychology of and for world-making. *Personality and Social Psychology Review*, 10888683221145756. https://doi.org/10.1177/10888683221145756.

Psaltis, C. (2011). From the epistemic to the social-psychological subject: The missing role of social identities, asymmetries of status, and social representations: Commentary on Sorsana and Trognon. *Human Development, 54*(4), 234–240.

Psaltis, C., Gillespie, A., & Perret-Clermont, A.-N. (2015). Introduction: The role of social relations in human and societal development. In C. Psaltis, A. Gillespie, & A.-N. Perret-Clermont (Eds.), *Social relations in human and societal development* (pp. 1–15). London: Palgrave Macmillan. https://doi.org/10.1057/9781137400994_1.

Rochex, J.-Y. (1998). *Le sens de l'expérience scolaire*. Paris: Presses universitaires de France.

Salvatore, S., De Luca Picione, R., Bochicchio, V., Mannino, G., Langher, V., Pergola, R. F., Velotti, P., & Venuleo, C. (2021). The affectivization of the public sphere: The contribution of psychoanalysis in understanding and counteracting the current crisis scenarios. *Subject, Action, & Society: Psychoanalytical Studies and Practices*, *I*(1), 2–29. https://doi.org/10.32111/SAS.2021.1.1.2.

Salvatore, S., & Valsiner, J. (2010). Between the general and the unique: Overcoming the nomothetic versus idiographic opposition. *Theory & Psychology*, *20*(6), 817–833. https://doi.org/10.1177/0959354310381156.

Sánchez, Á., Haye, A., & Sebastián, C. (2022). Affective learning as a higher psychological process: A microgenetic analysis of evaluative conditioning from a sociocultural approach (Aprendizaje afectivo como proceso psicológico superior: análisis microgenético del condicionamiento evaluativo desde un enfoque sociocultural). *Studies in Psychology*, *43*(2), 287–310. https://doi.org/10.1080/02109395.2021.1991132.

Saxe, G. B. (1981). Body parts as numerals: A developmental analysis of numeration among the Oksapmin in Papua New Guinea. *Child Development*, *52*(1), 306–316. https://doi.org/10.2307/1129244.

(1982). Culture and the development of numerical cognition: Studies among the Oksapmin of Papua New Guinea. In C.-G. Brainerd (Ed.), *Children's logical and mathematical cognition* (pp. 157–176). Berlin: Springer Verlag.

(1983). Piaget and anthropology. *American Anthropologist*, *85*(1), 136–143.

(1999). Sources of concepts: A cultural-developmental perspective. In E. K. Scholnick, K. Nelson, S. A. Gelman, & P. H. Miller (Eds.), *Conceptual development: Piaget's legacy* (pp. 253–267). New York: Psychology Press.

(2012). *Cultural development of mathematical ideas. Panua New Guinea studies.* Cambridge: Cambridge University Press.

(2015). Studying culture-cognition relations in collective practices of daily life: A research framework / El estudio de las relaciones cultura-cognición en las prácticas colectivas cotidianas: un modelo de investigación. *Journal for the Study of Education and Development*, *38*(3), 473–508. https://doi.org/10.1080/02103702.2015.1054669.

Scribner, S., & Cole, M. (1986). *Psychology of literacy*. Cambridge, MA: Harvard University Press.

Smith, L. B., & Thelen, E. (2003). Development as a dynamic system. *Trends in Cognitive Sciences*, *7*(8), 343–348.

Tisseron, S. (1995). *Le psychisme à l'épreuve des générations. Clinique du fantôme.* Paris: Dunod.

Valsiner, J. (2019). *Ornamented lives*. Charlotte, NC: Information Age Publishing.

(2020). *Sensuality in human living: Cultural psychology of human affect*. New York: Springer.

(2021). *General human psychology*. Cham: Springer Nature Switzerland AG.

Valsiner, J., & Van der Veer, R. (2000). *The social mind: Construction of the idea.* Cambridge: Cambridge University Press.

Van der Veer, R., & Valsiner, J. (1988). Lev Vygotsky and Pierre Janet: On the origin of the concept of sociogenesis. *Developmental Review*, *8*(1), 52–65. https://doi.org/10.1016/0273-2297(88)90011-1.

(1993). *Understanding Vygotsky: A quest for synthesis.* Hoboken, NJ: Wiley-Blackwell.
(Eds.). (1994). *The Vygotsky reader.* Hoboken, NJ: Wiley-Blackwell.
Vygotsky, L. S. (1931). *Imagination and creativity of the adolescent.* http://www.cddc.vt.edu/marxists/archive/vygotsky/works/1931/adolescent/ch12.htm#s02.
(1971). *The psychology of art.* Cambridge, MA: MIT press.
(1986). *Thought and Language* (A. Kozulin, Ed.). Cambridge, MA: MIT Press.
(2004). Imagination and creativity in childhood (M. E. Sharpe, Trans.). *Journal of Russian and East European Psychology*, *42*(1), 7–97.
Wagoner, B. (2017). *The constructive mind: Bartlett's psychology in reconstruction.* Cambridge: Cambridge University Press.
Werner, H., & Kaplan, B. (1963). *Symbol formation: An organismic-developmental approach to language and the expression of thought.* New York: John Wiley & son.
Wertsch, J. V. (1998). *Mind as action.* Oxford: Oxford University Press.
Zavershneva, E., & Van der Veer, R. (2018). *Vygotsky's notebooks: A selection.* New York: Springer.
Zittoun, T. (1996). Non sono tutti fascisti. Immagini di sé e degli altri nei ragazzi della scuola ebraica. *La Rassegna Mensile Di Israel*, *62*(3), 155–187.
(2016). A sociocultural psychology of the life-course. *Social Psychological Review*, *18*(1), 6–17.
(2019). *Sociocultural psychology on the regional scale: A case study of a hill.* New York: Springer.
(2020). Living memories in the wild. In B. Wagoner, I. Brescó de Luna, & S. Zadeh (Eds.), *Memory in the wild* (pp. 57–75). Charlotte, NC: Information Age Publishing.
(2022). A sociocultural psychology of the life course to study human development. *Human Development*, *66*(4–5), 306–324. https://doi.org/10.1159/000526435.
(2023). *The pleasure of thinking.* Cambridge: Cambridge University Press.
Zittoun, T., Cabra, M., Gfeller, F., & Grossen, M. (2024). Développement des personnes « âgées » et transformation des espaces vécus. In A. Iannaccone, E. Cattaruzza, & E. Schwab (Eds.), *Experiences socio-matérielles: Objets, interactions et espaces* (pp. 159–178). Paris: Editions Alphil.
Zittoun, T., Cabra, M., Pedersen, O. C., & Hawlina, H. (2022). Thinking the lifecourse through single cases. In S. Salvatore & J. Valsiner (Eds.), *Ten years of idiographic science* (pp. 203–217). Charlotte, NC: Information Age Publishing.
Zittoun, T., Cornish, F., Gillespie, A., & Aveling, E.-L. (2008). Using social knowledge: A case study of a diarist's meaning making during World War II. In W. Wagner, T. Sugiman, & K. Gergen (Eds.), *Meaning in action: Constructions, narratives and representations* (pp. 163–179). New York: Springer.
Zittoun, T., Duveen, G., Gillespie, A., Ivinson, G., & Psaltis, C. (2003). The uses of symbolic resources in transitions. *Culture & Psychology*, *9*(4), 415–448.

Zittoun, T., & Gillespie, A. (2022). A sociocultural approach to identity through diary studies. In M. Bamberg, C. Demuth, & M. Watzlawik (Eds.), *Cambridge Handbook of Identity* (pp. 345–365). Cambridge: Cambridge University Press.

Zittoun, T., & Stenner, P. (2021). Vygotsky's tragedy: Hamlet and the psychology of art. *Review of General Psychology*, *25*(3), 223–238. https://doi.org/10.1177/10892680211013293.

Zittoun, T., Valsiner, J., Vedeler, D., Salgado, J., Gonçalves, M., & Ferring, D. (2013). *Human development in the lifecourse: Melodies of living*. Cambridge: Cambridge University Press.

CHAPTER 9

Trauma in the Construction of a Collective Memory and Identity

Christina Alexopoulos

Introduction

> *The therapeutic work . . . would consist in ridding the piece of historical truth of its deformations and its support on the real present, and bringing it back to its place in the past. Just as our construction has no effect except by restoring a piece of the lost life story, so the delusion owes its convincing force to the bit of historical truth it puts in the place of the* rejected reality. (Freud, 1937, p. 72)

The relationship between collective and individual trauma is central to the theory and research presented in Part I of the book. The question of microgenesis, ontogenesis and sociogenesisis is part of a reflection on the construction of the relationship to oneself, to the other and to the object in conditions that can be turned upside down by a traumatic encounter. Psychoanalytic thought, for its part, has been very interested in the weight of history and its interpretations in understanding the present. While psychotics remain locked in an exclusive relationship with primary objects, in the grip of a very real past violence that they continue to project onto current situations, we are all affected by the reproduction of our relationship with the past in our perception of the present. Becoming aware of this, working on interpretations of one's own history and working out past traumas by differentiating them from current contexts are all necessary conditions for projecting oneself into a present and a future that are not confined to the traumatic reproduction of the past, of one's anxieties or of one's ways of relating to others.

Thinking about the subject's links to the group to which he or she belongs and to society as a whole in situations of individual and collective trauma presupposes first of all questioning the meaning of trauma as a psychic intrusion, then focusing on the movements of identification and the ways in which trauma is transmitted within communities of memory, and finally evoking the forms of memorial and narrative reconstruction of representations of oneself and one's relationship to the past in the groups concerned.

A Psychoanalytical Approach to Individual and Collective Trauma

Reflection on trauma is consubstantial with the birth of psychoanalysis. Freud's first hysterical patients suffered from reminiscences, and the talking cure revealed early experiences of seduction. Although Sigmund Freud initially supported a traumatic aetiology for his patients' disorders, on 21 September 1897, in his Equinox letter, he confided to his friend Fliess that he no longer believed in his Neurotica (Moussaieff Masson, 1985). For the father of psychoanalysis, fantasy reality took precedence over material reality. In the new approach adopted by the founder of psychoanalysis, it was not the traumatic event itself but the way in which the subject experienced a situation that had overwhelmed his or her defences that was important. We will attempt to understand the way in which trauma, both individually and collectively, undermines the ability to process conflictual situations, by encouraging a regression to archaic anxieties and defences. To do this, we will first look at the way in which psychoanalysis thinks about trauma at individual and collective levels, based on the distinction between material reality, or the state of facts, and phantasmatic reality, or the subjective interpretation of factual reality. It will then be important to look at the notion of the repetition compulsion, which is very present in traumatic dreams, in the construction of the symptom and in the representation of the aftermath or second stage of the trauma, which gives full meaning to the initial experiences. Finally, we feel it is essential to examine the archaic anxieties associated with the traumatic experience.

For Freud, the psychic construction of the subject is thought out from the outset in relation to the hypothesis of the unconscious, the instance of the first topic, which constitutes an attempt to represent the different psychic spaces: unconscious, preconscious and conscious. The Freudian unconscious represents what escapes the subject's consciousness. Its main mechanism is repression, which makes it possible to keep intolerable representations away from consciousness. This first topical approach was made more complex by the contributions of the second topical approach, which introduced the separation of id, ego and superego, while in the 1920s Freud introduced the notion of the death drive into psychoanalysis, defined as the tendency to return living beings to an inorganic state.

The death drive is particularly present in repetition compulsion. It drives the subject to reproduce traumatic experiences that are familiar to them, through symptoms or nightmares, no doubt because they are under their influence, in a passive position, or because they unconsciously identify with their tormentors, identification with the aggressor being a way of finding oneself in an active position. At the same time, repetition is a first attempt to elaborate or symbolise something of the trauma, to appropriate what has happened by linking fragments of one's history, to change the actors in the traumatic scenario, leading to a first form of differentiation.

In Psaltis's story (Chapter 5 in this volume), a frequent traumatic dream, linked to the arrival of Turkish soldiers who would seize his house, signals the presence of a fear of which the dream is both a symptom and an attempt at self-healing. It is to be understood as an initial effort to process the traumatic charge. After the age of 18, the traumatic dream that had accompanied him throughout his childhood disappeared; this signals a change in his relationship with the past and the ways in which he defended himself against it.

In the psychoanalytical approach, the perception, representation and interpretation of a situation are more important than the nature of the situation itself, and their meaning is always linked to a psychic work determined by the subjectivity of the actors. The subject's history and psychic organisation, as well as exogenous factors linked to the context of the traumatic encounter, play a decisive role not only when confronted with a traumatic experience but also when it is recorded in the memory and later narrated. Within the same family, each person has his or her own representation of what happened, even if there are links between the narratives of different people (Bruner, 1990). The resulting memory traces are determined by the individual's way of maintaining a psychological relationship with the experience, the essential thing being what each person does unconsciously with the traumatic encounter in relation to their internal resources. The clinical question of the forms of 'reminiscence' and 'reviviscence' (representation of the affect) thus refers back to a theory of memory, of its forms of inscription and conservation, but also of the forms of 'return' of previous traces of the subjective experience (Roussillon, 2003). This return concerns what had been repressed and buried in the unconscious or cleaved, denied and preserved in encysted form (Abraham &Torok, 1994).

The encounter with trauma often takes place in two stages. A first experience, the meaning of which escapes the subject, and a second temporality, that of the aftermath, which gives meaning to the traumatic experience a posteriori.

> The "aftermath" process is a theory in action. It contains the virtuality of theories of temporality, causality and generativity, all of which refer to the whole of advent-disappearance-resurgence . . . So the psyche is a factory of returns in its anti-traumatic function, and a factory of formations of the unconscious in its generative function. What emerges is a need to remember, a duty to multiple, unconscious memories. Memory reveals itself as the messenger of what compels it to inscribe itself as such, and of what threatens to erase it. It reveals itself as the memory of psychic processes, those that have already taken effect and those that are prevented or remain potential. The aftermath is a reminiscence of the processes that constitute it and the tendencies that constrain and animate it. It is a processual memory. (Chervet, 2009)

It may be possible to see traumatic repetition as an unconscious search for an aftermath that would link the fragments of the past and present, in relation to the questions left unanswered in the subject's history, to find out what lies behind them and try to make sense of them. Repetition obeys a logic of reconstituting the 'scene of the crime' with the unconscious aim of mastering its unfolding a little more, if not understanding its meaning.

While Freud often sees trauma as intrinsically linked to the human condition, with every human being experiencing experiences that psychically overwhelm them and attack their excitatory barrier, we find it interesting to note in his work the idea of *Hilflosigkeit* (Freud, 1926). This is the infant's 'original distress', which echoes in all our subsequent experiences of powerlessness. An infant's powerlessness in the face of a world on which he or she is entirely dependent at the beginning of life can confine a being to an imaginary omnipotence that is all the more difficult to dialectise (i.e. to develop something through a process of oppositions) and overcoming these oppositions (thesis, antithesis, synthesis), because he or she has not been able to experience sufficiently satisfying and containing responses from his or her environment. As Winnicott would later show, it is the ability of those around the child to help them experience a good enough response to their needs that will gradually enable the child to emerge from this delusion of omnipotence and become progressively disillusioned. Intrapsychic and intersubjective bonds are built by internalising the other person's good relational qualities. It is this introjection that enables the subject to psychically process the anxieties of early life and those of major traumatic experiences, which take us back to the quality of our first bonds and our narcissistic foundations.

The analogy between the primitive anxieties of the infant, exposed to a feeling of acute powerlessness in an environment that is not good enough, and the re-actualisation of this initial distress in the face of major collective disasters should not obscure the differences that exist between the two types of experience. This would be an epistemological pitfall to be avoided, as would the concept of cultural trauma, which confuses the experiences of victims, perpetrators and bystanders of traumatic events (Kansteiner, 2004). In one case, an under-resourced child must face up to a hostile world; in the other, a human community is plunged into the most extreme adversity. The two contexts are different, and to equate them would be to run the risk of denying the uniqueness of each situation, trivialising its seriousness and minimising its impact on those involved. Our aim, however, is to show that confrontation with collective trauma encourages massive regression and gives rise to anxieties and defences that can be found both in the mental world of the very young child and in the clinic of psychosis.

The question of archaic anxieties concerns the earliest stages of the subject's psychological construction, in a quasi-archaeological approach in which the earliest strata are more or less well buried.[1] These anxieties involve physicality, the infralanguage and early bonds. They concern the anxiety of collapse, of falling, of liquefaction, of fragmentation, of intrusion, of emptying.[2] In the wake of the thinking of Donald Winiccott and René Roussillon, we could call them agonistic.[3] Later, the anxieties relate to separation and the loss of an object, to be understood as the

[1] The presence of archaic anxieties is normal in infants, pathological and extremely disabling in psychiatry, and manifested by remnants, more or less well overcome, in the rest of the general population. Psychoanalysts refer to these anxieties as archaic because they were present before language was established. Their common evolution is to be overcome over the course of development. They are overcome, not totally resolved or forgotten. There are many sociocultural resurgences of these issues, which demonstrate their vigour in contexts of social regression. Pireyre, É. (2015). Les angoisses corporelles archaïques. In É. Pireyre, *Clinique de l'image du corps: Du vécu au concept* (pp. 141–156). Paris: Dunod.

[2] Fears of breakdown: these correspond to the most archaic of fears – the fear of annihilation. Fears of falling: these are linked to the infant's first sensations of weight by the infant. It's the fear of falling endlessly, of being sucked down into the ground. Fears of liquefaction: linked to a fragile representation of the limits of the body and skin. This anxiety is one of dissolution, of a body that could liquefy. Fears of fragmentation: the subject imagines his or her body as several 'pieces' that are not connected to each other. Fears of emptying and intrusion: the skin is perceived as a container, there is the beginnings of the constitution of a space, the beginning of a psychic envelope, but it is felt to be perforated. The anxiety is therefore that the body will be emptied or that there will be an intrusion, without the subject being able to prevent it. The child's mastery of sphincters calms this anxiety about going in and out.

[3] Roussillon, R. (2012). La terreur agonistique et le psychotique. In R. Roussillon, *Agonie, clivage et symbolisation* (pp. 138–158). Paris: PUF.

disappearance of the loved one. When all goes well, the archaic anxieties are relatively calmed and other anxieties more related to the oedipal crisis, such as castration anxiety, linked to the prohibition of incest and parricide, take over. Early traumatic experiences hinder both the creation of a feeling of internal security, which guarantees the ability to relate to others, and the more general ability to perceive others and otherness not as a threat to one's own integrity but as an intersubjective encounter, rich in emotional and intellectual exchanges.

If new layers are added to the oldest strata of the psyche, these remain accessible and determine subsequent constructions. To take this geological metaphor a step further, we would add that these layers can come to the surface during an earthquake, particularly in seismogenic terrain. Exposure to major trauma, such as an earthquake, puts to the test both the quality of the initial constructions and the solidity of the later buildings and soils involved. In the case of extreme trauma, primitive fears take over and are expressed by a disintegration of the drive to live and the drive to die. Confrontation with mortifying experiences encourages regression movements that sometimes lead to massive anguish and the mobilisation of defence mechanisms that are just as consequential, situated on the side of primary processes, namely the immediate and unbound discharge of psychic energy.

Some particularly hateful political discourse finds fertile ground in the emergence of these archaic anxieties and their defence mechanisms. To protect themselves, individuals or groups deny the violence on their own side, divide their relationship with the world into those who are all good and those who are all bad, and project everything that is bad onto the enemy group. The demonisation of the political enemy or an ethnically and culturally different group builds on these mechanisms of denial of our common humanity, of the Manichean dichotomy of the world and of the essentialisation of the other as the bearer of all evil.

The traumatic experience unravels the work of linking the inside and outside of oneself, whereas a therapeutic approach to trauma enables us to re-establish links between the present and the past, between our emotional experiences and our thoughts, between ourselves and others. Although Freud (1933, p. 82) said that crystal only shatters according to the fracture lines in its structure, our experience with patients who have lived through situations of war, genocide or torture shows us that in the face of experiences of massive dehumanisation, depersonalisation and derealisation, phenomena specific to psychosis can emerge and even persist. Non-psychotic subjects may also experience decompensation in the face of extreme experiences, taking on the appearance of psychotic disorders, with delusions and hallucinations.

People confronted with war, deportation or genocidal violence are caught up in a regression to the most primitive strata of their psyche. Some of them, younger when they were confronted with the trauma, may remain attached to problems linked to a stage in their psychosexual development. This is particularly the case with certain children for whom reality collides with fantasies in a collapse between the two that can be more or less long-lasting (Janin, 1996). Losing one's father at a time when strong feelings of unconscious hostility are present can plunge the subject into significant guilt, hinder the mourning process and even take the form of melancholic identification. Being exposed to a mother's depression in the first two years of life, when the children themselves are confronted with massive anxieties, theorised by Melanie Klein under the terms of schizo-paranoid anxieties and depressive anxieties, can make it much more difficult for them to cope, and can lead some children who have previously had a good enough environment to constantly try actively to 'repair' this distressed mother, or even to adopt sacrificial positions within the family and the community. Becoming a model pupil by trying to live up as closely as possible to parental ideals is also sometimes a way of remedying the parents' distress.

The context in which the trauma is experienced is very important, and the collapse of a certain symbolic order in the world, as in the experience of war, can play a drastic role in undoing what may have been established as relatively acquired, what formed the psychic and group envelope for the subjects. Didier Anzieu has referred to the 'group envelope' (Anzieu, 1972) as a way of thinking about the differentiation between the inside and the outside, following on from the notion of the 'ego-skin': 'Through its internal face, the group envelope enables the establishment of a transindividual psychic state that I propose to call a group Self . . . It is the container within which a phantasmatic and identificatory circulation will be activated between individuals. It is the Self that brings the group to life' (Anzieu, 1981/1999, p. 2).

The advantage of this approach is that it allows us to think about the various psychological functions that the group performs for the subject in terms of containment. The ego-skin is used to evoke any boundary, any interface that separates, unites and connects. Transposed to the group, these concepts make it possible to think about what constitutes a link and containment within a group in relation to the subject's psychic needs. They are particularly useful for thinking about all the attacks to which members of a group are subjected because they are members of that group. Anything that overflows the group's excitation barrier, and is therefore on the side of trauma, attacks the main functions of this protective interface and exposes the members of the group to very archaic anxieties.

For a family, the loss of their home or the intrusion of soldiers into it can be experienced as an invasion of the envelope that protects the 'good' psychic objects within the group. For the members of the group, hoping to find the lost house can mean rediscovering a moment of 'group illusion', of fusional euphoria where all members of the group feel good together and are delighted to form a good group (Anzieu, 1981). As time goes by, rediscovering the lost home, the way of life of yesteryear – an unattainable ideal, in short – becomes the emblem of all the aspirations, hopes and disappointments endured individually and collectively since the loss.

Confrontation with traumas that undo the symbolic order of the world, that legitimise unlimited violence, that attack the social meta-frameworks (René Kaës, 2009a, 2009b) as guarantors of the existence of protective laws, is capable of undoing what may have been achieved from the point of view of the psychic construction of the subject and the group. The trauma that attacks the subject's links to the group and, more broadly, to society is thus interesting to question in so far as it undoes a sense of belonging to humanity. At the collective level, as at the individual level, confrontation with trauma leads to a disintegration of the drive, a regression to the most archaic strata of the psyche and a deconstruction of the group's symbolising capacities through the mobilisation of massive defences of projection, cleavage and denial of otherness. The result is a weakening of the difference between inside and outside, accompanied by intense fears of persecution. The impact of this trauma is not limited to the generation directly confronted with it. It is passed on to subsequent generations through an interplay of identifications, projections and unconscious transmissions.

Between Identification, Projection and Unconscious Transmission of Trauma

How can we think about the mechanisms of identification and transmission within groups confronted with collective trauma? After a brief diversion into some Freudian reflections on the way institutionalised groups function, we will look at the processes of identification, projection and unconscious transmission of trauma within communities that are victims of mass violence.

In his work *Group Psychology and Analysis of the Ego*, Freud (1921) looks more specifically at the affective links between the individual and the collective, with a clear interest in both crowd movements and institutions that require the subject to identify strongly with the group and its leader, such as the church or the army. It is important here to emphasise the affective dimension of membership of these groups – in other words, the way in which they are psychically invested by the subjects. Their highly hierarchical mode of operation presupposes not only adherence to the dominant ideas and beliefs but also submission to the authority figures who determine their decisions, and implies strong conflicts of loyalty in the event of disagreement with some of their decisions. These are institutions responsible for perpetuating an established social order, which find their internal legitimacy in their ability to elicit a degree of identification with, or adherence to, the group's ideals from their members, and which have little tolerance for internal dissent or disobedience. They are also institutions that seem to guarantee a certain relationship to national identity at different times and in different places.

In Greece and Cyprus, the image of the army and the church is strongly linked to a certain version of Greek Orthodox national identity, which is not very open to the internal plurality of each place. The various ethnic, religious and cultural minorities thus seem to be ignored in the dominant narratives, with a semblance of cohesion for some taking place at the expense of recognition for others. A narrative that homogenises the demographic composition, multiculturalism and religious diversity of each country constructs a fixed, ahistorical and essentialist image of its national identity (Alexopoulos de Girard, 2017).

It is interesting to note that this ostracism of the other can relate to groups considered to be very different from one's own (Christians vs Muslims) but also to groups that are relatively close (opposition between centre and periphery). The question of the narcissism of small differences, which seems to us fundamental to thinking about the rejection of groups that are culturally or geographically close but outside one's own group, is largely explained by Freud in *Civilization and Its Discontents* (1930):

> It is always possible to unite a greater mass of men to one another by the bonds of love, on the sole condition that there remain others outside it to receive the blows. I once dealt with the phenomenon of neighbouring and even related communities fighting and mocking each other; for example, Spaniards and Portuguese, North and South Germans, English and Scots, etc. I called it 'narcissism'. I have called it the 'narcissism of small differences', a name that does little to illuminate it. It is a convenient and

> relatively harmless way of satisfying the aggressive instinct, which makes it easier for members of a community to remain together. From this point of view, the Jewish people, by virtue of the fact that they were scattered all over the world, served the culture of the peoples who welcomed them with dignity. (deMijolla, 2005, pp. 1134–1135)

It seems to us that sometimes relations between Greek Cypriots and Turkish Cypriots are thought of in terms of this racism of small differences, which accentuates everything that is not identical, deliberately minimising similarities in the interests of maximum differentiation. It is as if the identity of one group is based on its differentiation from another group, sometimes even, and especially, when the two are similar.

Freud's work on social psychology, while varying over time, highlights the psychological mechanisms at work in identification with the leader and in the adoption of an ideology in place of the ideal self. The libidinal bonds between peers, the love for the father figure of the leader and the idealisation of the leader constitute the very 'flesh' of political, military or religious commitment, in the sense that they literally embody the relationship between the different members of the group, giving it a libidinal basis. For Freud, identification with the figure of the leader or his co-disciples is seen less in terms of representations and more in terms of affects. It is very important to keep this idea of an embodied link to the ideological, religious or military fact in order to be able to think about the question of identification, as a psychic movement of appropriation of the traits of the beloved or hated figure, and projection as an attempt to get rid of everything that is thought to be intolerable for one's conscience.

Identification is classically defined as a 'psychological process by which a subject assimilates an aspect, a property, an attribute of the other and transforms himself, totally or partially, on the model of the latter. The personality is constituted and differentiated by a series of identifications' (Laplanche & Pontalis, 1967). Projection is defined as 'the operation by which the subject expels from himself and locates in the other, person or thing, qualities, feelings, desires, or even objects that he does not recognise or reject in himself' (Laplanche & Pontalis, 1967). In conditions of war, the group under attack experiences movements of projections and identifications constructed in response to archaic anxieties linked to threats to the group's survival. Achieving a dialectical vision of its relationship with the other presupposes introspective work on these movements of identification and projection. It means moving away from a compact, Manichean vision of oneself, one's group and those outside it to nuance one's view, admitting one's own dark side in individual and collective terms, while recognising the humanity of every individual and every group.

In his testimony, Psaltis (Chapter 5 in this volume) refers to various father figures in the persons responsible for his education, whether university or military. It is interesting to note the way in which these encounters shaped, constructed and transformed his thinking, from an approach that was rather close to the official Hellenistic-centric historiography to a gradual ability to emancipate himself from it. Meeting his future wife also enabled him to embrace some of her ideas, socialising with some of his teachers seemed to authorise him to think about things differently, and the confrontation with his military instructor came to determine a breaking point on the side of a shared rejection. Thought of as a Greek from the periphery, abused by this man in accordance with the operating world of the military, confronted with the absurdity of the army, Psaltis nevertheless managed to resist the alienation mechanisms of this institution as described by Françoise Sironi (1999, 2007).

This emancipation from monolithic and exclusive nationalist authority figures enabled him to construct a way of thinking oriented towards otherness. Integrating the point of view of the other, external to the group, also means breaking out of a relationship of control that refuses all forms of exteriority, to gain access to a dialectical vision of the historical role of each party. It is very important to be able to move away from a projective mode of operation, based on the exclusion of a demonised otherness, towards a capacity to recognise otherness in ourselves and identity in the other, without minimising the place of the affects of fear, hatred or despair that may have been present.

Projecting outside the group what is intolerable for oneself, or recognising one's own violence, is a very archaic mechanism that we find whenever there is a feeling of threat in real, symbolic or imaginary terms. While this mechanism initially helps us to form a kind of 'sacred union' with the group, it does not allow us to recognise the violence on our own side and freezes everyone in Manichean roles. Trauma can convey an overly compact vision of oneself, of others and of the past, silencing the internal polyphony of each human group.

The question of identification and projection is central to thinking about the relationship with trauma in terms of the memory issues at stake in our communities of belonging or reference, and more generally in the construction of imaginary communities (Anderson, 1983). It is important here to emphasise the unconscious transmission of trauma at work in the processes of identification and projection. The violence suffered is transmitted not only through verbal expression but also through a whole series of signs that consciously, but more often than not unconsciously, give shape to the trauma endured by previous generations. The younger generations thus identify with the distress of their parents, continue to project onto the enemy groups of yesteryear the image of a threatening and fundamentally 'evil' otherness, and receive from their families a transgenerational mandate to honour that commits them to a series of acts of loyalty.

When Psaltis's son tells him that the Turks are bad because they took their house, this phrase interprets the paternal grandmother's factual description of the spoliation. It brings back repressed representations, obeying a logic of identification with the discourse of his elders and of explicitation of its latent content. The child's projection of all that is 'bad' onto the enemy group allows him to give meaning to his family's painful experience by naming the negative experiences that have been kept silent, pointing the finger of blame and attributing responsibility for this painful experience to an 'evil' other.

At the same time, it speaks of a process of transmission in which Psaltis's self-censorship, carried out in the name of the ideal of preserving his child from any discourse of rejection of the other, is thwarted by the unconscious need of the son and grandparents to come and signify something of an unresolved original prejudice. If the grandparents' generation is imbued with a deep sense of prejudice, and the children's generation tries to rationalise this approach through scientific reflection on the causes and consequences of intercommunity violence, by advocating solutions that bring people together, it is fairly predictable that the third generation will recall the negative representations of the enemies of yesteryear that the parental discourse had tried to sweep under the rug. Overcoming this feeling of prejudice presupposes the explicit recognition and uncensored recounting of one's own suffering in the same way as that of the other side. If Psaltis's son felt the need to tell him that the Turks are bad, it was undoubtedly because Psaltis was following a logic of intercommunity rapprochement, trying to defend himself against the suffering and powerlessness he had once felt and to cut through his own mother's 'infant distress' and possible depression in the early years after the war. Psaltis failed to tell his son how psychically painful the loss of his home had been for him, how the fear of the return of the Turks had instilled itself in his heart, expressed through his many traumatic dreams, and how for his displaced parents this experience had been a nameless trauma and an endless sadness, having turned their lives upside down forever. Family trauma needs to be recognised as such, to be recounted and elaborated, so that it can then be considered in a more general context of condemnation of the violence committed by both sides and adherence to ideals of justice, peace and dialogue. Any rational discourse about overcoming conflict that fails to take account of the pain experienced by those involved blocks out a great deal of psychological work and can be found in encrypted form in the next generation.

The transgenerational transmission of trauma builds victim identifications at the same time as massive projections, which are very difficult to get rid of because they constitute a vital link with beloved figures whose narcissistic foundations and object relationships have been attacked. In a way, the unconscious transmission of trauma obeys a logic of force of attraction, where everything that is unrepresentable or unspeakable comes back as an unconscious problem for the subject and the group, sometimes leading to acting out. It is important, then, to think of the traumatic burden as a psychological and social fact that can prevent a bonding process based on the elaboration of the past, blocking the expression of negative affects and representations and hindering the effective recognition of the double trauma within memory communities. Emerging from victim identification and its transmission to the next generation in the form of encysted trauma (Abraham &Torok, 1994), which forms the basis of a 'narcissistic pact' – in other words, an internal image of the group that leaves no room for otherness – presupposes work on one's own violence and suffering. Telling the story of the past should enable us to work on the emergence of painful affects and repressed representations.

Reconstructing Memories and Passing on Trauma through Testimony

Recalling and recounting the past, as attempts to make sense of what has happened to oneself and by oneself, can help to avoid reproducing the trauma in favour of elaborating it. On the other hand, this can also obey a logic of reiterating patterns of thought that leave no room for otherness and that re-actualise the original feeling of injury. Lastly, this can oscillate between the two functions, at times becoming a form of expression as much as a way of concealing different memory issues. We will see how, by forming part of a polyphonic testimonial network, the telling of one's story and the recognition of its emotional charge open the way to a possible differentiation from the models with which we are familiar, heirs to a past of suffering and impasses.

The work of reconstructing our memories, which is partly unconscious, consists of trying to tell ourselves and others a certain version of what may have happened to ourselves and our loved ones. As Paul Ricœur (1984–1988) shows us, all narratives are selective. It is therefore important to be aware of the work of selection that sometimes takes place, even without our knowledge, when a testimonial is given. Depending on the framework in which it is expressed, this talk about the past may borrow from community matrices, by repeating a dominant discourse within the group, take the form of an interface that is both an opaque screen and a support for subjective speech, or take on a cathartic function by enabling the subject to be as close as possible to his or her internal reality. Very often, after a conflict ends, the discourse that relates to it embodies a heroic version of the facts and an idealisation of one's own camp, while gradually the axis of conflict shifts from the opposition between us and them to a capacity for self-criticism within one's own community or even within one's own history, between oneself and the other.

Recalling the past in a suitable therapeutic or research context is a way of revisiting what is still active in us, of becoming aware of it and sometimes of proposing a meta-analysis. Psaltis's nuanced account, which includes a significant reflexive approach to his journey and its links to the narratives of his group, shows that a narrative can have psychic and mental developmental values, and even give rise to an epistemophilic investment in the field of knowledge involved.

The way in which we remember as members of a group and as a society as a whole sheds light on our individual and collective relationship with authority figures, the ways in which we identify with discourse or ideas and the various forms of conscious or unconscious transmission to which we have been subjected. The memory of trauma is often transmitted by what is said, but also by unconscious attitudes. The formation of the image of the self and the other and the construction of a political and social memory of the past are the result of a twofold movement. There is a move from the factual to the interpretative, and vice versa, in such a way that every historical reality becomes the object of social and individual reconstructions endowed with an imaginary of their own (Wagoner, 2017). All the fantasies of an event consciously or unconsciously condition the perception and transmission of various facets of its reality.

Memory representations are social constructs with a group phantasmatic resonance and an individual unconscious anchoring. They evolve over time and maintain a causal and consecutive relationship with the discursive realities that frame them, since they are conditioned by them while in turn being likely to determine their contours. Discourses on the memory of the 1974 war, the intercommunity tensions of the 1960s and the experience of forced displacement within Cyprus are transformed into social objects that grapple with the endo-psychic and interpsychic issues of the subjects. They address themselves and the other at the same time, mobilising an enunciative act anchored in the here-and-now of the narrative while referring to a spatiotemporal elsewhere, and reflecting the internal polyphony of a plurality of memories divided inside and outside each community.

The transgenerational issues involved in the transmission of testimonies concern both the descendants and symbolic heirs of the witness and the researchers who take their testimonies and who find themselves confronted with the traumatic scare 'not experienced by the subject, expelled from the fray, which then crosses the generations of the descendants by creating a gap, an inhibition of the contact that would constitute speech likely to address the objects loved' (Altounian, 2004, p. 48). Working on one's own subjectivity as a researcher is necessary to understand the way in which our history determines our relationship with our objects of study. Becoming aware of it means identifying its strengths and limitations, based on what constitutes our desire: the assertion of loyalty to parental figures or those hierarchically assimilated to them, the expression of conflict in the face of what seems to us to be hindering the fulfilment of our desire (for peace, for a return to the land, for a national claim) or, on the contrary, the expression of conflict in the face of what seems to us to be hindering the fulfilment of our desire (for peace, for a national claim) or, on the contrary, the search for a solution that silences or partially conceals an intrapsychic or intersubjective conflict that puts us at odds with the dominant discourse of our group and/or our own ideals of the solution to be achieved – the search for possible ways of compromising between our aspirations and the principle of reality.

The recording of the testimonial accounts of those involved on both sides, the research carried out on issues of inter- and intracommunity conflict, the work of reflection and the writing of a meta-analysis of the data collected must contribute to a process of collective recollection that allows for the recognition of traumatic experiences on both sides. Recognition of the status of victims for all those involved in a conflict is essential if people are to rebuild their psyches by breaking away from the state of emergency or war into which the trauma plunges them. Stepping out of the victim's position to recognise the trauma suffered by others, particularly when they belong to the opposite group, presupposes that you feel that your own status as a former victim has been recognised. It is therefore a question of double recognition within communities of memory. However, it is difficult to escape from one's victimised position when the dominant narratives within one's group crystallise around victimisation, making it the basis of a narcissistic contract that also acts as a 'denial pact' (Kaës, 2014).

In the case of individual or collective trauma, it is interesting to consider the process of fetishisation in which the trauma is invested with the image of a partial, sacralised and fixed object. While this process can be found in both individual and collective trauma, it can be accompanied within a group by an attempt to instrumentalise the memory by public authorities constructing policies of remembrance based on the evocation of sacrificial and victim figures. This is the well-known martyrological nature of narratives of memory and official history in nationalist representational schemes, discourses and practices.

Finally, the recognition of double trauma, to be understood as the ability to acknowledge one's own share of responsibility and suffering, as well as those of the other within each community of memory, is a way of providing a point of exteriority to the narratives conducted within each group. It thus enables one to escape a compact vision of identity and leaves room for the internal polyphony of each community. By making room for the other, outside the group, we also allow ourselves to rehabilitate the voices within our own group, and vice versa.

Conclusion

This chapter has explored how psychoanalysis perceives trauma in its individual and collective aspects, with reference to the traumatic encounter, to the unconscious reproduction of what has broken into the subject's psyche and to the way in which each aftermath, sometimes unconsciously sought, remembers painful experiences that have been lived through without always being experienced. Repetition serves both to attach us to the past, possibly melancholising the link, and to replay the traumatic scenario, in an attempt to bring about some kind of transformation, however small. Changing our position and moving from a passive to an active role, by becoming the author of this play, thus represent the first attempt at subjective appropriation of a legacy that is heavy to bear.

In the history of the subject, the confrontation with early traumas, both in terms of too much excitement and emotional deficiencies, the absence of a sufficiently good and protective family environment, and repeated attacks on the envelope at individual and group levels hinder the passage through crucial stages of psychosexual and cognitive development by encouraging movements of fixation or regression. While archaic anxieties and the defence mechanisms deployed to deal with them are common to everyone, confrontation with major traumatic experiences can undo symbolisation capacities that had previously been successfully put in place. Trauma thus has a force of attraction that hinders separation from a painful past and can plunge the subject into very archaic modes of functioning.

In a group situation, confrontation with major collective trauma encourages the return of the archaic, the retreat of mental processing capacities and recourse to the reproduction of traumatogenic situations. It is as if very archaic mechanisms are summoned up, allowing a form of dehumanisation of the other: projection of the bad object outside the group, division between a very good self-image and a very bad image of the other, denial of the suffering and humanity of the enemy group. This mortifying, binary and projective logic encourages all kinds of violent acts, in a cycle of repeated violence from which it is important to find a way out.

To do this, it is vital to work on the dual recognition of trauma, specifically the ability to pass on to future generations a narrative of the past that leaves room for the internal and external polyphony of narratives without obscuring the emotional charge of what has been experienced. Integrating the point of view of the other, whether outside or within one's own group, also opens the way to expressing conflict within oneself and one's group by rejecting a compact, homogenous or monolithic vision of the identity and history of each group. Acknowledging the suffering of the other as well as one's own enables the individual and the group to emerge from a position of victimhood or screen discourse, to integrate the traumatic experience into a more dialectic and authentic vision of their history, and to project themselves into a less Manichean and more constructive vision of the future, opening the way to a process of co-creation.

REFERENCES

Abraham, N., & Torok, M. (1994). *The shell and the kernel: Renewals of psychoanalysis, Vol. 1.* (N. T. Rand, Ed.) Chicago: University of Chicago Press.

Alexopoulos de Girard C. (2017). *Représentationsmémorielles de la guerre civile grecque*, Paris: Classiques Garnier.

Altounian, J. (2004). De quoi témoignent les mains des survivants? De l'anéantissement des vivants, de l'affirmation de la vie. In J.-F. Chiantaretto (Ed.), *Témoignages et trauma, implications psychanalytiques* (p. 48). Paris: Dunod.

Anderson, B. (1983/2006). *Imagined communities: Reflections on the origin and spread of nationalism* (Rev. ed.). London: Verso.
Anzieu, D. (1981). *Le groupe et l'inconscient.* Paris: Bordas.
(1985). *Le Moi-peau.* Bordas, Paris.
Anzieu, D., Béjarano, A., Kaës, R., Missenard, A., & Pontalis, J.-B. (1972). *Le travail psychanalytique dans les groups.* Paris: Dunod.
Berger, P. L., & Luckmann, T. (1966). *The social construction of reality: A Treatise in the Sociology of Knowledge.* Garden City, NY: Anchor Books.
Bion, W. R. (1962). *Learning from experience,* London: William Heinemann.
Bowlby J. (1958). The nature of the child's tie to his mother, *International Journal of Psycho-Analysis, 39,* 350–373.
(1969/1982). *Attachment and loss: Attachment.* London: Basic Books,
(1973/1979). *Attachment and loss: Separation.* New York: Basic Books.
Brun, A., Chouvier, B., & Roussillon, R. (2019). *Manuel des médiationsthérapeutiques,* Paris: Dunod. https://doi.org/10.3917/dunod.brun.2019.02.
Bruner, J. (1990). *Acts of meaning.* Cambridge, MA: Harvard University Press.
Chervet, B. (2009). L'après-coup: La tentative d'inscrirece qui tend à disparaître. *Revue française de psychanalyse,* 73, 1361–1441. https://doi.org/10.3917/rfp.735.1361.
Duvernay Bolens, J. (2001). La théorie de la récapitulation de Haeckel à Freud. *Topique, 75,* 13–34. https://doi.org/10.3917/top.075.0013.
de Mijolla, A. (2005). Narcissisme des petites différences. In A. de Mijolla (Ed.), *Dictionnaire international de la psychanalyse* (pp. 1134–1135). Paris: Hachette Littératures.
Freud, S. (1914). On narcissism: An introduction. In J. Strachey (Ed.), *The Standard edition of the complete psychological works of Sigmund Freud* (pp. 67–102). London: Hogarth Press.
(1920). Beyond the pleasure principle. In A. Freud (Ed.), *The essentials of psychoanalysis: The definitive collection of Sigmund Freud's writing* (J. Strachey, Transl.). London: Penguin Books.
(1926). *Inhibition, symptôme et angoisse,* Paris: PUF.
(1933). *La décomposition de la personnalitépsychique, XXXI*[e] *conférence in Les nouvellesconférences sur la psychanalyse* (R.-M. Zeitlin, Transl.). Paris: Gallimard.
Freud S. (1934–1938). Moses and monotheism: Three essays (1939), *SE, XXIII,* 1–138.
(1937). Constructions dans l'analyse, OCF/P, XX. Paris: PUF.
Janin C. (1996). *Figures et destins du traumatisme.* Paris: PUF.
Kaës, R. (2009a). Le travail de l'intersubjectivité et la polyphonie du récit dans l'élaboration de l'expérience traumatique. In V. Altounian & J. Altounian (Eds.), *Mémoires du génocide arménien: Héritage traumatique et travail analytique* (pp. 209–235). Paris: PUF.
(2009b). *Les alliances inconscientes.* Paris: Dunod.
(2014). *Linking, alliances, and shared space: Groups and the psychoanalyst.* London: Routledge.

Kansteiner, W. (2004). Genealogy of a category mistake: A critical intellectual history of the cultural trauma metaphor. *Rethinking History*, *8*(2), 193–221. https://doi.org/10.1080/13642520410001683905.

Klein, M. (1984). *Envy and gratitude and other works 1946-1963*. London: The Hogarth Press.

(1996). Notes on some schizoid mechanisms. *Psychotherapy Practice Research*, *5*(2), 160–179.

Laplanche J., & Pontalis J.B. (1967). *Vocabulaire de la psychanalyse*, Paris: PUF.

Freud, S. (1985). *The complete letters of Sigmund Freud to Wilhelm Fliess, 1887-1904* (J. M. Masson, Ed. & Transl.). Cambridge, MA: Belknap Press of Harvard University Press.

Pireyre, É. (2015). Les angoissescorporellesarchaïques. In É. Pireyre (Ed.), *Clinique de l'image du corps: Du vécu au concept* (pp. 141–156). Paris: Dunod.

Radden, J. (2011). The depressive position: KLEIN. In J. Radden (Ed.), *The nature of melancholy: From Aristotle to Kristeva*. New York: Oxford Academic. https://doi.org/10.1093/acprof:oso/9780195151657.003.0027.

Ricoeur, P. (1984–1988). *Time and narrative*. 3 vols. Chicago: University of Chicago Press.

Roussillon, R. (2003). Historicité et mémoire subjective: La troisième trace. *Cliniquesméditerranéennes*, *67*, 127–144. https://doi.org/10.3917/cm.067.0127.

(2012). La terreuragonistique et le psychotique. In R. Roussillon (Ed.), *Agonie, clivage et symbolisation* (pp. 138–158). Paris: PUF.

Sironi, F. (1999). *Bourreaux et victimes: Psychologie de la torture*. Paris: Odile Jacob.

(2007). *Psychopathologie des violences collectives: Essai de psychologiegéopolitiqueclinique*. Paris: Odile Jacob.

Sommantico, M. (2008). Ce que les 'concepts-limites' d'Anzieuapportent à la cliniquepsychanalytique du couple et de la famille. *Le Divan familial*, *21*, 199–216. https://doi.org/10.3917/difa.021.0199.

Wagoner, B. (2017). *The constructive mind: Bartlett's psychology in reconstruction*. Cambridge: Cambridge University Press.

Winnicott D. W. (1958). The capacity to be alone. *The International Journal of Psychoanalysis*, *39*, 416–420.

Winnicott, D. W. (2016). Transitional objects and transitional phenomena. In L. Caldwell & H. T. Robinson (Eds.), *The collected works of D. W. Winnicott: Volume 3, 1946–1951* (pp. 447–462). New York: Oxford Academic. https://doi.org/10.1093/med:psych/9780190271350.003.0088.

CHAPTER 10

Reconciling Divergent Common Sense
Argumentation and Social Representation

Gordon Sammut

Introduction

The advent of modernity, followed by the post-modern era, precipitated certain cultural conditions in various societies that sought to establish a social order beyond traditional religious dogma on the one hand or feudal aristocracy on the other. At the centre of this cultural and philosophical upheaval was the rise of the individual, a thinking being in its own right endowed with a set of basic, inalienable human rights. As the authority of arguments replaced arguments of authority (Jovchelovitch, 2007), the individual emerged as the seat of reason, perspective, experience and free will. The fundamental consequence of this state of affairs was the rise and recognition of diversity. The individual was no longer noble or plebeian; anointed, infidel or heretic. Social class divisions were reconfigured along the lines of wealth and capital, whilst individuals became entitled to their own ideas, their personal opinions and their individual talents. These made them different from everyone else. Individuals also came to enjoy the right to exercise their freedoms, interests and pursuits despite their differences. Herein lies the American dream, that is, the aspiration to establish a social order where a self-reliant and determined individual, regardless of ascribed personal characteristics, can pursue an innovative idea or scarce talent that leads at once to the betterment of society as well as to unlimited personal success. In these conditions, diversity is positively connoted as the harbinger of innovation, which in turn enables progress. The absence of diversity leads to a stale order that grants social harmony but that preserves inequalities and fails to adapt to changing circumstances. The result of a lack of diversity that short-circuits innovation is deemed as potentially catastrophic.

Whilst the post-modern condition has, to some extent, taken root across the globe, it masks two critical fractures. Firstly, the recognition and respect of diversity is accompanied by a relativistic pluralism where any idea is, at least initially, held to be as good as any other. The merit of ideas hinges on their pragmatic utility and whether they are useful in practice regardless of moral considerations. Social order, however, necessitates a basic consensus with regards to some fundamental precepts. As Asch (1952) argued, one cannot have plural definitions in a single society of what constitutes a crime. The solution to relativism in post-modern societies that has replaced traditional forms of authority is black letter law, which is continually challenged, revised and updated. This is why politics is a highly charged and contentious activity. It is the process that diverse human beings engage in to legitimate and regularise their own ways. Secondly, humans have evolved a sense of self that helps them to identify friend from foe. In this way they are able to collaborate in mutually beneficial projects as well as avoid doing the same with enemies or cheats (Park & Van Leeuwen, 2015). This identification process pits them with some as well as distinguishes them from others when they are identified as members of some particular group. For this reason, individuals cultivate their identities to tap into the collaborative potential that group membership confers, that is, to tap a group's social capital (Sammut, 2011). Human psychology is thus fundamentally political. Whilst our sense of identity is meant to define our individuality in terms that delineate us from everyone else, we only ever achieve this by recounting who we are in terms of categories that we share with many others (e.g. mother, Muslim, middle aged, black, Maltese, Arsenal fan, etc.). Given this banded diversity, therefore, the postmodern condition leads to the recognition that, as Giddens (1991) famously noted, we cannot subscribe to any dictates without knowing, at the same time, that others in the same public sphere subscribe to wholly different and potentially opposing precepts. Postmodern societies are thus essentially imbued with the political challenge regarding whose dictates will ultimately prevail.

Identity Politics: Who I Am Is Who I Am Not

Identity politics – that is, the cultivation of identity in politically consequential ways (Fukuyama, 2018) – has replaced traditional party politics based on ideological criteria in many societies. The striving of subjects towards some utopic ideal that can only ever be approximated in reality but that can never be fully realised in practice has fuelled many political movements throughout history based on religious or national orders. Modernity has usurped these traditional orders. The freedom of association enjoyed by individuals today, enshrined in their basic human rights, also means that they are at liberty to establish coalitions to further their own aims and interests based on who they are or who they want to become. Membership in a social group confers identity and provides access to myriad resources associated with belonging. Human beings today enjoy the freedom to determine for themselves who they want to be for others. Crucially, this means that an individual is not fully identifiable through ascribed criteria alone (Cadge & Davidman, 2006). Rather, individuals have a choice when it comes to who they want to be identified *as*. The post-modern cosmopolitan identity, which becomes available in cosmopolitan publics marked by a high degree of interconnected diversity, is based on loose, fluid and individualistic identity criteria that are meaningful to the self but that do not require social recognition (Beck, 2002). In other words, I might be black and male, but I might also feel that I do not particularly identify either with my skin colour or with my masculinity. I might identify more strongly as a musician, or as a pet owner, and I use these criteria to associate in a public space that is so diverse that neither skin colour nor gender at birth serve as social markers of any kind any more than being into music or into pets does. Whilst this possibility is very real in highly diverse publics and offers some individuals self-enhancing and liberating possibilities in practice, it is worth noting that this state of affairs requires in any case a political commitment to the cosmopolitan vision (Bayram, 2017). I can only be gender fluid in a society that recognises gender fluidity, and this is by no means a political given. Recognition typically involves an emancipatory struggle, of a political nature, that opens new possibilities beyond established common sense.

The process of social identification thus bears political ramifications. One should note that negotiating a personal identity is an irreducibly social process, even in a cosmopolitan sense. I am not able to declare myself chairperson of any committee, no matter how much I might identify with the chair's role or how much I feel the designation truly reflects my personal attributes. The formal status I am able to achieve as a result of my self-declared identity depends very tangibly on its recognition by others. In this way, therefore, our identities serve to establish relations with similar- and different-minded others relative to some object of concern. This triangulation of social relations is modelled on the systemic conception of social representations (Sammut & Howarth, 2014) as a field of relational activity established between a minimal triad of two interacting subjects [S1, S2] concerned with an object [O] (Bauer & Gaskell, 1999; Sammut, 2015). A fourth element implicated in this relational activity is the project [P] that underlies the scope of interaction. The project essentially constitutes the social representations' political dimension and unites subjects relative to an object of mutual concern. In this way, according to Bauer and Gaskell (1999),

> Representations have a triple genitive; representations of the subjects, representations of the object, and representations of the project. Subjects, object and project form a system of mutual constitution; the third mediating between the other two. This structure is essential if we want to understand how in the object, the project of the subjects is represented; or how in the subjects the object appears in relation to a project; or how the project links the subjects and the object. (p. 168)

Individuals are implicated in social representations whenever they associate with others in pursuit of some interest of mutual concern. Like identity, interests are typically understood in exclusively personal terms but transpire as irreducibly social under further scrutiny. In its basic etymological sense, an interest instantiates a 'being together' (Arendt, 1958; Sammut, 2011). Whilst interests can be pursued alone, such as when a musician plays music at home without an audience, or a trekker hiking alone on a mountain trail, they always minimally associate a subject with an object. The involvement of another subject establishes a social representation linking the two interacting subjects to a mutual interest, which is understood as an object of a certain kind – the kind that mutually fulfils the separate interests of the independent subjects. Understood in any other way, the object fails to satisfy one or another interest (e.g. hiking as a physical challenge versus a relaxing pastime). The result of this is a disinterested subject that breaks the interrelational triad. To overcome this breakdown, the object will require re-presentation by the subjects (e.g. hiking as a relaxing activity involving a degree of physical exercise) (Chryssides et al., 2009; Buhagiar & Sammut, 2020).

The interested activity pursued in representational work of this kind instantiates a political project that aspires at serving mutual interests. In this way, the processes involved in social re-presentation are characteristically interobjective serving social constructionist aspirations (Sammut, Daanen & Sartawi, 2012). The understanding that inheres in established social representations serves as a common sense across implicated subjects and frames their individual interests. An individual coming from the outside who joins the established triad [S, S, O] in an effort to negotiate an inclusive identity with them partakes in this common sense and subscribes to the project entailed in the social representation. To the extent that this individual, however, holds discrepant interests to the other subjects that require accommodation through re-presentation of the object (e.g. hiking as a social activity), and where the re-presentation entailed is antithetical to the original project, then the members of the group will need to reformulate their project and revise their common sense in line or proceed with excluding the new interest to preserve the old. In such cases, the alien must pursue their discrepant interest by association with other non-belonging subjects – a competing coalition. This gives rise to a new project yielding an alternative common sense that satisfies the latter's interests and that may well collide with the former's.

To illustrate using the political context of Cyprus, a child growing up in Larnaca to parents who identify as Greek Cypriot internalises social representations of Cyprus as historically Hellenic and distinct from Turkey. The child goes on to assume a Greek Cypriot identity to the extent that she makes these representations her own and partakes in the political project of reclaiming Northern Cyprus from Turkey perceiving it as a commonsense reaction to the violation of national sovereignty suffered by Cyprus at Turkey's hands. The child may, however, encounter alternative representations of the conflict during its development and opt to negotiate a different identity, such as an inclusive Cypriot identity. This might contrast with that of her parents. The child, however, partakes in social representations that frame the conflict as a historical misfortune and the Cypriot nation as ethnically diverse. The project pursued by such identification would be a project of unification, not reclamation, sensitive to ethnic diversity instead of overlooking it or subjugating it. The latter project re-presents Turkish Cypriots [the object] in a different way than the former, as co-nationals rather than invaders, towards fulfilling a project with diametrically opposed aspirations.

Framed in this way, it is clear that political conflict of any kind involves discrepant projects based in competing common senses serving diverse interests. Conflict occurs when not all interests are, or can be, accommodated in the face of new demands, requiring subjects to pursue alternative means. This conception of conflict also makes clear that the negotiation of identity based on the political pursuit of interests is as much a process of inclusion as it is of exclusion. In other words, who we choose to be in terms of what we choose to do defines us as much as who we choose not to be and what we choose not to do. Both sides of this identity coin put us in coalition with some pursuing similar interests and in competition with others involved in contrasting pursuits. The post-modern drift of identity politics culminates in a-ideological populist deeds that are more concerned with who to leave out than with who to allow in (Zaslove, 2008).

Social Cognition and Social Influence

A frequent strategy pursued by politicians in instances of conflict is a call to dialogue. The idea behind dialogue is that through communication, parties pursuing different and conflicting ends acquire some sensitivity to the other side's aspirations and negotiate, in light of this understanding, mutually satisfactory solutions. In successful cases, dialogue averts the need for armed conflict (Sammut & Bauer, 2021). In practice, however, dialogue is no panacea and may not succeed in resolving an impasse that involves the forfeiture of some interests (Chryssides, 2018; Condor, 2018; Hopkins, 2018; Nesbitt-Larking, 2018). Aside from the fact that it might not be in some subjects' interest to yield – that is, take a loss of any kind for the other party to obtain a commensurate gain – as human beings we are ill-equipped to handle discrepant perspectives. Our social cognition relies on socio-cognitive strategies that discount the other's perspective so that we can march ahead with our own. Wason (1960) noted how evidence that confirms our hypotheses is given more weight than disconfirming evidence, leading to failure to reject false beliefs. Kunda (1990) observed how reasoning is motivated to fabricate arguments that justify the conclusions we wish to believe and to reject conclusions we are uncomfortable with. Ross and Ward (1996) argue that human beings are naïve realists – that is, they naturally assume that their subjective perceptions and experiences are in fact objective, and therefore others perceive and experience things in the same way that they do. Moreover, to the extent that others argue differently, their thinking must be at fault and if they had access to our own knowledge, they would necessarily agree with us. Sammut and Sartawi (2012) report attributions of ignorance on the part of those who hold contrasting beliefs to others, requiring education, not understanding. And Marques, Yzerbyt and Leyens (1988) observed how group members judge deviant in-group members more severely than they do out-group members who disagree with them.

These biased socio-cognitive processes, embedded in human psychology over evolutionary time, may well have proven adaptive during our ancestral environment when resources were scare and different coalitions competed in zero-sum strategies for evolutionary survival (Campbell, 1965; Jackson, 1993). These biases have seemingly enabled the cultivation of bonding social capital amongst group members (Sammut, 2011) that would have enabled a sharing of resources with other identified (and identifiable) group members, such as amongst extended kinship networks, which would have facilitated survival through reciprocity and altruism within the group. This also would have necessitated discrimination towards out-group members and withholding of prosocial relations outside of one's own group. In this way, social identity is evolutionarily adaptive and serves to consolidate projects over time that are self-serving and help dissenters to yield to mutual interests. Undoubtedly, these biases also get in the way of overcoming discrepancies in social representations and lead us down a path of conflictual standoffs in instances of discord, as both parties attribute ignorance to one another (Sammut & Sartawi, 2012).

Social cognition, in essence, fuels the spiral of conflict between differently interested social groups (Sammut, Bezzina & Sartawi, 2015). Interests, therefore, bind individuals together in collective projects (Sammut, 2011), which is how identity issues come to impact material interests (Moghaddam, 2010). These can only be secured if individuals stick to their guns and sustain their self-serving projects, personally and in collectives, over time. For this reason, if we must, we are able to socially re-present objects in ways that help our projects to survive in the face of challenge. There is perhaps no better example of this than Moscovici's (1976/2008) own study of psychoanalysis, re-presented by the Catholics in France as a form of confession. The Catholic Church's re-presentation strategy for survival is evident in other instances, such as its reconciliation with science through Pope John II's encyclical of *Fides et Ratio* or the re-presentation of The Shroud of Turin from the burial shroud used in Jesus' crucifixion to an iconic relic that invites contemplation of The Christ and His teachings. In this manner, social representation is an extension of motivated reasoning (Kunda, 1990) that enables the group's project to survive. In the face of challenge by discrepant perspectives, therefore, human beings are not always motivated to dialogue in an open-minded manner, questioning the validity of their own perspectives (Sammut & Gaskell, 2010). Rather, they are often motivated to adopt self-preserving strategies and seek to influence the other party to recognise the legitimacy of their own ways. This happens both when social groups are in a dominant majority as well as when they find themselves in a non-dominant minority. In a majority, social groups seek compliance for minorities to conform to their own ways. In their turn, minorities pursue strict internal conformity, ostracising dissenters (Marques, Yzerbyt & Leyens, 1988), to pursue conversion for the majority. In any case, they have at their disposal a range of social influence tactics, from crowd activism, to leadership, laws, authority, mass media, artefacts, persuasion strategies and others, to pursue the legitimation of their own ways. Failing social influence, social groups are also capable of hard power and fighting, literally, for the recognition and preservation of their own ways, including such group altruistic self-sacrificing strategies as suicide bombing and terrorism (Sammut & Bauer, 2021). Clearly, as the authors of the Harvard Method for conflict resolution advocate, when engaging another party in dialogue, it is always worth having a plan B (Fisher & Ury, 1981).

Positioning

In understanding how human beings orient themselves differently to social objects or events, the social sciences have traditionally relied on the study of attitudinal inclinations. Attitudes are conceptualised as the individual's evaluation of an attitude object. Consequently, knowing one's attitude towards some object or event reveals that person's alignment towards the object as well as relative to others holding similar or discrepant attitudes (Sammut, 2015). In this way, the study of attitude-based public opinion relies on aggregated scores that reveal the proportion of those who are favourably inclined, those are who unfavourably inclined and lastly those who are neutral towards the object of inquiry. In this conception, political activity emerges as a rhetorical exercise of social influence that aims to tip the scales of public opinion one way or another in an effort to secure a decisive majority. This conception is useful in understanding the political battle for hearts and minds that typically observes democratic principles when engaging opponents. The numerous public opinion polls in the run-up to democratic elections in Western countries demonstrate the utility of this pursuit. It is arguably less useful, however, in understanding conflict resolution strategies that incorporate elements of both hard and soft power across incommensurable divides.

Billig (1987) argues that a fundamental shortcoming of the attitude construct is that it does not adequately reveal alliances in the social domain. According to Billig, when individuals express a socially relevant attitude, they are doing more than articulating a personal disposition towards an attitude object. In certain circumstances, articulating an attitude serves in taking up a position and occupying a standpoint in social domains rife with highly charged controversies that are also materially consequential. The passive measurement of attitudes using the pervasive Likert scale fails to take these implications into account. Consequently, with regards to social controversies, the study of attitudes may not reveal much and provides little insight when it comes to understanding the nature of a dispute and identifying strategies for how to resolve it.

For instance, a social scientist may very easily measure individual attitudes towards salted-caramel chocolate bars. To do this, a researcher typically presents respondents with an item pertaining to the attitude object and asks individuals to evaluate the item using a rating scale from Strongly Agree to Strongly Disagree. The exercise will reveal how many are favourably or unfavourably inclined towards the object as well as how many are sitting on the fence and might be tempted, with some effort, one way or another. This exercise may be very useful when deciding how much stock of a given product to manufacture or acquire given the size of the market. The same method, however, may be less useful in understanding individual inclinations towards controversial events like Brexit, the American forces' withdrawal from Afghanistan, or the Cyprus–Turkey dispute. This is because some attitudes are not trivial. Rather, they are underlined by deep-seated standpoints on matters of controversy that position individuals for or against some issue and, consequently, with some people against some others in the very social domain they inhabit. In this way, changing attitudes is not merely an act of changing preferences. In certain cases this involves actually changing the environment in which the attitude is embedded, by constraining or legitimating contrasting positions which stand to overturn the prevalent order and usher in a new common sense (Sammut & Bauer, 2021). For instance, following Brexit, the British are no longer European. This is the new common sense standing across the Brexit divide (Andreouli & Nicholson, 2018).

It should be clear by now that not all positions regarding social controversies are reconcilable. Some involve trade-offs that benefit some at the expense of others. Others involve contrasting common senses that present different depictions of the social order and how it can or should be maintained. For instance, to the extent that one understands the present Cyprus–Turkey dispute in terms of a Turkish invasion of Cyprus, a strategy to dispel Turkish influence makes sense. But to the extent that one understands the dispute in light of the Greek military junta or as an ethnic problem of two conflicting nationalisms in Cyprus, one is able to see Turkish intervention in a new light. These nuanced levels of meaning are not revealed by attitudes but can be articulated as *accounts* (Harré & Secord, 1972) that provide insight into the sense that inheres in taking a stand, through adopting a certain attitude, for or against some controversial issue. Accounts provide a gateway to understanding a subject's point of view, which reveals how the subject perceives the issue relative to other perceiving subjects (Sammut & Gaskell, 2010; Sammut, 2015). That is, in furnishing accounts, subjects are able to articulate how they *see* things relative to how others are *seeing* the same thing and why the two points of view do not square up. Crucially, this understanding can be pursued across both sides of a conflict. The exercise ought to reveal discrepant realities, and if one is to pursue a reconciliatory strategy, the key must lie in fabricating solutions that are mutually satisfactory given the social representation of the issue already in place and the projects these have effectively sustained over time.

Bridging the Gap

In the rest of this chapter, I present a methodological procedure for reconciling divergent common sense that is based on a reformulation of social representations (Buhagiar & Sammut, 2020). The study of social representations has typically foregrounded disputed objects whose representations are studied amongst particular social groups towards a deep understanding. This tradition of social representations research can be traced back to Moscovici's (1976/2008) original study of psychoanalysis in France. In this study, the object of psychoanalysis was investigated amongst three group: Catholics, Communists and Liberals. This and many other studies in the social representations tradition (see Buhagiar & Sammut, 2020) follow the implicit formula of studying the Social Representation [SR] of an Object [X] held by Group [Y] in Context [Z]:

SR of X by Y in Z

Buhagiar and Sammut (2020) provide a reformulation of social representations that is intended to complement the one presented above. They argue that whilst the traditional formula is useful in understanding the content of an existent social representation, it does not provide any detail regarding how the social representation provides users with an objectification serving some particular purpose. In other words, if processes of social re-presentation (Chryssides et al., 2009) serve social constructionist aspirations, then social representations are re-presented over time by particular groups for the purposes of pursuing self-serving projects. In this way, social representations change and evolve to accommodate emerging realities in ways that enable the group's project to survive (Nicholson, 2017; Sammut, Tsirogianni & Wagoner, 2012) over time. Consequently, it is only natural for Catholics to elaborate a different representation of psychoanalysis than Communists or Liberals would. That elaborated by Catholics serves the Catholic project whilst that elaborated by Communists serves the Communist project, and similarly for Liberals. In this way, the French public sphere contended with three social re-presentations that objectified psychoanalysis differently at the time. Moreover, the three groups also elaborated *alternative representations* (Gillespie, 2008) of the other groups' own social representations that enabled each group to retain certain meanings whilst keeping others that threatened the group's underlying project. Formulated in this way, the study of social representations essentially involves the study of a Social Representation [SR] that serves Project [P] as Object [X] and Alternative Representation [AR] for Group [AY], by Group [Y] in Context [Z]:

SR for P as X + AR(AY) by Y in Z

To illustrate, in the Cyprus–Turkish dispute, one can readily identify three groups pursuing distinct political projects. Firstly, Greek Cypriots pursue a project of reunification of Cyprus by incorporation of Turkish Cypriots into the national population, as a minority, and the direct expulsion of Turkish intervention. Secondly, Turkish Cypriots pursue a project of reunification of Cyprus that involves a regional devolution of powers. Thirdly, non-aligned Cypriots persist in pursuing a Cypriot independence from both Hellenic and Turkish influences that melts and supersedes ethnic divides. To understand the conflict well enough to attempt a reconciliatory effort, one needs a deep understanding of how the social representations elaborated in pursuit of the different projects are justified and sustained in light of competing alternatives.

To this end, an empirical effort is required to unravel the different identity-positions entailed and to identify convergences that can be used towards fabricating mutually satisfactory solutions. The first step is to *elicit arguments* in favour or against an overarching project that all groups relate to. Arguments are typically elicited through qualitative interviews with subjects who are questioned about their views concerning a particular project. These interviews are analysed using an argumentation analysis (Sammut et al., 2018) that reveals their structural components. Crucially, the researcher is looking to identify claims that are supported by warrants and justified by data but that can also be qualified or rebutted. The claims represent the argument's conclusion and can be elaborated across different subjects who advance the same proposition. This first task needs to be undertaken separately for the different social groups that are identified as relevant players or stakeholders in the conflict.

The second step is undertaken once a list of claims has been elicited for the various groups. This involves a *thematic analysis* of claims to identify and categorise the ones that recur across the various groups. Limited claims that are proposed by less than the full range of groups involved are discarded, as these manifestly do not resonate with some groups and will thus serve no purpose in a reconciliatory effort. Some claims, however, will recur even if justified in different ways by different groups using different types of warrants or data. For instance, with regards to the Cyprus–Turkey dispute, one would expect the claim that 'The unification of Cyprus is not feasible' to emerge both amongst Greek Cypriots and Turkish Cypriots but to be justified differently by the two groups with reference to each other's actions over the years. Similarly, the claim that 'The unification of

Cyprus is the only legitimate way forward' would be expected to emerge in both groups, as one would expect at least some members of either group to endorse and elaborate this position even if in a minority, but that the claim would also be justified differently across the groups.

The third step is carried out once a full list of claims that resonate across the divide is identified and involves *rank ordering* the claims from those that support the project most to those that support the project least and/or those that oppose the project most. Rank ordering typically relies on experts and serves the purpose of devising an ecologically valid scale that includes practically extreme positions as well as other more or less polarised positions in between. For the sake of symmetry, the researcher should retain a similar number of claims for as against, with or without a neutral middle claim depending on the project's characteristics.

In the fourth step, the scale is administered in a survey with populations of the different groups to *measure the relative endorsement* of claims within the various groups. The exercise should involve measurement of the extent (a) to which an individual endorses each of the claims and (b) to which the individual thinks each of the other groups is inclined to endorse the same claims. This yields insight into alternative representations that may have been elaborated to dismiss alternatives presented by others that contradict the group's avowed project.

The fifth step involves an analysis of responses that is aimed at *identifying convergences* across groups in their endorsement of the claims as well as in their beliefs concerning the other group's endorsement of the claims with the other group's actual endorsement of the claims. For instance, this analysis might demonstrate diametrically opposite relative endorsement of claims, in which case the groups will converge with regards to the middle items. Alternatively, it might reveal similar general tendencies but differing proportional endorsements, in which case the range of items between one group's most endorsed option and that of the other groups will provide a common ground. Moreover, the group's beliefs about the other group and the other group's actual beliefs can be contrasted to identify misrepresentations. For instance, a particular group may oppose unification if holding a mistaken impression that the other group does not wish for this and will only seek advantage if this option is tabled. In this case, the strategy for intervention should not target any particular group's beliefs, but should instead target their attributions to other groups.

Finally, the identified convergences/common ground should be used for *staircasing mutually plausible solutions*. For instance, one group might lag behind another in endorsing some particular ends. In such a case, one group can be nudged up and another group nudged down towards a converging position. Alternatively, groups may be on the same page but hold contrasting representations of each other. In this case, their misperceptions of each other should be targeted to enable the groups to see eye to eye.

Fabricating a reconciliatory strategy utilising this empirically based method should (a) proceed from the most highly endorsed claim for the particular group in the direction towards the desired ends, like a staircase that enables movement up or down one step at a time, and (b) involve communicative appeals that resonate with the particular groups in their own terms. That is, appeals should utilise ecologically validated justificatory grounds as identified during the initial phases of research using this method, due to the fact that these are rooted in the particular group's own common sense. In this way, claims that traverse different common senses may nevertheless hold appeal across the divide by recourse to different justificatory grounds that are, however, sensible within their own context (Jovchelovitch, 2007). In this way, this empirically based method presents a sequence of palatable options to different groups that enables their movement towards a mutually satisfactory common ground (Table 10.1).

Table 10.1 *Bridging the gap: Staircasing towards mutually plausible solutions*

1.	*Elicit Arguments* Elicitation of arguments advanced by social groups in favour or against a project and analyse in terms of structural argumentation components with a focus on identification of Claims.
2.	*Thematic Analysis* Identify and categorise Claims that recur across different social groups.
3.	*Rank Order* Subject Claims to a rank-order exercise (typically expert ranking) to empirically determine order of Claims for and against the project in relative terms.
4.	*Population Measurement* Survey relative endorsement of Claims in a population constituted by different social groups along with extent to which one group thinks the other group(s) endorse(s) the respective Claims.
5.	*Identify Convergences* Analyse results to identify convergences or approximations in relative endorsement by respective groups along with correspondences of endorsement by one group relative to attributions of endorsement by other groups.
6.	*Staircase* Propose convergent arguments in terms of respective argumentation justifications proferred by the different groups to solicit agreement, then proceed to incrementally introduce ranked Claims in a staircasing order towards mutually plausible solutions.

Conclusion

The resolution of conflict that is rooted in different interests and aspirations requires a reconciliatory effort that avoids rewarding one group at the expense of another. Whilst a mutually satisfactory solution may not be evident, the empirical exploration of particular group projects and the social representations that are fashioned in their support may reveal convergences across conflicting groups that, if pursued in ecologically sensitive ways, may open up a window onto mutually satisfactory outcomes. This chapter has proposed an empirically based method for conflict resolution that is based on the investigation of social representations that are rooted in particular projects that grant individuals identity. The sobering reality of various age-old intractable conflicts across the globe (Bar-Tal, 2000) provides a stark warning against highly optimistic silver-bullet solutions based on limited success. More likely, there is no one-size-fits-all approach to conflict resolution. A more realistic aspiration seems to be the installation of reconciliatory projects in themselves (Nicholson, 2016, 2019), faithful to the diverse contexts involved as well as to the grievances and animosities perpetrated in the past. This chapter has articulated a method for pursuing a reconciliatory ends based in processes of social identification and social representation (Sammut, Andreouli, Gaskell & Valsiner, 2015). The effort, aside from an empirically based procedure, requires the implementation of a strategy for shifting common sense and changing social representations for the future (Sammut & Bauer, 2021). However daunting, the enterprise remains in any case preferable to the alternative of settling for long-standing and seemingly inevitable discord.

REFERENCES

Andreouli, E., & Nicholson, C. (2018). Brexit and everyday politics: An analysis of focus-group data on the EU referendum. *Political Psychology*, *39*(6), 1323–1338.

Arendt, H. (1958). *The human condition*. Chicago: University of Chicago Press.

Asch, S.E. (1952). *Social psychology*. New York: Prentice-Hall.

Bar-Tal, D. (2000). From intractable conflict through conflict resolution to reconciliation: Psychological analysis. *Political Psychology*, *21*(2), 351–365.

Bauer, M. W., & Gaskell, G. (1999). Towards a paradigm for research on social representations. *Journal for the Theory of Social Behaviour*, *29*(2), 163–186.

Bayram, A. (2017). Due deference: Cosmopolitan social identity and the psychology of legal obligation in international politics. *International Organization*, *71*(S1), S137–S163.

Beck, U. (2002). The cosmopolitan society and its enemies. *Theory, Culture & Society*, *19*(1–2), 17–44.
Billig, M. (1987). *Arguing and thinking: A rhetorical approach to social psychology*. Cambridge: Cambridge University Press.
Buhagiar, L. J., & Sammut, G. (2020). 'Social Re-presentation for…': An action-oriented formula for intergroup relations research. *Frontiers in Psychology*, *11*, 352.
Cadge, W., & Davidman, L. (2006). Ascription, choice, and the construction of religious identitites in the contemporary United States. *Journal for the Scientific Study of Religion*, *45*(1), 23–38.
Campbell, D. T. (1965). *Ethnocentric and other altruistic motives*. Lincoln NE: University of Nebraska Press.
Chryssides, A. (2018). Conditions for dialogue and illuminating inequality in multicultural societies. *Journal of Community & Applied Social Psychology*, *18*(4), 375–381.
Chryssides, A., Dashtipour, P., Keshet, S., Righi, C., Sammut, G., & Sartawi, M. (2009). We don't share! The social representation approach, enactivism and the fundamental incompatibilities between the two. *Culture & Psychology*, *15*(1), 83–95.
Condor, S. (2018). Multiculturalism, liberal fundamentalism and banal nationalism: Dilemmatic aspects of dissolving the diaspora. *Journal of Community & Applied Social Psychology*, *18*(4), 369–374.
Fisher, R., & Ury, W. (1981). *Getting to yes: Negotiating agreement without giving in*. New York: Penguin
Fukuyama, F. (2018). *Identity: Contemporary identity politics and the struggle for recognition*. London: Profile Books.
Giddens, A. (1991). *Modernity and Self-identity*. Stanford, CA: Stanford University Press.
Gillespie, A. (2008). Social representations, alternative representations and semantic barriers. *Journal for the Theory of Social Behaviour*, *38*(4), 375–391.
Harré, R., & Secord, P. F. (1972). *The explanation of social behaviour*. Oxford: Basil Blackwell.
Hopkins, N. (2018). Identity, practice and dialogue. *Journal of Community & Applied Social Psychology*, *18*(4), 363–368.
Jackson, J. W. (1993). Realistic group conflict theory: A review and evaluation of the theoretical and empirical literature. *Psychological Record*, *43*(3), 395–415.
Jovchelovitch, S. (2007). *Knowledge in context: Representations, community and culture*. London: Routledge.
Kunda, Z. (1990). The case for motivated reasoning. *Psychological Bulletin*, *108*(3), 480–498.
Marques, J. M., Yzerbyt, V. Y., & Leyens, J. (1988). The 'Black Sheep Effect': Extremity of judgments towards ingroup members as a function of group identification. *European Journal of Social Psychology*, *18*(1), 1–16.
Moghaddam, F. M. (2010). *The new global insecurity*. Westport, CT: Praeger Security International.

Moscovici, S. (1976/2008). *Psychoanalysis: Its image and its public.* London: Polity.

Nesbitt-Larking, P. (2018). Dissolving the diaspora: Dialogical practice in the development of deep multiculturalism. *Journal of Community & Applied Social Psychology, 18*(4), 351–362.

Nicholson, C. (2016). The role of historical representations in Israeli-Palestinian relations: Narratives from abroad. *Peace and Conflict: Journal of Peace Psychology, 22*(1), 5–11.

(2017). The role of collective memory in protracted conflict. *Culture & Psychology, 23*(2), 217–233.

(2019). Working together, living together: Jewish and Palestinian citizens of Israel crossing imagined group boundaries. *Journal of Social and Political Psychology, 7*(2), 959–977.

Park, J. H., & Van Leeuwen, F. (2015). Evolutionary perspectives on social identity. In V. Zeigler-Hill, L. Welling, & T. Shackleford (Eds.), *Evolutionary perspectives on social psychology* (pp. 115–125). Cham: Springer Verlag.

Ross, L., & Ward, A. (1996). Naive realism in everyday life: Implications for social conflict and misunderstanding. In E. S. Reed, E. Turiel, & T. Brown (Eds.), *Values and knowledge* (pp. 103–135). Mahwah, NJ: Lawrence Erlbaum Associates.

Sammut, G. (2011). Civic solidarity: The negotiation of identities in modern societies, *Papers on Social Representations, 20*(1), 4.1–4.24.

(2015). Attitudes, social representations and points of view. In G. Sammut, E. Andreouli, G. Gaskell, & J. Valisner (Eds.), *The Cambridge handbook of social representations* (pp. 96–112). Cambridge: Cambridge University Press.

Sammut, G., Andreouli, E., Gaskell, G., & Valsiner, J. (Eds.). (2015). *The Cambridge handbook of social representations.* Cambridge: Cambridge University Press.

Sammut, G., & Bauer, M. W. (2021). *The psychology of social influence: Modes and modalities of shifting common sense.* Cambridge: Cambridge University Press.

Sammut, G., Bezzina, F., & Sartawi, M. (2015). The spiral of conflict: Naïve realism and the black sheep effect in attributions of knowledge and ignorance. *Peace and Conflict: Journal of Peace Psychology, 21*(2), 289–294.

Sammut, G., Daanen, P., & Sartawi, M. (2010). Interobjectivity: Representations and artefacts in cultural psychology. *Culture & Psychology, 16*(4), 451–463.

Sammut, G., & Gaskell, G. (2010). Points of view, social positioning and intercultural relations. *Journal for the Theory of Social Behaviour, 40*(1), 47–64.

Sammut, G., & Howarth, C. (2014). Social representations. In T. Teo (Ed.), *Encyclopedia of critical psychology* (pp. 1799–1802). New York: Springer.

Sammut, G., Jovchelovitch, S., Buhagiar, L. J., Veltri, G. A., Redd, R., & Salvatore, S. (2018). Arabs in Europe: Arguments for and against integration. *Peace and Conflict: Journal of Peace Psychology, 24*(4), 398–406.

Sammut, G., & Sartawi, M. (2012). Perspective-taking and the attribution of ignorance. *Journal for the Theory of Social Behavior, 42*(2), 181–200.

Sammut, G., Tsirogianni, S., & Wagoner, B. (2012). Representations from the past: Social relations and the devolution of social representations. *Integrative Psychological and Behavioral Sciences*, *46*(4), 493–511.
Wason, P. C. (1960). On the failure to eliminate hypotheses in a conceptual task. *Quarterly Journal of Experimental Psychology*, *12*(3), 129–140.
Zaslove, A. (2008). Exclusion, community and a populist political economy: The radical right as an anti-globalization movement. *Comparative European Politics*, *6*(2), 169–189.

CHAPTER 11

Intergroup Relations and the Contact Hypothesis
A Multilevel Analysis of the Israeli–Palestinian Conflict

Cathy Nicholson

Background

The particular situational contexts of any conflict under discussion are key in acknowledging the role of the past in developing perceived social realities. A short chapter cannot take into account the complexities of such conflicts, but it can provide an introduction to possibilities of discussing these through a brief history, based on the author's interpretation from a wide range of sources. This serves to suggest how developing social representations can become embedded across communities, societies and their peoples.

Both Cyprus and Israel/Palestine have been subject to various forms of colonial rule over many centuries culminating in the Ottoman Empire dynasty until the First World War (1914–1918) when Britain, after defeating Germany with her allies, used its powerful global position to attain influence in both locations, amongst many others, for differently held strategies. In Cyprus, its geographical position was useful for Britain's continued colonial endeavours, leading to its independence in 1961 as the British Empire had been dismantled over previous years. The base of the Israel–Palestine conflict is similarly constructed around political power, competition over land rights and ethnic belonging. Palestine was pledged by Britain, supported by France and the United States, as a 'national home for Jewish people' in the Balfour declaration of 1917. Just 10% of the population at that time was Jewish, peacefully co-existing with the Palestinian Arab inhabitants. Promises of a wider independent Arab state were, at the same time, disregarded, and the division of lands gained by France and Britain following the First World War resulted in a new set of geopolitical power struggles across the Middle East (Barr, 2011; Smith, 2013). Although Britain and France have long given up their direct colonial enterprises in the area, legacies live on through the deeply embedded political cultural fabric created over time. With the rise of the United

Populations across mapped areas (2022/2023)

	Israel	West Bank	East Jerusalem	Gaza	Total
Israeli Jews	7.3m	475,000 Israeli Settlers	220,000 Israeli Settlers	0	**8m**
Palestinians	1.8m Israeli Arabs	3.1m	361,000	2.1m	**7.3**
Total	**9.1m**	**3.5m**	**581,000**	**2.1**	**15.3**

Sources: cbs.gov.il and pcbs.gov.il (accuracy not confirmed)

Occupied Territories (West Bank) post Oslo accords (1993)

West Bank: Area A: 18% Palestinian control

West Bank: Area B: 22% Joint Israeli/Palestinian control

West Bank: Area C: 60% Israeli control

Figure 11.1 Map and population groups across different areas.

States as a global power following the Second World War and the end of the Cold War in the late 20th century, a global political shift across the area, both in terms of US security and liberal democratic peace processes, has played a direct role. Since Israel's own self-claimed statehood in 1948, it has remained the more powerful partner in contrast to the Palestinian position. The complexity of geopolitical changes and further armed conflict inflicted over time has resulted in four separated geographical areas: that of Israel itself, the occupied West Bank (often referred to as Judea and Samaria by Jewish Israelis), Gaza and East Jerusalem. Within each area the intergroup relationship differs, resulting in a particular set of possible contact conditions, as outlined in Figure 11.1.

There have been several attempts at peace negotiations, most notably the Oslo Accords of 1993. During these negotiations, a shimmer of a sustained and peaceful future was envisaged with the setting up of a National Palestinian Authority as a first step towards Palestinian statehood and the division of the West Bank as illustrated in Figure 11.1. However, further fractures have resulted in a stalemate position, both within and across cultural and political structures. Palestinian resistance to Israeli hegemony through direct attacks on the Jewish population plus two intifadas have only served to strengthen Israel's military security systems and defensive attacks to defend their perceived, and often real, weakened status and vulnerability. Internal and antagonistic Palestinian politics developing between Hamas, in power in Gaza, and Fatah within the West Bank and East Jerusalem adds to this mix of political turmoil embroiled within the wider conflict. Palestine remains without sovereignty and statehood, under a continued military occupation and surveillance in the West Bank, a blockade in Gaza and annexation in East Jerusalem. Israel continues to increase its settler population against international and UN responses.

Within the state of Israel, 20% of the population are of Palestinian descent. Collectively known as Israeli Arabs or Palestinian Israelis who remained after the Nakba of 1948 at the time of the birth of Israel, they are given full Israeli citizenship. Two-thirds of the indigenous Palestinians fled or were forced out into refugee camp during the Nakba, to what is now the West Bank, Gaza and nearby states (Lebanon, Syria and Jordan), where their descendants remain. Israel is a democratic state, a member of the United Nations, with close ties with the West, particularly the United States, as both benefactor and supporter for security concerns against local and wider terrorist threats.

Focus on Intergroup Relationships

The relationship across and between conflicting groups is key to understanding the social and cultural maps that form the backdrop to any discussions. Each conflict bears witness to its own particular present and past circumstances, so any generalisation across contexts is fraught with challenges. However, certain processes are common across different contexts, highlighting a process approach over one of entity and structure (Wagoner, 2014). The process of the dynamic and dialogical nature of each group's representations of the other remains paramount (Liu, 2006) where each group remains embedded within their knowledge base of their history and culture. The epistemological significance of natural thinking and communication is at base dialogical, multidimensional, heterogenous and diverse (Marková, 2016). Any dialogue becomes a carrier of social representations for both individuals and the wider community that communicates and interacts with others in the pursuit and development of social knowledge. The complexity of any social reality can be explored through this dialogical trajectory, to take into account the relationship across groups as co-partners in conflict. Key is the maintenance of this base, coupled with points of any social change through communication, where the co-authoring of a relationship is dependent on perspectives about the other even when not necessarily in direct communication (Moscovici & Marková, 1998; Nicholson, 2020). This chapter takes this genetic framework as a base from which to explore how a complex concrete reality might be discussed through a lens of intergroup contact.

In the case of the Israeli–Palestinian conflict, both histories are parallel histories, where each group can be defined through their collective narratives of past, present and future aspirations, and which, for the most part, have followed divergent paths (Shlaim, 2009). The consequences of one group's acting out of those aspirations onto the other activates a response, which activates yet another, as members of both groups continue to be locked in a dialogical painful duet of mutual suffering (Nicholson, 2016, 2017). At base there is – and continues to be – a deep-seated asymmetry where the reins of power remain within the domain of Israel's political and religious practices and ideology. The backing of Western international support reflects how little change is forecast to foster Palestinian autonomy that satisfies Israeli security needs. The resulting political and cultural barriers across the two peoples remain hardened and antagonistic where any political shift to change to the status quo appears more and more distant. A semantic blocking of the realities of the other remains paramount (Gillespie, 2008, 2020). And yet during this long period there have also been incidents of intergroup contact that have resulted in the softening of intergroup boundaries, reflecting social change in action across these intergroup relationships (Nicholson & Howarth, 2018).

Levels of Explanation

Taking microgenesis, ontogenesis and sociogenesis (Psaltis, Part I in this volume) as a theoretical genetic base when discussing the concrete reality of the intergroup conflict in Cyprus, I turn to Doise (1980, 1986) and four levels of explanation to add a further theoretical and empirical perspective. The origins of his work were exploratory to monitor different levels across and between individuals taking part in social psychology experiments as reported in the first 27 volumes of the *European Journal of Social Psychology*. From this base a theoretical development was followed to reflect how these levels might be viewed to aid discussion of different empirical contexts. The first level (I), the intrapersonal, that of the individual and the ways in which perceptions are organised within a social context, remained the foundation of much of social psychology experimental work. The second level (II), the interpersonal and situational, follows the dynamics of any given individual in any given situation, although it is the individuals who remain the focus of analysis. The third level (III), the positional, explores the effects of differences in social positions between different categories that are represented within group behaviour. Finally, the fourth level (IV), the ideological, represents how society develops its own systems of representations, beliefs, values and norms. I suggest these levels correspond to a deepening of the analysis from the individual to the societal, from the microgenetic to the sociogenetic and the ontogenetic. It is not assumed that a particular social reality is structured around these levels, but by analysis of each of them, as in the case of protracted conflict, we can highlight combinations of perceived social relationships about the other. Doise (1986) suggested that any interactions in negotiations would require the discussion of analysis at levels II (interpersonal and situated) and level III (group membership). Any mediator would need to take into account the ideological aspects of the conflict, so the analysis of these levels II and III should be added at level IV (ideological) for a more comprehensive study of intergroup negotiations and relationships.

Intergroup Contact

The original contact hypothesis formulated by Allport (1954) has been widely used as a base for improved intergroup relations with an assumed plethora of positive effects – but only under certain conditions. The four base relational contexts that form the basic foundations of optimal contact – that of equal group status, common goals, intergroup cooperation and the support of authorities, law or custom – are key to the possibilities of what might be considered a way forward. An oft-cited extensive meta-nalysis of 515 studies (n = 250,000) (Pettigrew & Tropp, 2006) reported a significant reduction in prejudice following contact initiatives, more pronounced when contact situations were made through group friendships under a cloak of equality. However, marked differences between the perceptions of minority and majority groups are also evident, suggesting that the different groups might construe interaction differently (Swart, Hewstone, Christ & Voci, 2011). The erroneous notion that intergroup contact stands to produce improved relations between groups still persists. Assumptions of changing individuals' prejudice to ripple outwards to shape wider patterns of intergroup conflict and discrimination can lie at the base of the contact hypothesis, yet simple antipathy can be the exception rather than the rule. Prejudice can be seen as the manifestation perceiving a negative attribute and acting upon this judgment towards the outgroup as though it were objectively true (Hall, 1997). Yet prejudice is not simply experienced at the level of attitudes across individual interactions, but represents a complex array of underlying attributes that require further analysis and theoretical development. The metaphor of an iceberg (Duveen & Lloyd, 1990), reiterated by Psaltis (Part I in this volume), is useful to illustrate how the tip of the iceberg representing an individual prejudiced attitude towards others can result in only a partial analysis. The greater portion that lies submerged beneath the water, that of the group's layers of cultural and social values and all that is represented within that, needs to be explored to allow a fuller account to emerge.

Stigmatising representations can be understood as being ideologically constructed, communicated and resisted in systems of difference and privilege that constitute and communicate the social norms and consensual beliefs of a culture (Howarth, 2009) through the media, material culture, social spaces and embodied practices (Howarth, Nicholson & Whitney, 2013). Attempts at shifting these resulting representations across groups in conflict with one another remain at the basis of planned contact work. Yet unplanned contact also plays an important role within this discussion. The key is to explore contextual differences where the study of any form of prejudice cannot be considered worthwhile 'without taking into account of its life space' (Moscovici, 2011, p. 452).

The Context of Israel–Palestine Contact

The geopolitical context of Israel–Palestine remains central to contact discussions; the four distinct regions as described previously in Figure 11.1 present different contact scenarios, though all have in common different degrees of asymmetrical relationships. Through the lens of the four levels of explanation (Doise, 1980, 1986) different contact scenarios will be discussed to add to the comparison of contact opportunities between that of Cyprus and the Israeli–Palestinian relationship. Significant is the difference between planned and unplanned contact. The opening of the checkpoints in Cyprus in 2003 allowed for unplanned contact between Greek Cypriots and Turkish Cypriots as the two communities found ways of meeting each other with reduced prejudice and increasing friendship opportunities over time (Psaltis, Part I in this volume). One of the studies focused on extended contact, a form of indirect contact where cross-group friendships are imagined through knowing that other ingroup members have cross-group friends. These results align with the concept of imagined contact (Crisp & Turner, 2009) defined as mental simulation with members of perceived outgroupswhere actual contact is not possible, or as a means of preparing people for future face-to-face contact. In a meta-analysis of more than 70 studies, Miles and Crisp (2014) demonstrated that overall prejudice was reduced with imagined positive intergroup behaviour through these imagined contact scenarios. These studies, based on levels I and II of explanation, where individual perceptions of intergroup behaviour demonstrate shifts and development in imagining and thinking, stand out as pertinent developments within this context.

Unplanned Intergroup Contact in Israel/Palestine

Unplanned contact within the four geopolitical areas shown in Figure 11.1 demonstrates differences across all four levels of explanation. First, in Gaza, the Palestinian population is excluded from the rest of the region through an Israeli blockade. Wars between the political resistance party Hamas, denounced as a Palestinian terrorist group by Israel and most of the international community, and the Israeli military have continued over many years, resulting in high numbers of Palestinian deaths and loss of infrastructure throughout the region in 2008, 2012, 2014, and 2023. From 2008 to 2020, 95% of deaths through conflict were on the Palestinian side (UN Office for the Coordination of Humanitarian Affairs, 2021).

Second, within East Jerusalem, both Jewish Israelis and Palestinians, although living segregated lifestyles with security police evident, share the streets across the Old City and the surrounding areas. Recent research (Faibish et al., 2023) reports on unplanned encounters between Palestinian and Jewish Israeli students who choose to study at an Israeli higher education institution on a specially designed one-year preparatory programme for later studies within the Israeli education system. The levels I and II study explored how spontaneous intergroup encounters resulted in more positive attitudes towards more intergroup integration within the city of Jerusalem as well as higher cooperation with Israeli Jews. It was also found that the campus allowed a safe space for Palestinians to enable cross-group interactions (Halibi, 2022). However, there was no report that considered if Jewish Israelis were similarly changed by having these same opportunities to mix with East Jerusalem Palestinian students.

Third, unplanned contact encounters within the West Bank are not the norm, as the two communities remain separated through Israeli occupation and Jewish settlers scattered across the region, thus military checkpoints throughout the region serve as places of contact. Longo et al. (2014) explored whether contact at checkpoints between Palestinians and the Israeli military had the effect of supressing violence or perpetuating it, exploring levels I and II with reference to level III, based on individual and intergroup perceptions. Taking the opportunity of some checkpoints in the Jenin corridor being eased, an opportunity arose to examine political attitudes both before the easement and afterwards. Palestinians during easement were found to be less likely to support violence against Israel or support the militant Islamist group Hamas over the secular-nationalist Fatah. It was suggested that humiliation, rather than fear or financial loss, was a strong variable leading to support violence against Israel. This negative form of contact leading to possible negative consequences has also been observed in Cyprus (Psaltis, Part I in this volume) when Turkish Cypriots crossing into southern regions face a lukewarm or racist attitudes from Greek Cypriot police officers. As conditions of repression lessened, so did the subject population's preference for dissent. Living within Palestinian communities close to surveillance infrastructures was also found to have an effect on a range of attitudes around forms of action (Penic et al., 2024). Living in highly surveilled communities served to make support for forms of support for co-operative actions less likely, suggesting that the silencing of alternative narratives is key, eroding collective support for more local co-operative forms of actions. This is made more apparent when forced indiscriminate surveillance is enforced by a powerful and threatening outgroup (Adelman & Dasgupta, 2019; Ariyanto et al., 2010). Thus the aim of stemming violence to boost security might, in effect, undermine a social representation of pluralism, resulting in more aggressive and/or unilateral forms of action (Penic et al., 2024).

Fourth, within Israel where Jewish and Palestinian citizens of Israel c-oexist within the state (see Figure 11.1), there is surprising little research into unplanned contact yet an abundance on planned contact, addressed later. Israel is defined through its essence of Jewish ethnicity, allowing worldwide Jewry to freely immigrate to embrace its biblical language of Hebrew, with its particular institutions, official holidays and cultural symbols (Smooha, 1993). The Palestinian Israelis stand as a bicultural minority within this structure, where segregation amidst cultural divisions of separate systems of education, sociopolitical institutions, language (Arabic) and religious following (Muslim, Christian and Druze) form the base of their minority social and cultural reality (Yaftel, 2000). Military service is not obligatory as it is for all Jewish Israelis, although a small minority of Israeli Arabs choose it. Despite this, there are areas of co-existence where cross-group relational contact is visible, notably within the tertiary education sector and workplaces. For example, Weiss (2021) found that Jewish contact with a Palestinian medic tended to increase positive attitudes towards the minority group in general. Desivila (1998) explored professional relationships within a medical setting on levels of co-existence amongst Jewish and Palestinian Israeli physicians and nurses finding unplanned contact had resulted in satisfactory professional intergroup relationships. However, there were no changes across any perceived sense of changes in national identity across the groups. This result at levels I, II and III demonstrates how intergroup perceptions can remain positive under a cloak of professional equality and yet leave a boundary of divergent national belonging beneath this surface. My own work in this area explored how unplanned contact with both Jewish and Palestinian Israeli medics might be explored that takes into account their professional relationships in the workplace compared to their lives outside of that (Nicholson, 2019). Their shared work environment, based on medical ethics of life enhancement and healthcare through equality across all staff and patients was key to where respect and friendship flourished in a safe, equal and satisfactory work setting. However, this contrasted with the context away from the work setting where structural and social asymmetry tended to take precedence with the minority group affected by inequality through their Palestinian Israeli status. A sense of threat was picked up within some Jewish Israeli's narratives, highlighted by the war in Gaza (2014) six months previously, leading to some intergroup tensions that seeped into their relationships. Each group's narratives fell into distinct foundational bases, stemming from the far and near past, that affected their own and the other's understanding of these relationships, justifying each group's way of dealing with the complexity of the situation. These perspectives had shifted back to pre-war relationships at the time of the interviews, yet they had given a glimpse of the uncertainty stemming from the ease with which a threatening context can so easily shift the status quo to one of division rather than forms of co-existence. The study highlights the benefits of exploring the intergroup relationship within two specific contexts to determine their genetic developments with each other rather than taking one group as the focus of study. The four levels, from individual perspectives, to intergroup dynamics, to positioning of oneself in relation to others within this matrix, to the development of cultural norms and belief systems exemplify the utility of exploring these levels of explanation. These unplanned contact studies reflect how all four levels of explanation are intertwined within the societal context, demonstrating its utility in pursuing this mode of study.

Planned Intergroup Contact in Israel

Much of the contact research across the intergroup relationship within Israel has centred on co-existence movements within the state to offset right-wing power groups. Suileman (2004) directed such encounter groups over an extended period of time between Jewish and Palestinian Israeli students at Haifa University, a city in northern Israel, where intergroup co-existence was judged to be more prominent than in other cities in Israel. He reflected that attempts to play down political components led to the failure of meaningful intergroup contact across the asymmetry, as the sessions tended to reflect a microcosm of the external social reality where 'a basic contradiction exists between the structure of the encounter group and its potentiality to advance intergroup contents and processes' (Suileman, 2004, p. 325). Here the tendency is a focus on the first two levels, that of the intrapersonal and interpersonal, while the social, cultural and ideological positions with deeper representations held by the groups remained outside the remit of the group. Maoz (2011) addressed this examined contact work over a period of 20 years between Jewish and Palestinian Israelis, finding that particular ways of approaching encounter groups was key to reaching across group boundaries to gain intergroup knowledge and understanding. Encounter groups that followed programmes based on the sharing of narratives, as well as those that offered possibilities of confrontation, were found to be more successful in softening boundaries. The co-existence model is based on the spirit of the contact hypothesis (Allport, 1954) that promotes a sense of shared intergroup understanding and tolerance in order to reduce stereotypical representations of the other.

However, this approach also comes with a number of limitations. First, it ignores the institutionalised base of discrimination and concentrates more on changing group members' representations of the other. Second, the joint projects model is designed to cross intergroup boundaries to work together with superordinate goals to unite the group, but it ignores the significance of different identities, collective memories and social representations of their social realities and thus preserves the status quo by normalising existing power asymmetries. Third, the confrontational model is designed to modify constructions of group identities by encouraging awareness of the majority/minority positioning and the ensuing asymmetry, supposedly opening up the way for the Palestinian Israelis to bring up and voice, rather than ignore, aspirations of national identities, discrimination and asymmetry (Halabi & Sonnenschein, 2004). In practice, however, challenges in approaching key sensitive topics had the potential to result in verbal violence and degradation of the other, thus leading to distrust and disappointment at not being able to voice and discuss the intergroup relationship in any meaningful depth (Maoz, Bar-On & Yikya, 2007). Finally, the narrative model combines elements of the co-existence and confrontational models in an attempt to work through unresolved anger and pain. Sharing individual narratives opens a space for opportunities to build social representations of understanding through storytelling about individual experiences within the conflict, making it possible to build a more complex yet realistic image of intergroup relationships (Bar-On, 2000; Bar-On & Kassem, 2004).

These models suggest how different levels of enquiry produce different outcomes that reflect the depth to which individuals are compromised by their identification with one group established in the process of protracted conflict with another. Any shift in becoming open to the other assumes that a level where individual positioning, which includes a historical ideological component (level IV), is recognised within an intergroup dialogical relationship and remains central to the encounter. The development of these models demonstrates how the confrontational model supported by the narrative model has the potential to increase intergroup social knowledge encounters. On a smaller scale but offering possibilities for equalising intergroup relationships within Israel, educational developments such as the Hand in Hand schools, where Jewish and Palestinian children come together in equal bilingual and bicultural settings from nursery to high school, suggest a viable alternative route for the future. How they might fare when conducted outside that particular space, where the asymmetry is deeper and conflict narratives are never far from the public consciousness, remains to be investigated.

Planned Intergroup Contact with Israelis and Palestinians by External Agencies

Much of the planned contact between Israelis and Palestinians from the West Bank, East Jerusalem and Gaza are conducted through non-governmental organisations and international agencies as opportunities for intergroup peace building that bypass the political reality to initiate relationships at the local level as a starting point for possible political movement at a later stage. Three such initiatives are presented to exemplify all levels from I to IV. First, following the narrative approach, Hammack (2011) directed a summer camp in the United States with a group of young Palestinians and Israelis with daily meetings and social activities with a group of young Americans who acted as third-party mediators. All participants were encouraged to think about their own and the other's social identities, juxtaposed with those of young Americans through group exercises, social events and the writing of individual diaries. The overall approach was based on the softening of intergroup boundaries through these narratives around their social identities that had the potential for transformation towards more understanding of the other. These experiences were thought to be successful in achieving these aims. By opening new identity boundaries it was hoped that once they returned to their respective homes within a conflict zone, a path to better co-existence might be envisaged at some time in the future. However, a year later when revisiting the students, their previous home social identities began to take hold. The importance of this context was key, showing that the political structure of the conflict was a factor (Hammack, Pilecki & Merrilees, 2014), where pressure to remain loyal to the group took precedence as their newly found identities began to fade.

Second, White et al. (2021) collected seven years of data from Jewish Israeli and Palestinian youth participating in a 'Seeds of Peace' three-week summer camp in the United States. The aim of the organisation, financed by public donations, bases itself on conflict transformation where potential leadership plays a vital role in the future lives of its alumni of more than 8,000 'seeds' as they focused on their personal transformation in the context of wider societal change in the future. This study centred on intergroup relationship formation through joint activities: for example, sharing rooms, dining and dialogue groups. Previous research suggested competing theories for whether propinquity – that is, feeling a sense of kinship – is stronger in developing in-group or outgroup relationships. In this study it was found to be significantly more impactful for outgroup relationships. White et al. (2021) proposed that the actual sharing of an activity group can be influential for dyads that are more dissimilar, as it is less likely to spontaneously engage with outgroup members in ways that promote relationships, concluding that well-structured and meaningful engagement can counteract homophily. However, their data was obtained via surveys, based on levels I, II and III, where intergroup perspectives and positions were examined. By exploring level IV across societal and political developments, much needed data to chart deeper changes have been added. As a joint project model, the study exemplifies how the beginning of attachments can occur under optimal conditions, but less so how their ongoing friendships may or may not develop once back in their original asymmetric positions.

Third, the Olive Tree Project, took place in London, UK between 2004 and 2016, where academically successful Israeli and Palestinian students from all areas across the region were sponsored to follow a three-year undergraduate course at City University (Hollis, 2019). As part of this endeavour, students met weekly for group discussions and other programmed events, mediated by the director and an assistant, as well as other activities to support the programme. All models of contact as discussed by Maoz (2011) were evident: co-existence, joints projects, confrontational and narrative models. Levels I, II, III and IV (Doise, 1986) were integral to the students' group meetings and developing relationships by allowing communication between and across individual perspectives, set within the social, cultural, political and ideological fabric of their experiences. The object was not to change perspectives but to note shifts in the narratives of how the students reacted and related to one another over a relatively long time period. Ideas around theories of resolving the asymmetric conflict were not central to the programme. Instead, opportunities to explore the entrapment of group and personal narratives were encouraged, to retrieve a measure of agency.

The Narrative Trap

The narrative trap as introduced by Hollis (2019), reflecting levels I to IV, reveals how each group can enshrine a positive trajectory that relies on negative constructions of the other, with the participants moving towards increasingly more extreme behaviour. A survey carried out with Olive Tree students and young people, matched for age and education in Israel and the Occupied Territories, demonstrated how their narratives had shifted during their time away from their homeland, from a base of each group's narrative having its own internal logic, existing in parallel and blaming the other for forcing them to behave as they do, to a development change after ongoing and prolonged dialogue. Olive Tree Jewish Israelis accepted the legitimacy of a Palestinian nationalism by framing it as a response to the occupation rather than as a direct response to Zionism. The non–Olive Tree Jewish Israelis described Israel as a necessary safe place free from European and wider persecution, and the resulting conflict as a clash between two national movements, with the non–Olive Tree Palestinians harbouring resentment about their resulting losses. Non–Olive Tree Palestinians attributed the origins of the conflict to imperial powers dividing up this area in the Middle East after the First World War, whilst Olive Tree Palestinians perceived it through a lens of cycles of violence and retribution with Israeli settlements expansion and the resulting occupation. The development of the construction of alternative narratives through the unblocking of social and semantic barriers (Bar-Tal & Halperin, 2011; Gillespie, 2008, 2020) highlights genetic shifts that corresponded with the microgenetic at all four levels, the sociogenetic within the social, cultural and political frameworks and the ontogenetic which reflects these developments and change over time. No research to date has been carried out to explore any long-term social representations of the Olive Tree students' relationships with one other, political perspectives or career paths chosen since graduating.

Level of Explanation and the Genetic Framework in Intergroup Contact Research

Intergroup contact has traditionally been an avenue for the possibilities of developing more tolerant intergroup relations across an array of conflict-ridden contexts. In the case of the Israeli–Palestinian conflict as suggested here, results have been mixed. The social and political asymmetric context of planned contact lies at the base of how social change might be achieved to any satisfactory degree. Surface individual and intra-individual levels show some positive but also ambiguous or negative results, depending on the research strategy (Maoz, 2011). When deeper levels of identity positions within political and ideological constructs are included, some positive results show development, yet the long-term context within the asymmetric interdependent relationship exemplifies the complexities of such well-meaning initiatives.

Within the West Bank, contact programmes have achieved little political symmetry, leading to criticism from Palestinians attempting to build normal relations with Jewish Israelis in the present political climate. Paradoxically, positive intergroup contact experiences can contribute to perpetuating the status quo and entrenching inequalities as deeper levels are overlooked. Normalisation of the context at these levels can act as a sedative to social change by lessening motivation to engage in forms of peaceful resistance where asymmetry remains central (Albzour et al., 2019, 2023). Within the context of protracted and asymmetrical conflict we need to ask in what way the contact hypothesis might be a useful tool at all.

Durrheim and Dixon (2018) have argued that basing contact research on a form of utopian exercises to find an ideal world bears little relevance to the real complex world. In the case of intergroup conflict, the layers of mistrust and hatred, fuelled by communication of propaganda and strengthening of ingroup and outgroup identities, act as both cultural and semantic barriers to inhibit any softening of boundaries to permit equal contact. Within this framework using an approach that suggests intergroup harmony as a solution to conflict can be deemed simplistic and unrealistic (Dovidio et al., 2012). If the goals of contact research tend towards promoting social change by empowering the disadvantaged group, the Palestinians, there remains the issue of the advantaged group, the Israelis, not being in a position to support this endeavour. The intrinsic need to be liked by the other for their involvement in contact work (Bergsieker et al., 2010), as well as searching for intragroup commonalities rather than differences to protect one's own moral image (Knowles et al., 2014), can become a key concern. Furthermore, intergroup discussions focusing on group differences hold the possibility of heightening threat perceptions, leading to anxiety (Saguy et al., 2009). All of these practices may lead to remaining motivated to maintain the present status quo (Saguy & Kteily, 2014) rather than finding opportunities to move beyond it. And yet initiatives for social change often start at the individual level through personal experiences (Nicholson, 2020) that widens out to the societal levels leading to collective action (Tropp & Barlow, 2018).

The four basic relational contexts that form the foundations of optimal contact from the original work by Allport (1954), that of equal group status, common goals, intergroup cooperation and the support of authorities, law, or custom, remain relevant to these arguments. For each contact situation discussed in this chapter that have shown promise in crossing boundaries from an asymmetric base towards one of intergroup tolerance and some measure of understanding, these basic relational contexts have been present. And with a shift of the social context to one more embedded within an asymmetrical context, any positive move towards tolerance can easily become dislodged to reflect each ingroup positioning and group narratives and thus drawing away from possibilities of any desired political and social change.

REFERENCES

Adelman, L., & Dasgupta, N. (2019). Effect of threat and social identity on reactions to ingroup criticism: Defensiveness, openness, and a remedy. *Personality and Social Psychology Bulletin*, *45*(5), 740–753.

Albzour, M., Bady, Z., Elcheroth, G., Penic, S., Riemer, N., & Green, E. (2023). Talking to a (segregation) wall: Intergroup contact and attitudes toward normalization among palestinians from the occupied territories. *Political Psychology, 44*(1), 43–59.

Albzour, M., Penic, S., Nasser, R., & Green, E. (2019). Support for "normalization" of relations between Palestinians and Israelis, and how it relates to contact and resistance in the West Bank. *Journal of Social and Political Psychology, 7*(2), 978–996.

Allport, G. W. (1954). *On the nature of prejudice*. Cambridge, MA: Addison-Wesley.

Ariyanto, A., Hornsey, M., & Gallois, C. (2010). United we stand: Intergroup conflict moderates the intergroup sensitivity effect. *European Journal of Social Psychology, 40*(1), 169–177.

Bar-On, D. (2000*). Bridging the gap*. Hamburg: Koerber.

Bar-On, D., & Kassem, B. (2004). Storytelling as a way to work through intractable conflicts: The German-Jewish experience and its relevance to the Palestinian-Israeli Context. *Journal of Social Issues, 60*(2), 289–306.

Barr, J. (2011). *A line in the sand: Britain, France and the struggle that shaped the Middle East*. London: Simon & Schuster.

Bar-Tal, D., & Halperin, E. (2011). Socio-psychological barriers to conflict resolution. In D. Bar-Tal (Ed.), *Intergroup conflicts and their resolution* (pp. 217–239). London: Psychology Press.

Bergsieker, H. B., Shelton, J. N., & Richeson, J. A. (2010). To be liked versus respected: Divergent goals in interracial interactions. *Journal of Personality and Social Psychology, 99*(2), 248–264.

Crisp, R. J., & Turner, R. N. (2009). Can imagined interactions produce positive perceptions? Reducing prejudice through simulated social contact. *American Psychologist, 64*, 231–240. doi:10.1037/a001471.

Desivilya, H. A, (1998). Jewish-Arab coexistence in Israel: The role of joint professional teams. *Journal of Peace Research, 35*(4), 429–452.

Dixon, J., Levine, M., Reicher, S., & Durrheim, K. (2012). Beyond prejudice: Are negative evaluations the problem and is getting us to like one another more the solution? *Behavioural and Brain Sciences*, 35(6), 411–466.

Doise, W. (1980). Levels of explanation in the European Journal of Social Psychology. *European Journal of Social Psychology, 10*, 213–231.

(1986*). Levels of explanation in social psychology*. Cambridge: Cambridge University Press.

Dovidio, J. F., Saguy, T., Gaertner, S. L., & Thomas, E. L. (2012). From attitudes to (in)action: The darker side of 'we.' In J. Dixon & M. Levine (Eds.), *Beyond prejudice: Extending the social psychology of conflict, inequality and social change* (pp. 248–268). Cambridge: Cambridge University PressK.

Durrheim, K., & Dixon, J. (2018). Intergroup contact and the struggle for social justice. In P. Hammack (Ed.), *The Oxford handbook of social psychology and social justice* (pp. 367–378). New York: Oxford University Press.

Elcheroth, G., Doise, W., & Reicher, S. (2011). On the knowledge of politics and the politics of knowledge: How a social representations approach helps us rethink the subject of political psychology. *Political Psychology*, *32*(5), 729–758.

Faibish, N., Rajabi, N., Miodownik, D., & Maoz, I. (2023). Spontaneous contact and intergroup attitudes in asymmetric protracted ethno-national conflict. *Peace and Conflict: Journal of Peace Psychology* (Epub ahead of print). doi: 10.1037/pac0000683.

Gillespie, A. (2008). Social representations, alternative representations and semantic barriers. *Journal for the Theory of Social Behaviour*, *38*(4), 375–391.

(2020). Semantic contact and semantic barriers: Reactionary responses to disruptive ideas. *Current Opinion in Psychology*, *35*, 21–25.

Halabi, R. (2022). Palestinian students in an Israeli-Hebrew University: Obstacles and challenges. *Higher Education*. Advance online publication. https://doi.org/10.1007/s10734-022-00920.

Halabi, R., & Sonnenschein, N. (2004). The Jewish-Palestinian encounter in a time of crisis. *Journal of Social Issues*, *60*(2), 375–387.

Hall, S. (1997). *Representation: Cultural representations and signifying practices*. London: Sage.

Hammack, P. L. (2011). *Narrative and the politics of identity: The cultural psychology of Israeli and Palestinian youth, culture and identity*. New York: Oxford University Press.

Hammack, P. L., Pilecki, A., & Merrilees, C. (2014). Interrogating the process and meaning of intergroup contact: Contrasting theoretical approaches. *Journal of Community and Applied Social Psychology*, *24*, 296–324.

Hollis, R. (2019). *Surviving the story: The narrative trap in Israel and Palestine*. London: Red Hawk.

Howarth, C. (2009). "I hope we won't have to understand racism one day": Researching or reproducing 'race' in social psychological research? *British Journal of Social Psychology*, *48*(3), 407–426.

Howarth, C., Campbell, C., Cornish, F., Franks, B., Garcia-Lorenzo, L., Gillespie, A., Gleibs, I., Goncalves-Portelinha, I., Jovchelovitch, S., Lahlou, S., Mannell, J., Reader, T., & Tennant, C. (2013). Insights from societal psychology: A contextual politics of societal change. *Journal of Social and Political Psychology*, *1*(1), 364–384.

Howarth, C., Nicholson, C., & Whitney. T. (2013). Stigma. In L. Mason (Ed.), *Encyclopaedia of race and racism* (Vol. 4, pp. 140--145). Detroit, MI: Gale.

Knowles, E. D., Lowery, B. S., Chow, R. M., & Unzueta, M. M. (2014). Deny, distance, or dismantle? How white Americans manage a privileged identity. *Perspectives on Psychological Science*, *9*(6): 594–609.

Longo, M., Canetti, D., & Hite-Rubin, N. (2014). Checkpoint effect? Evidence from a natural experiment on travel restrictions in the West Bank. *American Journal of Political Science*, *58*(4), 1006–1023.

Lui, L. (2006). Sensitising concept, themata and sharedness: A dialogical perspective of social representations. *Journal of the Theory of Social Behaviour*, *34*(3), 249–264.

Maoz, I. (2011). Does contact work in protracted asymmetrical conflict? Appraising 20 years of reconciliation aimed encounters between Israeli Jews and Palestinians. *Journal of Peace Research, 48*, 115–125.

Maoz, I., Bar-On, D., & Yikya, S. (2007) 'They understand only force': A critical examination of the eruption of verbal violence in a Jewish-Palestinian dialogue. *Peace and Conflict Studies, 14*(2), 27–48.

Marková, I., (2016). *The dialogical mind.* Cambridge: Cambridge University Press.

Miles, E., & Crisp, R. J. (2014). A meta-analytic test of the imagined contact hypothesis. *Group Processes & Intergroup Relations, 17*(1), 3–26.

Moscovici, S., (2011). An essay on social representations and ethnic minorities. *Social Science Information, 50*(3–4), 442–461.

Moscovici, S., & Marková, I. (1998). Presenting social representations: A conversation. *Culture and Psychology, 4*(3), 371–410.

Nicholson, C (2016). The role of historical representations in Israeli–Palestinian relations: Narratives from abroad. *Peace and Conflict: Journal of Peace Psychology, 22*(1), 5–11.

(2017). The role of collective memory in protracted conflict. *Culture & Psychology, 23*(2), 217–233.

(2019). Working together, living together: Jewish and Palestinian citizens of Israel crossing imagined group boundaries. *Journal of Social and Political Psychology, 7*(2), 959–977.

(2020). Remembering traumatic experiences across time and place: How the dialogical turn echoes memory in the wild. In B. Wagoner, I. Brescó de Luna, & S. Zadeh (Eds.), *Memory in the wild* (pp. 107–25). Charlotte, NC: Information Age Publishing.

Nicholson, C., & Howarth, C. (2018). Imagining collective identities beyond intergroup conflict. In C. de Saint-Laurent, S. Obradović, & K. Carriere (Eds.), *Imagining collective futures: Perspectives from social, cultural and political psychology* (pp. 173–196). London: Palgrave.

Penic, S., Donnay, K., Bhavnani, R., Elcheroth, G., & Albzour, M. (2024). How does the geography of surveillance affect collective action? *Political Psychology, 45*(2), 319–340.

Pettigrew, T. F., & Tropp, L. R. (2006). A meta-analytic test of intergroup contact theory. *Journal of Personality and Social Psychology, 90*(5), 751–783.

Saguy, T., & Kteily, N. (2014). Power, negotiations, and the anticipation of intergroup encounters. *European Review of Social Psychology, 25*(1), 107–141.

Saguy, T., Tausch, N., Dovidio, J., & Pratto, F. (2009). The irony of harmony: Intergroup contact can produce false expectations for equality. *Psychological Science, 20*, 14–121.

Shlaim, A. (2009). *Israel and Palestine: Re-appraisals, revisions, refutations.* London: Verso.

Smith, C. D. (2013). *Palestine and the Arab-Israeli conflict: A history with documents.* Boston, MA: Bedford/St. Martin.

Smooha, S. (1993). Minority status in an ethnic democracy: The status of the Arab minority in Israel. *Ethnic and Racial Studies, 13*, 389–413.

Suileman, R. (2004). Planned encounters between Jewish and Palestinian Israelis: A social psychological perspective. *Journal of Social Issues*, *60*(2), 323–337.

Swart, H., Hewstone, M., Christ, O., & Voci, A. (2011). Affective mediators of intergroup contact: A three-way longitudinal study in South Africa. *Journal of Personality and Social Psychology*, *101*(6), 1221–1238.

Tropp, L. R., & Barlow, K. (2018). Making advantaged racial groups care about inequality: Intergroup contact as a route to psychological investment. *Current Directions in Psychological Science*, *27*(3), 194–199.

United Nations Office for the Coordination of Humanitarian Affairs (OCHA). (2021). www.statista.com/chart/16516/israeli-palestinian-casualties-by-in-gaza-and-the-west-bank.

Wagoner, B. (2014). A sociocultural approach to peace and conflict. *Peace and Conflict: Journal of Peace Psychology*, *20*(2), 187–190.

Weiss, C. M. (2021). Diversity in heath care institutions reduces Israeli patient-s'prejudice towards Arabs. *Proceedings of the National Academy of Sciences of the United States of America*, *118*(14), 1–6.

White, S., Schroeder, J., & Risen, J. L., (2021). "Enemies" become close: Relationship formation among Palestinians and Jewish Israelis at a youth camp. *Journal of Personality and Social Psychology: Interpersonal Relations and Group Processes*, *121*(1), 76–94.

Yaftel, O. (2000). *Ethnocracy and its discontents: Minorities, protests and the Israeli polity*. Chicago: University of Chicago Press.

CHAPTER 12

Thinking Critically with Others
Three Analytic Perspectives

Angela Bermúdez

Introduction

Psaltis proposes a genetic social psychological theory that integrates ontogenetic, microgenetic and sociogenetic analyses in order to capture three types of transformation involved in societal change. I find this proposal particularly enticing for scholars, like me, interested in investigating how to develop in youth a critical understanding of social conflict and violence that contributes to peacebuilding.

Throughout my research trajectory, I have struggled with the limitations of analytic frameworks that focus their attention only on the individual's mind, or on the influence of social context. Many of these struggles relate to concepts and propositions advanced by Psaltis in Part I of this volume, so engaging with his model allowed me to shed light on the challenges I faced and on the "solutions" I devised to overcome them. I thus decided to take his invitation to write a commentary on his chapters as an opportunity to trace the continuities and transformations in my own work, and to evidence the connections that exist between different parts of it that emerged at different times, in response to different methodological quandaries. My hope is that this self-reflective exercise also serves to illustrate the different components of Psaltis's model, and the importance of integrating them in a holistic way if we want research and practice to contribute to conflict transformation (Psaltis, Carretero, & Cehanic-Clancy, 2017).

This chapter is organized in three sections that describe the evolution of my work over time and the connections I draw with the three processes analyzed by Psaltis. The first discusses my research on critical thinking in the social domain and relates it to an ontogenetic perspective focused on analyzing the cognitive challenges that students face in understanding interpersonal conflicts and social controversies. I illustrate this with the analysis of an ostracism incident among adolescent girls in an American middle school. I then explain the limitations I faced with the cognitive approach I used, which could not account for how other factors, such as the construction of identities or social asymmetries, informed students' critical thinking. The second section explains how the previous quandary led me to adopt a discursive approach in order to situate students' performance of critical thinking in their relational and social contexts. I discuss the similarities between this phase of my work and the microgenetic perspective described by Psaltis, and illustrate it with a revised analysis of the ostracism incident and with a second case study of an online discussion about racism and police brutality among American high school students. The third section introduces my current research on the narrative normalization and de-normalization of violence and applies some of its ideas to an ongoing project on the memory and history of violence in the Spanish Basque Country. I draw parallels between this work and the sociogenetic perspective outlined by Psaltis, as it focuses on the societal level in which collective narratives are produced, disseminated, disputed, and transformed. The chapter ends with a brief recapitulation of the interconnections I see between the three analytic perspectives, in my own work and in the similarities with the model proposed by Psaltis.

Addressing Ontogenesis – Cognitive Tools of Critical Inquiry

I began my professional trajectory in Colombia, where I was born and raised. I am sure this shaped my interest in history education as a tool for peacebuilding. In one of my earliest studies, I analyzed how students progressively learn to integrate causality and intentionality in historical explanations, and how this shapes their understanding of agency in processes of social change (Bermudez & Jaramillo, 2001). My assumption at the time was that the development of an increasingly sophisticated understanding depended on the individual's capacity for historical thinking, which in turn was an expression of their intellectual experience reasoning about historical topics (Carretero & Voss, 1994; Dickinson, Lee, & Rogers, 1984). A similar view informed my work on moral education (Bermudez & Jaramillo, 2000). Research on the development of students' moral judgment informed the design of pedagogical guidelines proposed to engage teachers and students in exploring moral dilemmas related to issues typical of adolescent life in school and community: stealing, lying, engaging in risky or destructive practices, hurting others to achieve what you want. Drawing on Kohlberg's tradition (1984), our approach emphasized the limited reach of choices and solutions when dilemmas are addressed with a simplistic mindset – and the improvement that comes about when reasoning takes into account diverse perspectives, beyond the immediacy of time, space, and norms.

Important as this work was, and is still today, looking back, I see that our conceptual frameworks, with a focus on universal reasoning structures and operations, made context irrelevant or insignificant. In a social setting of pervasive corruption, violence, inequality, and abundant discourses to justify them, students' judgments were most likely influenced by their interactions with such context and discourses. But this did not capture our attention at the time. We had no room in our analytic models for the influence of context.

In 2001, I moved to start my doctorate at Harvard Graduate School of Education, and I brought this individual-centered constructivist mindset with me. Building upon educational interventions and datasets developed by Facing History and Ourselves (FHAO),[1] my dissertation investigated two cases of young people engaged in controversies about current and past violence: the Ostracism Case Study and the Twilight L.A. Case Study. Under the mentorship of Robert Selman and David Perkins, my goal was to analyze student learning to establish if an increasing capacity for critical thinking afforded a more sophisticated understanding of the dynamics of violence and its ethical problems. I developed an analytic model (Table 12.1) that established four tools of critical inquiry in the social domain, drawing upon different conceptualizations of critical thinking in the fields of cognitive and moral psychology, critical pedagogy, and historical thinking. The model reconciled a seeming divergence of approaches in four categories – *problem-posing, reflective skepticism, multi-perspectivity, and systemic thinking* – that capture the central intellectual operations that these traditions define as critical (Bermudez, 2015).

In this model, critical thinking consists of a set of reflexive cognitive operations with which individuals construct, confront, and transform knowledge. The four tools afford the means to recognize and work through various challenges, particularly vivid in situations of conflict and controversy. Individuals use these tools with different degrees of sophistication that define the quality of their critical thinking and the adequacy of their understanding. This approach to critical thinking is consonant with Psaltis's description of an ontogenetic analysis that is concerned with "the process of change of the representations of a single individual over time" aiming to map the development of understanding "from simpler to more complex forms, chiefly through a process of reflective transformation" (see Part I in this volume).

[1] FHAO is an organization dedicated to curriculum development and teacher education that fosters critical understanding and action regarding racism, discrimination, and violence (www.facing.org).

Table 12.1 *Tools of critical inquiry*

Critical Inquiry Tool • Shed light on	**Intellectual Operations**:
Problem posing: • Need and possibility of inquiry. • Personal and social relevance of historical knowledge.	✧ Generate questions to investigate matters of truth (epistemological) and justice (ethical). ✧ Establish connections between past, present, and future and between individual and society. ✧ Provoke emotional sensitivity and ethical reflection on the consequences and legacies of the past in the present.
Reflective skepticism: • Interpretive nature of social and historical knowledge. • Dialogic nature of knowledge construction.	✧ Evaluate the validity of truth claims and the plausibility of explanations. ✧ Evaluate the rigor of epistemic procedures, the evidence that supports explanations and interpretations, and the logic of argumentation. ✧ Stress the importance of disciplined procedures in the construction of knowledge.
Multiperspectivity: • Diversity of perspectives. • Beliefs that motivate individual/collective agency.	✧ Recognize the plurality of perspectives. ✧ Reconstruct the viewpoints of different people in the past and in the present. ✧ Situate the beliefs, practices, decisions, and actions of people in their contexts of meaning.
Systemic thinking: • Larger social systems and processes in which discrete events and practices are located. • Power relations that shape historical events and people's agency.	✧ Differentiate social, political, economic, psychological, and cultural dimensions of events and explain how they affect each other. ✧ Identify and coordinate multiple causes and consequences. ✧ Establish interactions between causality and motivated action. ✧ Identify continuity and change in historical processes. ✧ Uncover the social structures and forces that define the range of options available to historical actors.

The Ostracism Case Study

I first used this model in the Ostracism Case Study (Bermudez, 2014), focused on a real incident in a group of girls involved in a long grim story of bullying in an urban middle school in the United States.

> In December of 1995 Sue and Rhonda considered each other best friends. They belonged to a popular group of girls in the 7th grade. One day, Sue wrote a note to Ronda saying that she thought their friend Jill was "stupid

> to break up with her boyfriend." Also in the note, Sue asked Rhonda to keep the note private because she had not yet told Jill that she felt that way. Rhonda decided to tell Jill what Sue had written anyway. Jill confronted Sue and they argued in front of many peers. Their fight snowballed, and many students joined together against Sue. Rhonda, Tina and Patti sided with Jill, and influenced other girls to do the same. For over a year, they excluded Sue from their group, teased her, spread rumors, and wrote hurtful letters to her. Sue went from being a strong student to getting poor grades, not wanting to go to school, and seriously considering suicide. (Barr, 1998)

Researchers from FHAO interviewed seven girls involved in the incident in 1996 and again in 1997 and 2001. Each time, the girls reflected on the ostracism incident, and on other social and historical issues addressed in the curriculum. I was fascinated by the very different explanations that the girls gave of the incident and their own participation in it, and proposed to investigate how the girls' capacity for critical reflection defined their understanding of the conflict and their sense of responsibility in it.

I first coded the interviews from time 1, identifying excerpts that revealed how each girl used the critical inquiry tools to construct their initial account of the incident. The results for each girl were contrasted through comparisons that exposed the varying levels of complexity of their explanations (cross-sectional analysis). Next, I focused on Rhonda and Patti's interviews at times 2 and 3, using the analytic model to identify if their explanations gained complexity over time. These results were contrasted through comparisons with the critical complexity demonstrated in time 1 (longitudinal analysis).

Rhonda intrigued me more than any of the girls because, even though she had actively harassed Sue, she felt proud of her behavior. When first interviewed, she placed all the blame on Sue and didn't doubt the rightfulness of her own actions: Sue had violated their trust, and Jill deserved to know what her "friend" was saying behind her back. Her initial account of the incident showed a simplistic use of the critical inquiry tools. Rhonda never considered Sue's hurt or perspective (multiperspectivity). While she questioned the teachers' and Sue's judgment, she didn't question her own, nor the incongruence of questioning Sue for exactly the same thing she was doing: telling the story exclusively from her viewpoint (reflective skepticism). Further, Rhonda attributed the escalation of the incident solely to the personal motives of the girls, not recognizing her leadership and obscuring the power dynamics at play (systemic thinking).

One could argue that temporal proximity and Rhonda's own emotional involvement explained her difficulty in questioning her role. However, other girls, equally involved, did offer a more self-critical account. Rhonda's simplistic use of the critical inquiry tools offered an important clue to understand her limited sense of responsibility for hurting Sue. Confirming this, subsequent interviews showed a clear improvement in multiperspectivity and systemic thinking, in parallel with a growing acknowledgment of the hurt she inflicted, an expression of regret, and the consideration of alternative solutions (problem posing).

My cognitive interpretation of Rhonda's simplistic understanding of the incident seemed reasonable, but something did not fit well. Other sections of the interviews, in which she reflected about school and society, showed a more complex use of the critical inquiry tools. Already in early eighth grade, Rhonda was articulate about issues of discrimination and prejudice (problem posing and systemic thinking). She was surprisingly aware of stereotypes, skeptical of social conventions, and challenged what others saw as unquestionable truths or fair social arrangements (multiperspectivity and reflective skepticism). What puzzled me was the contrast between the sophistication of Rhonda's critical reflection regarding the social world around her and the simplicity with which she reflected on her own involvement in the conflict.

I shared my puzzle with some colleagues working from a critical race theory perspective, who contested my cognitive interpretation of Rhonda's simplistic and self-indulgent account of the incident. They underlined something that I knew but had no effective tools to address: Rhonda was a tall, thin African American girl with a broad smile, often wearing a red bandana wrapped around her head. She was the youngest of five in a close-knit working-class family. In school, she was one of the few black girls bused daily into an affluent school with a primarily white population. Despite being in the minority, she was popular and a strong leader in her peer group. Teachers described her as very smart and hardworking but sometimes insensitive to other people's feelings (Barr, 1998).

How did all that make a difference? The cognitive approach I had taken could not offer a convincing explanation, and in fact revealed a significant limitation: it had no means to examine how students' identities and the social asymmetries in which they find themselves play a role in their ways of making sense of social conflict. I had analyzed Rhonda as a "thinking individual," disregarding her sense of self, her relationships and her sociocultural context. Psaltis (Part I in this volume) describes this limitation as the weakness of an ontogenetic analysis that is conducted from a developmental perspective that fails to capture the situated nature of thinking and understanding. Drawing on the work of Duveen (2002), he identifies the roots of this weakness in the Piagetian assumption that individuals are able to fix their own inconsistencies through *reflective autoregulation*, disregarding the influence of the relations of *cooperation* and *co-construction* of which they are a part. Resolving this limitation requires, in their view, moving from the study of the *epistemic subject* toward the study of the *social psychological subject.*

In light of the interaction with my critical race theory colleagues, Rhonda's background information, irrelevant in the cognitive analysis, turned significant and raised a new question: *How did Rhonda's experience within the social dynamics of school and society influence her use of critical inquiry tools?* Selman, one of my dissertation advisors, recognized my struggle. His early work on the development of role-taking (Selman, 1980), rooted, among others, in Kohlberg's theory, had been subject to similar criticisms, and subsequent transformations of his theory took account of other noncognitive factors that affected children's relationships and the development of their social awareness (Selman et al., 1997; Selman, 2003). Selman introduced me to Helen Haste – who had recently started a visiting professorship at Harvard – considering that her Vygotskian and discursive perspectives on morality and civic engagement (Haste, 1993, 2004, 2014) could help me unlock the quandary I was in without forgoing my interest in analyzing individuals' capacity for critical thinking. She read my work and begun to raise questions that turned my thinking upside down and gave way to a long-lasting conversation.

Addressing Microgenesis – Discursive Processes in Controversy

Haste insisted that I needed to consider three domains of meaning-making, and their interactions, in order to get a better grasp of the complexities of people's engagement in social controversies: (1) the domain of the individual agent that makes meaning of social issues through active cognitive processes that take place "inside the head"; (2) the domain of interpersonal interactions in which the individual engages in dialogue, argumentation, and negotiation with others, drawing upon and shaping his or her individual reasoning and identities; and (3) the domain of the sociocultural production of narratives and discourses that are invoked by individuals and communities to make sense of issues within the frames of collective meaning (Haste, 2004). She then led me into the work of social psychologists Rom Harre (2003) and Michael Billig (1996) to understand their discursive perspective on controversy. They regard both thinking and discussion as relational and situated activities that must be analyzed within the interpersonal and sociocultural context in which they perform "function-oriented productions." Through them, individuals strive to accomplish a variety of social goals, not simply intellectual ones. For instance, they establish relationships of alliance, hostility, or subordination, and within these relationships they talk in ways that make language "do social work" such as establishing bonds, undermining someone's authority, or reifying an existing account. Three core discursive processes – *narrative*, *rhetoric*, and *positioning* – seemed the most relevant to analyze the ostracism incident taking into account students' identities, their positions regarding the controversial issues they were dealing with, and the impact of the relationships, power asymmetries, and struggles they were embedded in.

Narratives reflect the cultural systems of representation and construction of meaning that are particular to historical times and cultural contexts. Individuals draw upon the narratives available in their contexts to make sense of social events. They don't construct meaning through lonesome reflection, but through invoking, negotiating, and transforming these narratives (Haste, 2004). Narratives provide the language with which people think and talk about an issue. They define what elements of an issue are connected or disconnected, what aspects are placed in the foreground or background of an argument, and what is taken for granted, what is considered good or appropriate, or, conversely, strange or problematic. Therefore, the meaning of every single position expressed by an individual must be analyzed within the context of these larger social discourses. In controversies, in which multiple narratives collide, participants negotiate with each other the relevance, meaning, and trustworthiness of the different accounts.

Individuals engage with social narratives through the adoption of *rhetorical stances*. Billig (1996) claims that thinking is, primarily, a process of arguing with others or with yourself. Thus, participants adopt different rhetorical stances, depending on whether they seek to *expose* ideas that others *take for granted*, *challenge* the merits of a claim, *resist* its meaning and implications, or, alternatively, *justify* personal beliefs that are disregarded by others or *persuade* others of their value. Any statement implies another one that is being affirmed or disputed, and we can only understand its meaning if we grasp what it is arguing for or against.

Positioning: Narratives make certain identity categories available that allow participants to position themselves and others as being this or that kind of person. Harré uses the concept of positioning to capture the involvement of the self in the process of argumentation. In controversies, individuals take on and ascribe to others different identities and negotiate the implications that historical accounts have for their sense of self and for the management of interpersonal and social relationships. Therefore, the sense of "self" and "other" that individuals bring to a conversation is constantly redefined through the process of arguing (Harré & Moghaddam, 2003). The analysis of positioning reveals how the participants in a controversy relate to one another through the content of their arguments. Who you are is partly defined by what you argue for or against. Likewise, ideas are signified depending partly on *who* is claiming or contesting them.

This discursive perspective radically challenged my approach to the analysis of critical inquiry, highlighting the limitations of the cognitive-individualistic framework I had taken so far. If, as Billig (1996) claimed, the form and content of thinking and arguing are significantly defined by "outward dialog" rather than simply by the internal structures of the mind, I had to make room in my analytic model for the relational and sociocultural contexts in which individual reasoning operated and developed. Importantly, this discursive perspective that regards the individual as an *active* agent (rather than as a passive agent subject to external social forces) provided me with the categories to analyze the discursive activity of the individual, not by displacing my attention from the cognitive operations of critical inquiry, but by situating them in the relational and social dynamics that modulate the performance of critical complexity. This revised approach to critical inquiry resonates with Psaltis's conceptualization of microgenetic research. The integration of a discursive perspective in the analysis of critical thinking was my way to move from the study of the *epistemic subject* toward the study of the *social psychological subject.* Indeed, this move allowed me to capture the interplay between self-regulation and other-regulation that, as claimed by Duveen (2002), is "rendered intelligible by the embedding of the epistemic subject in group life in a network of symmetric and asymmetric social interactions" (see Psaltis, Part I in this volume).

Discursive Insights on Rhonda

The discursive analysis of Rhonda's narratives (Bermudez, 2014) paid special attention to her discussion of the larger social issues. Inequality, discrimination, power, and violence were rather stable in her experience, and therefore had a remarkable continuity across the three interviews. This analysis shed a different light on the source and meaning of her "simplistic and indulgent" interpretation of the ostracism incident.

The Organic Meaning of Critical Inquiry

Discursive analysis suggests that Rhonda's negotiation of her identity and relationships modulated her engagement in critical inquiry.

Rhonda talked sharply about her personal life, her school and her social milieu, and took active stances regarding them. As she reflected on the tensions she navigated daily, she evoked social narratives about racism, black identity, and white expectations and stereotypes about black people. Three pairs of narrative themes – *Fakeness/Authenticity*, *Bias/Outspokenness,* and *Exclusion/Independent agency* – revealed her perception of interpersonal and social relationships and delineated the sociocultural context of meaning of her arguments. Drawing upon them, Rhonda positioned herself and others in ways that helped her negotiate her black identity and minority status in a white affluent community in which she was placed in the margins and overburden with a social identity that she could not take for granted as the other girls did.

Several anecdotes stress Rhonda's perception that people were *fake.* They pretended to care about others more than they really did. In the face of conflict, they hid their views to avoid confrontation. Challenging their attitude and resisting their expectations, Rhonda positioned herself as *authentic.* At age 13, she stated that Rosa Parks and Harriet Tubman inspired her, or "anybody that sticks up for what they believe in." However, she knew that what she interpreted as being genuine, others read as being mean. Looking back, in her last interview she explains, "People say I was mean, but I didn't think I was mean. People say I'm mean now... maybe because I tell people what's on my mind."

Rhonda also talked profusely about her experience of *bias* in relationships. On the basis of skin color, she explained, black people are typified as a source of unease and concern, prone to crime, untamed sexuality, and slang-talk. These stereotypes prevented others from knowing who she truly was, so, in response, Rhonda positioned herself as *outspoken.* If others won't listen, she will speak loud and frankly to assure that she gets her point across. Throughout the three interviews she repeated, "I'll say whatever I want to. I don't care what other people think about me."

Adding to the negative stereotypes that pitted her against the normative criteria of what is good and desirable, Rhonda offered several examples of incidents of discrimination. Against the risk of *exclusion* and disempowerment, she presents herself as assertive and willing to do whatever is necessary to hold her place. Already in eighth grade Rhonda described herself as "an outgoing person who, like, thinks about themself first (sic), . . . independent, maybe."

From a cognitive perspective, I was struck by the disparity between Rhonda's "self-oriented critical thinking" and her "other-oriented critical thinking." However, discursive analysis revealed a remarkable similarity between Rhonda's moral claims regarding the conflict with Sue and her perception of relationships in school and society: Sue tried to keep an appearance of being Jill's best friend when in fact she "went behind," talking about her behind her back. In questioning Sue's fakeness and claiming that Jill deserved better, Rhonda asserted her own moral regard for authenticity and outspokenness.

Risk and Vulnerability of Critical Inquiry

Rhonda's use of the critical inquiry tools was informed by her sense of self and her management of positioning. The experience of living in the margins, together with her sense of authenticity and outspokenness, inclined her to differentiate her perspective from others' and to dispute stereotypes and biases. However, when she was called into question, sophisticated critical reflection seemed to make her vulnerable and to put her at risk in the negotiation of identities and relationships. Considering the effort Rhonda had put into resisting and challenging negative stereotypes about black youth, the open recognition of contending perspectives regarding the Ostracism Incident could have appeared to Rhonda as accepting the dominant views and values (e.g., black girls are too loud, too blunt, too insensitive) that placed her in the margins. Coordinating her views with other perspectives might have felt as "giving in" to the stereotypes that threatened to erode her sense of self-worth and her standing in peer relationships. In contrast, not caring about what others said about her helped her resist the weight of expectations that she did not share, and the deprecating effect of the identity labels laid on her.

Similarly, considering the disempowering context in which she found herself, overlooking the role she played in the dynamics of fear and peer pressure during the ostracism incident could have seemed necessary to protect one of the few sources of peer recognition available in her minority status. If Rhonda's strength in this context rested on her commitment to "stay true to herself," how could she scrutinize the consistency and validity of her own claims and motives in the conflict with Sue without threatening her sense of authenticity and leadership?

A situated view of Rhonda's use of the critical inquiry tools indicates that her simplistic and self-indulgent reflection about the ostracism incident may have seemed to her the best she could do to stay safe in a precarious environment. While from a cognitive perspective higher critical complexity in thinking and arguing is regarded as better, from a discursive perspective one must consider that the display of critical complexity by specific participants in particular contexts may generate vulnerability in the face of significant social and relational risks. This insight allowed me to understand that, for strategic reasons, Rhonda did not always use the critical thinking capacities she had. Critical inquiry turned out to be too costly for her, undermining her identity, her social relationships, and her management of the conflicts she was immersed in.

In turn, the analysis of Rhonda's case and the integration of cognitive and discursive perspectives led me to new insights that transformed my understanding of critical inquiry (Bermudez, 2014). People are not simply individual thinkers, but *thinkers-in-relation-to-others*, so the relational dynamics need to be considered when explaining how individuals "*think critically with others.*" Social controversies set in motion an *intellectual dynamic* in which individuals make use of critical inquiry tools to construct reliable knowledge of the issues at hand. Yet, controversies also set in motion a *social dynamic* in which individuals engage in discursive processes of affirmation, recognition, and contestation that intertwine with the intellectual processes.

The new interpretation of Rhonda's understanding and management of the ostracism incident illustrates well the effect of relocating the analysis of critical inquiry in a *microgenetic perspective* that pays attention to the interaction between individuals, the sociocognitive conflicts that emerge between their different social representations, and the transformations that emerge as they negotiate and (re)construct their representations, identities, and relationships (Psaltis, Part I in this volume). My transformed interest in the dynamics of *thinking-critically-with-others* echoes the claim that the significant structure to be studied is the functioning of the subject–object–other triad. Applied to Rhonda, the discursive manner of "embedding the epistemic subject in group-life" revealed the "interplay between self-regulation and other-regulation" that shaped her particular way of making sense of interpersonal and social conflicts and of her own and others' responsibilities in them.

The Twilight L.A. Case Study

With this new understanding of critical inquiry, I embarked in a second case study of an online discussion about racism and police brutality among diverse youth in the United States (Bermudez, 2012). The "Twilight L.A. Case Study" was based on the extensive documentation of a pedagogical discussion facilitated in 2002 by FHAO teachers on the 10th anniversary of the riots that followed the nonguilty verdict of the white police officers accused of beating African American Rodney King in Los Angeles. Over a hundred African American, Latino, and white students attending different high schools took part in heated controversies that spanned over a month. I used the cognitive and discursive approaches to critical inquiry to analyze the complexity of students' rendition of the riots and of police brutality, and the role that their identities, positions, and relationships played in their meaning-making and arguing.

One discussion thread involved 20 students arguing about the slavery roots of current racism and the value of historic legacies and memory.[2] The analysis of rhetorical stances showed that up until the middle of the discussion thread the controversy had divided pretty strongly into two discourses. One sustained that racism was a sore *reality* that had its roots in a long history of oppression of the African American people and other minorities (Latinos and Native Americans). These participants argued that racism was still alive in the inequalities, stereotypes, and discrimination that marked the life of these minorities in the present. The other discourse sustained that racism is a self-perpetuating *fiction*, resulting from black people's resentment against white people. For these participants, racism remained alive in the racial tension created by the attitude of African Americans who blamed their problems on white people. These different narratives operated as the larger context of meaning that framed participants' contending claims about the role and significance of the past in the present.

RightWinger: In a nutshell, the riots were minority groups protesting white men doing their job and defending their lives against a black felon.

Kit Koi: One thing to remember is that the Rodney King verdict was not the entire reason for people to react the way they did; it was also from oppression they had felt for quite some time then. This incident may just have been the breaking point.

This short interaction already evidences a significant difference in the representation of time. RightWinger's explanation of the riots as 'minority groups' protesting 'white men doing their job' confines the issue to discrete actions in the present. In contrast, Kit Koi explains the riots as "the

[2] All the names used by students in the forum where self-chosen pseudonyms.

breaking point" in an ongoing social experience of oppression. The controversy continued to build up as other participants chimed in, and what emerged as contrasting narratives about racism as *reality* or *fiction* evolved into contrasting narratives about the *continuity* and *discontinuity* between past and present.

JESSIE: In case you didn't know, the Rodney King incident was an opportunity. Many people came out of their shells to fight for what they believed in. [. . .] Did you know that the Mexican-Americans had to suffer through stereotyping of being trouble-makers during the zoot-suit riots?
JFOXX: Zoot suit riots had nothing to do with the King beating.
JESSIE: For your information it wasn't just the blacks that were involved in the riots. It was everyone in L.A., and the zoot suit riots did have something to do with it. The Hispanic community has been through a lot. The zoot suit riots were a root of why they jumped in.
JFOXX: How long ago was that?!? How many people that lived in the 90s were in it?!?!? Please let me know.
JESSIE: So what if the zoot suit riots were a long time ago? The woman's rights to vote were also a long time ago, and that's still a motivation for women to come out and do what they have too.

Jessie builds over the image of continuity suggested by Kit Koi. His notion of 'opportunity' extends the metaphor of a 'breaking point' and provides a concrete image: Hispanics "came out of their shells." He also explains that the experience of people in the past *motivates* the action of people in the present. In turn, Jfoxx challenges Jessie's temporal connection and states an explicit discontinuity between past and present. For him, events that happened long ago cannot motivate people who did not live through them, and with this he supports RightWinger's claim that the events of the present are to be explained within the present.

These narratives reflect larger social discourses and moral values that provide individuals the language to think, feel, and talk about particular issues, and in this way 'prescribe' and 'proscribe' their thinking and meaning-making. The discussion between these students reflects a larger controversy at the heart of American culture: The narrative that highlights continuity and fluidity between past and present resembles the Black Heritage discourse. The narrative that highlights discontinuity between past and present, and a present-future orientation, resembles the American Dream discourse. However, as the controversy evidences, the narratives invoked by participants become the object of discursive negotiations in which individuals play an active and creative role disputing established accounts and exposing the two-sidedness of the phenomenon.

Students mobilized the different identity categories made available by the respective narratives to position themselves and each other, and thereby achieve different constructions of self and other identities. The continuous and discontinuous views of past and present implicate different definitions of the boundaries and qualities of "I," "We," and "They."

> **NubiaQueen:** Jfoxx, you have no idea of what AFRICANS AMERICANS go through in our day to day lives. Your ancestors brought us over here to do your dirty work, they raped our women and killed our men. They would burn us inside of our own houses and they would hang our men right in front of our children. [. . .]. African American men are always being followed by police officers or we are always accused for something that we never did. [. . .] The white man took this land away from the NATIVE Americans and from MEXICANS. [. . .] Look into your ancestor background and you'll probably find out that you ancestors killed mine.

NubiaQueen blends the historic and the contemporary self. In describing the experience of African Americans, she moves fluidly between then and now, stressing the continuity between violence and oppression in the past and between discrimination and stereotyping in the present. A continuous "we" is victimized over time. The past lives with you. She also blends the individual and collective self. The boundaries between I/We are also fluid, so the experience of her ancestors is her own experience. She sees herself as part of a 'collective actor' that was 'brought over here' and 'raped.' Likewise, she positions Jfoxx as one of the "whites" that enslaved and harmed her people in the past. Not surprisingly, Jfoxx responds to Nubia's provocation with a very different management of identities.

> **Jfoxx:** Slow down there, Queen Latifa. My ancestors had nothing to do with anything. Before you start making assumptions about my heritage, can you guess where my heritage starts?? My grandpa came from England. He was born and raised there until he was about 10 years old. He then moved to Hawaii and then into the States. There he had my dad and my dad had me. So, what was that about me doing stuff to your ancestors?
> Wow, I never knew you are in slavery. . . . I'm sorry you feel that I had blacks do my "dirty work," and that I "raped" the black women and "killed" the black men. I have no recollection of myself ever doing that. I laugh when I hear people like you talk about what you go through because of slavery. You have never been through it. If you have, then you would be how old?? rrriiiiggghhttt.

Jfoxx resists how NubiaQueen positions him. He responds with facts about his ancestors, to prove that they were not involved in slavery and thus he cannot be blamed for it. Highlighting their individuality, Jfoxx makes a clear distinction between his ancestors and the general category of "white men." He then turns to challenge NubiaQueen's definition of herself. With irony he questions her use of the collective voice and her adoption of the experience of slavery and victimization of her ancestors as her own experience. By pointing to the chronological impossibility of her account, he positions NubiaQueen as ignorant or confused. A new participant builds off of Jfoxx to position NubiaQueen and her perspective as childish and immature

Holiday: NubiaQueen: you need to grow up and face the facts. Slavery is over!!! You will amount to nothing in your life if you can't let the past go. It's good to know the past, but don't live in it.

Holiday reinterprets NubiaQueen's connection with the past as not wanting to "accept reality" and a misleading strategy of blaming everything on others instead of taking charge of her own life and moving forward.

Taken together, these excerpts depict how the discourses of "*reality of racism+ past-present continuity*" and "*fiction of racism + past-present discontinuity*" also implicate a sharp contrast between *fluid* and *discrete identities*. In the discussion, the students that regarded the past as an indelible heritage that lives in you were confronted for being "too obsessed with the past." In turn, the students that regarded the past as a burden you must let go of were confronted for being "too stuck in the present." These discursive interactions help explain why some students were more inclined to situate the L.A Riots within a long-term process of race relations and others more inclined to connect them to the weight of individual's actions and choices in the present. The difference between them does not necessarily indicate a more developed cognitive capacity for systemic thinking on the part of some students, or the lack of such capacity on the part of other students. Rather, it indicates that the discursive context of controversy informs how students *make use* of the cognitive tools of critical inquiry, and of whatever capacities they had. Interestingly, these findings seem to echo Duveen & Lloyd's (1990) claim that "an adequate account of ontogenesis needs to describe how social representations become psychologically active for individuals" (cited by Psaltis in Part I of this volume). In the conflicting interpretations that RightWinger, KitKoi, Jessie, JFoxx, NubiaQueen, and Holiday make of the Los Angeles Riots of 1992, the particular reconstruction of their respective social identities appears to be what makes a given social representation become active for some of them but not for others.

Important insights gained on critical inquiry, such as the discrepancies that may exist between "self-oriented critical thinking" and "other-oriented critical thinking," or the social and relational vulnerability of "thinking critically with others," are clear manifestations of the importance of articulating the ontogenetic and microgenetic perspectives of analysis and, within that, integrate the role that identity, social asymmetries, and sociocultural context have in the development of a critical understanding of social phenomena.

Addressing Sociogenesis – Narrative Mechanisms in the Representation of Political Violence

In the Ostracism and in the Twilight case studies, I used the categories of *rhetoric stances*, *positioning*, and *narratives* to analyze how these three discursive processes played out in shaping interpersonal interactions and meaning-making in the discussion of controversial issues. In respect to narratives, I focused on how participants drew upon or invoked particular social narratives that gave authority and significance to their claims. Yet the Twilight forum highlighted the enormous power that narratives have to frame peoples' thinking, prescribing and proscribing their understanding of interpersonal and social conflict and their critical reflection about them. This increased my interest in studying the processes of narrative production and circulation, at a societal level, separately from the individual's discursive gestures of invoking available narratives to ground their claims in a controversy.

In 2011, I moved to the Center for Applied Ethics at Deusto University (Basque Country, Spain) to study the ethical potential of formal and informal history education. In particular, I wanted to deconstruct the narratives about violent pasts that are communicated to young people through artifacts of historical culture, such as school textbooks or museum exhibits, and to examine the implications they could have for conflict transformation and peace building. Historical narratives have powerful and often-unexamined ways of constructing and sustaining social representations that have meaning and practical value in the present. For instance, narratives about violent pasts do not simply describe or explain the occurrence of particular violent events; they also communicate social representations about the nature, functions, and meaning of violence in human relations over time, and these representations inform people's understanding and action in the face of current conflict and violence.

This last iteration of my research interests relates to what Psaltis characterizes as a sociogenetic analysis (and pedagogical practice) concerned with the "transformation of collective narratives of social groups about specific objects, in historical time" (see Part I in this volume). Indeed, a distinct contribution of history education to the construction of well-rooted cultures of peace rests in the possibility of fostering a critical interrogation of collective representations of conflict and violence. Educational interventions at this level can cultivate in students the capacities and dispositions necessary for a reflective engagement with the social narratives that are available in their communities, exposing the extent to which they open or close the possibilities of a critical understanding of their violent pasts (Bermudez, Sáez de la Fuente, & Bilbao, 2020). This kind of pedagogical work requires research that investigates the processes of production, dissemination, appropriation, and transformation of collective narratives.

In line with these considerations, it called my attention that most of the history taught to young people across the world is a history of violence. Textbooks are full of battles, conquests, and colonizing enterprises, dictatorships, and so forth. However, despite being a dominant motif, violence is rarely discussed or made the object of explicit analysis. Quite the contrary, it is most often treated as a natural trait of human affairs, an inevitable feature of historical processes that is not regarded as problematic and, therefore, requires no explanation. It is not that violence is hidden from the students. Much is said about it, but by avoiding an explicit analysis of its causes, consequences, and alternatives, textbook narratives tend to *normalize violence* and often hinder critical reflection on it (Bermudez, 2019). The analysis of textbook accounts on different episodes of the violent pasts of countries like Colombia, Spain, the United States, and Serbia led me to identify 10 narrative mechanisms involved in the normalization of violence (Table 12.2).

Subsequent research conducted in a memorial museum has shown that these mechanisms can be inverted, so to speak, to represent violent pasts in ways that invite critical reflection (Bermudez & Epstein, 2020). Thus, a new analytic model that integrates the two orientations of narrative mechanisms toward the normalization or de-normalization of violence is currently being developed for research and pedagogical purposes: the model may be used to deconstruct the narratives that circulate through formal and informal sites of history education or to design pedagogical mediations that engage students in a critical and ethical examination of violent pasts.

Table 12.2 *Narrative mechanisms to normalize violence*

1. ***Conflation of conflict and violence:*** Conflict and violence tend to be treated as inseparable, implying that where there is conflict, violence follows. Historical narratives rarely explain why an episode turned violent, how violence evolved, or how violence defined the development of historical events.
2. ***Narrative framing that justifies violence:*** Historical accounts frame the meaning of specific events by locating them within larger historical process. Most narratives portray violence as an unfortunate but necessary means to valued social ends, such as attaining progress, gaining independence, or building a nation.
3. ***Biased coordination of different narratives:*** Historical accounts tend to convey dominant narratives that marginalize alternative viewpoints. Events and perspectives that go against the dominant storyline that justified or sanitized violence are reframed, distorted, or entirely suppressed.
4. ***Marginalization of the perspective of the victims:*** Historical narratives tend to understate the extent and depth of violence leveled against certain sectors of the population (particularly if they belonged to an out-group). Thus, the accounts of a violent past come across as stories of violence with no hurt.
5. ***Marginalization of nonviolent alternatives:*** Historical narratives rarely represent the historical actors that expressed disagreement, actively opposed the use of violence, or advocated for nonviolent strategies to deal with the conflicts at stake. This silence suggests that there were no alternatives to violence.
6. ***Obscured depiction of human agency:*** Most historical narratives portray violence as a spontaneous and inescapable response to conflict, disguising the fact that violence was often socially constructed, that is, that it involved decision-making and operated as a deliberate and instrumental practice. In this way, historical narratives convey stories of hurt with no blame, in which violence is disconnected from authorship and responsibility.
7. ***Disjointed discussion of the social structures that propel and sustain violence.*** Violent practices are often described in a vacuum, disconnected from the complex interaction of social structures that generate conflict and trigger or motivate the use of violence as a means to manage tensions and contradictions.
8. ***Simplistic account of the destructive effects of violence:*** Beyond the number of human casualties, textbooks did not offer a comprehensive representation of the costs and losses generated by violence at different levels, including, for instance, psychosocial trauma, the destruction of cultural heritage, the loss of economic resources, or environmental devastation.
9. ***Omission of group-based benefits of violence:*** Historical narratives provide virtually no discussion of what was gained (by some) with the use of violence, who gained from it, and who paid for it. This silence concealed the "economy of violence," or the social interests and dynamics that mobilize the recourse to violence.
10. ***Disconnected Past:*** Historical narratives rarely make explicit connections between the violence lived in the past and its ripple effects in the present, between societal processes and individual experiences, or between "academic" knowledge of the violent past and collective memory of traumatic events. In this way, historical narratives cast a shadow over the purpose and potential of historical inquiry about the violent past.

Memory, History Education, and Peace Building in Euskadi

The model of narrative mechanisms involved in the normalization or de-normalization of violence is one of the foundations guiding the "Learning Community on Memory, History Education and Peace Building in Euskadi," an ongoing project led by the Center for Applied Ethics at the University of Deusto

Ten years after ETA's[3] final ceasefire, young people in the Basque Country, the first generation not to have firsthand experience of violence, complained that there were few safe environments where they could ask questions about and discuss the political violence that permeated the last six decades. Many of the university students that participated in the learning community referred repeatedly to the weight of a "legacy of silence" in their families, peer groups, schools, and community (Saéz de la Fuente, Bermudez, & Prieto, 2020).

> "Whenever I heard something about the Basque conflict, my mother told me not to talk, not to comment on it. [. . .] She said I should better shut up so I wouldn't get in trouble." (S.10)
>
> "My parents have not told me anything about what happened, on this subject there has only been silence." (S.1)
>
> "It's impossible to talk about the Basque conflict with my friends without arguing. [. . .] I have not experienced the Basque conflict in the first person, but I have felt the tension that continues and that remains today." (S.2)
>
> "When I hear 'Basque conflict' I feel afraid, it has always been a hidden topic that cannot be talked about." (S.7)
>
> I joined the learning community because I wanted to "learn about the 'taboo of the Basque conflict'. We, young people, know very little about it, and we feel uncomfortable talking about it." (E.3)

Aware of the detrimental effect of such forced silence on peacebuilding, the Center for Applied Ethics convened the learning community in 2019 with the goal of fostering a critical dialogue across generations and across political and disciplinary perspectives. During 2019 and 2020 it facilitated an exploratory year-long process of 10 youth from different ideological backgrounds who came together to share and explore their questions and reflections concerning the conflict and violence.

[3] ETA (*Euskadi Ta Askatasuna* / Basque Country and Freedom) was a nationalist terrorist organization that sought the independence of the Basque Country from Spain.

The Basque society is, like any other, plural. However, among the different narratives of the Basque conflict that have coexisted and rivaled for visibility and recognition, the leftist narrative that justified the armed struggle led by ETA has had a long-lasting and relatively dominant hold on public opinion (Sáez de la Fuente, 2011). According to it, the Basque people have been unwillingly subjected to an incessant historical conflict by the Spanish people, who have recurrently strived to invade and conquer their land and destroy their culture. Victimized by foreign oppressors, Basques have been forced at different times in history to resort to violence to defend themselves. ETA's armed struggle was only the last manifestation of a necessary and inevitable defensive strategy.

Despite their varied social and political backgrounds, many of the students that took part in the learning community recognized traces of this narrative in the fragmented memories they had inherited about the recent past. For instance, one of them recalled how her father tried to explain the conflict,

> "'Say this is a house, with different rooms. And someone comes into my house and settles in my rooms, and decides what he wants to cook and starts cooking [. . .] and decides at what time he has dinner [. . .] That's how they have entered and started telling us how we have to do things'. And that's his way, so simple, to explain the subject." (S.4)

Later on, in a workshop dedicated to analyzing a variety of sources (press articles, journalistic accounts, cartoons, and political statements of various actors), students promptly identified some of the key features and silences of this dominant narrative.

> "A central idea that appears in all the texts is that they [ETA] took-up arms because that is part of the history of Basque people. But they do not tell what that violence translated into. Not only do they try to justify what ETA did, but they discredit the complaints or criticisms made by the entire Spanish society and part of Basque society [. . .] We got that impression because . . . it seems that taking up arms and planting bombs is the normal thing to do, given the history we've had. We also noticed that there were immense gaps that can be manipulative [. . .] When they talk about the bombing of Gernika, they don't mention that Madrid was also bombed during the war because it was full of reds [communists]. So, it is as if suddenly in Madrid everyone went from being red to being Franco supporters. And the Basques were all resistant and we are still all resistant." (S.2 and S.7)
>
> "Well, we have seen more or less the same, on the one hand, the central idea of building the identity of a people, the Basque people, which comes

> from antiquity . . ., as it had always been there. And then also, the attempt to justify ETA taking-up arms. This is always the consequence, it is never an initiative but the consequence of other violent acts on account of which they have suffered oppression by different nations, peoples, ideologies . . . It is a victimist discourse, we are the victims and we, in legitimate defense, take-up arms and unite to fight against oppression . . . Another thing we observed is that there is a dichotomous logic of identity construction. There is 'us' and there is the 'others'. ETA understood 'us' in a way that didn't recognize that there were political differences [within the Basque people]. . . . ETA had the idea that there was a single identity of the Basque people, that there was no room for a plural identity. Basically, it was a 'us' or 'them', and 'them' is identified with evil, the oppressor, the first to attack, and the one who will continue to attack throughout history." (S.3)
>
> "We have seen an idea of a combat of historical roots, of the Basque people against the invaders. The Basque people, we see our identity as rooted in past generations that have not hesitated to die and kill. Those generations have served so that we today have our language and our identity. It is like justifying [violence] with its utility, it has been useful. And then also, with a sense of legitimate vengeance, we suffered with the flames of Gernika, the hatred we have is because we have suffered, and we want to √ our victims [. . .]. We also realized that in this story there is only one option, an absolute, unquestionable truth, which is ours. And if you do not share it, then you become part of the 'others', you are no longer part of 'us'." (S.4)

It is easy to recognize the narrative mechanisms at play in the accounts that the students refer to: they frame the recent violent past within a long-term story of victimization and legitimate defense. The perspective and experience of the victims of violence are lost in the heroic rendition of the armed struggle. The intentional agency of the perpetrators of violence is erased, as they were forced by others to take that path. Other possible accounts of the conflict are silenced, ridiculed, or stigmatized as foreign, evil, oppressive, and the like. The wide-ranging and costly consequences of ETA's violence are dismissed. In these different ways, the still dominant collective narrative of the Basque conflict normalizes and justifies violence.

It is nevertheless worth noting that the ways in which students distanced themselves from the texts they read, reinterpreted their meaning, and discussed them with each other reveal the development of significant fractures in the dominant narrative that open renewed possibilities to interrogate available discourses, express discrepancies, and raise controversies that many would say were improbable a decade ago. What happened in the learning community is, to a certain extent, the result of the active intellectual engagement of the students as they grow older (ontogenesis), and of the holding environment that the group developed to facilitate a collaborative exploration and a safe discussion of a deep-seated social taboo (microgenesis). However, it is also an expression of an ongoing social transformation that is eroding the hold that the dominant narrative had on Basque public opinion and historical culture (sociogenesis). This change is clearly evident in the recent boom of cultural productions that give voice to different perspectives and experiences of the conflict and violence and invite the public to recognize and engage constructively with the pluralism of the Basque society and of its memory of the violent past. A few examples of these productions are *Patria* (Homeland), the best-selling novel by Fernando Aramburu (2016), turned into a short HBO series that tells the story of two families in a small Basque town pitted against each other by ETA's ideology and violence, and describes in fine detail the traumatic experience of each of the members of the family that lost the father; *Maixabel*, a prize-winning movie directed by Iciar Bollain (2021) that tells the real-life story of one of the "restorative encounters" that brought together the wife of an assassinated socialist politician and one of the imprisoned ETA ex-militants that murdered her husband; or *Gesto*, a crowd-funded documentary directed by Xuban Intxausti (2022) that narrates the 30-year painstaking work of pacifist organization Gesto por la Paz. Also indicative are two new permanent museum exhibits on the topic, one housed at the *Centro Memorial de las Víctimas del Terrorismo* (Memorial Center of the Victims of Terrorism) that opened to the public in 2021, and *Plaza de la Memoria*, a 450-m^2 itinerary exhibit developed by *Gogora – Instituto de la Memoria, la Convivencia y los Derechos Humanos* (Remember – Institute for Memory, Coexistence and Human Rights) that since 2016 is placed in public spaces of different Basque towns.

The fractures in the dominant narrative, and the changes they bring about, are also visible in the assessment that students made of their year-long experience in the learning community:

> "I would highlight the process of dialogue, the fact that we have been in this community with people who did not always think the same, diverse people. My classmates had questions similar to mine, but some from a different prism, because of the conditions they had in their lives. . ., people who had lived in a more nationalistic environment, others who had not. . . It has helped me understand better." (E.7)
>
> "I take away a lot of experiences from many people, above all, I also take away a new capacity for understanding [. . .] At least in my case it has helped me to understand better and to be able to empathize with all kinds of people and points of view." (E.5)

"The good thing about the group was that there were people from different backgrounds, ages, and family backgrounds. [. . .]. Being able to talk to all these people in a safe environment, understanding how the conflict marked each family, has served me to have a broader vision, and also to understand that all the victims of violence have suffered a similar pain." (E.2)

"I have met a lot of people who wanted to talk about the subject, to discuss it, to express their points of view, to convince or to be convinced, simply to contrast opinions and also to contrast facts and do self-criticism, a little of everything [. . .]." (E.6)

"What I have found in the learning community has pleasantly surprised me. There are other young people like me quite interested in what has happened and in looking for solutions thinking about the future. And also to share it with older people, who have lived it, because in the end, we are the children or grandchildren of those who have lived it [. . .]." (E.4)

"I wanted to expose myself to other ideologies and other ways of seeing history and having lived history, and that was totally fulfilled [. . .]. In your close environment the opinions are usually more homogeneous and you are not exposed to opinions that confront yours. And yet in these last sessions studying the history of the conflict, our opinions clashed with each other, and that gave rise to doubts that would not come up if you are only in contact with people from your closest environment." (E.7)

"If I had to sum up the experience in one sentence, it would say that I had to unlearn what I had learned as a child [. . .] In my environment, the ideas were much more radical. Here I have found a space where I can openly discuss issues which might be uncomfortable outside. It has introduced me to new perspectives, and in the end to seeing different versions of the same conflict. I have come to rethink what I knew so far, what I have absorbed since I was little, I've had to question all my ideals." (E.4)

"To me, the most important contribution is that I can now see the conflict from another perspective. There is a hegemonic discourse that we all have in our heads, and this experience has helped me to demystify that discourse a little, to see what things are true, which are not so true, and to form my own opinion." (E.3)

The last sessions served us all to open our eyes, because at home, in class, with friends, only one version was told, and what we have seen in the learning community is that that version is distorted." (E.2)

Aiming to build off this work with young people, the Learning Community inaugurated in 2022 a new phase that convenes a group of historians, political sociologists, ethical philosophers, and pedagogues to develop educational resources that engage young people in a critical exploration of contending collective memories and their contrast with disciplined historical research. We anticipate using these resources to structure critical history–memory dialogues among diverse youth in universities, hoping to foster conflict transformation and peace building in the Euskadi. In turn, this will allow us to investigate not only how the narratives invoked by participants frame their engagement in critical inquiry and controversy about the violent past but also how guided critical inquiry may enrich the discursive negotiation of meaning among them, and thereby contribute to transform the representations of conflict and violence in their communities.

The vision of these memory–history dialogues brings together the three dimensions of change described by Psaltis, as it articulates the active and reflective intellectual engagement of young people, the propitious environment of a learning community that scaffolds productive controversy, and the wider dialog that unfolds from the sociogenetic dynamic of challenging *belief-based social representations* through their contrast with *knowledge-based social representations*. Illustrating this distinction proposed by Moscovici (1998), through the learning community we can see how representations grounded on beliefs tend to be "more homogenous, affective, impermeable to experience or contradiction, and leave little scope for individual variations," while social representations founded on knowledge are "more fluid, pragmatic, amenable to the proof of success or failure, and leave a certain latitude to language, experience, and to the critical faculties of individuals" (cited by Psaltis in Part I of this volume).

Conclusions

In this chapter, I discussed several challenges that I encountered in my research and how I tried to "solve" them by developing analytic frameworks that progressively integrated categories to account for the role of individual, relational, and social dynamics in the construction of a critical understanding of social conflict and violence. I attempted to show how the three frameworks, designed to analyze the use of critical inquiry tools, the discursive dynamics of controversy, and the narrative mechanisms of the normalization or de-normalization of violence, resemble the ontogenetic, microgenetic, and sociogenetic analyses conceptualized by Psaltis.

To be sure, there are also important differences in how we conceptualize particular elements of these processes and the particular methodologies we use to investigate them, but the analysis of such differences is far beyond the scope of this chapter and the depth of my experience with Psaltis's model. It is nevertheless striking that, coming from somewhat different disciplinary backgrounds and theoretical traditions, we arrived at a similar view of the limitations of research (and educational interventions) that focus only on individual's thinking, group interactions, or societal dynamics at the expense of capturing the intricate interplay of these dimensions and its impact both on understanding and on the possibilities of conflict transformation. I coincide with Psaltis on that each of the three perspectives of analysis are necessary because they give us important information that the other ones cannot yield. And each perspective also affords important insights on how to intervene, socially and pedagogically, if we aim to foster conflict transformation. Yet, both in research and in educational practice, the three perspectives must be kept in interaction with each other. As illustrated with a variety of examples, individual cognition is embedded in the discursive dynamics deployed in relationships and is framed by the narratives available in particular social contexts. And it is in the interaction between them that we find the possibilities of conflict transformation. Through guided critical inquiry and dialogue, individuals can mobilize their agency to reorient interactions with others and, in this manner, contribute to interrogating and transforming social narratives that sustain conflict and violence.

REFERENCES

Barr, D. (1998). Rhonda: A Case Study of an Eighth-Grader's Perspectives on Social Issues. Facing History and Ourselves. Unpublished manuscript, Brookline, MA.

Bermudez, A. (2012). The discursive negotiation of cultural narratives and social identities in learning history. In M. Carretero, M. Asensio, & M. Rodríguez Moneo (Eds.), *History teaching and national identities: International review of history education* (Vol. 5, pp. 203–219). Charlotte, NC: Information Age Publishers.

(2014). Integrating cognitive and discursive approaches in the analysis of critical reflection within relational and socio-cultural contexts. In *Sage cases in methodology* (pp. 1–21). London: Sage Publications.

(2015). Four tools for critical inquiry in history and civic education. *Revista de Estudios Sociales*, 52, 102–118.

(2019). The normalization of political violence in history textbooks: Ten narrative keys. historical dialogues, justice, and memory network. Working Paper Series, No. 15.

(2020). Narrative justice? Ten tools to deconstruct narratives about violent pasts. In M. Keynes, H. Åström Elmersjö, D. Lindmark, & B. Norlin (Eds.), *Historical justice and history education* (pp. 269–289.). Cham: Palgrave Macmillan.

Bermudez, A., & Epstein, T. (2020). Learning about the violent past in memorial museums: Ethical reflection and history education. *Journal for the Study of*

Education and Development. Special Issue: "Popular Uses of the Past and Education: The Effects of Fading Boundaries."

Bermúdez, A., de la Fuente, S., & Izaskun y Bilbao, G. (2020). *Contribuciones de la educación histórica a la deslegitimación de la violencia de motivación política en Euskadi*. Bilbao: Universidad de Deusto.

Bermudez, A., & Jaramillo, R. (2000) *Guía Pedagógica para el Análisis de Dilemas Morales a partir de la Serie Francisco el Matemático*. Caja de Herramientas "Vida de Maestro". Bogotá: IDEP.

(2001). Students' development of historical explanation: Relationships between historical agents, contexts and events. In A. Dickinson, P. Gordon, & P. Lee (Eds.), *Raising standards in history education: International review of history education* (Vol. 3, pp. 146–167). London: Woburn Press.

Billig, M. (1996). *Arguing and thinking: A rhetorical approach to social psychology*. Cambridge: Cambridge University Press.

Carretero, M., & Voss, J. (1994). *Cognitive and instructional processes in history and the social sciences*. Mahwah, NJ: Lawrence Erlbaum Associates.

Dickinson, A., Lee, P., & Rogers, P. (1984). *Learning history*. London: Heinemann Educational.

Duveen, G. (2002). Construction, belief, doubt. *Psychologie et Societé, 3*, 139–155.

Duveen, G., & Lloyd, B. (1990). *Social representations and the development of knowledge*. Cambridge: Cambridge University Press.

Harré, R., & Moghaddam, F. M. (2003). *The self and others: Positioning individuals and groups in personal, political, and cultural contexts*. Westport, CT: Praeger.

Haste, H. (1993). Morality, self and sociohistorical context: The role of lay social theory. In G. G. Noam & T. Wren (Eds.), *The moral self* (pp. 175–208). Cambridge, MA: The MIT Press.

(2004). Constructing the citizen. *Political Psychology, 25*(3) 413–440.

(2014). Culture, tools and subjectivity: The (re)construction of self. In T. Magioglou (Ed.), *Culture and political psychology* (pp. 27–48). Charlotte, NC: Information Age.

Kohlberg, L. (1984). *The psychology of moral development: The nature and validity of moral stages*. San Francisco, CA: Harper & Row.

Moscovici, S. (1998). The history and actuality of social representations. In U. Flick (Ed.), *The psychology of the social* (pp. 209–247). Cambridge: Cambridge University Press.

Psaltis, C., Carretero, M., & Cehanic-Clancy, S. (2017). *History education and conflict transformation: Social psychosocial theories, history teaching and reconciliation*. London: Palgrave MacMillan.

Sáez de la Fuente, I. (2011). *La opinión pública vasca frente a la violencia de ETA. Una mirada retrospectiva*. Bilbao: Bakeaz.

Saéz de la Fuente, I., Bermudez, A., & Prieto, J. (2020). *La historización de la memoria: Balance de la experiencia de una comunidad de aprendizaje con personas jóvenes en Euskadi*. Bilbao: Universidad de Deusto.

Selman, R. (1980). *The growth of interpersonal understanding: Developmental and clinical analyses*. Cambridge: Academic Press.

(2003). *The promotion of social awareness: Powerful lessons from the partnership of developmental theory and classroom practice*. New York: Russell Sage Foundation.

Selman, R., Watts, C., & Schltz, L. H. (Eds.). (1997). *Fostering friendship: Pair therapy for treatment and prevention*. Boston, MA: Aldine de Gruyter.

CHAPTER 13

Rethinking Social Knowledge Development from the Perspective of Genetic Psychology

Alicia Barreiro, José Antonio Castorina, and Mario Carretero

Introduction

In a now classic work, Doise (1982) explored the challenge of maintaining a dialectical understanding of individuals and society in studying social knowledge. Based on the different ways research on social knowledge translated this tension, Doise distinguished different intertwined levels of analysis, highlighting the field's heterogeneity. This chapter will focus on the intra-individual level of analysis because its specificity allows us to draw the relationships, similarities, and differences between the revisited genetic psychology, where our work is framed (Castorina & Barreiro, 2023), and genetic social psychology (Psaltis, 2015; Psaltis & Zapiti, 2014), with the aim of advancing the understanding of social knowledge construction. Such intention involves researchers being able to raise questions to grasp how individuals and cultures are linked in such a process and to delineate units of analysis suitable for empirically addressing them.

To study the development of social knowledge, it is necessary to consider, as in any other field of knowledge, researchers' philosophical assumptions that constrain the visible and the invisible in this process, allowing specific problems to be raised and making it difficult to delimit others. In other words, it is necessary to reflect upon an interconnected set of principles that emerge or operate in different instances of research, transcending theories and methods. These principles define the context in which theoretical concepts or methodologies are constructed and act implicitly in the everyday practice of science. They also influence the elaboration of explanatory models but do not determine the validity of research that follows specific criteria (Castorina, 2021a).

The dialectical perspective for studying psychological development, assumed by both Piaget and Vygotsky, involves a relational ontology (Castorina & Baquero, 2005). In such a worldview (Garcia, 2002), each element of human experience only exists by its constitutive relation with its counterpart, in a dynamic transformation process between the organism and the environment, nature and culture, individual and society. The intervention of such a dialectical framework makes the genetic social psychology epistemologically compatible with the revisited genetic psychology perspective (Castorina, 2017; Psaltis, 2024).

The levels of analysis from which each discipline deals with social knowledge development are different, giving them their theoretical and methodological specificity. Both disciplines assume the challenge of adopting an ontogenetic approach to studying social knowledge construction, being aware of its historical and collective dimensions. We agree with the following statement by Duveen and Lloyd (1990) when defining ontogenesis: "An adequate account of ontogenesis needs to describe how social representations become psychologically active for individuals … ontogenesis is a process through which individuals re-construct social representations, and that in doing so they elaborate particular social identities" (p. 7). However, revisited genetic psychology is dedicated to studying the cognitive mechanisms involved in such processes. In other words, the specificity of the genetic psychology's developmental approach is its focus on the conceptualization of the processes by which individuals reconstruct social knowledge as they appropriate it. It also implies explaining the constructive dynamics that allow appropriating collectively constructed knowledge during such a process. We understand that the study of such mechanisms constitutes the main contribution of revisited genetic psychology to genetic social psychology.

Finally, this chapter will analyze how these theoretical developments could provide helpful insight to design didactic interventions to develop social knowledge, specifically for teaching controversial historical processes that conform to current intergroup relations.

Social Knowledge Construction and the Revisited Genetic Psychology

As it is well known, Piagetian theory was mainly dedicated to the explanation of the process involved in the passages from one lower level of physical or logical-mathematical knowledge to a higher level, and it is necessary to introduce the analysis of the delimitation of the "social" character of knowledge by revisited genetic psychology. This assumption must be made explicit, as it can acquire different meanings depending on the adopted disciplinary approach. It is a problem that requires conceptual discussion and the production of empirical evidence to be fully interpreted.

Therefore, we will delimit from conceptual analysis the epistemological and methodological approaches that, for us, determine the specificity of the processes of social knowledge construction in a broad sense that encompasses different dimensions.

The constructivist epistemological perspective inherited from the Piagetian tradition, in which we critically inscribe ourselves, focuses on the constitutive relationship between subject and object of knowledge, understood as two inseparable poles of the activities carried out in the world. In knowledge development, the systems produced in subject–object interactions are not contained in the previous ones; that is to say, they allow for the construction of novelty.

In this framework, our perspective is inspired by Duveen (1994, 1998), who interprets social psychology from a relational worldview and critically approaches Piagetian tradition. In so doing, he affirms that the construction of individual theories or hypotheses is situated in the context of collectively constructed knowledge transmission. It is essential to clarify that foregrounding the social interactions in which knowledge construction processes take place and the appropriation of collectively constructed knowledge, such as ideological beliefs or social representations, do not imply neglecting the constructive processes that take place at the individual cognitive level. In other words, doing so does not imply abandoning the active character of the subject in this process, which is one of the central theses of Piagetian theory.

In this framework, the following questions arise: To what extent does the appropriation of collective knowledge processes involve a truly original construction of knowledge by individuals? What degree of freedom does someone who appropriates collectively constructed knowledge have? What is the dynamic through which an individual makes a collective belief or social representation his or her own? To answer these questions, it is necessary to investigate the relationships between social representations and the constructive dynamics of knowledge development – that is, to elucidate their ontogenesis (Barreiro & Castorina, 2017). In this sense, positing the existence of a process of individuation (Barreiro & Castorina, 2010; Castorina, 2017, 2010) in the framework of the ontogenetic process of social representations is not equivalent to the defense of an isolated subject or of an individual identity, based on the self and radically dissociated from society. On the contrary, our position holds that when a person appropriates the social representations constitutive of his or her social identity during interaction with others – both peers and adults – he or she engages in an individual cognitive activity. In other words, we highlight the constructive process widely recognized by Duveen (1994). From this perspective, we reject the idea that social beliefs are assimilated to an individual cognitive apparatus or are transformed by an individual subject detached from the social practices in which they participate. Foregrounding the existence of cognitive mechanisms, in line with the intra-individual level of analysis in Doise's (1982) scheme, does not imply the existence of an individual subject apart from his or her cultural environment.

Basically, for the revised Piagetian developmental psychology in which we frame our work, as for genetic social psychology, the subject is a constitutive part of a relational triad composed of a social subject, the object of knowledge, and alter (individuals, groups, or educational and normative institutional practices such as schools). Thus, throughout the unfolding of the research program of constructivist developmental psychology, the epistemic subject of the classical Piagetian tradition was progressively abandoned in favour of a psychosocial subject. This subject is constituted by his or her participation in social practices where the relations between him or her and the others, rooted in collective beliefs and practices, play a constitutive role. As we have already pointed out, it is precisely this dialectical epistemic framework that makes revisited genetic psychology and genetic social psychology compatible (Castorina, 2017; Duveen, 1994). Both share the relational and interactive character of the components of social experience – whether historical, moral, or political – assuming its components exist only in their interpenetration. As Psaltis and Marková point out in this volume, there was a theoretical shift from the dual subject–object dialectic in classic Piagetian works toward a triadic dialectical unity of analysis: subject–object–other.

Returning to Moscovici's initial contributions (Marková, 2010; Moscovici, 1961), social knowledge is constructed in a dynamic semiotic triangle ego–alter–object (representation/symbol). From the point of view of revisited Piagetian developmental psychology, this triadic dialectical unity becomes specific in terms of the study of the constructive dynamics involved in cutting out the object of knowledge through the inferences that the subject makes during social practices (Barreiro & Castorina, 2017; Horn et al., 2023). This approach allows for studying the developmental processes involved in the individual appropriation of social representations. The inquiry focuses on the individual inferential activity aimed to make sense of the object of knowledge. However, the social interactions in which both are immersed constitute this process (Barreiro, 2013a; Barreiro & Castorina, 2017).

The careful study of individual conceptualization processes amid social interaction, in which collective beliefs are constructed and expressed, is the object of the revisited genetic psychology study. In this way it coincides with genetic social psychology in the psychosocial character of the subject, leaving aside the decontextualized epistemic subject characteristic of Piaget's classic works. From a microgenetic level of analysis as discussed by Psaltis and Duveen (2006, 2007), to analyze the conversation types aimed at social recognition and cognitive change – for example, how social representations of gender modulate discussions about the conservation of quantities – social interactions are not only the context in which the equilibration process of cognitive structures unfolds but also provide the resources for them to emerge (Psaltis & Zapiti, 2014). In this empirical and conceptual perspective, the psychosocial subject (the subject of genetic social psychology) in its conversational interactions with others about a social object is taken as the unit of analysis. Even the precedence of social interactions of cooperation or constraint over cognitive achievements pointed out by Psaltis, which Piaget (1932/1948) studied as mutually necessary for moral development, does not prevent us from considering their cognitive specificity. The latter is expressed in the temporal duration and the cognitive effort that the ontogenetic process of appropriation of social representations requires, as shown by the studies from this perspective (Barreiro, 2013a, 2013b; Duveen & Lloyd, 1990). Nevertheless, the progressive equilibration of cognitive structures was proposed by Piaget (1975/1985) to explain the passage from structural preoperational thinking to operational. Therefore, the specificity of social knowledge brings us back to the question with which we began this section: If a psychosocial subject has replaced the Piagetian operational subject, can the equilibration mechanism be used to explain the development of social knowledge?

The Psychosocial Subject versus the Operational Subject in the Construction of Social Knowledge

At this point, it becomes necessary to reconsider the operational subject in the light of the postulate of a psychosocial subject whose development follows specific conceptual trajectories and who interacts with t polysemic objects of knowledge. On the one hand, in recent decades, a debate has occurred in Piagetian developmental psychology concerning the scope of the changes that lead to the construction of new acquisitions and knowledge: that is, whether development occurs in specific domains or is carried out by a general process of logical structure construction, affecting different knowledge domains as if they were isomorphic. In classical Piagetian constructivism, such a general process was the equilibration of thought structures culminating in formal operations. In Piaget's theory, structures have been clearly differentiated from contents.[1] It has been argued that the contents of knowledge are diverse, but the way of thinking about them is determined by the structures constructed by the subject, whether it is historical, physical, moral, or logical knowledge.

Thus, in a first and long period, the inquiries of Piagetian psychologists who dealt with the construction of social notions approached this process from a general domain perspective, focused on the study of a subject isolated from social interactions. Instead, the subject interacts with the object of knowledge in isolation, and cognitive development follows a universal sequence (Berti, 1994; Delval, 1994; Jahoda, 1979). From this perspective, it is assumed that the social and cultural context exerts some influence on the content of knowledge from the outside but does not affect the form of the cognitive process. That is to say, from such perspective, context does not intervene in the increasingly complex trajectory of judgments and arguments elaborated by individuals and sustained by the operational structures (Castorina, 2005).

By contrast, empirical research carried out in the past four decades (Castorina & Barreiro, 2023; Ferreiro & Teberosky, 1991; Martí, 2012; Smetana et al., 2014; Smetana & Villalobos, 2009; Turiel, 1983) has highlighted the existence and centrality of the so-called specific domains of development. Domains are knowledge sets about a class of phenomena that share specific properties. These studies have shown that it is possible to distinguish different domains of knowledge (moral, mathematical, historical, physical, and several others) that are defined by their conceptual organization, assuming their constructive paths about a specific field of experience. For example, Turiel (1983) identified three domains of social experience (moral, psychological, and conventional) based on the different characteristics of social interactions in each of them, together with the distinct developmental trajectories identified in children's justifications about how and why not respecting a social norm in such social interactions could be okay. When considering knowledge from the point of view of the

[1] It is worth noting that there were and still are misinterpretations of the notion of structure in Piaget's work. He was a theorist of actions on the world and not of structuresThus, logic does not determine actions; is embedded in actions. Logic is neither before nor after actions but is inherent to them. Structures cannot be separated from contents or the activities that express them. Piaget never considered bridges between operative structures and actions because the former does not float above the latter.

subject's activity, the notion of the domain is distinguished from its interpretation in terms of biologically determined internal representations, as well as from the peculiarity of cultural instruments or from reality. In our view, a domain is neither contextually given nor internal to the subject, but is constructed – that is, it is modified through interactions with social phenomena. From this perspective, social knowledge is the field of phenomena and relations about which individuals formulate ideas during their social experiences (Castorina & Faigenbaum, 2003; Castorina et al., 2010). Thus, the social domain is not constituted by a particular application of general individual knowledge systems, as in the classical Piagetian tradition. Therefore, it is possible to identify constructive paths specific to each field of societal experience (Barreiro, 2012, 2013a, 2013b; Horn, 2021; Turiel, 1983). Individuals construct domain-specific conceptual systems about social objects of knowledge during their experience with them within institutional practices. In this way, social practices and the beliefs that are expressed and transmitted in them constitute constraints to the construction of social knowledge by individuals, as they limit and at the same time enable this process (Barreiro & Castorina, 2012; Castorina & Faingenbaum, 2003; Castorina et al., 2010). The latter implies affirming that they are neither external nor associated with a general process of knowledge construction; instead, they constitute it. The objects of social knowledge are constituted as such in the social practices of individuals; therefore, without them, thinking is impossible (Castorina et al., 2010).

On the other hand, if the epistemic subject of knowledge is thought of as the expression of a general logical cognitive structure, even if this structure is embedded in social practices (Psaltis & Zapetti, 2014), we would be conceiving a subject with little flexibility to understand the social world. However, the knowledge necessary to live in a social world, particularly about others, is volatile, unpredictable, and variable. Similarly, if one adopts a classical Piagetian perspective, explaining the specificity of logical operational part–whole relations is problematic when it comes to knowledge about others in terms of the social groups to which they belong. In a pioneering study, Piaget and Weil (1951) attributed the problems that children had up to the age of 10–11 in understanding the notion of homeland and the relations with foreigners to the development of part–whole logical inclusion relations and of the relativity or symmetrical character of relations that allows them to coordinate perspectives. Both capacities would be the result of operational activities that are based on reciprocity. On the one hand, understanding that one's city is located within a country implies a process of cognitive decentering. Thus, the child would first understand the notion of the neighborhood, then that of the city, then that of the province, and finally that of the nation. Developing this intellectual coordination consists in mastering reciprocal operations. Piaget states that this understanding requires a cognitive effort and is slow to develop. Up to the age of 7–8, children think in terms of juxtaposed relations between their city and the country in which they live. Although they affirm that Geneva is in Switzerland, they still need to understand this affirmation in terms of the spatial and logical relations that it implies. Later, children can understand the spatial and temporal inclusion of Geneva in Switzerland, but this still needs to correspond to a relationship of inclusion, because they think that it is not possible to be Swiss and, at the same time, Genevan. In other words, the children do not accept the dual belonging to the city and the country. Regarding the construction of the notion of foreigner, Piaget focuses his analyses on the understanding of relativity (in this case, the symmetrical nature of the logical relations involved) as the result of an operational activity that allows the conversion operation to be carried out to transform $A = B$ into $B = A$. In other words, it is an operation of symmetry.

Inspired by Piaget, Psaltis resorts to the operational construction of part–whole relations when considering the possible reduction of prejudice through intergroup contact. He analyzes the individual possibilities of generalizing a social/national group feature from a single case in the future without considering the variability of the objects (the others in this case) toward which thought is directed in the domain of social knowledge. Part–whole relations, defined by the functioning of operational structures described by Piaget, refer to a logical category that would homogenize and stereotype the diversity of singular identities within a social group. The relations of necessity between logical classes – for example, in a set of roses and daisies, there are more flowers than daisies, even if there are more daisies than roses – cannot be extended to social knowledge. The whole and inclusion in the whole seems to presuppose the diversity of individuals' traits in that whole. People, even if they belong to the same national or ethnic group, are diverse and behave differently. More than operational arguments are needed to explain how subjects think about social phenomena such as nationality or homeland. It is necessary to appeal to the changing and diverse relations between individuals and social groups to conceptions that modify their meaning or specify it beyond operatory thought.

The logical necessity, the awareness of the necessity to which individuals arrive, is the indicator of logical operations in the logical-mathematical field. However, it is debatable whether its acquisition accounts for social knowledge development. Even if there were such a necessity in social thought, its transformation does not go in that direction – in other words, the genesis of social knowledge does not go in the direction of the conquest of logical necessity, but of conceptual systematicity. Developmental transformations in this field go toward social representations and other collective beliefs that circulate in individuals' social groups, driving their cognitive development. We are not saying that operational logical thinking ceases to be part of social knowledge, but rather that its development does not explain the specific ideas of this domain. From the subject's point of view, it is possible to speak of necessity retrospectively, but it is not a logical necessity. The subject who has advanced conceptually may believe that it is necessary to think in this way, but this results from a history characterized by its indeterminacy, much more significant than in the shaping of other knowledge domain, because of the nature of the practices in which he or she participates. Only once a subject conceptualizes a notion does it become the real object for them, and only then is it experienced as "necessary" by them. This necessity is very different from the one inherent to operational logic, according to which the nonexistence of a specific state of facts is not possible.

The indeterminacy and coexistence of the different meanings that an object of social knowledge can acquire constitute one of the basic principles of the social representations theory. Multiple meanings that can be given socially to the same objects because the social contexts in which they are included are also multiple, giving rise to a state of cognitive polyphasia (Moscovici, 1961; Wagner & Hayes, 2005). This implies that even contradictory meanings of the same object of knowledge can coexist. Thus, social psychologists explicitly criticize the postulate that thinking does not progress from pre-logical to logical states or from lesser to greater validity, but different logics of thinking coexist, even in adults. Everyday thinking involves the construction of representations with contradictory meanings to each other. However, such contradictions are not disturbing to individuals as long as the representations are locally consistent and not expressed simultaneously in their discourse (Wagner et al., 2006). In this sense, the logical framework of commonsense representations is reminiscent of the transductive thinking described by Piaget (1959/1999) in young children, whose reasoning goes from particular cases to particular cases without recourse to universality or logical necessity.

However, it is essential to note that when social psychologists speak of polyphasia, they generally compare scientific knowledge or disciplinary knowledge with commonsense knowledge (considered chiefly in terms of social representations) and contrast everyday thinking with scientific knowledge. Social psychologists do not generally accept individual appropriation elaboration of concepts, with the exception of Duveen, Leman, and De Rosa (Duveen & De Rosa, 1992; Leman, 1998; Leman & Duveen, 1996). However, we have identified the existence of processes by which subjects construct their knowledge about the world that are not exhausted in a passive incorporation of social beliefs because this is not immediate; that is, it is needed to recognize that individuals carry out a process of conceptual elaboration (Castorina et al., 2010). The results of empirical research in developmental psychology show that the construction of social knowledge, from the perspective of individuals, requires a prolonged effort of intellectual elaboration and reorganization of the framework of ideas. Such studies point to a constructive process that progresses from states of lower to higher differentiation and integration of knowledge. For example, in studying the ontogenesis of the social representations of justice, we found that the initial independent utilitarian (what makes me happy) and retributive representations (punish who did wrong) were held by children from 6 to 9 years of age. From 10 to 17, such independent representations are integrated, conforming to the social hegemonic representation of justice that prevails in Argentine society: justice is what makes everyone happy, and the method to achieve this is to punish who did wrong and to reward those who did good (Barreiro, 2013a, 2020; Barreiro & Castorina, 2016).

Similarly, the appropriation of historical master narratives (Carretero & Bermudez, 2011) or children's experiences with cultural artifacts charged with collective meanings cannot be explained by limiting them to logical structures. Moreover, Piaget described cognitive structures in analyzing the relations of people's activity with the physical world. As we said earlier, we do not deny the existence of operational logic and its intervention in, for example, the classification of social phenomena, as in the case of the part–whole inclusion relations applicable to the categories of city and country. However, it is not only through these relations that it is possible to explain the transformation processes of the meanings given to the objects of the social world, including the others. In this way, the concepts of foreigners or nations studied by Piaget would be products of operational structures, losing their specificity as social concepts. Operational classification is ahistorical, but social knowledge is historical, variable, and unpredictable. In other words, this knowledge is situated in a world of contingency, of a changing intervention of others on cognitive activity (what Habermas

[1987] called "the revenge of the object"), of historically constituted social practices that structure people's knowledge. Therefore, operational relations cannot capture signification, since, in historical knowledge, conceptual formations cannot be reduced to operational logic.

The ontogenetic transformation of a collective belief cannot be understood in terms of the development of operational reasoning because it is not an inferential process about logical categories, but concepts with specific referents. By contrast, logical categories are generic and universal. The explanatory model that leads to the necessary relations between classes, elaborated by Piaget, does not capture the specificity of a concept such as justice, defined in terms of its relations with other concepts and materialized in the social practices in which children participate. The specificity of generic logical categories allows us to understand the world conceived as scientific knowledge based on mathematics and logic. But it is problematic to apply it to knowledge in the social world, which operates on other logics, whether narrative (Bruner, 1986) or commonsense representations (Moscovici, 1961). In this sense, in order to account for the ontogenesis of social collective beliefs, it seems necessary to attend to the significant aspect of equilibration, considering the inferential processes named dialectical inferences that, according to Piaget (1980), allow for novel articulations of meanings or concepts (Barreiro & Castorina, 2017; Horn et al., 2023).

Is It Possible to Change Social and Historical Knowledge through Educational Interventions? The Case of History Education

Does questioning the explanation of the progression of social and historical knowledge as a function of the passage from one stage or logic of thought to another imply abandoning the assumption of a greater complexity of knowledge? Our answer is no. Let us start with our studies on social knowledge, because history understanding is always intertwined with social issues. Different studies show that knowledge of the social world is transformed toward more complex and abstract forms. Still, such studies also show that more is needed to explain them than appealing to the differences between preoperational and operational reasoning (Barreiro, 2013a, 2013b; Horn, 2021; Horn, Castorina & Barreiro, 2023). In the case of social knowledge, the progressive increase in abstract thinking in the passage from childhood to adolescence requires revising current explanatory models. For example, the meritocratic ideological belief in a just world (Lerner & Clayton, 2010), which refers to people getting what they deserve according to their actions, would be false if analyzed through hypothetico-deductive thinking. Yet, it is present from childhood to adulthood in subjects. Such belief conforms to an overarching explanatory frame for the social process; for example, it becomes essential in commonsense understanding of historical conflicts. Despite its persistence in adulthood, when analyzing its ontogenesis, it was possible to identify inferential processes that indicate increasing levels of abstraction in children's thinking (Barreiro, 2013b). In Piaget's (1980) terms, its ontogenetic developmental process, referring to the elaboration of logical structures, was driven by dialectic inferences, different from logical inferences, since the conclusion does not reiterate the premises, explaining the construction of conceptual novelties. We have identified such processes in the processes of appropriation of the social representations of justice (Barreiro & Castorina, 2017), the ideological belief in a just world (Barreiro, 2013b), and the children's right to intimacy in school (Horn et al., 2023). In the appropriation process of the belief in a just world, appealing to such mechanism, we have identified transformation ranging from the idea that objects can punish wrongdoing in children from 6 to 9 years to justifications based on processes of social reciprocity, from 10 to 17 years. Thus, there is clearly a step from minor to major in increasing conceptual relativization and integration, expressed in a complexification of individuals' arguments. Producing these more complex arguments involves processes of abstraction that reorganize previous ideas but cannot be characterized in terms of a sequence of general stages moving forward a single line of general development for all notions.

This way of understanding the transformations of social knowledge acquires great relevance for thinking about teaching processes. For example, in the processes of knowledge construction by students about historical processes, three different types of knowledge intervene: (1) commonsense knowledge (e.g., social representations, ideologies) proper to children belonging to social groups and which, therefore, are constitutive of their social identity; (2) school knowledge resulting from the didactic transposition (Chevallard, 1985) of scientific knowledge; and (3) knowledge resulting from individual intellectual elaboration when appropriating both. Thus, teachers' work with students' commonsense prior knowledge is not reduced to identifying it to try to eliminate or correct it. Nor is it a matter of making a previous diagnosis independent of the teaching situation; instead, students' knowledge emerges during the didactic situation. Students assimilate the knowledge to be taught according to the knowledge they have, facilitating or hindering their learning. At this point, didactic interventions on commonsense beliefs play a central role. The modification of collective knowledge in the learning knowledge in school depends on the nature of activities organized by the teacher, since the didactic situation defines the encounter between the different types of knowledge, enabling its reconstruction or problematization (Castorina, 2021b).

Now, we have characterized social domain knowledge as polyphasic, as a field in which different meanings coexist about objects of knowledge that may be contradictory to each other and that are highly resistant to change, since they involve the social identity of students. Thus, as we have stated when delimiting the concept of cognitive polyphasia, contradictory representations or beliefs about the same object of knowledge coexist without conflict among them, since they belong to different ways of thinking. The contradictions between them do not occur spontaneously but require the intervention of another, which makes it possible for them to become evident to the subject when they are expressed in his or her discourse. Therefore, constructing such contradictions may intentionally occur through teaching interventions within the framework of specific school contents – that is, in didactic situations. This process can be illustrated by the answers of María, an 8-year-old Mapuche girl, when asked about her knowledge of the Argentine historical process known as the "Conquest of the Desert,"[2] a military campaign carried out by the Argentine state at the end of the 19th century to conquer territories inhabited by indigenous peoples (for further details on this research, see Barreiro et al., 2020; Barreiro et al., 2017; Barreiro, Wainryb, et al., 2016, 2017). María tells us that the "Conquest of the Desert" was something that happened between the Indians [sic] and the people who lived there, and when asked if she thought it was right or wrong what each of those groups did, she answers the following:

> María: (. . .) And the Indians on the one hand. . . bad, because I uh. . . one day I read in a book too, that said that the Indians were good and bad. On the one hand. . . good and. . . on the other. . . bad. *And how would that be?* Let's see, were they good on one side because of what? . . . Let's see, how can I explain it to you? I read it in a book. . . I would say because the. . .

[2] It should be noted that the conquered territory was not a desert; it was inhabited by indigenous people. This type of military campaigns, and their consequences of incorporating enormous amounts of territory and attempting to exterminate the indigenous population, also occurred in other countries of America at the same time. For example, the United States and Canada also followed the same historical path. In other words, such historical process was central in the development of countries that have an influential position in the world today.

> those who were not Indians had stronger huts. And the Indians... on the one hand, I would say that they would fight for that hut. Because... I don't know... every time it rained water would fall [...] Because there are two kinds of Indians, I don't know what, but... My... my grandfather told me that there are two kinds of Indians: one that speaks Mapuche and another one that speaks... I don't know... all kinds... Let's see, how can I say? One part Indian and the other part Mapuche [...] They killed... they killed the horses and lived in tiny huts. *The Indians?* Yes and mhm... the Indians did not kill the horses, the others, the other Indians. *Ah! These two kinds of Indians you were telling me about...*

In María's answers it can be seen how the collective memory, typical of the official narrative of the Argentine state about what happened during the "Conquest of the Desert", which presents indigenous people as violent and uncivilized, whose domination was necessary to consolidate the nation ("the bad Indians"), enters into contradiction with her own experience as a Mapuche ("the good Indians"). At the beginning of her arguments, she becomes aware of the contradiction, moving from one knowledge to another, successively alternating cognitive centrations. This movement leads her to resolve the conflict by differentiating between "two types of Indians": the bad ones, who speak Mapuche; and the good ones, who do not speak Mapuche. María does not speak Mapuche, and although her family is fluent in this language, they do not use it in their daily exchanges. In this way she manages to integrate her previous knowledge into the dialogic intervention, thus constructing a new narrative about what happened during the "Conquest of the Desert." This narrative allows her to coherently include both the existence of "good Indians" and "bad Indians," thus preserving her social identity and the epistemic authority of the version of the past that she legitimizes by saying, "I read it in a book." Both pieces of knowledge are transformed by being integrated into a narrative about the past, which can be interpreted as a "beta" compensatory reaction, taking up the progression of ways of compensating for disturbances identified by Piaget (1975/1985) in the processes of cognitive equilibration. It is an incomplete compensation of the perturbation, which expresses the modification of the system to accommodate it. However, the integration of the disturbance occurs nonsystemically; therefore, it is a compromise solution that only works for a specific case, and does not imply a passage to a state of more stability in knowledge.

At this point, it is necessary to clarify that these interpretations diverge from the original Piagetian theory, given that we are using the theory of equilibration for explaining the process of appropriating collective beliefs, which is very different from the constructive processes of operatory thinking. In addition, the permeability of the knowledge to be taught and the collective beliefs could be more robust because students often tend to anticipate what teachers expect from them without committing or investing their personality in the didactic situation (Castorina, 2021b). It is difficult for students to take the necessary distance from their common sense to be able to problematize their beliefs to produce an epistemological rupture, since they are constitutive of their social identity. Thus, this kind of dialogical interventions on the students' beliefs or social representations usually fails to achieve their modification simply and directly in the teaching process. Their transformation does not follow a linear path toward the knowledge to be taught, wholly stripped of common sense.

Even if they do not abandon their commonsense knowledge, students may reach more complex representations on social and historical processes or recognize the existence of multiple perspectives about them. Moreover, teaching interventions must be aimed at providing more than just new or contradictory information that students already have, since such contradiction does not necessarily imply overcoming it. People already have these contradictory representations; therefore, what is essential is the way of accompanying the problematization of this contradiction, putting it into words within the framework of a dialogic process of making explicit the representations themselves, and, once they have been made explicit, guiding the way to resolve it (Castorina, 2021b).

This example shows how a dialogical intervention aimed at confronting two alternative versions of the same historical process makes it possible for Maria to become aware of the contradiction between her previous knowledge, which she had previously held independently. Recent and extensive reviews (Luis & Rapanta, 2020) and empirical work (Cantabrana & Carretero, 2021; Reisman, 2015) have shown the importance of adopting a dialogical approach in history education, emphasizing the potential of teaching historical issues in a context of constructive controversies and discussion in the classroom. Additional work has pointed to the success of this approach to civic, political, and historical topics (Freedman, 2020; McAvoy & Hess, 2013). Reconstructing knowledge in this field means not having a version of history imposed on students but instead increasing critical thinking. The latter implies that students become aware of their prior knowledge and can integrate it and approach the different ways a historical process or event can be understood. History teaching should be directed not only toward the knowledge of the past but also allow students to understand how the interpretations of what happened intervene in interpreting the present, defining rights and obligations, and supporting the vindictive claims of a particular social group. In this sense, history teaching should be directed toward the relations between the past and the present, looking toward possible futures.

Finally, it is essential to point out that while cognitive polyphasia results from the appropriation of collective knowledge, the interventions carried out at the individual level (ontogenetic) aimed to produce representational changes in students require processes of change at the social level (sociogenetic) aimed to transforming the social representation present in the society in which the students live. It should not be forgotten that states of cognitive polyphasia are expressed in individuals but originate in social contradictions that must also be problematized. In this sense, the dispute between different social representations or ideological beliefs is part of the discussions to be promoted for the conceptual change of social knowledge, which involves teachers taking a position on them (Castorina, 2017).

Acknowledgments

This chapter was carried out in the context of the research group www.histandmem.com, coordinated by the third author. Also, this work was made possible thanks to the Project Making Histories, 101086106, Marie Curie Staff Exchange (EU), and The Spencer Foundation Grant 202400098, "History teaching through dialogical controversies in synergy with documentary films: fostering historical comprehension, identity development and prejudice reduction."

REFERENCES

Barreiro, A. (2012). El desarrollo de las justificaciones del castigo: ¿Conceptualización individual o apropiación de conocimientos colectivos? [The development of justifications for punishment: individual conceptualization or collective knowledge appropriation?] *Estudios de Psicología*, *33*(1), 67–77. https://doi.org/10.1174/021093912799803845.

(2013a). The ontogenesis of social representation of justice: Personal conceptualization and social constraints. *Papers on Social Representations*, *22*, 13.1–13.26. https://psr.iscte-iul.pt/index.php/PSR/article/view/327.

(2013b). The appropriation process of the belief in a just world. *Integrative Psychological and Behavioral Sciences*, *47*, 431–449. https://doi.org/10.1007/s12124-013-9246-y.

Barreiro, A., & Castorina, J. A. (2012). Desafíos a la versión clásica del desarrollo en las investigaciones sobre el juicio moral [Challenging the classic version of development in moral judgement research]. *Infancia y Aprendizaje*, *35*(4), 471–481. https://doi.org/10.1174/021037012803495302.

(2017). Dialectical inferences in the ontogenesis of social representations. *Theory & Psychology*, *27*(1), 34–49. https://doi.org/10.1177/0959354316681863.

Barreiro, A., Castorina, J. A., & Van Alphen, F. (2017). Conflicting narratives about the Argentinean 'Conquest of the Desert': Social representations, cognitive polyphasia, and nothingness. In M. Carretero, S. Berger, & M. Grever (Eds.), *Palgrave handbook of research in historical culture and education* (pp. 373–389). London: Palgrave Macmillan.

Barreiro, A., Ungaretti, J., Etchezahar, E., & Wainryb, C. (2020). "They are not truly indigenous people": Social representations and prejudice against indigenous people in Argentine. *Papers on Social Representations*, *29*(1), 6.1–6.24.

Barreiro, A., Wainryb, C., & Carretero, M. (2016). Narratives about the past and cognitive polyphasia remembering the Argentine "Conquest of the Desert". *Peace & Conflict*, *22*(1), 44–51. https://doi.org/10.1037/pac0000150.

(2017). Power struggles in the remembering of historical intergroup conflict: Hegemonic and counter-narratives about the Argentine 'Conquest of the Desert'. In C. Psaltis, M. Carretero, & S. Cehajic-Clancy (Eds.), *History teaching and conflict transformation: Social psychological theories, history teaching and reconciliation* (pp. 125–145). New York: Springer. https://link.springer.com/book/10.1007/978-3-319-54681-0.

Berti, A. (1994). Children's understanding of the concept of the state. In M. Carretero & J. F. Voss (Eds.), *Cognitive and instructional process in history and social sciences* (pp. 49–76). Mahwah, NJ: Lawrence Erlbaum Associates.

Bruner, J. (1986). *Actual minds, possible worlds*. Cambridge, MA: Harvard University Press.

Cantabrana, M., & Carretero, M. (2021). Theatre of war: Lola Arias' documentary theatre as innovative tool for historical dialogue. In M. Carretero, M. Rodríguez-Moneo, M. Cantabrana, & C. Parellada (Eds.), *History education in the digital age* (pp. 217–234). New York: Springer.

Carretero, M., & Bermudez, A. (2012). Constructing histories. In J. Valsiner (Ed.), *Oxford handbook of culture and psychology* (pp. 622–648). Oxford: Oxford University Press.

Castorina, J. A. (2005). La investigación psicológica de los conocimientos sociales. Los desafíos a la tradición constructivista. [Psychological research of social knowledge: Challenges to the constructivist tradition] In J. A. Castorina (Ed.), *Construcción conceptual y representaciones sociales. El conocimiento de la sociedad [Conceptual construction and social representations: Knowledge of society]* (pp. 19–44). Buenos Aires: Miño & Dávila.

(2010). The ontogenesis of social representations: A dialectic perspective. *Papers on Social Representations*, *19*, 18.1–18.19. https://psr.iscte-iul.pt/index.php/PSR/article/view/397.

(2017). Relationships between revisited genetic psychology and the theory of social representations: A critical analysis. *Papers on Social Representations*, *26*(1), 5.1–5.22. https://psr.iscte-iul.pt/index.php/PSR/article/view/86.

(2021a). The importance of world-views for developmental psychology. *Human Arenas, 1*, 1–19. https://doi.org/10.1007/s42087-020-00115-9.
(2021b). El estudio de las representaciones sociales en el contexto didáctico. In A. Roso, P. A. Guareschi, A. Novaes, A. Accorssi, & C. dos Santos Goncalves (Eds.), *Mundos sem fronteiras. Representações sociais e práticas psicosociais* (pp. 385–413). Porto Alegre: Abrapso.
Castorina, J. A., & Baquero, R. (2005). *Dialéctica y psicología del desarrollo. El pensamiento de Piaget y Vigotsky* [*Dialectics and developmental psychology. The thought of Piaget and Vigotsky.*]. Buenos Aires: Amorrortu.
Castorina, J. A., & Barreiro, A. (2010). El proceso de individuación de las representaciones sociales: historia y reformulación de un problema. *Revista Interdisciplinaria, 27*(1), 63–75.
(2023). *The development of social knowledge: Towards a cultural-individual dialectic.* Charlotte, NC: Information Age Publishing.
Castorina, J. A., Barreiro, A., & Carreño, L. (2010). El concepto de Polifasia cognitiva en el estudio del cambio conceptual. In M. Carretero & J. A. Castorina (Eds.), *La construcción del conocimiento histórico Enseñanza, narración e identidades* (pp. 131–151). Buenos Aires: Paidós.
Castorina, J. A., Barreiro, A., Horn, A., Carreño, L., Lombardo, E., & Karabelnicoff, D. (2009). Las restricciones en la construcción de ideas sociales: revisión de un concepto, *Revista Irice, 20*, 79–88.
Castorina, J. A., & Faigenbaum, G. (2003). The epistemological meaning of constraints in the development of domain knowledge. *Theory & Psychology, 12*(3), 315–334. https://doi.org/10.1177/0959354302012003O.
Chevallard, Y. (1985). *La transposition didactique*. Grenoble: Le Pensée Savage
Deconchy, J. P. (1985). Sistemas de creencias y representaciones ideológicas [Belief systems and ideological representations]. In S. Moscovici (Ed.), *Psicología social II [Social psychology II]* (pp. 439–468). Barcelona: Paidós.
Delval, J. (1994). Stages in children's construction of social knowledge. In M. Carretero & J. Voss (Eds.), *Cognitive and structural process in history and social sciences* (pp. 77–102). Mahwah, NJ: Lawrence Erlbaum.
Doise, W. (1982). *L'explication en psychologie sociale*. Paris: PUF.
Duveen, G. (1994). Children as social actors: Social representations in development. In P. Guareschi & S. Jovchelovitch (Eds.), *Textos em Representaçôes Sociais [Texts in social representations]* (pp. 261–296). Petrópolis: Vozes.
Duveen, G., & De Rosa, A. (1992). Social representations and the genesis of social knowledge. *Papers on Social Représentations, 1*(2–3), 94–108. https://psr.iscte-iul.pt/index.php/PSR/article/view/95.
Duveen, G., & Lloyd, B. (1990). A semiotic analysis of the development of social representation of gender. In G. Duveen & B. Lloyd (Eds.), *Social representations and the development of knowledge* (pp. 27–46). Cambridge: Cambridge University Press.
Ferreiro, E., & Teberosky, A. (1991). *Los sistemas de escritura en el desarrollo del niño [Writing systems in child development].* México: Siglo XXI.

Freedman, E. B. (2020). When discussions sputter or take flight: Comparing productive disciplinary engagement in two history classes. *Journal of the Learning Sciences*, *29*(3), 385–429.

García, R. (2002). *El conocimiento en construcción. De las formulaciones de Jean Piaget a la teoría de los sistemas complejos. [Knowledge under construction: From Jean Piaget's formulations to the theory of complex systems]*. Buenos Aires: Gedisa.

Habermas, J. (1987). *La lógica de la Ciencias Sociales. [The logic of social sciences.]* Madrid: Tecnos.

Horn, A. (2021). What ideas do boys and girls construct about their right to privacy at school? *Educação e Pesquisa*, *47*. https://doi.org/10.1590/S1678-4634202147237848.

Horn, A., Castorina, J. A., & Barreiro, A. (2023). Dialectical inferences in the construction of social domain knowledge. *Human Arenas*. https://doi.org/10.1007/s42087-023-00341-x.

Jahoda, G. (1979). The construction of economic reality by some Glaswegian children. *European Journal of Social Psychology*, *9*, 115–127. https://doi.org/10.1002/ejsp.2420090202.

Leman, P. (1998). Social relations, social influence and the development of knowledge. *Papers on Social Representations*, *7*(1–2), 41–56. www.psych.lse.ac.uk/psr/PSR1998/7_1998Leman.pdf.

Leman, P. J., & Duveen, G. (1996). Developmental differences in children's understanding of epistemic authority. *European Journal of Social Psychology*, *26*(5), 683–702. https://doi.org/10.1002/(SICI)1099-0992(199609)26:5<683::AID-EJSP779>3.0.CO;2-R.

Lerner, M., & Clayton, S. (2010). *Justice and self-interest: Two fundamental motives*. Cambridge: Cambridge University Press.

Lloyd, B., & Duveen, G. (1990). A semiotic analysis of the development of social representations of gender. In G. Duveen & B. Lloyd (Eds.), *Social representations and the development of knowledge* (pp. 27–46). Cambridge: Cambridge University Press.

Luis, R., & Rapanta, C. (2020). Towards (re-)defining historical reasoning competence: A review of theoretical and empirical research. *Educational Research Review*, *31*, 100336.

McAvoy, P., & Hess, D. (2013). Classroom deliberation in an era of political polarization. *Curriculum Inquiry*, *43*(1), 14–47.

Marková, I. (2010). Gerard Duveen on the epistemology of social representations. *Papers on Social Representations*, *19*, 4.1–4.9. www.psych.lse.ac.uk/psr.

Martí, E. (2012). Thinking with signs: From symbolic actions to external systems of representations. In E. Martí & C. Rodríguez (Eds.), *After Piaget* (pp. 151–170). Piscataway, NJ: Transaction Publishers.

Moscovici, S. (1961). *La psychanalyse son image et son public*. Paris: PUF.

Overton, W. F. (2006). Developmental psychology: Philosophy, concepts, methodology. In R. M. Lerner (Ed.), *Theoretical models of human development: Handbook of child psychology* (pp. 18–88). Hoboken, NJ: Wiley.

Piaget, J. (1932/1948). *The moral judgment of the child.* New York: Free Press.
(1959/1999). *Play, dreams and imitation in childhood.* London: Routledge.
(1975/1985). *The equilibration of cognitive structures: The central problem of intellectual development.* Chicago: University of Chicago Press.
(1980). *Les formes elementaires de la dialectique* [The elementary forms of the dialectic]. Paris: Gallimard.
Piaget, J., & García, R. (1989). *Psychogenesis and the history of science.* New York: Columbia University.
Piaget, J., & Weil, A. M. (1951). The development in children of the idea of homeland and of relations with other countries. *International Social Sciences Bulletin, 3*(3), 561–578.
Psaltis, C. (2015). Genetic social psychology: From microgenesis to ontogenesis, sociogenesis ... and back. In C. Psaltis, A. Gillespie, & A. N. P. Perret-Clermont (Eds.), *Social relations in human and societal development* (pp. 71–94). London: Palgrave Macmillan.
(2024). Genesis y estructura: un cuento de dos ciudades y la Psicología Social Genética [*Genesis and structure: a tale of two cities and Genetic Social Psychology*]. In A. Barreiro & M. Carretero (Eds.), *La construcción del conocimiento en el campo psicológico. Celebrando a Tono Castorina I [The construction of knowledge in the psychological field. Celebrating Tono Castorina I]* (pp. 141–164). Buenos Aires: Tilde.
Psaltis, C., & Duveen, G. (2006). Social relations and cognitive development: The influence of conversation type and representations of gender. *European Journal of Social Psychology, 36*, 407–430.
(2007). Conservation and conversation types: Forms of recognition and cognitive development. *British Journal of Developmental Psychology, 25*, 79–102. https://doi.org/10.1348/026151005X91415.
Psaltis, C., & Zapiti, A. (2014). *Interaction, communication and development: Psychological development as a social process.* London: Routledge.
Reisman, A. (2015). Entering the historical problem space: Whole class, text-based discussion in history class. *Teachers College Record, 117*(2), 1–44.
Smetana, J., Jabom, M., & Ball, C. (2014). The social domain approach to children's moral and social judgements. In M. Killen & J. Smetana (Eds.), *Handbook of moral development* (pp. 23–45). Abingdon: Taylor & Francis.
Smetana, J., & Villalobos, M. (2009). Social cognitive development in adolescence. In R. Lerner & L. Steinberg (Eds.), *Handbook of adolescent psychology: Individual bases of adolescent development* (Vol. 1, pp. 187–228). Hoboken, NJ: Wiley.
Turiel, E. (1983). *The development of social knowledge: Morality and convention.* Cambridge: Cambridge University Press.
Valsiner, J. (1997). *Culture and the development of children's action.* Hoboken, NJ: Wiley and Sons.
Wagner, W., Duveen G., Verma, J., & Themel, M. (2006). Polyphasie cognitive et transformations culturelles Cognitive polyphasia and cultural transformations]. In V. Hass (Ed.), *Les saviors du quotidian. Transmissions,*

appropriations, répresentations [Everyday knowledge. Transmissions, appropriations, representations] (pp. 157–172). Rennes: Presses Universitaires de Rennes.

Wagner, W., & Hayes, N. (2005). *Everyday discourse and common sense: The theory of social representations*. London: Palgrave Macmillan.

Conclusion: Rejoinder

Charis Psaltis

Introduction

I would first like to thank all the contributors for their commentaries and their thoughtful reflections, insights and critiques. I found all commentaries extremely useful in helping me to sharpen my proposal for a genetic social psychology. The development and presentation of the genetic social psychology framework have been a journey of intellectual exploration that started together with some of the colleagues that offered their commentaries whilst all pursuing our studies in Cambridge University in the 'triangle' reading group in the period 2000–2005. In this group, with Alex Gillespie, Flora Cornish and Tania Zittoun, we would discuss classical texts of psychology (mostly social and developmental psychology, American pragmatism and epistemology) all under the direct or indirect influence of the late Gerard Duveen. Later, Brady Wagoner would also join our discussions in this reading group. Some of these earlier explorations were published as Psaltis (2005), Zittoun et al. (2003), Zittoun and Psaltis (2006) and Zittoun et al. (2007) and more recently in Power et al. (2023).

In Part I of this volume I outlined the pressing need for an interdisciplinary social and developmental psychology with historical depth, poised to address the complexities of societal change and human development that can come into dialogue with anthropology, politics, sociology, economics and cultural evolution. What I propose as genetic social psychology is a holistic approach to understanding human development and societal change through a historical lens that integrates insights from key theorists like Piaget, Vygotsky, Moscovici, the social Genevans, Furth and Duveen, among others. Genetic social psychology emphasises the need for a multidimensional analysis that includes the intrapersonal, interpersonal, intergroup, ideological and inter-societal levels of analysis.

I believe that in the 21st century, considering the nature of polycrisis mentioned by Gillespie (Chapter 7 in this volume), such a discipline can contribute meaningfully to both understanding and changing the societal dynamics, marked by increasing conflict, inequalities, fragmentation and the spread of misinformation. My proposal is based on the case study of the Cyprus conflict. This deeply divided society in the Eastern Mediterranean where east meets west, Christians meet Muslims and share an island is a case study to explore a situation beyond what Henrich (2015, 2020) calls WEIRD societies. Cyprus, with its conflicting past, offers many opportunities to study various developmental pathways in a rapidly changing society (especially after joining of the EU in 2004) with a mix of characteristics that are neither eastern nor western (Uskul et al., 2023). However, I identify three distinct microgenetic paths as processes of social representing that I believe are universal, as they are based on the quality of human social relationships that can essentially take three forms independent of any part of the world one finds themselves in: (1) the submissive-traditional, (2) the dominant-individualist and (3) the co-operative.

In each society or country all pathways of development can be found, but some become more or less likely depending on the external inter-societal relationships, internal political economy of a country and the level of socio-economic development and historical trajectory of each society, with family, education (formal, informal and non-formal) and the media being the epicentres of socialisation. These three pathways are directly mediated by attachment style in infancy, parenting styles (authoritarian, laissez faire, authoritative), family dynamics, in-group norms (family, school and the wider context), threats and specific value priorities and configurations. In-group norms and intergroup contact regulate how wide the ethical horizon of an individual becomes, as well as collective identifications.

Ontogenetically, there are developmental constraints on how wide the ethical horizon is in the period from birth to age 10–11 years, but after this age the 'group nous' (Abrams et al., 2009) and quantity and quality of intergroup contact will regulate how wide or narrow the horizon of each individual will actually be. The role of history teaching and values attached to it is crucial, as it regulates semantic contact with the out-group perspective (Gillespie, 2020) and has a key role in formulating the developmental pathway to be taken in each nation state. The traditional submissive position is supported by one-sided victimisation narratives and religiosity which forms part–whole relations where the individual is submitted to the group. The domination-individualist one is a position where the individual–group part–whole relationship tilts towards an unchecked individualism, egocentrism and machiavellianism. The co-operative is the position of mutual respect at the interpersonal level, equality at the inter-group level and balance between the individual and the group in part–whole relations (Piaget, 1995).

Sociogenetic changes in historical time (period and cohort effects) of social representations largely depend on exogenous factors to the individual (war, ethnic conflict, geopolitics, economic development and relations of production, urbanisation, diminant denomination of religion in each country and how central religion is in society as an institution). However, changes in values can also support the emergence of new norms and institutions following the opposite evolutionary path (Henrich, 2020).

The real challenge, and the most complex task ahead for this proposal, is the innovation of new methods of data collection that will do justice to the study of the articulation of the processes of microgenesis, ontogenesis and sociogenesis in real-world contexts. Through the various commentaries run some common threads to which I would like to offer a rejoinder that follows.

Epistemological Issues, Different Developmental Pathways and Domains: Is There Linear Development?

In the commentaries by Marková (Chapter 6), Gillespie (Chapter 7), Zittoun (Chapter 8) and Barreiro et al. (Chapter 13) there seems to be the critique that given the strong Piagetian basis of genetic social psychology, we need to abandon the assumption of linear development. Marková views the dialectic epistemologies of Piaget and Goldmann I discussed in Part I as emphasising evolution and the transformation of knowledge. Just like the dialectic of Marx or Hegel, they assume the hierarchical development of less advanced into more progressive stages. These kinds of dialectic are based on the idea that evolutions and histories strive towards predetermined goals. For Piaget, the dialectic hierarchical progression is completed when the child achieves formal operations. Marková rejects this epistemological stance and proposes the alternative of an open-ended dialogical epistemology that rejects both the predetermined end of development and the hierarchies. She situates Moscovici's and Duveen's work in this camp. I think this argument is premised on collapsing ontogenetic and sociogenetic processes that need to be differentiated.

It is interesting to note that usually theoreticians do not challenge the notion of less or more advanced, progressed or powerful knowledge in discussions about ontogenesis of human beings. Even if they reject the idea of stage-like development and that the end state is what Piaget proposed as formal operational stage, they would still espouse some kind of more powerful knowledge in a trajectory from less to more differentiation, one-sided to more multi-perspectival view of the world and less to more complex understandings (Zittoun & Gillespie, 2022). It seems to be accepted that we expect and indeed find differences in cognitive and emotional development from birth to adulthood. It would simply be absurd to suggest otherwise, as it would be tantamount to disregarding the findings of developmental psychology.

When we move to sociogenesis, however, the issue can certainly be contested, and we should recognise that change is an open-ended process with no predetermined end, as it depends on the quality of norms and institutions and the kind of subject–object–other configurations they sustain. Nevertheless, certain structural historical changes (e.g. economic development, urbanisation, setting up institutions of formal education) as suggested by Patricia Greenfield can have predictable changes in the values of communities, quality of social relationships and learning environments (Greenfield, 2009). We argue this takes place through the mediating role of changes in the quality of social relationships between people or changes in the microgenetic processes of *subject–object–other* configurations within and between groups. In this sense Duveen was right to claim that microgenesis is the motor for ontogenesis and sociogenesis.

Protesting the idea of historical progress seems legitimate when stage-like ideas from the individual level of analysis are projected onto whole groups or countries to serve powerful group's interests, raising the spectre of ethnocentric or even racist views. It is when forms of knowing become an instrument for human rights violations, submission, domination or exploitation (e.g. colonialism, imperialism) that people legitimately object to the notion of more and less progressed knowledge.

From a process account of social representations (significant structures as forms of representing) like the one of genetic social psychology, there is no basis for one-to-one linkages between the three basic structural ways of representing that we identified (submission, domination, co-operation) and any collectivity, because these forms of representing can be identified in different institutions or social networks in various countries of the world, albeit in different proportions in varying domains of social life. For example, most countries have hierarchical institutions like the army. In such institutions in-group norms sustain forms of submission and domination, and to deny this would amount to negating the possibility of any ideological critique of institutions within each country or nation state.

In some domains of knowledge, especially under conditions of central control by governments like history teaching, it is again possible to locate a greater emphasis on submission to a romantic kind of master narrative controlled by a central authority. Barreiro, Castorina and Carretero (Chapter 13) offer a critique of traditional divisions in psychology. Their commentary underscores the need for a more integrated approach that bridges the often-artificial divides between cognitive, social and emotional domains of human experience. Their discussion of domain-specific vs. domain-general knowledge is very insightful and allows for further deepening of some of the connections between representations of the past or history and Piagetian thinking. The tension between domain-specific and domain-general knowledge is similarly discussed in some of the recent work by Zittoun et al. (2023), who propose that in adult learning and development both the processes of differentiation and distanciation are crucial. The process of differentiation and progressive integration entails some notion of development. In contrast to normative propositions, the 'norm' ('better' expertise or knowledge) is given by a criterion related to the system itself: it is about the acquisition of more stability of the system (e.g. equilibrium) or towards – at least locally – more stable organisation. The process of distanciation through semiotic elaboration can be said to occur on three main dimensions: progressive generalisation, relation to time and imagination (Zittoun et al., 2023).

In the case of representations of the past and history teaching, differentiation and distanciation from the concrete in a domain could be threatening to the self or collective identity. As a consequence, the potential for generalisation and more abstract thinking is obstructed. History teaching is a very good example. For example, in Cyprus a narration that threatens the master narrative which relativises the pain or the perspectives of the two communities would cause resistance to be accepted, and thus a multiperspective structure of thinking would become more difficult to achieve in this case. In contrast, in the case of mathematics, such resistances are somewhat less likely albeit not impossible as we know from the work of Guida de Abreau under the supervision of Gerard Duveen. As Barreiro et al. posit, this is an instance in which thinking cannot be separated from contents, or from the activities of which they are a part. The activities in this case could be school nationalist commemorations, reenactments of collective victimisation or participation in collective activities that serve national or patriotic interest and vindication. This would be an enunciation of what Barreiro et al. find in Piagetian thinking as precausal and transductive thinking according to which reasoning is constructed by going from particular cases to particular cases, without recourse to universality or logical necessity. As they say, there could be necessity here, but it would be the necessity to support the nation state and its cause, not a logical necessity. Agreement with this approach steers clear of the murky waters of postmodern relativism, as it recognises that this necessity to support the nation state through this instrumentalisation of history teaching will be consequential for various other dimensions of the significant structure under formation. In this way it fundamentally changes the way students will construct their collective self, feelings of threat, prejudice, distrust and a value system, in a way that undermines their critical thinking (Bermúdez, Chapter 12 in this volume).

Genetic social psychology is certainly not in favour of cultural relativism or postmodern ideas of the kind that 'everything goes'. On the contrary, one of the main aims of genetic social psychology, as mentioned by Gillespie (Chapter 7 in this volume), is emancipatory, to bring to the surface the submerged part of the iceberg of these significant structures so that a critical distance can be taken towards them and act on the world on the basis of the consequences of each one for human and societal development.

A particular example of the genetic social psychology perspective on this issue can be given from the sphere of history teaching in Canada. In 2015, the Truth and Reconciliation Commission of Canada (TRC) identified that education plays a central role in developing new, reconciliatory relationships between Aboriginal and non-Aboriginal peoples. This education would involve learning about residential schools and their assimilationist policies but would have a broader focus on transforming education into a place where Indigenous experiences would be integrated, racism and coloniality would be rejected, and equal respect for Indigenous and Western epistemologies could be demonstrated (TRC, 2015b).

The aim of reflecting on history teaching in Canada for reconciliation in this case is certainly praiseworthy; however, the reference to 'Indigenous and Western epistemologies' seems to me to be flirting with cultural relativism which can in fact end up undermining the aim of reconciliation in the first place. It seems like a recipe for 'fighting' colonialism by paradoxically appropriating its ideological machinery of essentialist thinking. For example, some Indigenous scholars, such as Marker (2011), claim that Western historiographies with an emphasis on historical evidence, human agency, progress and modernity disregard Indigenous understandings of the process of time and principles of ecological knowledge systems. Marker has identified four characteristics of Indigenous ways of knowing: (1) the circular nature of time and ways of telling oral histories, with recurring events merged in a non-linear fashion; (2) the central relationship between humans, landscape and animals as a source of knowledge and wisdom; (3) the emphasis on local landscape as containing the full meaning of time and place; and (4) Indigenous narratives as both physical and metaphysical journeys that challenge histories of colonization.

As rightly pointed out by both Peter Seixas (2012) and Stephan Levesque (2016, 2017), the historical thinking approach in Canada is well suited to develop the narrative competence of students by incorporating the voices and perspectives of aboriginals in teaching. But this, I would add, in no way implies accepting any voice or narration as true without evaluation or because the tradition and the chiefs of the community present it as 'true'. The historical approach should not be downgraded to a 'heritage' approach that essentialises the culture, historical consciousness or epistemology of aboriginals. First, as I mentioned in the previous paragraph, we should never assume homogeneity of any form of representing (submission, domination, co-operation) in any collectivity, and in that sense there is no homogeneous aboriginal culture, historical consciousness or epistemology, as there is no homogeneous western culture, historical consciousness or epistemology. In fact, when such an in-group–out-group grammar is evoked, essentialist identities imbued with feelings of realistic and symbolic threat take the upper hand that furthers antagonism, competition and conflict between the groups, taking us far away from the goal of reconciliation.

The words of Moscovici (1993) from his acceptance speech of the honorary PhD he was awarded from the university of Seville with the title "Reason and Cultures" here are germane:

> All cultures have good reasons, past, present or future, to believe they are incomparable. And indeed, they are. But when it is stated that they are so because of their identity, because of their mentality, because of their ethnocentrism or because of their incommensurability, or because of any type of attributions of the same style, deep down, it starts from the principle that they are separable or that they only see in the others what distinguishes them, defining themselves outside of all reflexibility. As if they kept asking themselves Goethe's question: 'How can I be myself if another exists?' which arouses the desire for absolute singularity or irreconcilable difference. For such a difference can only reveal fragility, hide the obsession of a closed 'self'. Organizing collective memory, transforming history into an instrument in charge of legitimizing separation, continues to be a permanent temptation.

The application of relations of co-operation could overcome essentialist ways of thinking and could fruitfully encompass a number of policies: (1) a joint committee for the writing of history textbooks by both Indigenous and Euro-Canadians; (2) the promotion of multi-perspectivity in history teaching; (3) reflecting on master narratives of various groups and their role in promoting essentialist identities, threats and prejudice; and (4) the role of colonialism, nationalism and various other 'isms' in instrumentalising narratives of the past for submission, domination and exploitation, and (5) mutual interactions and influence on values, and ideas and practices through contacts between members of different groups.

Marková (Chapter 6) also criticises the hierarchy of knowledge forms in the dialectical epistemologies of Piaget and Goldmann, proposing as an alternative the idea of heterarchy from Moscovici's work. Heterarchies are defined as decentralised organisations which safeguard a degree of freedom and establish reflexive relationships among components of the system. Here there seems to be a collapse of two different types of hierarchies into one. A hierarchy of knowledge, however, is altogether different from hierarchies relating to part–whole relationships in groups, so there is no reason why rejecting the one should also mean rejecting the other.

One of the major challenges for genetic social psychology is the articulation of these two types of hierarchies through microgenetic processes. This is something that we have explored experimentally with Duveen around social representations of gender and social interaction on Piagetian tasks between asymmetrical dyads in terms of knowledge on the same tasks in same and mixed sex dyads (Psaltis & Duveen, 2006, 2007). But even if the intention of Marková in her commentary is to reiterate Moscovici's reluctance to place scientific knowledge on top of common-sense knowledge, one has to recognise that from a processual account of *social representing*, Moscovici does favour more reflective and decentred ways of representing otherness. This is clear in his studies of representations of Gypsies with Perez (Moscovici, 2011) and his masterful talk for his honorary doctorate at the University of Seville quoted above (Moscovici, 1993) that we take as aligned with our idea (Psaltis, 2012) that a hierarchy of knowledge can be located in ways of thinking within cultures but not between cultures, since cultures are not homogeneous entities.

I thank Ivana for reminding me of the work by Galam and Moscovici (1991, 1994, 1995) because I believe there is a lot of inspiration to be taken from this work in unifying Moscovici's genetic models of social influence with his social representations theory, an idea discussed by Marková (2021) herself elsewhere. I take the main message of this work to be the importance of 'asymmetry breaking' as the process that leads to individual and societal innovations. Their complex systems way of thinking reminds us that there are processes of emergence at the group level that we need to account for on the basis of social interactions or social influence between people. In our work with Duveen we revealed exactly this complex process of emergence of a co-operative relationship in conditions of conflicting asymmetries of knowledge and status in what we identified as the 'Fm' effect. This was when non-conserving boys were interacting with conserving girls (6–8-year-olds). In these interactions we observed longer discussions, more socio-cognitive conflict, but also forms of intersubjectivity that entailed reflection and novelty (Psaltis & Duveen, 2006, 2007; Duveen & Psaltis, 2008). More recently, in the context of intergroup contact in Cyprus, we applied an agent-based model (ABM) that simulated interaction between members of the two communities projecting aggregate reductions in prejudice at the communal level on the basis of varying impact of contact in prejudice reduction and percentage of people crossing the checkpoints.[1] There is certainly much more to be done in terms of capturing the complexity of transformations with the help of systems or complexity theory, and we have started exploring some of this complexity by mapping belief networks using a new method proposed by Carpentras et al. (2021).

The vision of Galam and Moscovici can easily be extended to be tested with ABM, as it includes agents who have internalised norms and social representations in various degrees. This internalisation creates a personal field that orients the agents into certain beliefs or actions. At the same time in-group norms create pressures to conform to certain beliefs or actions. One source of influence is a central authority figure (leader of a state, god, etc.) with which an aggregate of individuals may comply even if they do not actually interact with each other. Another source of influence is the idea of a small group where individuals know each other and interact on a regular basis. These two forms of social influence according to their view lead to two different forms of polarisation. They also identify three forms of power corresponding to three phases of group organisation that they call the 'paradigmatic, transitional and agonal' stages. Small groups can be seen as the prototypical case where conformity to in-group norms is the usual function. Then, as the group becomes bigger in a transitional stage, there is more conflict which leads to the emergence of power in the form of central forms of authority demanding compliance or conformity without the need for direct social interaction between members of the in-group. Finally, once groups learn to be resilient to conflict and appreciate diversity for its

[1] The model can be run from: https://modelingcommons.org/browse/one_model/7189#model_tabs_browse_in.

generativity and innovation, then, in the agonal stage, conformity pressure lessens and reflexivity, novelty and innovation are favoured by conflicts of perspectives in societies. It could be argued that our post-industrial societies are now at this agonal stage where our historical wager is to promote the co-operative position described in Table 2.1, which overcomes the Scylla of submission-traditional and the Charybdis of rugged individualism-domination.

In the same 'Reason and Cultures' speech, Moscovici (1993) had a chance to explain with clarity the relationship between rationality and culture. He reiterated that we need a social psychology which resembles an anthropology of our everyday lives aiming to know how people elaborate their culture, resist it or dominate it. This is something that justifies a line of 'genetic research', as he says, and something that we described as the need for the study of part–whole relations in this book. It is a line of research capable of describing and understanding cultures when they are being developed. Once again, in this talk he believes there is something important in the ideas of Lévy-Bruhl regarding the opposition between collective representations stemming from beliefs and representations based on knowledge. He sees this distinction as constituting the seed of a social psychology of belief that can be verified and applied, which will give it its main attraction. We see asymmetrical relations as largely promoting representations based on belief and co-operative symmetrical social relations as largely promoting representations based on knowledge. However, real social interactions are always messy and are formulated as co-operative or asymmetrical in the process of negotiating various knowledge and status asymmetries in social interaction (Psaltis, 2005; Duveen & Psaltis, 2008).

The challenge for Moscovici consists in replacing what has been learned by comparing societies and cultures with each other with the most vivid contrast that exists within a society – a culture that is within ours and includes both representations based on belief and representations based on knowledge. What we need to do with our genetic approach, he argues, is to follow the transformations of one into another in order to capture the transformations of society and culture in themselves. Duveen (2007/2013) saw culture as a system of social representations, and in his last paper (Duveen, 2008) he further extended this discussion about heterogeneity in our current societies by proposing that the three communicative genres identified by Moscovici in the second part of his book on psychoanalysis support three different types of social groups. Propagation supports a way of relating that he calls communion, propaganda supports a group based on solidarity, and diffusion supports a group based on sympathy. For him this was a way to challenge the notion of a social group which became mainstream due to Tajfel's Social Identity Theory. The way to overcome the homogenisation of the notion of culture and nationalism or racism that promotes such homogenising notions of the collective is not only to recognise the heterogeneity of communicative genres or positions in the representational field of each community, country or society but, maybe more importantly, to render intelligible the processes of internal transformation from one position to the other (Psaltis, 2012). We see the proposal in this book as offering one possible answer to this challenge.

In this book what I proposed as submission, domination and co-operation can also be seen as being supported by different communicative genres or types of social groups. They are all living generative representations. They are not a 'representation of the world' but '*for* the world' as Moscovici (1993) argues. Even if the elements of each configuration are fleeting and illusory, they keep form, meaning and power of action that converge in a social reality. Different forms of historical consciousness relating to each position regulate connection between past, present and future orientations in different ways.

Social Representations and Conflict Transformation: The Role of Emotions

Both Zittoun (Chapter 8) and Alexopoulos (Chapter 9) suggest that genetic social psychology engages more closely with the role of emotions. Zittoun reproaches me when I claim that there is no place in genetic social psychology for individuation, as she argues that 'genetic social psychology can only account for human development if it accounts both for the development of knowledge and the development of person who builds, experiences, feels and lives through that knowledge'. Let me first give some context to my claim on individuation. I was referring to a word used by Castorina (2010) in one of his two commentaries on Duveen's work and genetic social psychology. Castorina (2010) wrote in his commentary something that both Patrick Leman (2010) and myself (Psaltis, 2024) found objectionable: he wrote about 'the significance of some of his [Duveen's] empirical studies which link psychological development to social identity' as describing a process of individuation in social psychology.

Leman (2010) replying to Castorina wrote that to cast the individual as a unit of theoretical interest is a mistake: the individual is often necessarily an empirical focus, but development is, always, a social process according to Duveen (1997/2013). This was the sense in which I wrote that there is no place in Duveen's writing where the process of internalising social representations could be described as individuation, and thus there is no place in genetic social psychology for individuation. There are at least two reasons for this: (1) Duveen was describing the process of the ontogenesis of social representations as the emergence of the social actor and the internalisation of a social identity, not a personal or ego identity – Duveen was interested in the social-psychological and not the psychological subject; (2) even in the original genetic psychology of Piaget his research interest was with the epistemic subject which is not an individual subject but a mere abstraction dealing with the coordination of actions irrespective of whether these take place intra- or interpersonally. In other words, the study of idiosyncratic or individual trajectories of individuals did not seem to be the priority for Duveen despite his own interest in psychoanalysis and the ethnographic method. There is no doubt that what is proposed by Zittoun in her study of diaries or Valsiner as idiographic science can offer a lot of insights in the service of developing our understanding of the articulation of microgenesis, ontogenesis and sociogenesis, but, at least for me, this is one of the various methodologies to help in this articulation and not an aim in itself. Indeed, I see the autobiographical method that I proposed in this book as valuable in helping to realise some important points about this articulation: (1) The image of Varoshia as 'hostage' in my early childhood is acting as a guiding principle for the rest of my life. My efforts to build the home for co-operation in the buffer zone could be seen as some kind of substitute for the loss of my home. (2) Technological innovation is crucial in life trajectories. Would I have been in a position to locate Duveen and his work and eventually study with him were it not for the internet that just appeared and made possible my locating his work. (3) Hierarchical relationships not only have superficial influence on people but can actually lead to the opposite results. Hazing in the army in Greece led me to develop a distaste for hierarchies and the army itself.

My autobiographical analysis also shows that both Zittoun and Alexopoulos are correct in requesting further integration of emotions in my theoretical framework. Although I am personally not vested in psychoanalysis in any way, it is important to recognise that foundational ideas for the formation of genetic social psychology directly relate to Freud's work through the influence of Hans Furth on Duveen. As I showed in Chapter 1 of this book, Furth, who was Duveen's first supervisor, was a psychoanalyst and offered Duveen a vision of genetic social psychology of the need to insert a role of identity/social relational dynamics in knowledge construction. I believe Duveen's turn to the study of social interaction and cognitive development in that sense was no coincidence. For him to understand the role of social interaction in cognitive development was a way to understand the role of emotions in cognitive development also. In fact, I was struck by some of the arguments made by Piaget in his *Intelligence and Affectivity*. He used the exact same argument about the role of emotions in cognitive development with the role of social interaction in cognitive development when commenting on the work of the social Genevans' (Doise, Mugny & Perret-Clermont, 1976) in the special issue for his 80th birthday (see Psaltis & Zapiti, 2014). In short, like social interaction, emotions are offering the energetics and dynamogenic dimension but not the structure of knowledge.

Now, from the perspective of the study of the epistemic subject that Piaget was interested in and his definition of changing knowledge as change in operatory structures, this is probably correct. However, from the perspective of genetic social psychology interested in the study of the social psychological subject, emotions have a more constitutive function in the three significant subject–object–other significant structures of representing identified (submission, domination, co-operation), as they are integral parts of a socio-emotional and cognitive configuration described in Table 2.1 of Chapter 2 in this book. The further and deeper step in the study of emotions requested by Zittoun that hinges on the study of extreme cases of emotions (child trauma, PTSD, etc.), which is certainly relevant in post-conflict settings, is a new avenue for exploration which I hope to explore more in collaboration with colleagues from clinical psychology in the future.

Genetic Social Psychology for World-Making and Its Application: The Limits of Intergroup Contact

Gillespie (Chapter 7) rightly recognises the need for a psychology that empowers humans to critically reflect on and collectively navigate changes, focusing on creating possibilities and distributing world-making tools fairly. In line with our recent proposal with colleagues (Power et al., 2023), social psychology as a historical science (e.g. Muthukrishna, Henrich & Slingerland, 2021) should focus on 'world-making' in two senses. First, people are future oriented and often are guided more by what could be than what is. Second, social psychology can contribute to this future orientation by supporting people's world-making as well as critically reflecting on the role of social psychological research in world-making. This endeavour is fundamental, for example, in Furth's work when he draws on Castoriades and his radical imaginary. In any emancipatory proposal, as also shown more recently by Zittoun and Gillespie (2015, 2018) and Glăveanu (2020), the role of imagination and creativity is crucial. Recent work by anthropologists and archaeologists (Graeber & Wengrow, 2021) shows that in the history and prehistory of humanity all possible forms of social organisation (egalitarian, hierarchical, matriarchal, patriarchal, etc.) were possible, many times co-existed and often varied seasonally even within a single society. There is no specific historical necessity for complexity to lead to power, and indeed Galam and Moscovici's work shows that more complex heterarchic organisations, resilient to conflict of ideas that view diversity as opportunity for innovation, novelty and richness, are possible in our post-industrial worlds. One does not need a lot of imagination to see the value in what Piaget was proposing in 1932 as co-operative relations (Piaget, 1932) in his *Moral Judgment of the Child* as a solution to post-industrial dilemmas. To the west of the Federation of Switzerland,[2] in New York, he witnessed the rugged individualism and the Wall Street Crash of 1929, and just next to his country he saw rising fascism in Italy and Nazism in Germany. About 100 years later the challenge remains the same. Let us hope that humanity will not need a nuclear holocaust to rediscover the importance of co-operation over competition, as this realisation was probably a phenomenon related to the shock caused by the Second World War (see Figure 5.1).

It is our belief that family structures, education and the media hold the key to cultivating what is 'possible' and the imagination of a better society. Genetic social psychology proposes interventions on the basis of direct and indirect forms of intergroup contact, semantic contact through media and co-operative relationships at all levels of analysis. Interventions like the ones proposed by Bermúdez, Sammut and Nicholson in this volume are at the heart of a way forward.

Bermúdez (Chapter 12) offers a compelling example of how integrating ontogenetic, microgenetic and sociogenetic analyses can enrich our understanding of societal change and the development of critical thinking about social conflict and violence. Her reflection on the evolution of her research underscores the importance of considering individual cognitive processes, relational dynamics and societal narratives collectively. Her perspective highlights the value of a holistic approach to theoretical frameworks that aims to address complex social issues. Her current research on how

[2] I often wonder about whether the fact that Switzerland is a successful federation could be related to Piaget's work and his social psychology in this country.

collective narratives around violence are produced, disseminated and transformed at the societal level in the Spanish Basque country suggests more ways of applying our framework in various other contexts of post-conflict settings beyond Cyprus. For example, like the Basque country, in Cyprus there is also a secessionist feeling in a certain community that at some historical point took up arms to make this a possibility. Unlike Cyprus, in her example there was not a powerful neighbour to support this claim militarily, and therefore the situation evolved differently. In either case, the loss of life is a tragedy, and what is proposed by Bermúdez as a way to critically evaluate the normalisation of violence is compatible with our approach to promote co-operative relationships. Methods like the one proposed by Bermúdez and Sammut are desperately needed to connect theory to praxis. Sammut (Chapter 10) similarly reveals the complexities of reconciling divergent perspectives rooted in contrasting world views which shape social order and relations. Sammut argues that human action is inherently self-interested and oriented towards social relations that support collective projects. These projects are legitimised by common sense, which grants meaning to social objects and events. Overcoming conflict requires unpacking contrasting action strategies in terms of supported projects and logical perspectives. The argumentation analysis protocol proposed by Sammut is promising in identifying convergent claims in a contested terrain. While these claims do not reconcile contrasting projects, they provide building blocks for mutually satisfactory solutions and reveal targets for social representations interventions.

The possible limitations of contact theory and contact interventions are brought to the surface in Nicolson's commentary (Chapter 11) that focuses on the Israeli–Palestinian conflict through the lens of genetic social psychology, specifically examining the potential for societal change through various forms of intergroup contact. Nicholson explores the complexities of this protracted conflict by applying a multilayered analysis that considers individual, intergroup and societal ideological contexts. The commentary emphasises the importance of acknowledging asymmetry in intergroup perceptions and actions, using empirical findings to discuss the role of intergroup prejudice and its impact on the microgenesis, ontogenesis and sociogenesis of social representations of the conflict.

Nicholson advocates for a comprehensive approach to understanding the Israeli–Palestinian conflict, highlighting the need to consider individual experiences within broader intergroup and societal contexts and underscores the critical role of power asymmetry in shaping intergroup contact and its outcomes. Nicholson points out that this aspect is often overlooked in discussions of the contact hypothesis, yet it significantly influences how groups perceive and interact with each other.

Indeed a recent meta-analysis by Kende et al. (2018) of 660 samples across 36 cultures suggested that egalitarianism at country level moderated the expected contact-reduced prejudice association, as it led to stronger contact–prejudice associations. Higher cultural hierarchy values and social dominance orientation corresponded with weaker contact–prejudice associations. Nicolson's work shows that in unplanned encounters under conditions of military occupation the challenges could be even higher. Nicholson's sensitivity to the historical and geopolitical background of the conflict is setting the stage for a discussion on the possibilities and challenges of intergroup contact, the differences between unplanned and planned contact scenarios and highlighting differences in perceptions and outcomes between minority and majority groups.

Indeed, as we have seen in Cyprus, contrary to what one might expect on the basis of other findings where numerical minorities benefit less than numerical majorities from prejudice reduction through contact (Pettigrew & Tropp, 2005), prejudice reduction for Turkish Cypriots through contact was equal if not bigger compared to the one for Greek Cypriots in the period after the opening of the checkpoints. In a condition of a warm and escalating conflict like the 2023–2024 conflict in Israel and Gaza, one can easily see the limitations and maybe even failure of these unplanned interventions in earlier periods because of the highly asymmetrical and challenging situations of occupation in the Israeli–Palestinian conflict described by Nicholson. In such contexts planned contacts in safe environments would probably produce much better results.

All in all, commentaries from Nicholson, Sammut and Bermudez encompassing different conflict and post-conflict settings offer valuable perspectives on the complexities of intergroup relations and the potential for societal change through contact, argumentation and dialogue. By applying a multilayered analysis, all three commentaries enrich the discussion on genetic social psychology's applicability to real-world conflicts. They all emphasise the importance of considering asymmetry, societal context and the nuanced dynamics of intergroup contact in understanding and addressing protracted conflicts.

Conclusion

The proposal in this book of a genetic social psychology puts forward one way that psychology can be seen as a historical science (Muthukrishna,

Henrich & Slingerland, 2021). What Henrich (2020) describes as the dark matter of psychology that prepares the ground historically for the emergence of new institutions is actually social representations. But there is a struggle between representations to define the future on the basis of different visions and projects that we identified as significant structures. They are significant structures in the sense that they are enduring forms of social interaction with a predictable pattern of relationships between values, ideas and practices. We proposed three distinct significant structures (submission, domination and co-operation) that can be mapped on positions in the representational field of a certain conflict. Our aim should be to understand the processes that lead to some of these structures becoming more or less strengthened due to historical, political and economic developments. In the early years after conflict it is expected that significant structures of submission and domination take the upper hand and form a certain equilibrium that will tend to freeze representations around a more traditional ethos of conflict (Bar-Tal, 2023). However, a process of conflict transformation must be put in place that will increasingly favour the co-operative structure. Such a process will probably be taking place in parallel with historical processes of socio-economic changes (urbanisation, rise in GDP) and unexpected events (financial crises, pandemics, wars) that also influence value change in certain directions discussed in this book. International non-governmental and intergovernmental organisations tasked with promoting peace and stability can offer external help when internal dynamics are very difficult. The motor for positive ontogenetic and sociogenetic change is microgenesis as predicted by Duveen and Lloyd (1990) and the major institutions that can support microgenetic processes of co-operation is family the educational system and the media with increasing importance of each in a human life trajectory.

As we are reminded by Duveen (2001/2013), social identities are a function of representations and are concerned both with identifications and being identified; they can be construed as positions within the symbolic field of a culture. Thus the three positions in the representational field that we identified in the Greek Cypriot community in 2007 and the four positions in 2017 form the 'thinking society' of adult expectations of the 'being identified' part for students in the microgenetic process of social interaction between parents and students and teachers and students depending on their social network. In Cyprus, as in other parts of the world, only a minority of people are close to political parties. Thus, only a minority of students would be exposed to views more or less politically articulated (as I was from my father; see my autobiographical note), but the majority will be influenced by some of the grassroots understandings that we have seen earlier. Given the multiplicity of positions, one could assume that students extract their sense of in-group norms from the stance of the majority of their teachers and the official policy and rituals of the school.

Microgenetic processes of social influence and the development of agency will be regulated by the forms of recognition between subject and other, with closer and deeper interpersonal relationships having a stronger influence on the consciousness of students in either direction although relations of constraint will be more likely connected with the 'superficial layer of beliefs' (Duveen, 2002/2013) in Piagetian terms than reconstructed knowledge as depicted in Chapter 2 here (Table 2.1).

Children in childhood and adolescence become agents in the field of ethnic identity in the sense that they start choosing their friends by seeking or avoiding intergroup contact. This makes clear the dialectic between social representations and identities. The role of gender is not unrelated to the emergence of ethnic conflict. Representations of gender and gender identities are ontogenetically formulated first and probably form a template of asymmetrical expectations formulated in the first two to three years of life that become the core on which later forms of asymmetry are formed. Challenging patriarchal structures of asymmetry equals challenging the heart of asymmetrical militaristic and nationalistic structures also (Hadjipavlou & Mertan, 2010; Demetriou & Hadjipavlou, 2020).

As noted by Duveen (2001/2013), Lucien Goldmann (1976) saw so penetratingly that the identities that emerge in the course of development constrain the representations which individuals or groups might accept. In his terms the limiting case was one where the conditions for the acceptance of a new representation entailed the dissolution of an existing identity. But identities here are not understood as simply a categorisation or the strength of identification or importance of belongingness to a group as in Social Identity Theory. As proposed by Duveen (2008) in his last published paper, we should reconceptualise our notion of group and identity in social psychology by recognising heterogeneity of social groups that depend on the communicative genre or position supporting each representation. This will lead to the realisation that there are in fact more similarities between certain social networks of people across societies or social divides and countries than social networks within societies, countries or communities. In Cyprus, for example, the pro-reconciliation positions in both communities share many similarities in the definition of the

Cyprus history, current feelings and trust for the other community and reduced feelings of threat. Thus, a position of co-operation is an identity itself that might carry more social-psychological weight in the sociopolitical sphere than being Greek Cypriot or Turkish Cypriot.

As we have seen in Chapter 1, there has been some theoretical engagement with genetic social psychology beyond the positive commentaries by Moscovici (2013), Valsiner (2013) and Nicolopoulou and Weintraub (2009), by Juan Antonio Castorina (see Psaltis, 2024 for a more extended dialogue). Based on previous commentaries and the seven commentaries in this volume I see some avenues for further work on genetic social psychology and some contributions it can make to more traditional disciplines. There is certainly a need for more ethnographic work in the school context to understand everyday processes of constructing representations of ethnic conflict. Ethnographic work, mostly through in-depth interviews, can shed more light on autobiographical stories of people belonging in all birth cohorts of interest in a certain conflict case. Experimental ethnography that sets up conditions of social interaction under conditions of conflicting asymmetries is also needed. Analysis of how children and students give meaning to media news and social media that present aspects of a conflict is also of crucial importance for the future.

Hopefully, the genetic social psychology framework proposed here will facilitate theoretical expansions in various other disciplines and areas of interest. In social developmental psychology it could help to overcome the fragmentation of mini models of developments in various domains. The Piagetian tradition can turn its attention to further refinements of the work of Piaget and Weil (1951) that was stopped short due to concerns by the Genevan public in the Cold War climate of the times. Social representations theory can attain a more critical edge, as it often ends up just being a descriptive enterprise failing to find a place for power and its critique in its theoretical model. The field of history didactics can also enlarge its understanding of historical consciousness through an articulation of the processes of microgenesis, ontogenesis and sociogenesis. Finally, the field of conflict transformation can obtain a better understanding of both opportunities and challenges in the process of reconciliation in post-conflict settings from a better engagement with the developmental literature. At the same time further developments in these fields will naturally enlarge the purview of genetic social psychology itself.

REFERENCES

Abrams, D., Rutland, A., Pelletier, J., & Ferrell, J. M. (2009), Children's group nous: Understanding and applying peer exclusion within and between groups. *Child Development*, *80*, 224–243. https://doi.org/10.1111/j.1467-8624.2008.01256.x.

Bar-Tal, D. (2023). *Sinking into the honey trap: The case of the Israeli-Palestinian conflict*. Washington, DC: Westphalia Press.

Carpentras, D., Lueders, A., & Quayle, M. (2021, September 29). Response Item Network (ResIN): A network-based approach to explore attitude systems. https://doi.org/10.31234/osf.io/uzdcg.

Castorina, A. (2010). The ontogenesis of social representations: A dialectic perspective. *Papers on Social Representations*, *19*(18), 1–18.

Demetriou, O., & Hadjipavlou, M. (2020). Women and peace negotiations in Cyprus. In O. P. Richmond & G. Visoka (Eds.), *The Palgrave Encyclopedia of Peace and Conflict Studies* (pp. 1–9). Cham: Springer International Publishing.

Doise, W., Mugny, G., & Perret-Clermont, A. N. (1976). Social interaction and cognitive development: Further evidence. *European Journal of Social Psychology*, *6*(2), 245–247.

Duveen, G. (1997/2013). Psychological development as a social process. In S. Moscovici, S. Jovchelovitch, & B. Wagoner (Eds.), *Development as a social process: Contributions of Gerard Duveen* (pp. 90–111). London: Routledge.

(2001/2013). Representations, identities, resistance. In S. Moscovici, S. Jovchelovitch, & B. Wagoner (Eds.), *Development as a social process: Contributions of Gerard Duveen* (pp. 182–195). London: Routledge.

(2002/2013). Construction, belief, doubt. In S. Moscovici, S. Jovchelovitch, & B. Wagoner (Eds.), *Development as a social process: Contributions of Gerard Duveen* (pp. 112–123). London: Routledge.

(2007/2013). Culture and social representations. In S. Moscovici, S. Jovchelovitch, & B. Wagoner (Eds.), *Development as a social process: Contributions of Gerard Duveen* (pp. 198–216). London: Routledge.

(2008). Social actors and social groups: A return to heterogeneity in social psychology. *Journal for the Theory of Social Behaviour*, *38*(4), 369–374.

Duveen, G., & Lloyd, B. (1990). *Social representations and the development of knowledge*. Cambridge: Cambridge University Press.

Duveen, G., & Psaltis, C. (2008). The constructive role of asymmetries in social interaction. In U. Mueller, J.Carpendale, N. Budwig, & B. Sokol (Eds.), *Social life and social knowledge: Toward a process account of development* (pp. 183–204). Mahwah, NJ: Lawrence Erlbaum.

Fonseca, L., & Jovchelovitch, S. (2024). The long hard road of reconciliation: Prefiguring cultures of peace through the transformation of representations of former combatants and identities of urban youth in Colombia. *European Journal of Social Psychology*, *54*, 1–16. https://doi.org/10.1002/ejsp.2967.

Galam, S., & Moscovici, S. (1991). Towards a theory of collective phenomena: Consensus and attitude changes in groups. *European Journal of Social Psychology, 21*(1), 49–74.

(1994). Towards a theory of collective phenomena. II: Conformity and power. *European Journal of Social Psychology, 24*(4), 481–495.

(1995). Towards a theory of collective phenomena. III: Conflicts and forms of power. *European Journal of Social Psychology, 25*(2), 217–229.

Gillespie, A. (2020). Semantic contact and semantic barriers: Reactionary responses to disruptive ideas. *Current Opinion in Psychology, 35*, 21–25.

Glăveanu V. P. (2020). *The possible: A sociocultural theory.* Oxford: Oxford University Press.

Graeber, D., & Wengrow, D. (2021). *The dawn of everything: A new history of humanity*. London: Penguin .

Greenfield, P. M. (2009). Linking social change and developmental change: Shifting pathways of human development. *Developmental Psychology, 45*(2), 401.

Goldmann, L. (1976). The epistemology of sociology. *Telos, 1976*(30), 201–210.

Hadjipavlou, M., & Mertan, B. (2010). Cypriot feminism: An opportunity to challenge gender inequalities and promote women's rights and a different voice. *Cyprus Review, 22*(2), 247–268.

Henrich, J. (2015). *The secret of our success: How culture is driving human evolution, domesticating our species, and making us smarter.* Princeton, NJ: Princeton University Press.

(2020). *The weirdest people in the world: How the West became psychologically peculiar and particularly prosperous.* New York: Farrar, Straus & Giroux.

Kende, J., Phalet, K., Van den Noortgate, W., Kara, A., & Fischer, R. (2018). Equality revisited: A cultural meta-analysis of intergroup contact and prejudice. *Social Psychological and Personality Science, 9*(8), 887–895.

Leman, P. J. (2010). Commentary: Social psychology and developmental psychology: Conversation or collaboration? *Papers on Social Representations, 19*(1), 19–21.

Lévesque, S. (2016). History in an age of 'truth and reconciliation'. *Public History Weekly, 4*(29). https://doi.org/10.1515/phw-2016-7043.

(2017). History as a'GPS': On the uses of historical narrative for French Canadian students' life orientation and identity. *London Review of Education, 15*(2), 227–242.

Mannheim, K. (1952). The problem of generations. In P. Kecskemeti (Ed.), *Essays on the sociology of knowledge: Collected works* (Vol. 5, pp. 276–322). New York: Routledge.

Marker, M. (2011). Teaching history from an Indigenous perspective: Four winding paths up the mountain. In P. Clark (Ed.), *New possibilities for the past: Shaping history education in Canada* (pp. 97–112). Vancouver: University of British Columbia Press.

Marková, I. (2021). 'La dissidence d'un seul': Relations between social representations and minorities' innovation. In N. Kalampalikis, D. Jodelet,

M. Wieviorka, D. Moscovici, & P. Moscovici (Eds.), *Serge Moscovici: Un regard sur les mondes contemporains* (pp. 117–132). Paris: Éditions de la Maison des sciences de l'homme.

Mifsud R., & Sammut, G. (2023). Worldviews and the role of social values that underlie them. *PLoS ONE, 18*(7), e0288451. https://doi.org/10.1371/journal.pone.0288451.

Moscovici, S. (1993). *Reason and cultures. In University of Seville, solemn act of investiture as Doctor Honoris Causa by the University of Seville* (pp. 44–94). Seville: University of Seville, University Extension.

(2011). An essay on social representations and ethnic minorities. *Social Science Information, 50*(3–4), 442–461.

Moscovici, S., Jovchelovitch, S., & Wagoner, B. (2013). *Development as a social process: Contributions of Gerard Duveen*. London: Routledge.

Muthukrishna, M., Henrich, J., & Slingerland, E. (2021). Psychology as a historical science. *Annual Review of Psychology, 72*, 717–749.

Nicolopoulou, A., & Weintraub, J. (2009). Why operativity-in-context is not quite a sociocultural model. *Human Development, 52*(5), 320–328.

Pettigrew, T. F., & Tropp, L. R. (2006). A meta-analytic test of intergroup contact theory. *Journal of Personality and Social Psychology, 90*(5), 751.

Piaget, J. (1932). *The moral judgment of the child*. London: Kegan Paul.

(1977). *The development of thought: Equilibration of cognitive structures*. Oxford: Basil Blackwell.

(1995). *Sociological studies* (L. Smith, Ed.). London: Routledge.

Piaget, J., & Weil, A. M. (1951). The development in children of the idea of the homeland and of relations to other countries. *International Social Science Journal, 3*, 561–578.

Popescu, A. (2019). The brief history of generation – defining the concept of generation: An analysis of literature review. *Journal of Comparative Research in Anthropology and Sociology, 10*(2), 15–30.

Power, S. A., Zittoun, T., Akkerman, S., Wagoner, B., Cabra, M., Cornish, F., . . . & Gillespie, A. (2023). Social psychology of and for world-making. *Personal Sociology and Psychology Review, 27*(4), 378–392. https://doi.org/10.1177/10888683221145756.

Psaltis, C. (2005). Communication and the construction of knowledge or transmission of belief. *Studies in Communication Sciences, 209*, 228.

(2012). Culture and social representations: A continuing dialogue in search for heterogeneity in social developmental psychology. *Culture & Psychology, 18*(3), 375–390.

(2024). Génesis y estructura: Un cuento de dos ciudades y la psicología social genética. In M. Carretero & A. Barreiro (Eds.), *Construcción de conocimientos en el campo psicológico: Celebrando a Tono Castorina-Volumen 1* (pp. 141–164). Buenos Aires: Tilde editora.

Psaltis, C., & Duveen, G. (2006). Social relations and cognitive development: The influence of conversation types and representations of gender. *European Journal of Social Psychology, 36*, 407–430.

(2007). Conversation types and conservation: Forms of recognition and cognitive development. *British Journal of Developmental Psychology*, *25*, 79–102.
Psaltis, C., & Zapiti, A. (2014). *Interaction, communication and development: Psychological development as a social process*. London: Routledge.
Seixas, P. (2012). Indigenous historical consciousness: An oxymoron or a dialogue? In M. Carretero, M. Asensio, & M. Rodríguez-Moneo (Eds.), *History education and the construction of national identites* (pp. 125–138). Charlotte, NC: Information Age Publishing.
Thorpe, C., & Inglis, D. (2019). Do 'global generations' exist?: From Mannheim to Beck and beyond. *Youth and Globalization*, *1*(1), 40–64.
Tropp, L. R., & Pettigrew, T. F. (2005). Relationships between intergroup contact and prejudice among minority and majority status groups. *Psychological Science*, *16*(12), 951–957. https://doi.org/10.1111/j.1467-9280.2005.01643.x.
Truth and Reconciliation Commission of Canada (TRC). (2015b). *Final report of the Truth and Reconciliation Commission of Canada, Volume One: Summary: Honouring the truth, reconciling for the future*. Toronto, ON: James Lorimer & Company.
Uskul, A. K., Kirchner-Häusler, A., Vignoles, V. L., Rodriguez-Bailon, R., Castillo, V. A., Cross, S. E., ... & Uchida, Y. (2023). Neither Eastern nor Western: Patterns of independence and interdependence in Mediterranean societies. *Journal of Personality and Social Psychology*, *125*(3), 471–495.
Valsiner, J. (2013). Introduction: The idea that will live: Genetic social psychology. In S. Moscovici, S. Jovchelovitch, & B. Wagoner (Eds.), *Development as a social process: Contributions of Gerard Duveen* (pp. ix–x). London: Routledge.
Zittoun T. (2024). *The pleasure of thinking*. Cambridge: Cambridge University Press.
Zittoun, T., Duveen, G., Gillespie, A., Ivinson, G., & Psaltis, C. (2003). The use of symbolic resources in developmental transitions. *Culture & Psychology*, *9*(4), 415–448.
Zittoun T., & Gillespie A. (2015). *Imagination in human and cultural development*. London: Routledge.
(2018). Imagining the collective future: A sociocultural perspective. In C. de Saint-Laurent, S. Obradovic, & K. R. Carriere (Eds.), *Imagining collective futures: Perspectives from social, cultural and political psychology* (pp. 15–37). Cham: Palgrave Macmillan.
(2022). A sociocultural approach to identity through diary studies. In M. Bamberg, C. Demuth, & M. Watzlawik (Eds.), *Cambridge handbook of identity* (pp. 345–365). Cambridge: Cambridge University Press.
Zittoun, T., Gillespie, A., & Bernal Marcos, M. J. (2024). Development and vulnerability across the lifecourse. *Culture & Psychology*, *30*(4), 813–840. https://doi.org/10.1177/1354067X231201384.
Zittoun, T., Gillespie, A., Cornish, F., & Psaltis, C. (2007). The metaphor of the triangle in theories of human development. *Human Development*, *50*(4), 208–229.
Zittoun, T., & Psaltis, C. (2006). Socializing developmental interactions. *The American Journal of Psychology*, *119*(3), 487–496. https://doi.org/10.2307/20445355.

Index

For EU product safety concerns, contact us at Calle de José Abascal, 56–1°,
28003 Madrid, Spain or eugpsr@cambridge.org.

www.ingramcontent.com/pod-product-compliance
Ingram Content Group UK Ltd.
Pitfield, Milton Keynes, MK11 3LW, UK
UKHW021305011225
465572UK00030B/1148
* 9 7 8 1 0 0 9 3 9 3 1 5 7 *